IRAN AND THE UNITED STATES

IRAN AND THE UNITED STATES

An Insider's View on the Failed Past and the Road to Peace

Seyed Hossein Mousavian
with
Shahir ShahidSaless

Bloomsbury Academic
An imprint of Bloomsbury Publishing Inc

B L O O M S B U R Y
NEW YORK · LONDON · OXFORD · NEW DELHI · SYDNEY

Bloomsbury Academic
An imprint of Bloomsbury Publishing Inc

1385 Broadway	50 Bedford Square
New York	London
NY 10018	WC1B 3DP
USA	UK

www.bloomsbury.com

BLOOMSBURY and the Diana logo are trademarks of Bloomsbury Publishing Plc

First published 2014 by Bloomsbury Publishing Plc
Paperback edition first published 2015

Library of Congress Cataloging-in-Publication Data
Mousavian, Hossein.
Iran and the United States : an insider's view on the failed past and the road to peace / Seyed Hossein Mousavian, Shahir Shahidsaless.
pages cm
Includes bibliographical references and index.
ISBN 978-1-62892-007-9 (hardback)
1. United States–Foreign relations–Iran. 2. Iran–Foreign relations–United States. 3. Iran–Politics and government–1979–1997. 4. Iran–Politics and government–1997- I. Shahidsaless, Shahir. II. Title.
E183.8.I55M829 2014
327.73055–dc23
2014010015

ISBN: HB:	978-1-6289-2007-9
PB:	978-1-5013-1206-9
ePUB:	978-1-6289-2760-3
ePDF:	978-1-6289-2870-9

Typeset by Fakenham Prepress Solutions, Fakenham, Norfolk NR21 8NN
Printed and bound in the United States of America

I would like to offer my sincere thanks to all of my colleagues at the Woodrow Wilson School of Public and International Affairs at Princeton University for supporting my work, especially Professors Frank von Hippel, Christopher Chyba, Zia Mian and Daniel Kurtzer. I also want to offer my gratitude to the Rockefeller Brothers Fund and the Ploughshares Fund, for generously supporting my work with grants to Princeton University. I am also grateful to Emad Kiyaei, who has worked with me as my research assistant. Lastly, I dedicate this book to all victims of more than three decades of US-Iran hostilities, and my beloved family, who endured great hardship as a result of my unjust arrest in April 2007. I am forever grateful for their unrelenting support, dedication, and trust in me. The publication of this book coincides with my wife's birthday, which I consider a good omen.

Last but not least, I want to extend special thanks to Shahir Shahidsaless. His sound theoretical base, extensive knowledge of international relations, specifically Iran and the US domestic and foreign policy, as well as his analytical skills, were paramount to the completion of this project.

CONTENTS

A PREFACE TO THE NEW EDITION

November 4, 1979 is the most important day in US-Iran relations from the American perspective. This is the day Iranian students seized the US embassy in Tehran. It started a 444 day ordeal that humiliated Americans as we watched the daily news accounts of our hostages and the physical, emotional and mental threats they endured. This was something new for Americans. They felt helpless and humiliated by what was perceived in the United States as a strange religious leader who was leading enormous rallies of people chanting "death to America." Unfortunately, Americans knew little or nothing about Iran until the "Iranian Hostage Crisis." This experience has shaped the perception of several generations of Americans about Iran and it is very negative.

On the other hand August 19, 1953 means nothing to Americans but it may be the most important day in US-Iran relations from the Iranian perspective. This was the day that the US CIA and the British Secret Intelligence Service orchestrated the over throw of the democratically elected government of Iran and Prime Minister Mohammad Mosaddegh.

Iran and the United States have been struggling to recover from these tragic mistakes. There are legitimate grievances on both sides of this troubled international relationship. If we ever hope to improve relations with Iran it is important for Americans and our political leadership to learn more about Iran's view of the United States.

In law school I learned that the first thing a good lawyer does to prepare for settlement negotiations or a law suit is to learn all the facts. You want to know the other sides best arguments. You want to know their deepest desires, needs and motivations. You also want to know their strongest hopes, fears and aspirations.

Regrettably very few Americans, even our elected officials, know much about Iran and their legitimate grievances with the US. We have a duty to learn! It is for this reason that I highly recommend *Iran and the United States: An Insider's View on the Failed Past and the Road to Peace.*

Seyed Hossein Mousavian has the unique benefit of having worked for more than 30 years as an Iranian diplomat. He knows and has worked with Iran's President Hassan Rouhani and Iran's Foreign Minister Javad Zarif.

In this wonderfully written book Dr. Mousavian shares important insights about the events either long forgotten or never understood by Americans that have shaped US-Iran relations since the overthrow of Mosaddegh in 1953. It is important that we understand many current leaders of Iran either personally or had family members who suffered terribly at the hands of the Shah's secret police that had been trained by the CIA or Mossad, the Israeli security agency.

I have met key leaders in Iran who are veterans of the Iraq-Iran war that cost more than 200,000 Iranian lives between 1980 and 1988. Some were victims of gas attacks launched by Saddam Hussein. Iranians have not forgotten that the US was on Iraq's side during this tragic war that was started by Saddam in September 1980. Few Americans remember that the US and some European allies helped Saddam. Americans have also forgotten about the USS Vincennes, a warship fighting in the Persian Gulf that mistakenly shot down an Iranian civilian airline killing all 290 persons on board in 1988.

Dr. Mousavian reminds the reader of these important events and others that have helped shape Iran's view of the US over the last 35 years. He also shares some of the important attempts made by both sides to improve relations that were missed or rejected by the other side. Perhaps the biggest missed opportunity was in 2001 following the defeat of The Taliban in Afghanistan. Iran had assisted the US and coalition forces defeat the Taliban and reasonably expected some reciprocation from Washington but instead President Bush included Iran in the Axis of Evil in his State of the Union Address on January 29, 2002. As Dr. Mousavian points out this statement by President Bush persuaded some important leaders in Iran that it was impossible to deal with the US.

Iran has also missed overtures on the part of the US during Democrat and Republican administrations. As you read this book and reflect on the grievances on both sides, the missed opportunities to reset relations and common interests long ignored, one must ask how many more chances will we have to get it right.

As I write this we are living through an historic time in US-Iran relations. After 35 years of intense animosity it appears that for the first time both the President of the United States and the President of Iran have embraced diplomacy as a way to improve relations between our two countries. Significant progress has been made but much more is needed. The terms of the Joint Plan of Action agreement of November 24, 2013 have been complied with and this success provided a foundation for the framework agreement announced on April 2,

2015. Skeptics on both sides were surprised at how much progress had been made in the negotiations to resolve the perplexing nuclear issue over the last 18 months.

Negotiators know that many details must be settled before a final verifiable agreement between Iran and the P 5 + 1 can be signed. But there is hope in Washington and Tehran that where there is a will there is a way. After all, the Supreme Leader has forbid the possession of nuclear weapons in a fatwa (a religious command) as against Islam. The US and its negotiating partners are pushing hard for verification procedures that will simply confirm that the supreme leader's religious command is being followed by all branches of the Iranian Government and society.

There are forces in the United States and Iran who are opposed to the framework agreement. Ironically, hardliners in Iran, Israel and the US are on the same side. If the forces committed to a long overdue rapprochement are going to succeed it is important for them to read and reflect on the information presented in this timely book. I do not agree with all of Dr. Mousavian's conclusions but I find his perspective to be vitally important for Americans to understand. It is must reading for all who recognize the importance of preventing a nuclear Iran and the disastrous nuclear arms race in the Middle East that would surely follow.

It is time for all Americans to engage in the Iran debate and learn the facts. *Iran and the United States* is a great place to begin.

Jim Slattery\
Former Member of Congress\
Kansas 2nd district 1983–95\
Member of Abrahamic Dialogue with Iran\
2004 to Present

FOREWORD

Hossein Mousavian is a good friend and brings to this book a set of ideas and assessments worth considering even if we are not entirely in agreement. With agreement of a preliminary text and now a framework, his book is even more relevant and apposite. I met him some four years ago or more at a fascinating discussion which he details in the book regarding the Khobar Towers incident in Saudi Arabia. We met again at Princeton on several occasions and later attended conference meetings and platforms together.

We see eye to eye on many matters, particularly the critical importance of finding a way to get the US and Iran speaking together. Hossein's intellectual work during the last five years has been enormously valuable for senior American legislators and senior-level Washington executive branch leaders in gaining a better understanding of Iran. We have had the opportunity to discuss together and think through various approaches to the issue of bringing Iran and the US into closer contact and to finding answers to the matters that divide them, beginning with the nuclear issue.

While many have contributed to that process, it has been the unusual advantage of having Hossein here in the United States which has made its own, important and unique contribution to how Iran views the US. Hossein was able to present insights, points of view, historical details, and frank assessments from an Iranian point of view that helped to broaden horizons, inform policy-makers, and introduce new and useful ideas. Most importantly, he was able to convey thoughts about the Iranian cultural context and ways of thinking about the issues which definitively helped in closing the gap and opening the talks.

Iran–US relations have become the locus of perhaps the most important contribution to foreign affairs in this decade by both countries. The 36-year estrangement has been characterized by, indeed suffused with, mistrust and misunderstanding. Both countries in their own way play a special role in world affairs. Iran is a key regional power, major oil producer, and the leading Islamic state and the major Muslim power where Shia Islam predominates. The future of the Middle East is very much linked to Iran and its role, just as it is linked to Egypt, Saudi Arabia, and Israel. The United States is a major world power. Its security posture, economic strength, and traditional adherence to values and principles which have guided the country since 1776 are all sources of global and regional influence. Both countries will play a critical role with others in the future of the Middle East.

This book tracks and amplifies the reasons just noted above as to how and why its author has played his own special role in Washington, New York, and in many other cities in this country and Europe in providing a greater understanding of Iran. An Iranian diplomat in Germany, a senior official in Tehran, and a leader in the revolutionary movement to inform and reform Iran, Hossein Mousavian deserves our attention to what he says on key issues. We will not agree with everything, but we should be aware of his views, take them into account, understand where we agree and disagree, and use that information to help shape a constructive path to the future with Iran.

In the few words to follow, I want to do several things to put this book in perspective and share with you some thoughts and ideas which might make going forward by our two countries more understandable and even possible. I've spent over a dozen years looking at the issues posed by the differences between the United States and others with Iran over its nuclear program and other issues. There are several conclusions one can draw that might help with building understanding and progress between Iran and the US.

Direct contacts between the parties to the issue and especially between the United States and Iran are essential. They were, in order to conclude the November 24, 2013 Joint Plan of Action (JPAG). They have been and will be, to reach a conclusion to the current negotiations on a comprehensive agreement.

The parties are separated by over 30 years of mistrust, sporadic contact, and misunderstanding. This book, from the Iranian point of view, seeks to set that right. It is important to know how opposing sides view each other's ideas and intentions.

The reality is that no perfect agreement is achievable. However, the elements are in place to achieve an arrangement in which Iran can pursue a peaceful nuclear program and the US and others have more than reasonable confidence that the program is peaceful and civilian—that is, not being diverted to use in a nuclear weapon.

This takes place against a backdrop of deep suspicion on both sides arising out of the period of mistrust and misunderstanding; on the side of Iran, a sense that the objective is to effect regime change in their country. And there is evidence in the minds of Iranians for that view, as you will read in the pages ahead. On the other hand, a suspicion exists on the part of the United States, fed by some elements raised in the book, and which

I will try to summarize, that Iran's real objective is to construct a nuclear weapon. In part, both of these views are based on some "evidence"— the parties have not been scrupulous in eschewing misstatements and missteps—and in part based on, "that was what I would be doing if I were on the other side" kind of thinking and assessment.

At this stage, two conclusions seem to be possible with regard to this issue. First, the US (and Israeli) intelligence communities seem to agree, and the US has reported each year since 2007, that there has been no Iranian decision to make a nuclear weapon based on what it calls strong evidence. Second, it is clear that Iran has acted in ways that are likely to give it the technology, information, and hardware to proceed in that direction with some confidence should such a decision be made.

Let me now write a word or two now about how I interpret the book and its messages. Mousavian has done a good job in blending what he knows and understands from long service with his government. And he has done so in a way that is in accordance with what he has learned in over four years in the United States at Princeton University and well beyond that about US ideas and attitudes toward Iran and its nuclear program.

Diplomats get paid as much to listen as to talk. It is the essence of their profession to understand what the other side is saying and how that informs their task of getting a resolution to problems and disputes. Listening is thus essential and in my view ought to consume well over a majority of a diplomat's time interacting with others at home and abroad. This book is first and foremost a good volume for listening to the writer and understanding his views and most importantly what he has to say about Iran, its attitudes, and how they have been shaped by the interactions, good and bad, with the US and others.

But listening is a complicated affair. In the first instance, it involves understanding what is being said clearly and directly. But even more importantly—and this is where skill and experience comes in—it means trying to understand what is really meant by the words you are hearing or reading. In some instances, that is not always the same thing. Often, those involved in negotiations have settled on what they believe is the best explanation of their views and approach. But behind it, with careful analysis, it is possible to predict what the underlying objectives are and how one might use that understanding to find an approach that can lead to mutual understanding and eventually to agreement.

In part, what Mousavian has written for us raises that challenge clearly and I leave it to the reader to understand the challenge and to make her or his own judgments. To say that I do not agree with all that is set down is true. But to say also that what is set down is essential for understanding both how Iranians see the issue and therefore for understanding how it might be dealt with is also critical.

There are in looking at this issue several current conundrums which I believe are worth considering as we contemplate, Iran and the United States, how to move ahead together for the future both on the nuclear issue and beyond.

Fundamental to understanding the issue is a difference of view I detect over the interpretation of the Non-Proliferation Treaty of 1966.

On the Iranian side, the view appears to be that the treaty permits and even authorizes any action which does not result in the diversion of nuclear material to a nuclear weapon. That is a view quite broadly shared by a number of states, but often if not exclusively based on the argument that the action being taken—especially in sensitive or dual use technologies (enrichment and reprocessing)—is justified by a civilian or permitted non-weapons purpose. Examples include the production of highly enriched uranium for use in research reactors (now thankfully very largely if not completely abandoned) or for use in naval propulsion reactors. A more dangerous example in my view is the reprocessing of spent nuclear fuel to separate the plutonium produced in that fuel. The argument goes that this is not only an excellent way to reduce the total amount of dangerous material in spent fuel from a safety and even non-proliferation point of view, but also allows fuel to be burned in reactors as a mixed oxide fuel and its "fuel value" extracted. The truth is that the environmental argument can be satisfied in a much less dangerous way—long-term underground storage—and that the fuel costs are so expensive in its preparation as to make it non-competitive for the long-term future with low enriched uranium (LEU) for the same purpose. And LEU poses little or no proliferation risk.

On the other side of the ledger is the requirement, happily agreed to in the Joint Plan of Action, that a peaceful civilian program will be jointly reviewed and agreed by Iran and its negotiating parties and become the basis for defining an ongoing Iranian program. Thus, what does not serve or establish a peaceful program does not meet the strictures of the treaty, a view clearly implied in the first approach to this issue (outlined in the preceding paragraph) and which clearly fits the view that if it isn't a part of a peaceful program then it doesn't fit the treaty in intent or specificity. This issue will continue to be a part of the underlying differences, but to a degree that it can be reconciled, it will help reach an overall rapprochement.

A second issue has to do with the tactical approach of dealing with parts of the negotiations in this context. The US has taken the view that in an outcome which permits some enrichment (and no reprocessing), the best goal is to secure the longest possible time between any possible future decision to "break out" of the civilian program and go for a nuclear weapon. The JPAG arguably achieved a part of that purpose in enlarging the time period from a matter of some 4–6 weeks to some 3–4 months to produce in Iran a significant quantity of highly enriched uranium (for a weapon). The time periods will be disputed, but the rough proportions are right.

Iran takes the view that this is not their negotiating objective and they have not accepted that approach. They have said they believe that a program with limits defined by agreement on the size of a civil program now and for the life of a comprehensive agreement, buttressed by robust inspections and monitoring by the International Atomic Energy Agency of the United Nations (IAEA), which they say in principle, they are ready to accept, is the basis for going ahead.

There should be a path to agreement here if both sides, as I believe they are, are now serious about finding a common approach. What motivates the approach for success is how well we can accord our approach on break out time with the Iranian acceptance of a limited program of enrichment in quantity and quality defined by civil needs and purposes and robustly inspected by the IAEA.

A third issue also lies out on the horizon which ought to be looked at carefully and constructively. Iran, for reasons of pride in its success in its program and perhaps for other reasons, has, in connection with limitations on its enrichment program, taken a strong position that it is not willing to destroy centrifuges and associated equipment in that program. While from my perspective that approach would represent a better and more secure way to proceed, it can also be looked at in perhaps a different but analogous context. Such equipment could be stored, mothballed, or disconnected in ways that would meet the objectives of the negotiations from both sides—a program limited to civil needs on the Iranian side, and with increased time to break out on the US side. Similarly, proposals to convert the underground Fordow site to R and D purposes might also serve the same purpose.

Looking ahead to what would happen should a breakout be seen to be occurring is a problem unlikely to have to be addressed in an agreement. Also, it would seem likely and useful that extended time would provide an longer time for the use of non-military measures to resolve any such issue should it occur.

While nuclear questions are at the heart of present differences with Iran, they are not the only issues that need to be addressed. Both sides have agreed to keep the nuclear issue at the center of the current negotiations for a comprehensive agreement. But at some point in the future, other questions, as noted in this book, will also have to be considered if the nuclear talks are successful.

Among them are regional questions. These include Afghanistan, where there are shared views. Both sides oppose the Taliban, and see a need to recognize the role of all groups, including the Shia Hazara. They both seek a sovereign, united, and independent Afghanistan at peace with its neighbors and playing a constructive role in the region. Similar views are shared on Iraq, but with potential differences over the degree to which the rights of the Sunni and Kurdish minorities should and have to be accommodated. Syria represents a wider gulf, but even here both agree that Sunni, fundamentalist, terrorist organizations like ISIS or Da'esh pose a threat to the future of Syria and the region.

Beyond these, there are other questions which must be addressed: regime change; the Mossadegh overthrow; the regional role of Iran; how to deal with the USS *Vincennes*' shooting down of Iran Air Flight 655 in 1988; the US hostage-taking; funds left over from the Shah's regime in US hands; and how and in what fashion, if things proceed well, the US and Iran might find a path to closer contacts and eventual resumption of full diplomatic relations.

As an American negotiator, it is my experience that quite often negotiating with Washington and its friends and allies consumed more of my time than negotiating with the other parties at the table. This is no doubt part of the US approach with Iran. While I cannot speak for the Iranian side, this book shows evidence of their having the same problem.

One issue which has now reached prominence is the question of the level of enrichment which Iran might pursue in its future, peaceful, civil program. Much ink has been spilled and many words exchanged over this issue. Prime Minister Netanyahu of Israel, some of our key Arab friends, and a significant group in the US Congress, have all engaged in that discussion and have concluded in favor of "zero enrichment."

Most, if not all, of those who have engaged in this process believe that "zero" would be a preferable course. But a number also believe that given Iran's commitment and expenditure on their program of enrichment, no combination of leverage and pressure over time will achieve the zero goal. They also make the case that limited enrichment under inspection would be an acceptable approach in terms of getting a good overall agreement.

But it is not really enough to assert that the idea is not acceptable and cannot be negotiated without looking more carefully at some of the key reasons. One of those is that once achieved, mastery of enrichment is not something that can be taken out of the heads and experience of Iranian scientists and technicians. So zero, in terms of hardware and operation, while desirable, is not a complete answer. That means that two things might take place. First, it is unlikely that it will be possible to achieve zero, and one possible requirement in getting there which we cannot accept might be less stringent inspection—IAEA standard safeguard procedures unenhanced by the Additional Protocol which allows for inspections on a broader, more comprehensive basis. That would be a poor bargain. Under those circumstances, Iran might choose or be driven toward a clandestine program—there has been evidence of this in the past. (Indeed as far as we know, all such efforts have been discovered well in advance of their being declared by Iran. And that fact would have to be factored into a risk of discovery by Iran with all the consequences of such an action). Second, it would also be true that without an ongoing monitoring program, such a clandestine approach might be more difficult to detect, because there would be next to no possibility of the transfer of people, information, or equipment from an overt program to a clandestine one without being seen.

It will be important to do all that can be done through inspection and monitoring to deter any such efforts to go "underground" literally and figuratively. Unilateral intelligence, National Technical Means in US–Soviet parlance, can also enhance the uncertainty regarding discovery for any party wishing to try to go the clandestine route.

Further, it may be valuable to look at multilateralizing any enrichment operation in Iran. On the one hand, a number of regional countries might want to consider this both as a potential additional deterrent to a rapid breakout by promoting transparency, and on the other hand, as a source for fuel for research and similar-type reactors. Large investors over time might also find this prospect of interest.

We are presented with a unique gift in Mousavian's thorough examination of this issue from his perspective. This is a gift of greater understanding and of a significant opportunity to find a positive result in the negotiations which lie ahead.

Iran–US relations will play a huge role in the future of the Middle East. There will need to be a clear understanding with our friends and allies as we proceed. Many of these remain concerned that the United States, by engaging Iran, is somehow dedicated to turning the careful balance in the region on its head. They too have differences and problems with Iran, some in a theological context, some in a historical context. The truth is that the United States does not wish or is able to change essential balances in the region—and the region these days already presents us with numerous challenges in this regard, following the shifts in Egypt and Syria to mention only a few.

The immediate purpose with Iran is to avoid a nuclear arms threat in the region and the potential for a nuclear arms race that such a development might engender. A solid agreement with Iran, carefully limited and monitored, but respectful on both sides of a civil program, could be a model and not a threat, and indeed represent progress rather than disruption. And it is for the government and people of this region to determine their future relations within the region. Those organizations already functioning among them could well be the basis for their future relations and the United States should, and I feel confident will, support a balanced, equitable, and peaceful future for the Middle East. It is in our national interest to do so. It is clearly the desire of those in the region. Words are important in reaching such arrangements, but even more so, actions are essential. The right actions can help condition the disappearance of misunderstanding and build a barrier to continued mistrust.

The answers on the nuclear question, if they come, will open the door to greater possibilities for agreement on the many issues which still divide us, including Afghanistan, Iraq, and even Syria, where there is more than a modicum of overlap in our national interests. And while that is beyond the scope of the present volume, it is prefigured by its helpful aspects.

I am grateful to have had the opportunity to write this foreword.

Ambassador Thomas Pickering

INTRODUCTION

Filling the Gap

After studying as an undergraduate in the United States, I returned to Iran in 1979 during the upheavals of the revolution. At its victorious conclusion, I joined the new revolutionary government where I remained engaged for three decades in varying official positions working on foreign, security, and domestic policies. This remarkable experience exposed me first-hand to knowledge of the challenges faced by Iran's foreign policy. At the heart of those challenges was conflict between Iran and the West, but more specifically, Iran and the US.

I finally came back to the US in 2009 and began my postdoctoral research career at Princeton University. This new chapter in my life provided opportunities for me to meet hundreds of American and European current and former foreign policy experts and journalists. I worked with the think tanks in the US, EU, Asia, and the Middle East. Moreover, at Princeton I had the opportunity to engage in Track II diplomacy between Iran and the US, conducting a tremendous amount of work aimed at resolving the crisis over Iran's nuclear program, and ultimately reconciliation between Iran and the US. The conflict has had an important impact on the region and the worlds peace and stability. Due to the uncompromising stance between the two states, this struggle could spiral out of control and wind up in a military confrontation, potentially endangering many lives. Additionally, its economic consequences, such as a likely rise in energy costs, could affect millions of lives around the world.

The tenor of Iran–US relations has a tremendous impact on numerous key issues in the Middle East region: the stability of the Persian Gulf, and thus the security of energy; future of extremism in the region and throughout the world; fate of the Arab Awakening; destiny of the Middle East free from weapons of mass destruction;

the Israeli–Palestinian peace process; and weak states such as Iraq, Afghanistan, Lebanon, and Syria.

The stability and peace in the Persian Gulf and the Middle East is crucial to the entire world, including the West. If the current crisis in countries such as Iraq, Afghanistan, and Syria spiral into total chaos, forfeiting command and control to the unorganized masses, regional and international terrorist organizations are likely to take up residence within their borders. The geography of this region also lends itself to organized crime, serving as a major route for drug trafficking to the West via Turkey and Central Asian countries. Without governance, the region is also primed for the production of drugs. Moreover, chaos, sectarian war, and civil war may spill over into the neighboring countries and destabilize them, thus widening terrorism and organized crime even further.

Numerous books have been written by Western experts, mainly American, looking at the root causes of the conflict between Iran and the US. However, none of them has presented an immediate look at this complex relationship from within Iranian culture, society, and, most importantly, the Iranian policy-making system. This gap has been the cause of misanalysis, followed by the adoption of US policies that have failed to achieve their objectives. Furthermore, these policies have elevated hostilities between the two countries while creating and perpetuating a state of non-compromise between them. This is the gap that this book intends to fill. Former Secretary of State Condoleezza Rice once remarked,

> I think … [Iran is] a very opaque place and it's a political system I don't understand very well … And I'll just say one thing, one of the downsides of not having been in Iran … is that we don't really have people who know Iran inside our own system … So that's a problem for us …[1]

Western views on the Iran–US conflict will be discussed in this book, but the intention is not to offer equal attention to both sides of the conflict. The primary purpose of this book is to shed light on the Iranian side of the story which is hardly covered in the West in order to bring a better understanding, thus paving the road to resolving this conflict.

Having served for almost three decades within the Iranian political system, I have pooled my experience and knowledge in search of an answer to the central question of why Iran and the US remain unable to reach a stable compromise. This impasse has existed since the Iranian revolution, despite numerous opportunities for both countries to resolve the conflict, including several attempts at rapprochement. Yet, the fact that the two states, under the tenure of every president of the United States, have pursued reconciliation suggests that the desire for better relations has always existed. This fact has inspired me to write this book, hoping that better understanding of Iran's politics and society would contribute to the actualization of the two nations' aspirations to restore friendship.

Kenneth Pollack, a former CIA analyst and Iran expert, and Ray Takeyh, a former State Department official and advisor on Iran issues, admit that "it [is] exceptionally difficult for outsiders to perceive Iranian motives and intentions ... the best that outside observers can do is guess at Tehran's motives."[2] In this respect, Hamilton Jordan, President Carter's Chief of Staff raises a valid question. Writing about the Embassy seizure, he posited: "we didn't understand that country and its people. How in the world do you negotiate under those circumstances?"[3]

The good news is that for the first time since the Iranian Revolution, Iran and the US have conducted meaningful talks and reached an interim agreement over Iran's nuclear crisis in November 2013. However, caution should be exercised since until the final agreement is reached, there are many hurdles to jump and as a friend and expert said: "The road to a final settlement is long and rocky."

Having been engaged over four years with US foreign and domestic policy experts, I now realize that we, Iranians, also misread the American political system. Like Americans, we are also heavily influenced by our perceptions, misperceptions, and biases. Consequently, we place too much importance on statements by American officials, which lend themselves to further intensification of the conflict. Many Iranian decision-makers are not familiar with the Western culture. This is a mirror image of the situation in the United States, where many American Congressmen have not visited any foreign country, and even boast that they have no passport.[4] This has sometimes caused major problems in the Iranian understanding of the US push-and-pull policies. In fact, the breakthrough in Iran's nuclear dossier in 2013 is due partly to a better understanding in Tehran and Washington, perhaps due to forces on both sides: in the US, the combination of Obama, Kerry, and Hagel and their "engagement policy"; in Iran, the new president, Hassan Rouhani, elected in June 2013, a cleric from Qom with a PhD from UK, his foreign minister, Javad Zarif, with a

PhD from US and the head of the Atomic Energy Organization, Ali Akbar Salehi, also with a PhD from US.

Nevertheless, the majority of Iranian policy-makers become confused by contradictory statements from the Obama administration on the one hand, and the US Congress on the other. They do not see that there is infighting and disagreement within the US government on their foreign policy, just as there is in Iran. They view it as a clear manifestation of hypocrisy and duplicity. The Iranian leadership views these contradictory statements, at best, as signs of a plausible explanation for the US government playing a game of good cop, bad cop.

It is noteworthy that even the proponents of a realist theory in international relations who view the international system as anarchic, in a state of constant antagonism and struggle for survival, do not rule out minimal cooperation between competing states, as was the case during the Cold War era. Nevertheless, in the case of Iran and the US, there have only been a few piecemeal deals and short-lived periods of cooperation followed by renewed hostile postures toward each other. In other words, the dominant characteristic of their relationship has been one of non-compromise.[5] Even during the Cold War, the state of relations was not so poor. At that time, the US maintained diplomatic relations with the USSR and its allies in the communist bloc, despite fierce disagreements between them, and ultimately, diplomacy was successful.

Points of Contention

The conflict between the Islamic Republic of Iran and the US is complex. From the American perspective, the major elements of conflict include: Iran's provoking anti-Americanism; the potential export of the revolution in one of the most important geostrategic regions of the world (given its huge energy resources, amongst other things); Iran's potential threat to the Arab–Israeli peace process and security of Israel; its nuclear program; its role in terrorism; and its violation of human rights.

The major elements of the conflict identified from the Iranian perspective include: adoption of a humiliating approach toward Iran including the language of threat and intimidation; US regional hegemony and denial of Iran's role as a regional power; ignoring Iran's interests in the region; and, orchestrating international, multilateral, and unilateral coercive policies against Iran.

The Conflict as seen from Tehran

In Iran, there are mainly three schools of thought on the Iran–US conflict. All three share two key grievances: first, that the US does not respect the Islamic identity of Iran; and second, that the US has constantly interfered in Iran's affairs and wielded any instrument at its disposal to harm the Iranian government. Nevertheless, the three schools depart from each other over whether or not this US perspective can be altered.

The first school, most notably subscribed to by Iran's Supreme Leader, Ayatollah Ali Khamenei, maintains that the US is addicted to hegemonic status. This school of thought believes that because Iran's Islamic establishment rejects foreign domination, the US seeks regime change in an effort to establish a puppet state and exploit Iran's natural resources.[6]

This school of thought neither categorically rejects dialogue with the US nor opposes a healthy relationship. It is *pessimistic* about the prospects of the formation of a relationship based on an equal footing, non-interference, common interests, and mutual respect. In March 2013, Ayatollah Khamenei opined that he was "not opposed" to direct talks with the United States—although he remarked that he was "not optimistic," either.[7]

The second current of thinking, advocated by the radical right and left, asserts that there is an inherent antagonism between Iran and the US. The ultra-right focuses on the deep contrast between the Islamic and Western values, while the ultra-left's emphasis is on the clash between Iran's desire for independence and what they call the imperialist nature of the US. The ultra-left was the dominant current in the first decade after the revolution, and the ultra-right emerged after the end of Iran–Iraq War. While the ultra-left has almost disappeared, the ultra-right (i.e. "hardliners" in this book) has remained a relevant political force, although they are not big in terms of the number of followers.

The ultra-right argues not only that reconciliation is impossible between Iran and the US, but, more importantly, that reconciliation would conflict with Islamic values. In their view, negotiation with the United States must be considered as the red line. Even the United States' repeated demands for Iran to "change its behavior" are interpreted as a prelude for stripping Iran of its Islamic identity and, more importantly, undermining Iran's position as the spearhead of the war against "global arrogance" led by the United States. Hossein Shariatmadari, manager of chief editor of the daily newspaper *Kayhan* and a staunch proponent of this school of thought, views any talks with the US as "a huge strategic mistake."[8] "Talking to America," he states, "is [tantamount to] shaking hands with the devil and dancing with the wolves."[9]

The third school of thought, represented by Iran's former president Ali Akbar Hashemi Rafsanjani and incumbent President Hassan Rouhani, agrees with the notion that the American system, if it can, will harm Iran's Islamic establishment. However, they remain optimistic about altering the US perspective, as well as the possibility of achieving normalization in relations while protecting Iran's national interests. This school of thought is prepared for serious and comprehensive efforts for maximum engagement with the United States based on mutual respect, non-interference, and advancing mutual interests as the best way to serve the national interest of Iran. The group, described as "centrist," "moderate," and "pragmatist," supports a free market economy and favors privatization of state-owned industries. Proponents of this third school of thought intend to invest in common interests between Iran and the US.

They assert that a negotiation-based resolution can be a win-win situation that offers huge rewards for both countries. They also assert that negotiations between Iran and the US can minimize or eliminate serious threats to both countries which originate from each other's policies, as well as from external forces such as Salafi extremists.

Since the conclusion of the Iran–Iraq War in 1988, the first and third schools of thought have vacillated between cooperation and rejection, while the second has relentlessly sought to prevent the development of relations between Iran and the US.

Elements Obstructing Dialogue and Conciliation

Mistrust: Widely discussed, but ignored in practice

Material factors such as competition over power and interests play a major role in the conflict. However, a sense of profound mistrust is largely responsible for the longevity of deadlock, as well as perpetuation of the hostile, often uncompromising relationship between the two states. The mistrust has now gained an independent life in the relationship between Iran and the US, almost detached from competition over power and interests.

Mistrust has been one of the major reasons Iranians have shied away from engaging in lasting dialogue and negotiations with the US. They fear deception and humiliation by what they perceive as a powerful propaganda machine, without any opportunity to defend itself or confront such propaganda on an equal footing. Ostensibly, in the absence of enduring dialogue, it is illogical to expect a negotiated solution. Most destructively, mistrust has obstructed the development of meaningful and sustainable talks.

Iranians initially lost trust in the US after its admitted role in the 1953 coup d'état which overthrew Mohammad Mossadegh, Iran's popular, democratically-elected prime minister. For the following 25 years, the US supported the Shah, and also supported Iraq's invasion of Iran in September 1980.

The US mistrust of Iran began in 1979 with the seizure of their embassy in Tehran by radical students followed by 52 Americans being held hostage for 444 days. The mutual mistrust has reached the level of dogma. This has elevated the entangled narrative to such a degree that each government has tried to justify destructive policies toward the other in efforts to cripple capabilities and inflict harm.

This mutual mistrust stems from the US treatment of and policies toward Iran, and from Iran's behavior and its reactions to those policies. Surprisingly, many American experts and policy-makers admit that mistrust largely affects Iran–US relations, yet the policies that they propose or adopt only serve to intensify the mistrust between the two states.

Regime change policy

The "regime change" policy of the US, as perceived by all of the Iranian politicians and policy-makers across the political spectrum, is the primary factor that continually fuels the high level of mistrust toward the US, and rejection of any compromise. There is a cornucopia of offenses to choose from: paralyzing economic sanctions; allocating budgets under the banner of supporting freedom in Iran;[10] covert operations to create chaos in Iran;[11] CIA activities inside the country;[12] including Iran in the "Axis of Evil"; clear rejection of security guarantees to Iran,[13] and more. Iranians view all of these as clear signs pointing to a regime change outlook and policy. President Obama's statement that he would "never take military action off the table,"[14] coupled with the toughest sanctions in the last three decades imposed during his presidency, have convinced Iranians that, despite the change in leadership, the same regime-change doctrine is in motion. Major changes in the foreign policy of Iran and the US since the latter part of 2013 have engendered hopes that there might be "a crack in the wall of mistrust."[15]

Misperceptions and misanalysis

Misperceptions of the two countries' policy-makers have undoubtedly contributed to the failure of policies and initiatives aimed at détente between them, resolving the two countries' conflict over Iran's nuclear issue, and most importantly, establishing a meaningful dialogue between the two governments.

James L. Richardson, an international relations expert, offered a definition for misperception as "faulty, inaccurate or incorrect perception of a situation: it is perceived to have characteristics which are not present, or which are present to a significantly lesser or greater extent than perceived."[16] This definition is useful because, as will be discussed in this book, numerous positions and policies adopted by the two states that are largely responsible for the perpetuation of the conflict are based on miscalculations, and misanalysis of the situation.

Outstanding among misperceptions of American policy-makers as well as misanalysis by the analysts is the use of "coercive diplomacy" to change the behavior of the Iranian government. To fulfill this objective, the US "is committed to a dual-track policy of applying pressure in pursuit of constructive engagement, and a negotiated solution."[17] Sanctions are central to this dual-track diplomacy. The language of intimidation and threat of military action under the mantra of "all options are on the table" is also part of the US coercive diplomacy. Isolation, both regionally and internationally, is another element of the US coercive policy toward Iran. This book broadly assesses these "coercive policies" and why they have failed and will continue to fail. These policies are based on the flawed premise that Iran will surrender to pressure. American policy-makers entirely ignore the pervasive role of "pride" in Iran's politics. Hassan Rouhani, during his swearing-in ceremonies, repeated this major but constantly ignored demand by Iranians: "I say this straightforward. If you seek a suitable answer, speak to Iran through the language of respect, not through the language of sanctions."[18]

For better or worse, Iranians are a proud nation. This characteristic has roots in Iran's long history and civilization. Pride and national pride are ubiquitous in Iranian culture and discourse. The notion of pride is linked to empowerment rather than submission. That is the reason Iran fiercely resists coercive policies, particularly the sanctions.

John Limbert, former Deputy Assistant Secretary in charge of Iranian Affairs at the State Department during 2009–10, describes the weakness in this US approach as follows: "Since 1979 … [w]e've used sanctions against Iran. They're something we know. They're something with which we have experience … [But] changing the unproductive relationship that we've had with Iran for the last 30 years [is something] that we do not know how to do. That's hard."[19]

The risk of misperceiving that coercion will eventually work is that at some point, Iran's patience may wane to the point of abandoning its rationality, and responding to those US pressures in a hostile manner. This would most likely lead to a destructive war.

Some may argue that sanctions encouraged Iran to return to the negotiation table in 2013. This assertion is wrong. The realization of an interim agreement in November 2013 was the will of Iran's new moderate administration seeking rapprochement with the West, in particular the US, its neighbors, and the rest of the world. In addition, it reflected the change of the US position toward Iran's nuclear program from "no enrichment of uranium" to "no nuclear bomb." Iran has not left the negotiating table since talks began in 2003, even during the tenure of Mahmoud Ahmadinejad. While I was a member of the Iranian nuclear negotiating team from 2003 to 2005, Iran was not faced with crippling sanctions, yet in March 2005, Iran suggested measures similar to those stipulated in the November 2013 interim agreement between Iran and the P5+1, to ensure that the country would not divert its nuclear program toward weaponization. The 2005 talks failed because, as I was told by the European negotiators, the US position was "zero enrichment" in Iran. This claim is verifiable. If the US goes back to the similar approach of "no enrichment in Iran", it would be unlikely to reach a settlement on the nuclear issue, despite the imposition of paralyzing sanctions.

Domestic political struggles

Domestic political struggles in Tehran and Washington have repeatedly undercut efforts for engagement. One of the main problems with Iran–US rapprochement is the lack of consensus for a genuine engagement in both capitals. Since the 1979 Revolution, neither the US nor Iranian administrations have released any realistic study on the balance of costs and benefits of rapprochement.[20] Instead, both capitals' political systems have been locked in a Cold War model. It has been constant pull and push on both sides. In other words, there has been no real, strategic foreign policy. It has dominantly been domestic politics that seems to determine foreign policies toward one another.

Spoilers

Last but not least, spoilers have played a major role in blocking diplomatic efforts, not only for rapprochement, but even for cooperation on issues of common interest. Hardliners, in Iran, the United States, and Israel, as well as some Arab countries in the region and the terrorist group Mojahedin-e-Khalq (MEK[21]), have constantly sabotaged the relations between the two states. We observe a pattern of intensification of efforts to neutralize attempts at reconciliation between Iran and the US right at the very moments when hopes for an improvement in relations appear on the horizon. The harsh reactions of the Israeli government, including threats of military action, and the pro-Israel lobbying group, American Israel Public Affairs Committee (AIPAC), urging the Congress to pass a new sanctions bill after the interim Geneva agreement on Iran's nuclear program was signed between Iran and the P5+1 (the five permanent members of the UN Security Council plus Germany) in November 2013, are clear examples of such efforts.

Structure of this Book

Iran and The United States: An Insider's View on the Failed Past and the Road to Peace is structured chronologically. It analyzes the key events and figures that have shaped the hostile Iran–US relationship as well as describing the conflict between the states as viewed from Tehran. The book demonstrates the influence of psychological and cultural factors on the Iranian mindset. These factors have remained opaque to the US analysts and policy-makers who advocate reconciliatory solutions, but as is customary, focus merely on economic and political tradeoffs. Based on its findings, the book offers a realistic and feasible road map to peace to address not only substantive but also cultural-psychological factors.

The first chapter is a condensed review of three very different periods in the shared history of these two states. Without proper knowledge of the actual history of relations between the two nations, one might believe that the United States and Iran have, from the outset, been locked in disputes.

The second chapter reveals how profound mistrust and misperceptions on both sides shaped the hostage crisis, with effects that
few could have imagined would be so long lasting. The significance
of the hostage crisis lies in the fact that it marks the big bang, the
beginning of time in the hostile relationship between the Islamic
Republic of Iran and the United States. Identifying the root causes
of the hostage crisis leads us to understand the underlying causes of
both the emergence and perpetuation of the conflict between Iran and
the US. This is because many of current points of contention between
Iran and the US either did not exist or were insignificant at that time.
There was no competition over hegemony in the region between
the two countries, cultural differences had not emerged, the issue of
Israel was a non-factor, and there was no dispute over Iran's nuclear
program.

Chapter 3 focuses on Iran–Iraq War from 1980 to 1989, although it
also addresses other events such as the bombing of the Islamic Republic
Party's headquarters and attempts on my life.

US aid to Saddam, which is detailed in this chapter, and the US
absolute silence after Iraq's criminal use of chemical weapons against
the Iranians solidified hatred toward the US among the Iranian power
elite. The leadership embraced the belief that the US, no matter the
cost, was determined to change the Iranian system (*nezam*).

The strategic thinking of late Ayatollah Khomeini, the Leader of the
1979 Revolution, was that the war would end only when the "heretic"
Saddam was overthrown. Ayatollah Khomeini viewed Saddam as a
permanent threat to the whole region that had to be rooted out. To
achieve this, the Islamic Revolutionary Guards Corps (IRGC) prepared
a plan. However, some high-ranking figures, despite the objection
of many politicians, finally convinced the Leader of the Revolution
to accept a ceasefire and to end the War. While Tehran defeated
Saddam's plan to dismember Iran and bring about a regime change, it
failed to remove the aggressor. What Ayatollah Khomeini considered
as "drinking [a] chalice of poison" and the developments up to the
acceptance of the ceasefire are described in this chapter.

Chapter 4 discusses the eight-year presidency of Ayatollah Akbar
Hashemi Rafsanjani. Rafsanjani, a pragmatic centrist and moderate
conservative, took office in 1989. He sought economic development
through the free market model, active and productive relations with
the West, and the reestablishment of relations with the US. Rafsanjani
sought to use Germany as a doorway to implementing full diplomatic
and economic relations with Europe and détente and normalization

with the US. My mission as Iran's ambassador to Germany was to help actualize these objectives.

However, due to the lack of reciprocation by the West toward the Iranians' overtures, Ayatollah Ali Khamenei, Iran's Supreme Leader, supported a less flexible stance. Thus emerged the thesis of "the West minus the United States." This heralded the emergence of two distinctive schools of thought within the system (*nezam*) which have endured for the last 25 years.

From high hopes to total disappointment, the chapter tells how Rafsanjani's plans and my efforts for positive interaction with the West ended in failure. We see how terror events, broken promises, and policies based on misperception and misanalysis, all contributed to Rafsanjani's failure in his efforts at closing the gap between Iran and the United States.

The eight-year presidency of the reformist Mohammad Khatami is explained and analyzed in Chapter 5. By highlighting some unprecedented attempts at rapprochement, proposed from both sides and extraordinary cases of cooperation between the two governments, the chapter reveals how perceptions, misperceptions and misanalysis ultimately blocked the success of those efforts.

Through spotlighting some major developments of this period, the dynamics of Iran's foreign policy decision-making are decoded. Contrary to the Western vision, the Supreme Leader's will is not the only force that determines the tenor and direction of foreign policy. He constantly monitors the two opposing camps and then decides. In this chapter, based on my knowledge of Ayatollah Khamenei's mindset, I answer the key question: "Why does Ayatollah Khamenei oppose renewing the relationship with the United States?"

The revelation of Iran's nuclear program escalated the Iran–US conflict to new heights. As the former spokesman of Iran's negotiating team, I provide an insight into the developments, debates, and visions within and ouside the government of Iran. I demonstrate the hidden but significant role of the US in the failure of the negotiations between the moderate administration of Khatami and the Europeans.

A factional struggle between moderates and radicals dating back to the late 1980s led to the emergence of Ahmadinejad followed by the radicalization of the government after 16 years of the moderates' rule. In Chapter 6, the causes of this transformation are reviewed. However, the aggressive policies of the George W. Bush administration were arguably the decisive factor in the rise of radicalism in Iran.

The straw that broke the camel's back was the failure of the West to accept Khatami's moderate team's attempt to secure Iran's nuclear program. This, as I was informed by the Europeans, was directly linked to the US behind-the-scene activities. Chapter 6 also discusses the conflict at the intersection of Ahmadinejad and the presidencies of George W. Bush and Barack Obama. Obama's election gave hope for change in the US offensive policies toward Iran. The chapter illustrates why Obama's rapprochement failed. In the aftermath of Iran's 2009 disputed presidential election, due to the lack of knowledge about Iran's politics and misanalysis of the situation in Iran, thus overestimating the power and misreading the nature of the so-called Green Movement, by both American policy-makers and analysts alike, the Obama administration suddenly adopted extremely coercive policies intended to either change the behavior of the Islamic Republic of Iran or to bring about regime change.

A host of other issues, such as the cost of ignorance as well as miscalculations on the part of the Iranians, and the reasons why Iran's position was strengthened in Iraq during Ahmadinejad's presidency, are also discussed in this chapter.

Chapter 7 explores the major issues of the conflict between Iran and the US including terrorism, Iran–Israel conflict and the human rights. While the West has accused Iran of state-sponsored terrorism, that country has also been victim of terrorism and served as a key partner to the US in combating terrorism in the Middle East, especially following the tragic events of September 11, 2001. Based on analysis, I prescribe a way forward for the two states in combating their common enemies.

Iran's hostile stance toward Israel is not limited to the Rafsanjani period. But, it has became a major factor in Iran–US relations. The chapter discusses the views of Tehran and explains the root causes of Iran's hostility toward Israel. Finally, the chapter discusses the dispute over human rights, details the views of the two states in this respect and offers solution to this complex dimension of the conflict.

Chapter 8 is a road map to peace. The current precarious state of affairs cannot be sustained. If no common ground is created between Iran and the US, one of two scenarios, both with similar outcomes, is likely to occur. As pressures build over time, patience for long diplomatic processes will diminish and, most likely, military confrontation could take the place of diplomacy. Or, as the US tightens sanctions and, ultimately, the *nezam*'s survival is threatened, once they feel that they have nothing more to lose, Iran's retaliatory actions such as desta-bilizing American allies in the Persian Gulf, destabilizing US interests in the region, and disrupting the passage of oil through the Strait of Hormuz may lead to an inadvertent or deliberate war. The rewards for normalization of relations would be substantial for both countries. In cooperation, the two sides could address the concerns of the United States' Arab allies, stabilize Iraq, Syria, and even Afghanistan, secure a sustainable and stable flow of oil, create more security for Israel, fight Salafi-Al-Qaeda terrorism, and its more violent offshoot, ISIS, and narcotic trafficking, and put an end to Iran's economic difficulties.

Although there are more issues involved than nuclear development, a peaceful resolution to that *one* issue should be considered as a key starting point for peace between the two states. However, "[p]eace on the nuclear issue alone while other cases of conflict remain unresolved would be unstable."[22]

As a proponent of the "maximum engagement" school of thought between Iran and the West/US, based on 35 years of experience in diplomacy, in order to address mistrust and promote better and enduring friendly relations between Iran and the West/US, my aim is to formulate a workable, realistic, win-win road map to resolve the protracted standoff in Iran–US relations. I wish to substitute friendship and peace for hatred and hostilities between the two great countries of Iran and America. This is the aim pursued in *Iran and The United States: An Insider's View on the Failed Past and the Road to Peace.*

Chapter 1

IRAN-US RELATIONS: FROM FRIENDS TO FOES

Following the Islamic Revolution of 1979, relations between Iran and United States have been typified by heightened animosity and mistrust, at times teetering on the brink of confrontation. However, this has not always been the case. Prior to this period, from the origins of formal Iran–US relations dating back to the mid-1800s, two other vastly different periods define the interaction between the two nations.

During the first period (1856–1953), Iran viewed the United States as a benevolent international power whose intent was to support the independence and sovereignty of a weaker nation threatened by imperial powers. However, following the Second World War and the ensuing rise of the United States as a superpower—as well as its increasing tensions with the Soviet Union—its interest in preserving the independence of Iran quickly dissipated. The newfound international position of the US shifted its foreign policy objectives, particularly in the resource-rich region of the Middle East, focusing more on energy security and containing the spread of Soviet influence.

The 1953 coup that toppled Iran's first democratically elected government marked the beginning of the second period of relations (1953–79). The US supported the ousting of Iran's Prime Minister, Mohammad Mossadegh. Ironically, it was US assistance in building institutions to strengthen reform and representative rule in Iran that had planted the seeds of democracy. By installing Mohammad Reza Shah in the aftermath of the 1953 coup, Iran–US relations entered a new chapter characterized by a patron–client relationship and intrusive involvement by the US in Iran's domestic affairs.

With the victory of the Islamic Revolution in 1979, Iran entered the third period, which will be comprehensively discussed in this book.

Cordial Relations: 1856–1953

The beginnings of Iran–US relations dates back to 1856, when the two nations signed a Treaty of Commerce and Friendship based on mutual understanding and friendship.[1] At the time, Americans were viewed favorably by Iranians, who had come to praise the United States for the growing charitable work of American missionaries in the country.[2] Initial American involvement was well received in Iran because it was in the midst of staving off British and Russian pressure on its territorial integrity. Iran sought to establish relations with Washington to offset their influence.[3] The United States was widely regarded as a charitable international power whose foreign policy doctrine was based on protecting the weak from imperialist powers.[4] What began as an economic treaty between the two nations in 1856 led to formal diplomatic relations, with the opening of the US diplomatic mission in Tehran in 1883 and the first Iranian representative arriving in Washington in 1888.[5]

Relations between the two countries remained cordial; there was no interference by the United States in the internal affairs of Iran, giving them no reason for distrust. The US retained its spectator role and refrained from intervening during the Iranian Constitutional Revolution of 1905–11. The uprising took place in response to the failure of the Qajar[6] monarchy to improve the socio-economic and political conditions of the people. This popular movement brought together all parts of Iranian society—the clerics, merchants, intellectuals, nationalists, and socialists—in an effort to curb the powers of the monarch. The national effort culminated in the establishment of a constitutional monarchy in Iran.[7]

American heroes of Iran

While the US government avoided a public stance on the situation and refused to get involved in the Constitutional Revolution in Iran, nonetheless, from the ashes of the struggle to achieve independence, an American hero emerged for the Iranians: Howard Baskerville. In the early 1900s, Howard Baskerville emigrated to Iran as a Presbyterian missionary, teaching at the American Memorial School in Tabriz, at the time second largest city of Iran, and, during the Constitutional Revolution, actively supporting the constitutionalists who were fighting against the royalists. He gave his life in the ensuing battle.

Baskerville's ultimate sacrifice for Iranian independence and democratic movement in Iran not only made him a hero, but also bolstered Iran's conviction that the United States supported the rights of the people and their thirst for freedom. Baskerville's example also gave rise to the idea that Americans viewed the "other" on an equal footing. His statement that "[t]he only difference between me and these people is my place of birth, and this is not a big difference"[8] was the manifestation of that egalitarian view.

In response to the revolution, the British and Russians put their differences aside to ensure that their mutual interests in Iran were not jeopardized. Their efforts resulted in the Anglo-Russian Treaty of 1907, in which northern Iran would come under Russian influence while the south would be controlled by Britain.[9] This foreign imposition made the reform and strengthening of institutions a critical necessity for the new government.

To spearhead the reform initiative, the Constitutionalists looked for a foreign partner that would actively and willingly assist in building an independent nation without ulterior motive. The natural choice was the United States, as it was the only major power that could be entrusted with such a task, particularly since the memory of Baskerville was fresh in the minds of the Constitutionalists and the US had established that its intentions in Iran were not to encroach on Iran's sovereignty.

This belief on the part of the Constitutionalists led to the Iranians requesting Washington to recommend a financial advisor who would assist Iran's restructuring of its financial sector. The advisor was to be given the authority and scope necessary to perform the task. Washington accepted the request and on their recommendation, the Iranians recruited William Morgan Shuster, a lawyer with experience in financial matters. Shuster was not an employee of the American government but came as a private citizen, further deepening the perception that the United States had no wish or policy intention to meddle in Iran's domestic affairs, yet would extend its help to the country.[10]

Shuster arrived with a small team of financial advisors in 1911 and was shortly thereafter appointed by the Iranian parliament as the Treasurer General of Persia. Shuster's devotion, dedication, and honesty in assisting Iran to the best of his ability engendered great respect from the Iranians, and contributed to the growing admiration for the ethical manner in which the United States operated. However, the Russians and the British grew impatient with his outspoken opposition to their intrusion in Iran's domestic affairs. In Shuster's invaluable book, *The Strangling of Persia*, which detailed the events that led to the collapse of the Constitutional Revolution and described the British and Russian encroachments in Iran, he stated: "It was obvious that the people of Persia deserve much better than what they are getting, that they wanted us to succeed, but it was the British and the Russians who were determined not to let us succeed."[11]

The independent stance Shuster adopted toward the imperial powers resulted in a Russian ultimatum to Iran to oust Shuster or face the consequences. The Iranians resisted the ultimatum. The Russians retaliated by invading northern Iran and marching onward toward the capital, Tehran. Only then was the decision reluctantly made to expel Shuster. The parliament was consequently suspended.

While Iran paid a high price, Shuster's stance and commitment to improving the Iranian economy and standing up for values such as equality, dignity, and freedom reinforced the positive perception the Iranian people had of the United States. Shuster later wrote: "The Persian people, fighting for a chance to live and govern themselves instead of remaining the serfs of wholly heartless and corrupt rulers, deserved better of fate than to be forced, as now, either to sink back into an even worse serfdom or to be hunted down and murdered as 'revolutionary dregs.' British and Russian statesmen may be proud of their work in Persia; it is doubtful whether anyone else is."[12]

There were other Americans who contributed immensely to the development of Iran. In the education sector, Dr. Samuel Martin Jordan was seen as the pioneer who laid the foundations for the modern education system in Iran. Jordan devoted his life to improving the educational system in Iran by serving as the principal of the American High School in Tehran from 1898 to 1941. In the medical field, Dr. Joseph Plumb Cochran was the founder of Iran's first modern College of Medicine in 1879.

These examples and various others cemented the notion that the United States was interested in fostering better relations, advancing the Iranians' cause of independence, protecting the weak, and promoting democratic ideals. Yet it must be noted that US foreign policy toward Iran was also driven by a reluctance to challenge the vital interests of Britain and Russia, as evidenced in the dismissal of Shuster.

Saving Iran from British rule

At the onset of the First World War in 1914, Iran declared its neutrality and made numerous efforts to avoid the war. However, Iran's declared neutrality failed to protect it from the invasion of its territory by the belligerent powers of Russia and Britain. Owing to its strategic location,

Russia and Britain (Allied Powers) used Iranian territory to counter Ottoman (Central Power) forces as well as to guarantee that supplies from India would reach the British forces. Iran was destitute as its sovereignty was trampled on and its territory became a fighting ground between the opposing forces, leaving thousands of Iranians killed and its economy in tatters.

At this time, Iran once again reached out, asking for US assistance to safeguard its independence and to help maintain its neutrality. The United States responded with assurances to Iran that it would "lend its good offices to assist in doing whatever it may properly do to alleviate the conditions resulting from the situation existing in Europe."[13] This was in line with President Wilson's proclamation that the United States would confirm that the weaker nations would be protected from the Allied powers' imperialist tendencies in the aftermath of the war.[14] With this response, there was an air of optimism in Iran that the US would deliver on the promise.

This hope sustained Iran's positive image of the US. On the humanitarian front, the tensions on the western borders of the country required urgent relief; however, Iran had no capacity to respond. US groups created the Persian Relief Committee in 1916, which led the drive in soliciting relief aid for Iranians, with resounding success. This act of kindness was greatly appreciated by Iranians and was seen as another indicator of US generosity toward Iran. The creation of the American Persian Relief Commission in New York in 1918 continued relief efforts until the crisis was over.

The most significant test of the US commitment to weaker nations and evidence of its promise to protect Iran's independence came in the aftermath of the war.

The British were eager to solidify their hegemonic aspirations in Iran. The Bolshevik Revolution in 1917 had resulted in a weaker Russian influence in the region; the British moved to take advantage. To achieve their goal, the British had negotiated a secret treaty with the Iranian Prime Minister Vosuq al-Dowleh that, if ratified by the Iranian Parliament (*Majlis*), would in essence have made Iran a protectorate of Great Britain.[15] At this time, Iran's independence undoubtedly was on the line, and it was then that the United States took a firm stance against the British imperialist policy in Iran.

Two statements were sent from US Secretary of State Robert Lansing to the US ambassador in Tehran. The first outlined the American government's opposition to such a deal between Iran and Britain while the second reassured the Iranians of US support for Iran's independence by stating that "the United States has constantly and consistently showed its interest in the welfare of Persia."[16] These statements provided the backing the Iranians needed to take a bold position. The *Majlis* rejected the treaty.

This event brought about great changes in Iran–US relations: Iran perceived the US as a counterbalance to British influence, and was determined to court the Americans with economic and political incentives to ensure America's continued support for the independence of the country.

America helps to build modern Iran

In the aftermath of the First World War, Iran's economy was in ruins and the government of the constitutional monarchy was eager to solidify its authority in the country. The Iranian government sought to attract foreign investment in the country. The commodity that could provide the greatest incentive was oil; however, the British, through earlier agreements, had secured oil concessions that were entirely one-sided in favor of themselves. The case in point was a 1901 agreement that gave oil concessions in the southern Iranian fields to the British financier William Knox D'Arcy, leading to the establishment in 1908 of the Anglo-Persian Oil Company (APOC) – later renamed Anglo-Iranian Oil Company (AIOC). In 1914, through an Act of Parliament, the British government took effective control of the APOC. The terms of the agreement gave Iran a meager share of the net revenues, just 16 percent, while the Iranian government was not afforded access to the financial records of the company.[17] These arbitrary and demeaning terms fueled anti-British sentiments in Iran. The Iranian government would seek to procure more favorable conditions in future oil concessions.

A military coup d'état, led by British- and Russian-supported Colonel Reza Khan,[18] succeeded in February 1921. By 1925, Reza Khan had consolidated both the political and military power that ended the Qajar dynasty. He subsequently proclaimed himself as king, Reza Shah Pahlavi, and established the Pahlavi dynasty in Iran, ushering a new era for the country.

As the Iranian financial sector was in disarray once again, Tehran requested Washington to assist in recommending individuals to serve as the country's financial advisors. Following the success the Shuster mission had previously accomplished, the US was a natural choice. The US responded to Iran's request by proposing a team of American financial advisors led by Arthur C. Millspaugh, a former official at the US State Department's Office of Foreign Trade.[19]

In the next several years, Millspaugh worked with prodigious dedication to restructure the Iranian economy. He is credited with overhauling the taxation system, increasing government revenues, cutting deficit, and putting the finances of Iran on a sound basis. Secure finances led to the implementation of the Trans-Iranian railway project among other infrastructure developments and reforms.[20] Millspaugh's term ended after five years in 1927 due to his disagreement with Reza Shah, who wanted him to increase military expenditure. Relations between the United States and Iran remained cordial from the mid-1920s to the outbreak of the Second World War in 1939. The US unfailingly maintained its position of non-interference in the domestic affairs of Iran.[21] Meanwhile, Reza Shah had consolidated his power, and spearheaded the strengthening of central government and the military capability of the country. He had become attracted to the rapid industrialization of Germany and began to improve relations with Berlin, particularly because the Germans grew increasingly hostile toward the British and the Russians.[22]

At the onset of the Second World War, Iran once again announced its neutrality and aimed to protect its sovereignty and independence. However, as was the case in the First World War, the Allied forces of Britain and Russia invaded Iran in 1941, on the pretext of curbing German influence in the country. The actual intention behind the invasion was to assure that their supply routes and oil fields were secured.[23] At the same time, Moscow and London made a decision to remove Reza Shah because of his support for and collaboration with the Germans. Reza Shah was expelled from Iran and was replaced by his son, 22-year-old Mohammad Reza.[24]

Iranians still considered the United States to be a nation of ideal-istic values, which included protecting the weak and maintaining the independence of sovereign nations. Therefore, Tehran continued to pursue its policy of courting the United States in order to maintain the balance of power and mitigate the influence of Russia and Britain in Iranian affairs. Iran deduced that there was an urgent need for a strong advocate to ensure that the Allied adhered to the Tripartite Agreement, signed with Tehran in 1943.[25] This treaty stipulated that Allied forces would remove their troops in the aftermath of the war and provide adequate reparations in exchange for using Iran's territory and resources for their war operations.

Iran–US relations further developed as the government of Iran solicited the services of American advisors, leading to the return of Millspaugh and other advisors, not only to assist with the financial sector but to oversee the military, police, transportation, and food security.[26] However, owing to internal divisions, instability, and the growing disagreements between Mohammad Reza Shah and Millspaugh, the advisory missions failed and became a source of friction between Washington and Tehran, resulting in the termination of these missions in 1945.[27]

In a 1943 military operation, the first US troops landed on Iranian soil to assist in securing supply routes to the Soviet Union. This event marked an end to the hands-off policy of the US toward Iran.[28] However, Iranians continued to believe that in any eventuality, the United States would support their right to self-determination. Two events in the period 1945–6 further supported this view. In the course of the 1943 Tehran Conference, the leaders of the US, USSR and the UK had reaffirmed their commitment to Iran's sovereignty and acknowledged its invaluable contribution to the Allied war effort.[29] Moreover, following the war, in 1946, the British forces fulfilled their commitment and withdrew from Iranian soil under the Tripartite Agreement, although the Soviets refused to comply.

The six-month period of grace duly passed and there was no sign of the Russian troops leaving. President Truman issued a warning to the Russians that if they did not remove their troops, the US would send its forces to Iran. The Soviets, pressured by the US, eventually removed their troops in May 1946.[30] Truman's action served to reaffirm Iran's trust in the United States.

Twenty-Five Years of US Domination: 1953–79

In the years following the war, the United Stated adopted a cautious, yet emboldened approach to Iran. Originally, the US was hesitant to engage fully with their Iranian counterparts, partly due to the complications of balancing the growing tension with the Soviets in the Cold War, the extensive reconstruction effort underway in Europe to counter communist influence, and the avoidance of blatantly encroaching on the British sphere of influence in Iran.

Nevertheless, the developing importance of oil, the strategic location of Iran, the history of cordial relations, and proclamation of the Truman Doctrine, which provided economic support to nations to offset communist and separatist movements, spurred the US to be more intimately involved with Iran. The Truman Doctrine materialized for the Iranians through an initial military aid package on June 20, 1947 of $25 million to train the Iranian army and provide weapons. This event formed the basis of the growing military and economic relations between the two countries, encouraging the US to vigorously pursue strategic relations with Iran.

The tipping point

In the aftermath of the Second World War, Iran was confronted with chronic economic problems that had led to depleted government resources and an inept government with weak institutions headed by an inexperienced young king, Mohammad Reza Shah. Previous promises of reparations for Iran's wartime assistance never materialized. The situation was further exacerbated by the unfavorable oil arrangement between Iran and the Great Britain that gave rise to the British Petroleum Company (BP), which later became a source of humiliation and resentment for Iranians.[31] These one-sided conditions set in motion the aspiration for Iran to have more control over its natural resources and main source of revenue, namely oil.

In the pursuit of control over its oil resources, the Iranian Parliament (*Majlis*) in 1949 began to contemplate new terms for the oil agreement with AIOC. The person who championed this cause was Dr. Mohammad Mossadegh,[32] whose attempts at negotiations failed, mainly due to British reluctance to adjust the terms of the agreement.[33] During this time, Iran once again turned to the United States to play a mediating role and uphold their independence in the face of British aggression. Initially, the Truman administration sympathized with the Iranians and placed pressure on Britain to reform its agreement on oil concessions. However, the British refused to compromise, and there was no headway. In these circumstances, it was inevitable that Iran would nationalize its oil.[34]

By 1951, the oil issue had enraged the nation and a wave of popular nationalism swept the country, culminating in the *Majlis* announcing the nationalization of Iranian oil in March 1951. A month later, pressed by popular demand, the Shah appointed Mohammad Mossadegh as the new Iranian Prime Minister.

The Iranian decision to go ahead with the nationalization of its oil industry unleashed the British move to orchestrate sanctions in the form of an international boycott of Iranian oil, freezing Iranian assets, and taking steps to increase Iran's international isolation.[35] The British also undertook covert measures to oust Prime Minister Mossadegh, and turned to the United States to assist them with the plan. President Truman rejected the initial request by the British for US cooperation, asserting "We don't overthrow governments; the United States has never done this before, and we're not going to start now."[36]

Eventually, the British dragged the US into their deceptive gambit by using the anti-communist fervor of the Cold War and false propaganda to advance the unsubstantiated claim that Prime Minister Mossadegh was leaning toward the Soviet Union and was backed by the Iranian Communist Party (Tudeh Party).[37] This position gained traction with the election of President Eisenhower in November 1952, who came to power partly because of his passionate opposition to communist Soviet expansion.[38]

Eisenhower's administration, fearing that communism would gain a foothold in Iran and would contribute to the spread of nationalistic tendencies and communism in the region, decided to support the British plan to oust Prime Minister Mossadegh. The British MI6 and American Central Intelligence Agency (CIA) began to devise the plan, codenamed Operation AJAX, which included the use of negative propaganda against the Mossadegh government, rigging elections, bribing officials, and creating civil disturbance through hired gangs and the financing of a military coup led by former General Fazlollah Zahedi, with the blessing of the Shah.[39]

The first attempt at the coup failed on August 15, 1953 and the Shah fled to Italy, while Colonel Fazlollah Zahedi, who was tasked with leading the coup, went into hiding, only to be encouraged by the CIA and MI6 to initiate another attempt on August 19. The second effort, supported by CIA and MI6 agents, succeeded in bringing to an end the budding democratic movement in Iran and ejecting Prime Minister Mossadegh.[40]

The coup d'état was the single most pivotal event in shaping Iran–US relations for decades to come. Whether it was geostrategic imperatives and fears of a communist takeover, Soviet influence, or oil resources that motivated the US to intervene, the coup changed the psyche of Iranian society and destroyed Iranians' positive image of the United States. The humiliation and frustration felt by Iranians laid the foundations of the anti-Americanism that ultimately produced the 1979 Islamic Revolution.

The US: Senior partner

In the aftermath of the CIA and MI6 coup, Mohammad Reza Pahlavi returned from Italy and was reinstalled as the Shah of Iran. The ousted

Prime Minister Mossadegh was sentenced to a three-year jail sentence. Mossadegh spent the rest of his life under house arrest. The Shah took immediate measures to gain full authority in the country by placing the nation under a military curfew. He subsequently attempted to purge all dissent. He launched a wave of arrests, imprisonments, torture, and death sentences that affected nearly all of Mossadegh's supporters, sympathizers, and opposition figures.[41] Furthermore, all opposition parties were outlawed and political organizations and gatherings were banned. The *Majlis* was not spared. The limited authority and powers it had were stripped away and the Shah crafted a puppet "two-party" system that saw both political parties aligned with him and under his full control, rendering the parliament impotent and ineffective.

Concessions were made to the Americans for their role in reinstating the Shah, primarily securing their energy interests in Iran in the form of oil concessions. This was reflected in the United States taking a 40 percent share in the oil consortium.[42] These concessions ushered in greater US involvement in the domestic affairs of Iran, increased US reliance on Iranian oil, and an American desire to strengthen the Shah's domineering rule over the country.[43] The Eisenhower administration also intended to curb communist encroachment in the Middle East by bolstering the Shah. Despite the communist threat, the US made a strategic mistake by investing in a harsh dictator as a counterbalance.

The US and the British had control over a pro-Western Shah with staunch anti-communist tendencies. To ensure the West would maintain their hold on Iran in the face of the Soviet threat, immediately following the coup, the CIA helped create a new Iranian intelligence agency and trained virtually all of the first generation of its personnel.[44]

Sazeman-e Ettela'at va Amniyat-e Keshvar, [The Organization for National Intelligence and Security], popularly known by its Persian acronym "SAVAK," was established in 1956 and became the most feared component of the Shah's power structure. Right or wrong, Iranians associated SAVAK with the backing of the United States. The level of terror unleashed by SAVAK and the impunity with which they operated in the country made the organization one of the most brutal foundations of the Shah's power. In the perspective of the Iranian public, SAVAK was regarded as inseparable from American interference in Iran's affairs and the Tehran government's repressive control. A portion of those arrested and tortured included members of the religious establishment, both clerics and non-clerics. Many of these individuals later directed the opposition movement in the late

1970s, and subsequently, in the aftermath of the 1979 Revolution, took the most prominent positions in the new establishment. These included high-ranking Mujtahids such as late Ayatollah Montazeri (one of the main constitutional architects of the Islamic Republic) and political religious leaders such as Ayatollah Khamenei (Iran's second and current Supreme Leader), Ayatollah Rafsanjani (former President and current head of the Expediency Council), Ayatollah Mahdavi Kani (former head of the Assembly of Experts who passed away in 2014), Ayatollah Beheshti (first head of the Judiciary), and Mr. Karroubi (former Majlis Speaker of the parliament). These men held a deep sense of animosity toward the US for its support of the Shah.

The Shah was perceived favorably by Washington and seen as a loyal supporter of US interests in the region. In return, the Americans embarked on an extensive program to bolster the Shah's power and rule, providing vast military aid, with scores of advisors and trainers sent to Iran between 1952 and 1961, helping to build a formidable military force for the Shah.

By the early 1960s, the Shah had consolidated his power and was expanding the reach of SAVAK to guarantee that any dissent would be crushed. However, there was growing unease in the US regarding the stability of the Shah's rule, as Iran began to experience rampant inflation and high food prices. While the economy had grown considerably, wealth was concentrated in the hands of Shah's royalists, foreign businesses, select sectors, and urban centers of the country, thus increasing the disparity with the rest of the country and its people. Furthermore, stifled political freedom and brutal suppression of any form of dissent resulted in growing restlessness among Islamists and among the politically conscious educated population.

The Shah's first and foremost goal was to Westernize the country. However, fearing widespread revolution in Iran, the Kennedy administration in the early 1960s, urged the Shah to implement socio-economic reforms. The outcome was a far-reaching program of political, social, and economic reform—the Shah's so-called White Revolution.

The White Revolution aimed to transform the Iranian economy from an agrarian to an industrial one through land reform to end feudalism, privatization of government-owned enterprises, extension of voting rights to women, and curbing the influence of the religious establishment in the education sector by initiating a literacy drive and an overhaul of the education system. The Shah's heavy dependence on on US economic advisors had characterized the reforms of the White Revolution as distinctly Western, with insufficient attention given to the social and religious fabric of the Iranian society and its traditional resistance to Western dominance. This had roots in Reza Shah's decision to prohibit the use of hijab by women as well as reform of the judiciary and the education system based on Westernized models and standards of the late 1920s and 1930s, a system which was predominantly under the control of the clergy.[45]

A segment of the clergy, headed by Grand Ayatollah Ruhollah Khomeini, began to voice their disagreement with the White Revolution based on religious grounds, arguing that the reforms had stripped the country of its religious and cultural identity. Granting suffrage to women was viewed by this segment of the clergy as fake, deceptive and aimed at Westernization of the country. There was also mounting opposition within the urban working class and intelligentsia. They were critical of reforms that had not translated into meaningful political rights and participation in the country's governance.

The growing disagreement and opposition to the Shah's policies boiled over in June 1963. In a sermon, Ayatollah Khomeini openly criticized the Shah and his White Revolution as un-Islamic, in violation of the constitution, spreading moral corruption in the country, and submissive to America and Israel. In particular, Ayatollah Khomeini addressed two issues: women's behavior was a matter for Islamic guidance, and making capitulatory concessions to foreigners—namely granting special status and judicial immunity to foreign military personnel.

This infuriated the Shah, who consequently ordered the arrest of Ayatollah Khomeini. In response, protests broke out in major cities throughout the country, where people began chanting anti-Shah slogans in support of the imprisonment of their Marja-e Taqlid (*Source of Emulation* on religious matters). What transpired was to mark the beginning of the end of the Shah, when armed forces opened fire on and killed a number of protestors, and subsequent arrests and executions were carried out by SAVAK. Former US diplomat William Miller told me: "in Qom, the Shah sent paratroopers who killed Mullahs. These deaths prompted the march of many dressed in shrouds from Qom to Tehran. I saw this march and the riots in Tehran."

Under pressure, the Shah decided to release Ayatollah Khomeini after two months' imprisonment, yet he continued to be an outspoken critic of the Shah and his repressive regime. Ayatollah Khomeini had ascended from this protest in Qom to become one of the key voices of opposition to the regime. And as things turned out, he came to be an essential factor in the demise of the Shah's rule 15 years later.

The Shah: America's pillar in the Middle East

The Shah pressed the United States to assist his build-up of the military. To further strengthen his case, he relied on the Cold War mentality sweeping the United States, and voiced concerns that he could come under threat from the Soviet Union and Arab countries. By this time, Iran had become an important strategic ally of the United States. Growing economic, social, political, and military ties were intended to be a buffer against the spread of communism to neighboring Arab countries. In order to secure the military aid from the US, in October 1954 the Shah first fast-tracked a Status of Forces bill through the *Majlis*, infamously known as the "capitulation law," effectively granting US military personnel stationed in Iran and their dependents full diplomatic immunity. The passage of the bill was instrumental in heightening anti-American sentiments in Iran, as the bill clearly infringed Iran's sovereignty and conjured up memories of nineteenth-century capitulation laws which exempted Europeans from domestic Iranian law. Subsequently, President Johnson's administration removed barriers to providing sophisticated armaments to Iran.

The US military and regional alliance with Iran developed even further during President Richard Nixon's tenure of office (1969–1974). To ensure that Iran would be up to the task of acting as a buffer against the USSR expansionism in the region, President Nixon traveled to Tehran in 1972 to negotiate arms agreements including the sale of highly-advanced jet fighters, the most sophisticated conventional weapons, with an extensive team of military advisors and technicians.

The Shah, eager for Iran to become a regional powerhouse, was alacritous to accept the high-tech military aid and began an ambitious drive for expansion of the Iranian military capability, which saw military bases popping up on the northern borders to monitor Soviet ICBM missile test activities in addition to bases in the south to secure transit of oil from the Persian Gulf, ensuring secure transit of oil from the region. Armed with the revenues from rising oil prices of the early 1970s, Iran was in a position to spend lavishly on its military expansion; and the US was enthusiastic about providing the hardware and expertise. Within a few years, tens of thousands of American military advisors and technicians were stationed in Iran and a large amount of oil revenue was committed to military expenditure, mostly directed to the United States.

The end of the Pahlavi dynasty

The solid support and backing of the West, particularly the United States, the abundance of petrodollars, Westernization, a ruthless secret service, and a formidable military establishment made the Shah confident at the turn of the 1970s. Yet there were ample indications of widespread dissent brewing throughout the country, and plentiful evidence of the failure of his regime's economic, social, and political reforms. The White Revolution had failed, and the gulf between the rich and the poor had widened due to extensive corruption, nepotism, and economic mismanagement of oil revenues.

The Pahlavi dynasty's unyielding attempt to secularize and liberalize Iranian society, and its open war with Islamic values—to the extent of replacing the Islamic calendar with an imperial calendar—stirred up fury among the clergy. The clergy's opposition to the Shah's regime was initially more social than political. Until mid-1970s, the vast majority of the clergy were apolitical, neither opposing nor supporting the Shah openly. However, ultimately they joined the revolutionary movement, led by Grand Ayatollah Khomeini, mainly because the regime had failed to deal with moral decadence.

Naturally, the grassroots of society, who backed the clergy and passionately believed in Islamic values and traditions, also opposed the Shah's Westernization programs. Religious conservatives overwhelmingly came from the poor and those with low incomes. The Shah's system collided with this segment of society because it was indifferent to social justice and would undermine their identity. Ayatollah Khomeini highlighted the cultural decadence and spectacularly mobilized the masses by a reinterpretation of Shi'a theology fused with anti-Americanism.

Furthermore, the repression of political freedom and the increasingly brutal actions of the SAVAK, coupled with the Shah's lavish expenditure on luxuries while inequality was growing in the country, provoked discontent and resentment among the intelligentsia. The Shah's staunch pro-Western policy, manifested in a more pervasive American involvement in the domestic affairs of Iran, also collided with the nationalist sentiments of the Iranian people. In the eyes of many Iranians, the 1953 coup transformed Iran from an independent democracy into a puppet dictatorship.

These factors contributed to a deep abhorrence of the Shah and his abject subjugation to the West, in particular the United States. The Shah's decision to grant immunity to US military personnel seemed to have dealt the final blow to the long history of Iran's struggle for self-determination and independence. Finally, the establishment of a single party system in 1975 left the Iranian population without any hope of political reform.

It was in this environment that the Iranians rose in protest to force a structural change that would bring about an era of self-determination and independence from foreign powers while building a more egalitarian society. However, signs of discord did not ring alarm bells in Washington until it was too late.

Economic and military ties between the US and Iran were steadily increasing even when, beneath the surface, Iran was smoldering. The belief in the Shah's ability to withstand domestic dissent was evident when, on 31 December 1977, at the Niavaran Palace in Tehran, President Jimmy Carter raised a toast and stated: "Iran, because of the great leadership of the Shah, is an island of stability in one of the most troubled areas of the world. This is a great tribute to you, Your Majesty, and to your leadership and to the respect and the admiration and love which your people give to you."[46]

Within a few days of Carter's public endorsement, a small anti-Shah demonstration took place in the holy city of Qom, in protest against an article that had smeared Ayatollah Khomeini.[47] The protestors were violently suppressed, leading to a nationwide outbreak of protests. Even then, there was confidence in some quarters in Washington that the Shah was in a strong enough position to withstand domestic dissent.[48]

With every violent repression of the protests, further dissent was fueled, culminating on September 8, 1978 in what became known as Black Friday, when the Shah's troops fired on demonstrators at Zhaleh (Jaleh) Square in South Tehran. There is no reliable report about the number of dead and injured, but the effect of Black Friday in terms of intensifying the demonstrations followed by a widening crackdown by the state is undeniable. The wave of protests could no longer be controlled, and spread all over the country. The economy came to a standstill. The Shah's last-ditch attempts to deal with past grievances and reconcile the protestors by appointing a new prime minister and promising elections made no impression on the protest movement.

In the midst of the chaos engulfing Iran, Ayatollah Khomeini, still in exile in Iraq, issued fervent messages of opposition against the dictatorial and Western-dominated rule of the Shah. His charisma, religious piety, indefatigable stance against the Shah, and history of resistance, propelled him to become the undisputed leader of the protest movement in the country. His increasing popularity and drive to bring about the demise of the Shah's regime made Saddam Hussein wary of his continued stay in Iraq. Saddam eventually forced his departure on October 3, 1978. After a failed attempt to reside in Kuwait, Ayatollah Khomeini arrived in France, where he would continue to orchestrate the revolution in Iran.

Meanwhile, Washington was caught off-guard with the fast-paced changes occurring in Iran. They had the impression that the Shah would be able to quell any dissent, particularly since, thanks to the Americans, he had built up a formidable military capability and intelligence apparatus. This led to widespread confusion in Washington on the course of action to take. Some US officials advocated a last-minute military coup to salvage their interests and restabilize the country, whereas others feared that any US action would only deepen the already zealous anti-Americanism sweeping the Iranian society.[49]

In any event, throughout the events that unfolded, the United States reassured the Shah that they would back him until the end. Even after the massacre at Jaleh Square on Friday, September 8, 1978, President Carter called the Shah to assure him of his support. The White House reaffirmed the special ties between the US and Iran but regretted the loss of lives in Jaleh Square.[50] Ultimately, the Carter administration came to the conclusion that the Shah had no chance of surviving the upheaval. This led the American government to adopt a cautious position in order to deal with the new administration that would take control.

In January 1979, Iran was seized by a revolutionary spirit. Millions poured onto the streets, workers went on strike, and symbols of the Shah were vandalized and burnt. There was no longer any place for the Shah, leading him to finally take the decision to leave the country on January 16, and to hand over the government to Prime Minister Shapour Bakhtiar. Less than two weeks later, on February 1, Ayatollah Khomeini, after 14 years in exile, returned to Iran from France, with millions of citizens thronging the streets of Tehran to welcome him back. His return galvanized the revolution.

Addressing hundreds of thousands of people at Tehran's main Cemetery (Behesht-e Zahra), he voiced his staunch opposition to the newly appointed Prime Minister Shapour Bakhtiar: "These people are trying to bring back the regime of the Shah or another regime. I will strike [with my fists] at the mouths of this government." This speech paved the way for the rapid disintegration of the government system. Subsequent to the victory of the revolution on February 11, 1979 and a national referendum, the Islamic Republic of Iran was born on

April 1, 1979. The Shah's rule, and with it the ancient institution of monarchy, came to an end, together with the US domination of Iran. The emergence of the Islamic Republic in Iran and the US reactions to this unparalleled, obscure reality marked the beginning of an era of hostility between these two states.

Era of Animosity: 1979 Onwards

The 1979 Iranian Revolution was a popular movement that encompassed a wide spectrum of political, social, and economic groups that shared a common agenda to secure freedom from the suppressive regime of the Shah, elimination of foreign domination of Iran, and social justice. However, as the revolution evolved, its ideological characteristics became defined more clearly as anti-imperialist, nationalist, anti-dictatorship, and Islamic revivalist. These were crystalized in the revolution's dominant slogan of "Esteghlal, azadi, jomhuri-e-Eslami," meaning Independence, Freedom, Islamic Republic. The revolutionary masses viewed the demands for a reduction of the gulf between the rich and poor, and respect, protection, and promotion of Iranian culture to be encompassed in the notion of an Islamic republic.

It merits notice that in the aftermath of the revolution, Iran did not sever its ties with the United States, while the US also recognized the new revolutionary government. This was a clear indication that the two states intended to open a new chapter in their relations. However, this phase was short lived. A few months after the victory of the revolution, radical Muslim students stormed the American Embassy in Tehran and took 52 Americans hostage. Few could have imagined that the effect of the hostage crisis would be so long lasting. That was the beginning of a new era in the relationship between Iran and the United States, characterized by intense hostility and mistrust. These mutual sentiments of hatred and mistrust; leading both governments to justify destructive policies carried out in an effort to cripple the capabilities of the other to do harm.

While this book seeks to answer the essential question of why, despite numerous rapprochements by the two states, they are locked in such a relationship, this section considers their respective grievances, as they see them. Although the American side of the story will also be covered, as is the objective of this book, the focus will be on the Iranian side. It is worth noting that this discussion does not aim to justify or refute any aspects of the two perspectives.

The American perspective

Neither Iran nor the US dispute the nature of the relations during first period (1856–1953). With regard to the second period (1953–1979), the US has officially admitted that its involvement in the 1953 coup and support of the Shah was a mistake.[51] Therefore, there is no longer any major argument or disagreement over the second period, either. What remains in dispute are the activities of each party during the third period (1979 onwards) and their share in the formation of the conflict-ridden relationship between the two states since the 1979 Revolution. This is our focus in the following pages.

According to the United States, tensions with Iran are an outcome of its conduct regardless of the origins of the conflict between the two governments. Americans, unlike Iranians, do not focus on the history of hostilities, although they might have registered them somewhere in their minds. As the US State Department has commented: "The United States has long-standing concerns over Iran's nuclear program, sponsorship of terrorism, and human rights record … Iran still has not recognized Israel's right to exist and has hindered the Middle East peace process by arming militants, including Hamas, Hezbollah, and Palestinian Islamic Jihad."[52]

With regard to terrorism, the US accuses Iran of the following terrorist acts: the Beirut military barracks bombing on October 23, 1983 that targeted US and French military personnel, with a total of 299 killed, among them 241 US military personnel; the Khobar Tower bombing on June 25, 1996 in Saudi Arabia that killed 19 US Air Force personnel and injured 372 others; a slew of assassinations throughout Europe of Iranian dissident figures in the late 1980s and early 1990s, including the assassination of Iranian-Kurdish opposition leaders at a Greek restaurant in Germany on September 17, 1992; support for organizations such as Hezbollah, Hamas, and Islamic Jihad,[53] all three groups designated as Foreign Terrorist Organizations (FTO) by the US State Department and as such constituting part of the "war on terror";[54] support for extremist groups in Afghanistan and Iraq;[55] an assassination attempt on the Saudi Arabian ambassador on US soil;[56] and multiple assassination attempts and bombings targeting Israelis in countries such as Bulgaria, India, Thailand, and Georgia in 2012. Tehran has denied all these accusations. In the following chapters, some of the most critical terror cases will be analyzed and their complexities revealed.

One of the main issues for the US has been Tehran's opposition to the Middle East peace process. According to the US State Department, arming and supporting militant groups opposed to peace between Israel and Palestinians is an indication of deliberate attempts to prevent peace from becoming a reality. Moreover, the emergence of the mantra of the "export of revolution," shortly after the Islamic Revolution's victory, became a major cause of tension between Iran and the Gulf Cooperation Council (GCC) countries and Iran and the United States. Although Iran emphasized that the export of revolution would be by word and not by sword,[57] the US and its regional allies viewed the revolutionary and Islamic nature of the Iranian system as a threat to the stability of Arab Muslim regimes of oil-rich countries that maintained close ties with the United States.

The human rights situation in Iran has been a constant point of contention between Iran and the US. American allegations of human rights violations in Iran began in the aftermath of the Islamic Revolution and have grown steadily since the Iranian elections of 2009. The June 2012 *Country Report on Human Rights Practices* by the US Department of State explicitly points to Iran as a perpetrator of state-sanctioned torture.[58] According to the report, in the aftermath of the 2009 disputed presidential elections, the Iranian government utilized "beatings, stress positions, denial of medical attention, and prolonged solitary confinement" against human rights defenders, journalists, activists, and others related to social movements. The allegations of torture were also expounded by the United Nations Special Rapporteur on the state of human rights in Iran, Ahmed Shaheed.[59] Other human rights issues, such as discrimination against women, lack of freedom of expression, and a significant increase in known executions in Iran, are also raised by the US and the UN.[60]

Finally, the issue of weapons of mass destruction (WMD) has remained one of the major disputes between Iran and the US since 1979. Almost all US administrations have accused Iran of harboring WMD ambitions. At the heart of this dispute lies Ian's nuclear program. Since the revelation of the program in 2003, the US official position has been that it is apprehensive about the real nature of the program. Due to the IAEA reports, the US maintains that Iran should halt its uranium enrichment activities until the concerns about its nuclear project are addressed.

The Iranian perspective

The Iranian system (*nezam*) believes that, for its part, the US as the global superpower has applied almost all possible instruments at its command, short of an outright military invasion, to attain the goal of bringing down the Islamic Republic. Since the 1979 Revolution, these instruments, the Iranian government believes, have included a combination of subversion policies, sanctions, covert operations, support of militant groups, military action, support for regional aggression against Iran, cyber war, accusing Iran of terrorism, human rights violations and seeking to acquire WMD, and last but not least, cultural aggression.

Subversion

The United States unleashed a propaganda war to incite internal opposition in Iran against the Islamic Republic, as well as galvanizing anti-Iranian sentiment in the US and the international community shortly after the revolution. To reach Iranians in Iran and strengthen anti-government elements inside and outside, the US set up Farsi-language TV and radio stations. Meanwhile, with the goal of destabilizing the Iranian government, it officially allocated a budget under the Iran Freedom Support Act to back the Iranian opposition and exile television stations.[61] Voice of America has dedicated a considerable amount of air time to the opposition figures who are openly and closely working with the West to spread rumors and misinformation while openly passing instructions to the Iranian people on how to create chaos within the country and organize protests.

Demonizing statements by US officials, from the president down, have resulted in the creation of a damning image of Iran internationally. One high-ranking Iranian official told me that "history paints a different picture of who were the exploiters, instigators of violence, and supporters of despotic regimes." What has exacerbated this view has been that the US mainstream media have increasingly attacked the Iranian government and portrayed them as irrational fundamentalists, whose goal is to harm Americans. It is worth noting that in the eyes of the Iranian leadership, there is no distinction between the American media, which is privately owned, and the government. For them, it is unfathomable that the media should write or say something that is not favored by their government.

Sanctions

Sanctions have obviously played a fundamental role in American coercive policy toward Iran. Iran views increasing pressure by the US to be in pursuit of two aims: first, immediately after the victory of the Islamic Republic, to uproot Islamic revivalism and prevent it from spreading to the region, and by the collapse of the Islamic Republic, make an example to others who might seek similar change; second, to regain its foothold in the country and implant a pro-Western, client government.

Economic sanctions came into effect against Iran right after the hostage crisis in November 1979. On November 14, 1979, President Carter, through executive order 12710, banned imports of Iranian oil, froze some $12 billion in Iranian assets in the US, and later banned all US trade with and travel to Iran. The effects of the US sanctions were felt immediately in Iran, particularly since the revolution had created havoc in government institutions and their ability to function. In this regard, President Carter's executive order had an adverse effect. It diminished the pro-West and moderate faction within the Iranian government, that is, the base that the US aimed to empower, and instead strengthened the growing anti-American sentiments and hardened the revolutionaries and helped them to reinforce their position in Iran's political structure.

The US uses allegations of support for terrorism, human rights violations, and nuclear ambitions to justify the implementation of sanctions against and coercive policies toward the Islamic Republic. Iran has felt the burden of US economic, scientific, military and political sanctions for three decades. There are examples of the application of the sanctions that have been negative for the US image, particularly the prohibition placed on Iran's aviation sector, resulting in Boeing's inability to sell aircraft and repair parts and equipment in respect of Iran's aging fleet of passenger planes, mostly purchased from the US during the Shah's rule. These sanctions have placed civilian lives in danger and have once again intensified animosity between the two countries.

Since the actions of the Carter administration, subsequent US governments have broadened the scope and depth of the sanctions imposed on Iran. Iran was invaded by Iraq's Saddam Hussein on September 22, 1980 which led to an eight-year war. The US added further sanctions including arms sales and dual-use goods and technologies. During the War, while Iran was under immense pressure, under congressional pressure, President Reagan, under congressional pressure, banned all US imports from Iran in 1987.

The sanctions continued unabated, and increased in the 1990s, with the Clinton administration expanding their range by banning all American investments in Iran, particularly in the petroleum industry. The sanctions were based on the charge that Iran was a "state sponsor of terrorism," and a suspicion that the country was seeking to acquire weapons of mass destruction. To increase the potency and reach of the sanctions, the Clinton administration began to expand US unilateral sanctions by placing pressure on Iran's trading partners to follow suit. This led to the passing of Iran and Libya Sanctions Act (ILSA) in 1996 to urge foreign companies not to invest in Iran's oil and gas industry, the main source of government income.

During his tenure, President George W. Bush introduced further wide-ranging sanctions on Iran. At this time, the Iranian nuclear program had become of international concern, and the failure of negotiations had led Washington to develop sanctions significantly, particularly with the passage of the Iran, North Korea, and Syria Nonproliferation Act in 2006.

US President Barack Obama, immediately after taking office, signaled his willingness to enter into a dialogue with the Islamic Republic on a wide range of issues, aiming to remove 30 years of hostility, and create "a new beginning" between the two countries. The new beginning, as will be discussed in this book, was botched as a result of insulting statements by President Obama, as perceived by the Iranian leadership, and under the pressure of the pro-Israel lobby and Congress, Obama's engagement policy was practically abandoned, leading to the imposition of the most draconian sanctions on Iran during Obama's first term of office (2009–13).

In June 2010, President Obama signed the Comprehensive Iran Sanctions, Accountability, and Divestment Act (CISADA). As a result, Iran could not purchase refined petroleum products, such as petrol, while major Western oil companies severed their ties with the Islamic Republic.

In November 2011, President Obama expanded the sanctions to target the Iranian Central Bank and curtail oil exports, citing Iran's lack of cooperation with the International Atomic Energy Agency (IAEA) and doubts regarding the peaceful nature of its nuclear program. President Obama further tightened the screws on Iran by signing an executive order in February 2012, which included provisions requiring US institutions to freeze Iranian assets and further isolate Iran's Central Bank.

The number and effect of the measures adopted during the Obama administration dwarfed the impact of sanctions applied over the previous three decades. Following the last round of US sanctions on Iran's Central Bank and oil industry, the European Union, UK, and Canada followed suit.

In January 2012, the European Union, under pressure from the United States, placed sanctions on Iran's Central Bank and approved a phased oil embargo that would go into effect in June 2012. The increase of sanctions on Iran was compounded by Washington's pressure on other nations for compliance or risk being barred from the US market for their dealings with Iran's Central Bank and oil sector. One of the harshest blows to the Iranian financial system came with the US Congress threatening to place sanctions on the Belgian-based Society for Worldwide International Financial Telecommunication (SWIFT) unless they cut ties with all Iranian banks. The world's major banks use SWIFT to send secured messages crucial to making international transfer payments. Unsurprisingly, the EU yielded to US threats and consequently cut off the Iranian Central Bank from the international financial system.

The United States also spearheaded four rounds of United Nations Security Council sanctions on Iran from 2006 to 2010, once again justifying them on concerns about Iran's nuclear program.

However, the unilateral sanctions applied by the United States, its pressure on other nations to apply similar measures, and the spearheading of UNSC sanctions on Iran did not have any success in changing Iran's behavior. In fact, they resulted in a significant expansion and development of Iran's nuclear program. Addressing Iran's policy in a speech in New York in January 2012, Obama announced that he had rallied the world powers and built an "unprecedented" sanctions regime against Iran, claiming that US-led sanctions had reduced Iran's economy to "shambles." Indeed, some experts maintain that under economic sanctions, Iran had suffered 30 percent inflation and 20 percent unemployment.[62] Obviously, the poor and the middle class would pay a high price.

Covert operations and support of militant groups
Operation Ajax, the code name for the covert action to overthrow the democratically-elected government of Prime Minister Mohammad Mossadegh, was the first CIA operation against Iran. Covert operations against Iran have been expanded to include the utilization of stealth surveillance drones, purportedly penetrating 600 miles into Iranian territory. One super-advanced RQ 170 drone was downed in Iran in December 2011.

Covert activities are not only limited to surveillance operations. The Iranian Ministry of Intelligence and National Security (MOIS) has overwhelming evidence that confirms several reports in the Western media of the US allegedly supporting Baluchi group Jundolloh, one of the most brutal terrorist organizations, against Iran.[63] There have been multiple reports revealing that the US has been providing training and intelligence to the group to enable it to "stage attacks across the border into Iran on Iranian military officers, Iranian intelligence officers, kidnapping them, executing them on camera."[64]

One objective of the US covert operations, as mentioned in the media reports, is to destabilize the Iranian government. But when it comes to separatist groups, another goal is to jeopardize the territorial integrity of the country. These US policies have created more distance between Tehran and Washington. It is the view of Tehran that provoking ethnic and religious disputes in Iran is a modern adoption of the old British doctrine of "divide and rule," in practice, building up weak internal forces in a client–patron relationship to allow them to challenge the regime.

According to Iran's MOIS, the United States intelligence agencies have been involved in providing training and material support for separatist groups in an effort to undermine the Islamic Republic. Some reports in the Western media support this accusation.[65] These groups are clandestinely supported to advance US interests within Iran, being used for intelligence gathering, covert operations, and sabotage.[66]

In 2006, the PEJAK (Party for a Free Life in Kurdistan), a terrorist, separatist militant group, conducted a deadly attack in which 24 Iranian security personnel were killed. The attack prompted former US Representative Dennis Kucinich to question the ability of the PEJAK to launch such an attack from Iraq without prior US knowledge.[67] According to another report, US intelligence sources have indicated US financial, material, and tactical support for the PEJAK to place internal pressure on the Iranian government, and that the group was provided with "a list of targets inside Iran of interest to the US."[68]

The foremost terrorist group that has inflicted harm on the Iranian society is the *Mujahedin-e Khalq* (MEK). The MEK earned a terrorist group designation on October 8, 1997 when the US State Department established the Foreign Terrorist Organization (FTO) list.[69] It is important to note that a member of the MEK had gone to Najaf and met with Ayatollah Khomeini in the early years of the 1970s, seeking his permission and blessing for armed action against the officials of the regime as well as the Americans stationed in Iran. Ayatollah Khomeini, however, completely opposed such actions and considered it un-Islamic.[70]

Following the 1979 Revolution, in a bid to take over the reins of power, the MEK turned their opposition toward the newly found Islamic Republic in a slew of terrorist acts that cost the lives of thousands of

Iranian civilians, military, and political figures. In addition to its lethal terrorist attacks within Iran, the MEK moved its headquarters to Iraq in 1986 and joined the war effort with Saddam Hussein against Iran. MEK was financially and militarily backed by the Iraqi dictator until his fall in 2003.[71] The group was used by Saddam to provide intelligence, fight Iranian soldiers, and assist in the bloody crackdown on Iraqi Shia and Kurdish populations.[72]

Making matters worse was the move by the Obama administration on September 21, 2012 to remove the MEK from the US Foreign Terrorist Organization List. How this happened is an interesting story in itself.

A *Guardian* investigation, drawing partly on data researched by the Centre for Responsive Politics—a group tracking the impact of money in US politics—has identified a steady flow of funds from key Iranian American organizations and their leaders into the campaign to have the People's Mujahidin Organization of Iran removed from the list of terrorist organizations. The campaign to bury the MEK's bloody history of bombings and assassinations that killed American businessmen, Iranian politicians, and thousands of civilians, and to portray it as a loyal US ally against the Islamic government in Tehran, has seen large sums of money directed at three principal targets: members of Congress, Washington lobby groups, and influential former officials.[73]

The conclusion drawn by Iran's leadership is that frequent talk about human rights and terrorism is essentially nothing but a foreign policy tool that the US utilizes to bring down those governments that are not submitting to its hegemony and are seeking independence. According to some reports, the group has been provided with training and access to covert military operational knowledge inside the US, at Department of Energy sites in the State of Nevada.[74]

These covert operations have been backed by substantial financial resources, including a purported $400 million fund to destabilize Iran authorized by former US President George W. Bush, focused on a campaign of "propaganda, disinformation, and manipulation of Iran's currency."[75]

Military actions
Direct military action against Iran has been a significant factor in maintaining and elevating mistrust and hostility between the two

nations. A significant direct military event was the downing of Iran Air passenger flight 655 by the USS *Vincennes* in July 1988. All 290 civilians, including 66 children, perished due to the attack, which the US first had justified by arguing that the plane was believed to be a military fighter jet, was outside civilian flight corridors, and did not respond to radio calls. Subsequent investigations showed that the plane was in fact within civilian air corridors and was flying away from the American warship.[76] The Iranian government referred the matter to the International Court of Justice, arguing that the attack constituted gross negligence and recklessness amounting to an international crime.[77] The United States government has expressed regret for the loss of innocent life; it has, however, not apologized for the attack. From the Iranians' perspective what makes the whole scenario bizarre is that instead of accepting responsibility for the tragic event or apologizing to Iran, the US denied any wrongdoing and awarded medals to the USS *Vincennes* crew.[78]

The United States Navy was also involved in attacks against Iranian oil platforms as part of Operation Praying Mantis (April 1988), the largest naval combat operation by the US since the Second World War.[79] The attacks partially destroyed the Sassan and Sirri oil platforms, resulting in the loss of several ships and many lives. Iran sued for reparations at the International Court of Justice, stating that the United States breached the 1955 Treaty of Amity. The court dismissed the claim but noted, "The actions of the United States of America against Iranian oil platforms on October 19, 1987 (Operation Nimble Archer) and April 18, 1988 (Operation Praying Mantis) cannot be justified as measures necessary to protect the essential security interests of the United States of America."[80]

Support for regional aggression against Iran
All revolutions produce upheaval and the 1979 Revolution in Iran was no exception. Coupled with the changes in national leadership, the revolutionary reorientation of Iran caused chaos in the army. The Shah's generals fled from the country, and "control and command" was almost non-existent. Saddam Hussein grasped this opportunity in September 1980 and launched an all-out assault against Iran. The US originally claimed neutrality in the War. However, despite knowing Saddam Hussein for his track record and lack of any moral principles, the US became increasingly supportive of the Iraqi war effort and even allowed chemical and biological warfare-related dual use exports to Iraq.[81]

Tens of thousands of Iranian troops and civilians lost their lives and many more were horribly injured as a result of the use of chemical bombs by Iraq. This US behavior has been engraved in the minds of the Iranian leaders, whose scars have not disappeared to this date. While the US was on the verge of a military strike against Syria in September 2013 for the use of chemical weapons which killed 1,400 Syrians, it was the sole country that opposed—and blocked—UN condemnation of Iraq's use of chemical weapons.[82] According to evidence disclosed in August 2013, the US was aware of Saddam Hussein's chemical attacks against Iran, the worst in recent history, yet continued to assist his government.[83]

Cyber war
The United States and Israel launched the first state-planned cyber war in history against Iran's nuclear program. According to the *New York Times*,[84] from his first months in office, President Obama ordered acceleration of waves of cyber attacks against Iran. Sources told the *New York Times* that the US cyber attack, part of a larger sabotage operation called "Olympic Games," was a joint project of the US and Israel.

Following the *New York Times* report, leaders of the Senate and House intelligence committees released a statement noting, "We have become increasingly concerned at the continued leaks regarding sensitive intelligence programs and activities, including specific details of sources and methods."[85]

Republicans accused the White House of "intentionally leaking information to enhance President Obama's image as a tough guy for the elections."[86] President Obama refuted the allegations. "The notion that my White House would purposely release classified national security information is offensive. It's wrong," he said.[87] However, surprisingly, the substance of the *New York Times* report was not denied by the US administration.

Leading cyber experts maintain that the consequences of a massive, successful cyber attack on US infrastructure and/or the banking system would be devastating.[88] Clearly, the adverse potential of a serious cyber attack is not a secret. To that end, two possible scenarios should be considered.

First, the cyber attacks against Iran are continuing. Beginning with the Stuxnet, the Flame, and later Mini-Flame, hit Iran. According to the *Guardian*,[89] "Two leading computer security laboratories—Kaspersky Lab and Symantec—have been studying a series of powerful cyber weapons used against targets including the Iranian nuclear program and Lebanese banks accused of laundering money for Iran and its ally Hezbollah. They are now convinced that all were probably created by a national government or governments working together."

Considering all these, the Iranian government will almost certainly conclude that the strategy of "regime change" is in motion again, albeit a hi-tech version. They may opt to retaliate, possibly through the employment of foreign experts. Common sense dictates that such a trend could initiate a tit-for-tat chain of punitive events. While retaliations deteriorate, it is plausible, even likely, that a large scale Iranian cyber attack against the US would ultimately provoke a military response against Iran.

We now realize that the tragic events of 9/11 prepared the ground and were used as the pretext to attack Iraq, despite the absence of any connection between Saddam's regime and the attacks on New York and Washington. In reality, there are certain states and non-state actors hostile toward the Iranian government. Therefore, the second plausible scenario would be that a third party might stage a "false flag" attack, assigning blame to the Iranian government and justifying a US military response. There are active terrorist organizations within Iran that might be able to effect such a development with the help of Iran's regional adversaries to the Iranian government. In an atmosphere filled with hostility and distrust, and with emotions running high, a false flag attack would leave Tehran vulnerable to accusations of responsibility.

Misreading Iran: A Chronic Problem in US Politics

A close review of the three periods of Iran–US relations leads us to a better understanding of the root causes for the failure of US policies during the second and third periods of relations between the two countries. One of the central factors that has not only created and perpetuated the hostile and uncompromising relationship between Iran and the US, but has also pushed Iran's domestic politics toward radicalization, is that US policy makers unceasingly misinterpret Iran. This is what led to the 1979 Revolution, planting the seeds of mistrust and hostility that remain in Iran–US relations.

Failure to understand Iran's culture of resistance to foreign domination and intervention culminated in the 1953 American-led coup. From that point onward, successive US administrations supported the Shah because they firmly believed that his survival was key to blocking Soviet expansion, securing oil supplies, and reinforcing and expanding US intelligence capabilities on Iran's borders with the Soviet Union. Over time, this view became so rigid and sacred that

Americans would not even consider an alternative to the Shah. Instead, they relentlessly and unconditionally supported his regime to achieve these goals.

Astronomical arms sales were intended to bolster the Shah's regime but also significantly contributed to the US economy. In the fiscal year 1977, US arms sales totaled $9.9 billion worldwide, out of which $5.5 billion went to Iran. Some 700,000 jobs were at stake in the United States.[90] Americans benefited from interfering in and dominating Iranian affairs in the short term. However, in-depth knowledge of Iranian history and culture would have revealed US short-sightedness. They should have known that disdain for foreign domination would dramatically damage US interests in the long term.

A major element that contributed to this misunderstanding of Iran was the total disconnect of Americans from realities on the ground in Iran. In 1977, one year before the eruption of the revolution, a CIA study analyzed the stability of the Shah's regime. The study concluded: "The Shah seems to have no health or political problems at present that will prevent him from being the dominant figure in Iran into and possibly through the 1980s."[91] In fact, he suffered from cancer, and from serious political problems.

One year before the collapse of the Shah's regime, in a report titled "Iran after the Shah," the CIA declared that, "Iran is not in a revolutionary or even a 'prerevolutionary' situation."[92] The report also suggested that "those who are in opposition, both violent and non-violent, do not have the capacity to be more troublesome."

In January 1979, only four days before the Shah's departure from Tehran and just a month before the fall of the Pahlavi dynasty and the victory of the revolution, a CIA memorandum noted the protests. However, in its final assessment, it concluded that "Opposition to the Shah of Iran has never been a cohesive movement. It is a collection of widely disparate groups with differing ideologies and rival leaders."[93]

Ironically, the CIA's knowledge of the dynamics of Iranian society was based largely on information from SAVAK, the Shah's intelligence and repression apparatus. An Iranian journalist astutely pointed out to an American expert: "You [Americans] thought you understood Iran because the Shah spoke English and because his cabinet had read Shakespeare ... You thought he was good because you could see a reflection of yourself in him but he understood Iran as little as you did, and that is why you both failed."[94]

The Shah, dazzled by the industrial development of the West, and encouraged by Kennedy and Johnson administrations, launched his ambitious westernization project. The project would try to "westernize" Iran and thus marginalize the traditional and Islamic culture. This caused the emergence of a resistance movement by the religious conservatives led by the clergy.

In preceding pages, I have already dealt with the arrest of Ayatollah Khomeini and the June 1963 uprising and its bloody repression. Following this upheaval, the US administration did not discourage the Shah or encourage him to rethink the dangerous path that he had taken. In a personal letter to the Shah, Kennedy instead wrote: "I share the regret you must feel over the loss of life connected with the recent unfortunate attempts to block your reform programs. I am confident, however, that such manifestations will gradually disappear as your people realize the importance of the measures you are taking to establish social justice and equal opportunity for all Iranians." He went on to add: "I also know that you would agree that a vigorous and expanding economy would provide the best backstop for the basic reform program you are undertaking."[95]

Kennedy emphatically impressed upon the Shah the advantages of the US economic model. Neither Kennedy nor Johnson recognized that the Shah's program of westernization began to isolate him from his former conservative supporters and from the clergy.[96] Not only was he isolating himself, but as time went on, he grew more and more aggressive due to an overconfidence that the American support engendered in him.

The Westernization project started with "The Shah–People Revolution" (popularly known as "The White Revolution")[97] and then evolved into "Reaching the Gates of the Great Civilization."[98] From the cultural perspective the project climaxed in the Shiraz Festival of Arts (*jashn-e honar-e Shiraz*)[99] as well as the Great Celebration of 2,500 years of monarchy[100] in Iran in 1971.

Anthony Parsons, then British ambassador to Iran, described in his memoir a bizarre scene at the Shiraz Festival of 1977:

> As I have mentioned before, the Shiraz International Festival had for many years been a subject of controversy because of the startling nature of some of the avant-garde performances staged in a traditional Muslim environment. Brazilian dancers biting the heads off live chickens and the presentation of the Shi'ite passion play, the Ta'ziye, as a stage performance for the entertainment of a mainly foreign audience are two examples which come to mind. The Shiraz Festival of 1977 excelled itself in its insults to Iranian moral values.

For example, according to an eye-witness, a play was enacted which represented, as I was told, the evils of military rule and occupation. The theatre company had booked a shop in the main shopping street of Shiraz for the performance, which was played half inside the shop and half on the pavement outside. One scene, played on the pavement, involved a rape which was performed in full (no pretense) by a man (either naked or without any trousers, I forget which) on a woman who had had her dress ripped off her by her attacker. The denouement of the play, also acted on the pavement, included a scene where one of the characters dropped his trousers and inserted a stage pistol up his backside, presumably in order to add verisimilitude to his suicide. The effect of this bizarre and disgusting extravaganza on the good citizens of Shiraz, going about their evening shopping, can hardly be imagined. This grotesquerie aroused a storm of protest, which reached the press and television. I remember mentioning it to the Shah, adding that, if the same play had been put on, say, in the main street of Winchester (Shiraz is the Iranian equivalent of a cathedral city), the actors and sponsors would have found themselves in trouble. The Shah laughed indulgently.[101]

The regime intensified its attempts to revitalize a partly-fabricated history of monarchy in Iran and promote chauvinistic sentiments toward the history of Iran that predated Islam. While the history books at schools as well as the state media relentlessly promoted the "2,500 years of monarchy" history, beginning with the reign of Cyrus the Great (590/580 BC–530 BC), the reality was that for at least six centuries, Muslim-Arab Caliphates ruled Iran between the seventh and thirteenth centuries.

The official culture the regime promoted was assembled in parts taken from Iran's ancient history but also from the West. This culture clashed with the religious values of the traditional society. Americans were completely out of touch with this aspect of Iranian society. The religious conservatives' worldviews, their demands, their aspirations, and most importantly, their strength and potential in formulating the political equations, were wholly foreign to the US leadership.

America's push for Westernization in Iran was also accompanied by a sudden increase in the university student population both inside and outside Iran. This new social force would gradually become the center of protest against the Shah's iron-fist policies. They were the avant-garde of the society who would demand freedom. They would protest against rampant corruption in the privileged aristocracy, against eclecticism, and against nepotism. The fundamental problem was that while those connected to the regime enjoyed wealth and high positions, the rest of the people were treated as second-class citizens.

By the beginning of the 1970s, Iran's major universities were producing an army of writers, painters, artists, and poets who demanded change: freedom of expression, equal opportunity for all, and an end to the American domination. In tandem with students inside Iran, Iranian students in Europe and the United States organized themselves in leftist and Islamic organizations all aiming to topple the Shah. As the intellectuals'/students' movement gained momentum, SAVAK began to confront them in a more brutal manner. The intellectuals and students viewed America's support for the Shah as support for the evil actions carried out by the SAVAK—and they were not wrong.

"Direct links between the CIA and Savak developed to the point that in 1972 the CIA was actually training 400 Savak operatives at its headquarters in Langley, Virginia."[102] In May 1977, shortly after William Sullivan was appointed as ambassador to Iran, he met with President Carter and his National Security Advisor, Zbigniew Brzezinski. During that meeting, Sullivan asked Carter that, given the human rights situation in Iran and SAVAK's reputation of using brutality against the dissent, whether the cooperation between the CIA and SAVAK should continue. Carter responded that he had examined the issue and come to the conclusion that the intelligence that the US received was so critical that SAVAK–CIA cooperation should continue.[103]

Even the assessment that if the Iranian people become materially better off, opposition to the Shah's regime would diminish or disappear was inaccurate. The cultural character of resistance to and rebellion against injustice and inequality had been a feature of social and political change throughout the history of Iran. This does not mean that material factors played no role in social and political change. It only means that Iran's society was sensitive to the notions of inequality and injustice. The post-Islamic history of Iran was full of bloody movements rising against inequality and social injustice.

Understanding the role of the clerics in Iranian politics

I am convinced that Americans do not understand how the revolution happened, or how the clergy operate in the Iranian society; in short

" how the nuts and bolts work." Since the 1979 Revolution, clerics have held a dominant role in ruling Iran. Because of this, it is not surprising that the US and the West have failed to deal with the Iranian government. The Islamic Republic of Iran represents the world's first experience during the modern era of a government shaped by and founded upon the paradigm of "political Shia," dominanted by the clergy. Therefore, understanding the clergy's role in Iranian society has become essential in order to deal effectively with Iran. At the same time, it is equally important for those clerics to gain a better understanding of the West in order to best serve Iran's interests in today's world.

America's failure to understand the clergy's role in Iran has been a major drawback to analyzing the Iranian society. American analysts and policy-makers do not give credence to the Shia clergy in Iran's political calculations. This might be because their knowledge and understanding of the Islamic world was primarily derived from the Sunni Arab world, with which they are more familiar. But there are major differences between these two Muslim religious schools.

The Shia clergy have historically been a powerful social force as protectors of the masses against the actions of the state, as well as in resistance to foreign domination. The clerical organization encompasses the entire country; from the smallest villages in remote places to the largest cities. Unlike Sunni Islam, religious authority in the Shia clergy is centralized. Through *Maraje-e Taqlid* (Sources of Emulation— the highest-ranking authority of the Twelver Shia community), the clerics at different levels have an organic relationship with each other and can work in harmony together and mobilize the masses to achieve goals set by those authorities.

One of the biggest and most powerful ideological-political parties in the world is arguably the Shia clerical organization that has been shrouded in mystery. While the functions, structure, and influence is unlike mainstream party political party models, its influence and capability far surpasses others.

A clear manifestation of the dynamics of clerical organization was seen in Iran's 1979 Islamic Revolution. The Shia clerical establishment played the major role in galvanizing the masses to revolutionary zeal, ultimately bringing down the Shah. During the revolution, messages from Ayatollah Khomeini, the highest Shia authority, were disseminated first from Iraq, then Paris, and finally, upon his return to Iran, from Tehran. These messages promoted and invited the masses to resist and topple the Shah's regime.

No political group, movement, or party could match this widely extended, yet naturally centralized organization. It is no wonder that backed by such a network, Ayatollah Khomeini was able to assume an unmatched position among all opposition groups, from left to right, nationalist, Marxist or otherwise, to lead the revolution.

To better understand the vast influence of this religious establishment, in addition to the 1979 Islamic Revolution, the anti-imperialist tobacco boycott and the oil nationalization movements provide some insight.

The decision in 1891 by Nasir al-Din Shah, the Qajar King (1831–1896) to grant the monopoly of the Iranian tobacco trade to the British sparked widespread protests; the populace saw the concession as a clear violation of Iran's sovereignty. Nasir al-Din Shah stood his ground on this decision. By issuing a *fatwa*, or religious edict, Grand Ayatollah Mirza Hassan Shirazi forbade the use of tobacco as a religious duty. Things took a new turn, and even the servants of the Shah refused to prepare his pipe. Ultimately, the Shah, unable to stop the protests, was forced to nullify the agreement with the British.

The tobacco boycott also highlights the strength of anti-foreign-domination sentiments in Iran. These sentiments mobilized nineteenth-century Iranians in defiance of the British incursion, and are deeply rooted in Iran's history, but have yet to be fully appreciated by the US government, even up to today.

The Shia clergy also played an integral role in the Constitutional Revolution (1905–6) and subsequently oil nationalization movement, opening a new chapter in Iran's recent history in the early 1950s. While the democratically elected Prime Minister of Iran Mohammad Mossadegh has been rightfully credited with championing the cause of oil nationalization, the role of the Shia religious establishment has been less recognized. Mossadegh received significant support from the revered Ayatollah Sayyed Abol Qasem Kashani, a leading figure in the anti-imperialist movement against the British.[104] Kashani's popularity was matched only by Mossadegh. It has been noted that when Kashani was permitted to return to Iran from exile in June 1950, he received a hero's welcome.[105] Mossadegh was among the massive crowd that welcomed him. On his way from Tehran's Mehrabad Airport to his home, "the crowds became delirious, sometimes even lifting his car off the road."[106] With his patronage and support of the oil nationalization, Kashani transformed the movement into a widespread struggle that engulfed the country.[107]

The turning point in the struggle came with declaration of a *fatwa* by Ayatollah Kashani on December 21, 1950 that directed all "sincere Muslims and patriotic citizens to fight against the enemies of Islam and Iran by joining the nationalization struggle."[108] Within days, thousands joined Mossadegh in the streets of Tehran, and three months later the Iranian oil industry was nationalized.

Kashani's influence also manifested itself during the events of July 1952. Following Mossadegh's dismissal by the Shah and the appointment of Ghavam-o-Saltaneh as the new prime minister, Ghavam asked Khashani for his support in shaping an anti-Mossadegh front. He offered Kashani and his close supporters a significant role in the government, but Kashani refused the deal. In a harsh letter to Hossein Ala, former Iranian ambassador to the United States (1946–50) and a close confidant of the Court, Kashani threatened that "Unless Mossadegh is reappointed in twenty-four hours, I will personally aim the sharp edge of the revolution toward the Court itself." Mossadegh was reappointed that night.[109]

Although tension and differences were to emerge between Mossadegh and Kashani, resulting in the failure of the anti-imperialist movement of the Iranian people, Khashani's influence and prominent role in the history of oil nationalization is not disputed by historians.

The decisive role of clerics in Iran has been the driving force behind the Iranian political establishment's resistance to American pressure. The culture of resistance originates from Islamic, and more specifically, Shia teachings. The culture urges people to *resist* when they are subjected to pressure and humiliation. Drawing upon Shia teachings, clergy members, including the two successive Supreme Leaders (Ayatollah Khomeini and Ayatollah Khamenei), have constantly preached about the superiority of believers (*momenin*) over worldly people (*aafiat-talaban*) in defending their values. Meanwhile, Ayatollah Khamenei has portrayed himself as a symbol of resistance to the United States and Israel. His ruling power and stature, as Guardian Jurist (*vali-e faqih*) and a symbol of resistance to the US and Israel, among his own followers, including the Muslim (particularly Shia) world, would dissipate or dissolve if he surrendered to US pressures under humiliating conditions. It is no wonder that the language of threat and intimidation has indeed been a major obstacle to talks and negotiations, heightening hostility between the two states.

Chapter 2

HOSTAGE CRISIS: CLIMAX OF MISTRUST MISPERCEPTIONS AND WRONG ANALYSES

The Episode

The American Embassy in Tehran is situated in a large, park-like 27-acre lot on Taleghani Street (formerly Takhte-Jamshid). Construction of the elongated, two-storey brick building was completed in 1951. The architecture of the building mimicked that of American high schools, and staff referred to it as Henderson High, a reference to Loy W. Henderson, the first American ambassador to Iran, who started his work in that building. Apart from the main building, there are several other buildings, including the ambassador's residence and the consular section, as well as a pool and tennis court.

When the embassy first opened, Takhte-Jamshid, a street running east–west, was one of the northernmost streets of Tehran, but by 1979, due to city's expansion, it was closer to the city center than to its northern limit. When the compound was first constructed, it was enclosed by fences rather than walls. People walking in Takhte-Jamshid Street could see the lush, green American Embassy complex from outside. Conversely, the Russian (Soviet) and British embassies looked mysterious and nondescript from outside. This exuded the impression to Iran's people that Americans were open and frank; different from the British and Russians who had historically demonstrated an interventionist character to the Iranians. And up to that point, Iranians were right in their judgment.

Fast-forward 28 years. It is October 1979. The space and streets around the American Embassy are filled with people discussing what should be done in response to the US allowing the Shah to visit for medical purposes. Very few amongst them believed that the purpose of the Shah's visit to the US was to receive medical attention. The Shah entered the US on October 22—eight months after the revolution on February 11, 1979.

Despite strong warnings from the US Embassy in Tehran, President Carter decided to admit the Shah. From the perspective of the US Embassy staff in Tehran, it was absolutely the worst thing that the US president could do, simultaneously preventing the improvement of relations between the two countries and jeopardizing the safety and security of Americans in Iran.[1]

Young Iranians, whose convictions ranged from those sympathizing with leftist groups to radical Muslims, gathered in front of the Embassy's main door on a daily basis and shouted slogans against the Shah and the US, demanding the Shah's extradition. The number of protestors increased by the day, reaching several thousand toward the end of October.

Back in July 1979, the Islamic Associations of 22 universities had held a gathering at Tehran Polytechnic University (now Amir Kabir University) to create an organization that would "protect the achievements" of the revolution. A manifesto was also released pursuant to the unification of all Islamic Associations under one umbrella, thus coordinating their goals and actions.

The first elected Central Council of the new organization, then called the Office for Strengthening of Unity between the Islamic Associations of the Universities and Theological Seminaries (later simply called the Office for Strengthening of Unity or OSU), consisted of Mohsen Mirdamadi, Ebrahim Asgharzadeh, Habibollah Bitaraf, Mahmoud Ahmadinejad, and Mohammad Ali Sayyed Nejad. From the OSU's inception, it was apparent that Mirdamadi, Asgharzadeh, and Bitaraf were the key figures who dominated decision-making within the Central Council. In practice, the representatives of three universities—the University of Tehran, Sharif University, and Amir Kabir University—dominated and crafted OSU policies. Key to connecting the OSU with Ayatollah Khomeini, the Revolution's Leader, was a radical cleric called Mohammad Mousavi Khoeiniha.

The person who first brought up the idea of seizing the American Embassy was Ebrahim Asgharzadeh, while Bitaraf and Mirdamadi also supported him. During August and September, Ahmadinejad argued that communists were the main enemies of the Islamic Revolution and that the USSR Embassy should be seized. A week before the seizure, Asgharzadeh and the other two met with Mr. Mousavi Khoeiniha in his office at the Iranian national TV headquarters where he supervised the TV programs as Ayatollah Khomeini's representative.

The purpose of the meeting was to ask Khoeiniha to seek Ayatollah Khomeini's opinion regarding the plan. Khoeiniha welcomed the plan but rejected the students' strategy. Khoeiniha asserted that Ayatollah Khomeini faced political constraints which prevented him from approving the seizure, proposing that the group go ahead with the plan and then seek Ayatollah Khomeini's response. If he supported the group's actions, they would remain. If he objected, they would vacate the compound. In any case, Khoeiniha argued, the students would have expressed their opposition to American policies, thus attracting the world's attention to their cause.

The American Embassy had actually been occupied in February 1979, when leftist groups were involved. After Ayatollah Khomeini was informed about the event, he ordered the Provisional Government of Mehdi Bazargan to force the leftist elements out of the embassy. In response to the OSU leaders' concern about repeating the February episode's reaction, Khoeiniha argued that this situation was quite different. First, because by this time the Shah had been accepted on US soil, and second, because the students were devout Muslims not communists. So the group of four, which now included Khoeiniha, collectively decided to execute the plan without informing any high ranking officials or other influential figures including Ayatollah Khomeini. The details of the episode as related to me years later were presented to me by a number of students involved in the seizure of the Embassy, were as follows.[2]

The group formed reconnaissance units shortly after that meeting. One unit entered the compound as visa applicants. They were tasked with preparing a sketch of the compound including the buildings. Another unit assembled on nearby rooftops overlooking the Embassy. They assessed the number of security personnel, including US Marines and Iranian police, guarding the Embassy, and drew a diagram of building locations from above and the locations where cars were parked. Another unit located all of the entrances to the compound.

Two more events accelerated seizure of the US Embassy. News broke on November 1 of a meeting between Iran's Prime Minister, Mehdi Bazargan, and his Foreign Minister, Ebrahim Yazdi, with President Carter's National Security Advisor, Zbigniew Brzezinski in Algiers. Bazargan and Yazdi were both considered as pro-Western, liberal figures, while Brzezinski was perceived as a mysterious figure in Carter's administration. All of them were attending the events marking the 25th anniversary of the Algerian Revolution. News of this meeting provoked a huge sense of resentment among all revolutionary factions, including radical Muslim students, then the dominant political force on the streets of Tehran. The next day, in a fiery statement addressed to the clergy and students, Ayatollah Khomeini implored them to "expand with all their might their criticism against the United States." Ayatollah Khomeini insisted that the US should freeze the Shah's assets and extradite him back to Iran.

The statements left no doubt among leaders of the OSU that it was time for action. The OSU Central Council decided to select 100 to 150 trusted students from each of the main four universities in Tehran, Amir Kabir University, Sharif University, and the National University of Iran (later Shahid Beheshti)—for the operation. A small committee, appointed by the OSU Central Council in each of the four universities, would interview potential student candidates to execute the embassy plan. They would ask them only two questions: "Can you stay out of your home or the university dormitory 48 hours?," and, "Will you participate in a protest move against the United States?"

Those who said "yes" to both questions were asked to attend a briefing meeting. At the meeting, they were informed of the plan to seize the American Embassy. The Embassy's occupation was planned to last between 48 and 72 hours. The aim was to attract international attention to the issue of a perceived US conspiracy against the Revolution.

November 4, 1979 was the first anniversary of high school students' demonstrations at the University of Tehran, protesting against the Shah, which ended in the killing of a number of students. As a tribute to their memory, a massive demonstration was organized. In order to be distinguished from other demonstrators, the 400 students who were designated to participate in the plan seizure of the Embassy carried a picture of Ayatollah Khomeini with an armband on which it was written, "Muslim Students Following the Imam's Line."

They gathered at an intersection one kilometer east of the Embassy at 6.30 in the morning, and final briefings were presented by the leaders. At 10.30 the group walked toward the Embassy, pretending to join the demonstrators at Tehran University a few kilometers away to the west of the American Embassy. Only 50 were intended to enter the Embassy, the rest remaining outside to prevent the masses from joining their action, which would only create chaos inside the compound.

The students continued on their way, passing the main entrance of the Embassy. After walking 50 meters beyond the main door, embassy guards were caught by surprise as protesters returned to attack the gate. A few female students had hidden metal cutters under their long veils (*chadors*). The gate's chains were quickly cut and opened while others climbed over the walls. As soon as the main group entered the Embassy, the gate was secured again with locks and chains prepared in advance.

The students broke into the main building where they faced marines who guarded the embassy and were ready to shoot at them. A male and a female student shouted in English: "We are not here to hurt you! We just want to sit-in!" The marines, afraid of the seemingly angry students, shot tear gas. But because they were inside the building, the tear gas penetrated upstairs and throughout the building, making the situation intolerable for staff and the marines themselves.

The students then began to search for secret documents that would reveal the espionage operations of the embassy, but found nothing. Another small group entered a corridor at the end of which there was a steel wall. I was told by the witnesses that they heard a low noise behind the wall and suspected that there was something happening behind it. They concluded that it might be a door rather than a wall, and asked one of the hostages to open the door, as it was coded in a complex way.

When the door opened, their jaws dropped. Before them, the students saw tons of secret documents in the form of papers, microfilms, and microfiches. The noise they had heard had been shredders and incinerators. The students shut down the machines and guided the operators out of the room. Later, they painstakingly reconstructed those documents that had already been shredded. By 1.30 in the afternoon, the radical students controlled the entire compound.

The streets surrounding the embassy were now filled with thousands of angry people chanting against the United States, with their fists clenched, demanding the Shah's extradition. Thousands remained on the streets that night and for several nights afterwards. The atmosphere was so hysterical that an outside observer might have wondered if calm could ever be restored.

As I was told by Ayatollah Beheshti, at the time the second most powerful man in the revolutionary establishment after Ayatollah Khomeini, no one knew about the plan. He was shocked. Mssrs. Hashemi Rafsanjani and Khamenei, Iran's current Supreme Leader, were both on a pilgrimage to Mecca, Saudi Arabia. The Council of Revolution and the government also did not know about the planned seizure. Ayatollah Beheshti also told me that the Iranian leaders' immediate reaction was to argue that the students should evacuate the Embassy. But what transpired next changed the direction of events.

Ebrahim Yazdi, who had just come back from Algeria, rushed to the holy city of Qom, where Ayatollah Khomeini resided. Ayatollah Khomeini's first question was, "Who are these people?" Yazdi told him that they were students who introduced themselves as Ayatollah Khomeini's followers. After Yazdi explained the situation and the way the incident could become problematic internationally, Ayatollah Khomeini said firmly: "Kick them out."[3]

While Yazdi drove back, Khoeiniha called Sayyed Ahmad Khomeni, the Ayatollah's son and confidant. Khoeiniha assured Sayyed Ahmad that all of the students were devout Muslims who truly were the Ayatollah Khomeini's followers. He added that following Ayatollah Khomeini's statement about intensifying resistance to US intervention, the students decided to occupy the embassy in order to seek the Shah's extradition and to stop US intervention in Iranian affairs. To assess the real situation on the ground, Ahmad Khomeini flew to Tehran by helicopter.

When the crowd saw Ahmad Khomeini, they hoisted him above their heads while chanting in support of Ayatollah Khomeini and against the US. The frenzy on the streets shocked Ahmad Khomeini. On his return to Qom that same night, he reported to Ayatollah Khomeini about the hysteria in the streets of Tehran. He also reported on the mass of secret documents seized by the students, and the attempted destruction of many of the confidential papers.[4]

The next day, November 5, Ayatollah Khomeini called the US "The Great Satan," and the Embassy "a den of espionage." He elaborated: "That center that our youth went to, as we have been informed, has been a center for espionage and conspiracy." Tehran no longer controlled the course of events. As anti-American hysteria increased, with almost daily revelations by the students on national television of evidence of American espionage and efforts to intervene in Iran's affairs, it was almost impossible, even for Ayatollah Khomeini, to end the crisis. In an interview in November 2013, Asgharzadeh said, "We, ourselves, became hostages of hostage-taking." Ayatollah Beheshti told me that with the revelation of these espionage documents, no one could take any action to resolve the situation.

In 2010, the latest edition of *Documents from the U.S. Espionage Den* (*Asnad-e laneh-e Jasusi*) was published by the Political Studies and Research Institute in Iran. It comprised eight volumes and approximately 8,500 pages in total. These books featured telegrams, correspondence, and reports from the US State Department and Central Intelligence Agency, revealing detailed US intelligence about political figures in Iran. There were also accounts of meetings between US intelligence agents and liberal/moderate elements of the Bazargan cabinet, and detailed narratives of at least three CIA agents who were involved with an information-gathering project titled the Special

Reporting Facility (SRF). Some experts maintain that these documents "reveal nothing more than the routine, prudent espionage conducted at diplomatic missions everywhere."[5]

A few days later, the moderate cabinet of Mehdi Bazargan resigned, thus beginning the tumultuous years of Iran–US relations. Nobody could have imagined that the aftershocks from that earthquake would last more than 30 years.

The Role of Mistrust, Misperception, and Wrong Analysis in the Iran–US Conflict

The US lost Iran with the 1979 Revolution and fall of the Shah. It lost its privileged position in the Iranian political and economic system. The cancellation of $7 billion worth of unfulfilled arms contracts would seriously affect the US balance of payments. Americans also lost two sensitive listening posts used for monitoring the Soviet ballistic missiles program in order to verify the Soviets' commitment to the newly signed SALT (Strategic Arms Limitation Talks) Treaty. Furthermore, they no longer possessed reliable human intelligence in Iran, leaving them ignorant of Iranian current events.

In the meantime, Iran was determined to maintain relations with the US, but with several conditions. The US would have to recognize Iran's new government and accept its Islamic identity, accept a mutually respectful relationship, abandon the patron–client relationship model, and genuinely adopt a non-interference policy toward Iran. From the Islamic Republic's inception, Ayatollah Khomeini did not ban a relationship with the US. He only disallowed relations with South Africa, which was an apartheid regime, and Israel. All of the influential, high-ranking officials, including Ayatollah Beheshti, as well as the Provisional government, sought a relationship with the US. Let us not forget that the first time the embassy was seized, in February 1979, it was Ayatollah Khomeini who ordered its evacuation, and the revolutionary guards secured the location.

Despite Iran's efforts to maintain a relationship, the US was transfixed by the Cold War and was unable or unwilling to conceive of anything other than a means to meddle in Iran's politics in order to confront Soviet expansionism and protect US economic interests in Iran. The sudden rise of communist influence in Afghanistan and the existence of a pro-Soviet Iraq only made America more determined to pursue this line.

The backbone of Bazargan's administration consisted of highly educated, pro-Western, liberal-minded personalities, some of whom had lived and received education in the West. From the formation of Bazargan's provisional government, there was tension between his administration and their opponents. Bazargan and his administration believed that the revolution had come to an end and argued that it was time to build relations with foreign countries, particularly the West. Ayatollah Khomeini's view was that the revolution was incomplete, and that Iran still needed to root out US interference in its politics. I believe that Iran could have constructed a diplomatic relationship with the US and at the same time prevented its domestic affairs being influenced by Washington. Even during the height of the Cold War between the Communist and Western blocs, the US not only negotiated with its adversaries, but also maintained diplomatic and economic relations with them.

In order to reduce tensions, the US sought to foster a link to the pro-Western elements of Iran's new system. However, what they failed to understand was that executing these efforts behind the backs of the revolutionaries would be interpreted as conspiring to undermine the Revolution and its leadership. To have been successful, the US should have pursued the opposite track: they should have advanced a policy of openness, thus eliminating deep-rooted Iranian suspicions about American objectives.

A closer look at the root causes of the embassy crisis is of paramount importance. This incident marks the beginning of protracted hostility between Iran and the US. The combination of perceptions and misperceptions of the influential actors within the two states, misanalysis of the situation in Iran by the American policy-makers and experts, and an accumulation of decades of perceived betrayals have resulted in profound mutual mistrust, and have been largely responsible for the failure of all initiatives aimed at détente and peace between Iran and the US. Let us take a more in-depth look at the hostage crisis, and observe how these factors played a role in bringing about that event.

To begin with, Carter and his administration completely failed to grasp the profound, anti-American sentiment that dominated the revolutionary climate within Iran in the aftermath of its 1979 Revolution. Hamilton Jordan, Carter's advisor during the hostage crisis, admitted that the administration "didn't understand that country [Iran] and its people."[6]

A few weeks before the Embassy takeover, when Ebrahim Yazdi was informed by Henry Precht, head of the Iran Desk at the US State

Department, about the Shah's pending arrival in the US, he had warned Precht that "You are playing with fire."[7] For a while, Carter resisted the notion of admitting the Shah even though he was pressured by Henry Kissinger, David Rockefeller (then Chairman and the CEO of the Chase Manhattan Bank), and Brzezinski, Carter's National Security Advisor. In October, Carter is reported to have said to his advisors, "What are you guys going to advise me to do if they overrun our embassy and take our people hostage?"[8]

Nevertheless, his comments a few weeks after the seizure of the Embassy indicated how little he knew about what was going on in Iran. In a news conference in February 1980, he was asked by a reporter if "it was proper for the United States to restore the Shah to the throne in 1953 against Iran's popular will." Carter replied: "That is ancient history, and I don't think it's appropriate or helpful for me to go into the propriety of something that happened 30 years ago."[9]

Carter was dead wrong. The memory of the 1953 coup was so alive that every move of the United States was viewed and assessed and considered in the light of its involvement in the 1953 coup. Another misanalysis on Carter's part was that despite his objection to the admission of the Shah, out of fear of the Embassy being "overrun," he relied upon guarantees from Iran's Provisional government, namely Foreign Minister Ebrahim Yazdi, that the Embassy's security would be ensured. Due to Carter's ignorance of Iran's political environment, he and his administration overestimated the authority of Bazargan's administration, and under-estimated the power of the radicals.

Americans had already experienced one takeover of the Embassy, in February. At that time, Yazdi was able to kick the attackers out. But in the months that followed, many things had changed. Iran's large cities housed competing political groups, some of them armed. In minority areas, there were tensions and even armed struggle. Many perceived the United States, and specifically its Embassy, to be at the root of the unrest. Persuaded by the 1953 experience, many Iranians viewed the widespread turmoil as American preparation for bringing down the Revolution.

Generating more hostility among Iran's leadership was their claim that American statements contained no sign of recognition or support for the Revolution. The US was also not willing to condemn its previous policies. Iran's leadership argued that Americans were not prepared to supply the spare parts and arms worth $400 million for which Iran had already paid. Also there were no signs of the return of the Shah's or his family's funds that had been illegally seized from the Iranian nation.

In May 1979, Senator Jacob Javits, whose wife allegedly had financial connections to the Shah's system, sponsored a Senate resolution condemning executions by the Iranian government. Javits accused the Iranian government of killing Jews after they executed Habib Elghanian, a Jewish businessman. That condemnation stirred a great deal of resentment amongst the Iranian leaders. One revolutionary official told me that Elghanian was the only Jew who was executed at that time, and the reason was not because he was a Jew, otherwise thousands of Jews who lived in Iran should have been excuted. Rather it was because he had close ties to the former regime.

The Carter administration also condemned the executions. The issue of human rights was a major element in Carter's foreign policy. "Carter had refused to continue the past practice of overlooking the human rights abuses" of US allies "and was particularly tough"[10] on a handful of countries, including Iran under the Shah's rule.

Ayatollah Khomeini and Iran's revolutionaries viewed this stance as the continuation of US interference in Iran's domestic affairs. This perception affected the Iranian leadership in two ways. First, they thought that Americans refused to acknowledge Iranian national identity, which entailed rejection of foreign domination, and had been a major cause of the Revolution. And second, this perception raised fears that the US would not change its policy of interference in Iran's internal affairs. Interestingly, both of these perceptions still persist today.

Misperception was not limited to the Americans. Iranians became extremely paranoid as soon as the Shah entered the US in October 1979. Many, including the radical Muslim students, did not believe that the Shah was ill. Ayatollah Khomeini became extremely angry, his statements turning increasingly hostile. He, like many other Iranians, firmly believed that another 1953 was in the making. The students believed that the Shah's admission into the United States signaled another imminent coup attempt. I can attest that Muslim students concluded that the Revolution was under serious threat, and that by seizing the Embassy they could prevent a repeat of 1953. The whole thing was a misperception. The ailing Shah was terminally ill and died less than a year after the hostage-taking.

The straw that broke the camel's back was the unpublicized 75-minute meeting between Bazargan, Yazdi, and Brzezinski in Algeria. Students were afraid that liberals would compromise with the US, thus paving the way for a US comeback. The reality is that Bazargan advocated a "step-by-step" (*gam be gam*) policy to bring change to the structure of the government and the management of the country. He criticized radical changes and viewed them as counterproductive.

This view was discordant with the revolutionary climate which dominated the country and demanded swift and structural changes. Bazaragn also misread the situation and met with Brzezinski without consultation with the Council of Revolution. Bazargan and his colleagues criticized the interference of religion in the management of the state, directly conflicting with the outlook of the Leader of the Revolution. Bazargan later wrote: "The goal of establishing the Provisional (or transitional) government was to serve Iran via Islam and due to Islam's order, while Mr. Khomeini had adopted [the policy of] serving Islam via Iran to accomplish his own mission."[11] A conflict clearly existed between the two worldviews: Bazargan was a liberal reformist; Ayatollah Khomeini was a revolutionary.

Many experts have hypothesized that the hostage-taking event was more about factional infighting between radicals and moderates than the fear of another US intervention. But this argument is flawed on a number of counts.

First, neither Ayatollah Khomeini nor any other high-ranking official, revolutionary or otherwise, had any prior knowledge about the plan of seizing the Embassy. Second, Bazargan had already resigned three times, the last time being on November 2, that is, two days before the incident, and was just waiting for Ayatollah Khomeini's acceptance of his resignation. Also, Bazargan was not a militant or a revolutionary. He was a religious-liberal nationalist and mellow-tempered technocrat who desired to serve his country. He was not "clinging" to power and there was no need to force him out. Even if radicals had wanted to force him out, it would have been mainly because of a fear of US influence being restored. They were afraid that the Revolution was in jeopardy.

Third, Ebrahim Asgharzadeh, mastermind of the seizure, said in a 2011 interview that: "The move of the students in seizing the American Embassy was entirely a student movement. It was amateurish and unprofessional which had nothing to do with either opposition to the Provisional government, nor was it based on ideological grounds. I admit that there was a negative perception toward the American policies … however, the central problem that led to that incident was nothing but the Shah's admission into the US."[12]

Others have argued that Muslim students were afraid that leftists would initiate a seizure of the Embassy by taking advantage of the anti-American environment. But it is important to remember that the whole plan revolved around a 48-hour occupation of the compound. They were not planning or expecting to stay in their embassy more than 48 to 72 hours. And what could be achieved in such a short period in terms of defeating the leftist groups? Nothing would have dramatically changed in their favor.

Although the hostage crisis later stood for something much larger than a student uprising, the initial motivation emanated from a misperception on both sides. Herbert Kelman[13] rightfully states that "international conflict is a *process driven by collective needs and fears*, rather than entirely a product of rational calculation of objective national interest on the part of political decision makers" (emphasis in the original).[14] According to John Burton,[15] another prominent international relations scholar, "These needs include not only material ones, such as food, shelter, physical safety, and physical well-being but also psychological needs, such as identity, security, recognition, autonomy, self-esteem, and a sense of justice."[16]

Mistrust also played a key role in the Embassy's seizure. The admitted role of the US in the 1953 coup is central to the debate on mistrust between Iran's post-revolution government and the US. Resisting the Shah's policies of Westernization, an Islamic movement under the leadership of Ayatollah Khomeini emerged. Iranians believed that they were victims of US policies. Meanwhile, Ayatollah Khomeini's perception of the US, formed by his own experience in confrontation with the Shah's American-supported regime, of the Shah, was dominant in forming his mistrust of the United States. Nikki Keddie,[17] an Iran expert, maintains that "for every strange-seeming character trait [of the Iranians], as with 'mistrust' or 'paranoia,' one can nearly always find partially explanatory causes in Iranian history" (emphasis in the original).[18]

In September 1979, in an interview with an Italian journalist Oriana Fallaci, Ayatollah Khomeini was asked if there was any good thing about the West, to which he replied: "We were bitten by the snake so we also fear a string that looks like a snake from afar … now we have every reason to fear the West."[19] According to Robert Jervis, a professor of international affairs, "Historical analogies shape people's, as well as decision makers', understanding of politics … This is especially relevant when people have first-hand experiences."[20] From the onset of the Islamic Republic, the fear of "regime change" shaped the Iranian system's profound sense of mistrust of the United States. This fear was shared not only by Iran's leadership, but grassroots supporters of the system as well.

An unexpected consequence of the seizure of the American Embassy was the disclosure of classified documents, which served only to deepen Iranians' mistrust of the United States. Not all the documents were related to CIA operations in Iran, some instead focused on the Soviet Union, Turkey, Pakistan, Saudi Arabia, Iraq, and Israel. But overall, the documents reinforced Iranian fears about America.

Among the published volumes were copious CIA documents indicating efforts to generate covert ties with Iranian officials, two of them code-named SDLURE and SDROTTER. The exposure of these documents solidified the perspective that was related to me by one of the prominent leaders of the Revolution, that the United States was addicted to *khooye estekbari* (arrogant mentality) and thus could and would not leave Iran alone "until it is either able to actualize a permutation and transformation in the independence-seeking nature of the system, or topple the system (*nezam*) altogether."

One further development raised the Iranians' mistrust to a new level. A few days after the Embassy was seized, President Carter froze billions of dollars' worth of Iran's assets in the United States. This move helped Rockefeller's Chase Manhattan Bank by preventing the Iranians from withdrawing their funds out of the bank. The Chase move stunned Iranians and rumors began to spread among them that Rockefeller's direct involvement in the Shah's admission to the United States had been carefully planned to provoke the Embassy's seizure and in response freeze Iran's money. This view was reinforced when the Iranians found some correspondence from the Embassy indicating that the Carter administration had been warned about the danger of the seizure of the embassy in response to the Shah's admission to America.[21]

In his memoir, Rockefeller wrote that the Iranian "government did reduce the balances they maintained with us during the second half of 1979, but in reality they had simply returned to their historic level of about $500 million."[22] Rockefeller added that "Carter's 'freeze' of official Iranian assets protected our position, but no one at Chase played a role in convincing the administration to institute it."[23]

There is another largely ignored element that reinforced mistrust in Iran–US relations. A study of Iranian culture reveals a deep rooted "culture of conspiracy." This socio-psychological characteristic has largely influenced Iranian culture as well as politics. According to Ahmad Ashraf, an Iranian sociologist, the popularity of conspiracy theories has deep historical roots arising from a combination of complex historical experiences. In particular, Ashraf contends that "since the beginning of the 20th century Persians from all walks of life and all ideological orientations have relied on conspiracy theories as a basic mode of understanding politics and history."[24]

Historically, the great powers' covert interventions in the country's affairs have been responsible for the formation of this worldview. According to another Iranian sociologist, late Mehrdad Mashayekhi, this relatively high degree of mistrust of Iranian' culture is variously referred to by observers as "paranoid styles," "conspiracy-mindedness," "xenophobia," and "suspiciousness."[25] Events that followed the Islamic Revolution, including the documents seized from the American Embassy, as well as the US policies, only solidified this socio-psychological streak.

The deep-rooted conspiracy illusion in Iranian culture is a notable factor in shaping the political worldview of both the common people and the elite.[26] Within this setting, it is understandable how the sense of mistrust may intensify when experiences and observed evidence, in the eyes of the Iranian leadership, seemed to validate their suspicions.

Since the hostage crisis, the US has never tried to address the issue of mistrust. On the contrary, it has used every opportunity to directly or indirectly suggest to the Islamic Republic that its survival is at stake unless it "behaves," as the Americans wish. The deep mistrust of the United States, arising from a combination of the Iranian leadership's historical experience, US coercive policies, and the culture of conspiracy, has been largely responsible for the failure of initiatives, negotiations, and outreaches, and for a lack of purposeful dialogue between Iran and the US. And in the absence of meaningful dialogue, it is unreasonable to expect any change in the mutually hostile position assumed by both governments. On the contrary, it is reasonable to expect the conflict to be prolonged.

It is undeniable that the hostage-taking incident created a sense of mistrust in the United States, exhibited in questioning the rationality of the Iranian government.

The 444-day Iranian hostage crisis humiliated America in the eyes of its own people and of those around the world, and created a certain perception of the Iranian government in the American political establishment that has continued to this day. As Sick explains, "The underlying belief [was] that we were dealing not only with a government that had flouted the laws of nations ... but with a regime that was historically illegitimate, unfit, despicable."[27]

Mistrust has assumed a life of its own in the relationship between Iran and the US, almost detached from material factors such as competition over power and interests. As Anthony Cordesman et al. maintain: "Both sides harbor both legitimate and exaggerated grievances that have reinforced mutual mistrust. This mistrust now affects every aspect of US–Iranian competition over energy, economics, trade, sanctions and the nuclear issue."[28] The hostage crisis created a cycle of mistrust that has not been addressed, let alone broken, to this date. In fact, the cycle has probably only intensified due to issues such as Iran's nuclear program. A consequence of this cycle has been the creation of what the Iranian President, Mohammad Khatami, called a "wall of mistrust."

Emergence of the "Enemy Narrative"

Associated with the Embassy's seizure, the "enemy narrative" emerged in the political discourse of the Iranian government and its leaders. This discourse has remained one of the central elements of Iran's foreign policy. Many Western analysts indeed believe that the Iranian government uses the "enemy narrative" against the US (and the entire West) as a "justification for cracking down on any form of dissent or free expression."[29] Ray Takeyh, an Iran expert, maintains that "Self-serving domestic calculations likely play a part in generating [the] conservatives' statement about America's permanent ideological hostility to Iran." These assertions and related policies helped … justify political repression in Iran.[30] In other words, the Iranian regime needs the US as a permanent enemy, otherwise its "ideological foundation will be weakened."[31] However, this argument fails to convince.

First, in a "cold war" environment, where suspicion and mistrust dominate, it is more likely than not that Iran's ruling elite will use the "enemy narrative" when and where it finds it applicable. Still, this is not a fabricated reaction. On the contrary, it reflects a combination of genuine fear, mistrust, and maybe even to some extent paranoia rooted in the culture of conspiracy referred to earlier. Iran's government does not require access to confidential documents about US harboring intentions to achieve regime change. Just reading the *New York Times* and the *Washington Post* can serve to validate their fears. For example, a February 2011 article in the *New York Times* observed that the Obama administration "[had] all but encouraged protestors [in Iran] to take to the streets"[32] in the aftermath of Iran's 2009 disputed presidential election. The report added that a senior administration official maintained that "This isn't a regime-change strategy. But it's fair to say that it's exploiting fractures that are already there."[33]

Or, for instance, a further justification for Iranians to fear US intentions was the statement by former Secretary of State Condoleezza Rice that "Security assurances are not on the table" in exchange for Iran halting its nuclear program.[34] One of Iran's high-ranking officials subsequently remarked to me that "There is no clearer way to say that our [i.e. the US's] strategic plan is to overthrow the system (*nezam*) at some point."

Second, the notion that Iran requires a permanent enemy is in direct conflict with observations "on the ground." Iranian peace overtures have been made very public, including, for example, the "grand bargain" in 2003 which advanced a proposal for an all-encompassing detente with the United States. The US rejected this proposal outright. Iran cooperated closely with the US, offering intelligence and logistical support, as well as conducting a range of secret talks with US officials, before, during, and after the US-led operations in Afghanistan to topple the Taliban, also in the hope of normalizing relations. Again, in close cooperation with the US, Iran played a major role in the formation of the new Afghan government at the Bonn Conference in 2001, hoping to pave the way to a normalization of relations with America. As I was told by James Dobbins, who led the American delegation at the Bonn Conference, without Iran's support, the Conference was unlikely to have succeeded. All of these efforts resulted only in Iran's inclusion as a member of the "Axis of Evil" in George W. Bush's State of the Union address just weeks later.

The Hostage Saga Concludes

If there were no plans in advance to take the American hostages, why did it require 444 days to have them released? This is a major question posed by many observers. Indeed, it was a complex set of developments that transpired after the Embassy's takeover that prolonged the crisis.

Ebrahim Asgharzadeh has offered this explanation:

> Our plan was a student plan—temporary. But our activities at the embassy were met with support from, and subsequent imposition by the Imam, who had no knowledge [of our plan] in advance. The case became one of national recognition ... people gathered around the

Embassy and we were under siege … Following the second day, the case was out of our hands. People had even come from other cities to demonstrate in support of our actions. If we had left the Embassy, it would be [perceived as a] betrayal to the people"[35]

In other words, within the span of two days the episode grew way beyond a simple protest. National support appeared so strong that nobody, including the Revolution's Leader, could make a quick decision about releasing the Americans. As days passed, the espionage documents were exposed with a dramatic fashion by the students in order to justify their own act of taking control of "the Den of Spies/ Espionage," and the crisis became even more complicated. To Iran, America's conspiracy against the Revolution was no longer a matter of rumor or conjecture.

As already noted, eight days after the takeover, President Carter issued an executive order to freeze Iran's assets in the US and imposed the first round of sanctions, including a ban on oil imports from Iran. The Chase Manhattan Bank also froze Iran's assets. Whether it was a conspiracy theory or a reality, Iranians concluded that the American President was being manipulated and controlled by big business. This concerned Iran's top ranking decision-makers. They thought that a weak and vulnerable President might do whatever he considered necessary to overthrow the Islamic state in the interest of big oil companies who had lost their influence in Iran, thereby increasing mistrust between Iran and the US. But more importantly, the issue of frozen assets and the Americans' subsequent claims against the new Iranian government took on new life. It complicated the crisis by tethering it to a multi-billion-dollar dispute.

Following the resignation of Iran's Provisional government, two more factors negatively affected the crisis. First, there was no mediator to bridge the gap and moderate the conflict between Iran's revolutionary leadership and the United States. And second, with the exit of the moderate Bazargan administration, radicalism and anti-Americanism became dominated/gained dominance.

As direct and indirect negotiations were ongoing, Iran asked, as one of the conditions for releasing the hostages, that the US admit guilt and apologize for its past policies. Carter was fiercely opposed to that. In the meantime, the crisis escalated and became a symbol of pride for Iranians in opposition to "Americans who had supported the Shah and had ignored the Iranian people." It became increasingly difficult for Iran's leaders to agree to the release of US hostages against the backdrop of the ever-growing damage to Iran resulting from the freezing of its assets.

In February 1980, three months after the initial incident, Ayatollah Khomeini, now hospitalized due to heart-related problems, passed responsibility for deciding the fate of the American hostages' future parliament (*Majlis*). There has long been speculation that in so doing, Ayatollah Khomeini intended to ensure that the only remaining branch of the government, the *Majlis*, was established before the hostages were released. Two months later, in April 1980 and only a few weeks away from the first parliamentary elections, Iranians were stunned by Operation Eagle Claw, ordered by President Carter in attempt to rescue the hostages. The operation failed and eight Americans lost their lives in the course of the attempt. But, the failed attempt cultivated more hostility in Iran.

The initial meeting of the parliament took place at the end of May. The Shah had by that stage left the US for Egypt, but the delay had done its damage. "If the US had chosen to ask the Shah to leave sooner and before taking harsh actions such as freezing Iran's assets and imposing sanctions the crisis would have been definitely over," said Ebrahim Asgharzadeh. "Our main problem was the Shah but the US closed its eyes on that solution and instead chose coercive solutions," he added.[36]

Throughout June, the *Majlis* was busy organizing itself. Since this was the first parliament of the Islamic Republic, none of its representatives had relevant experience. Akbar Hashemi Rafsanjani, who was elected Speaker of the Majlis, was eager to conclude the hostage issue, but he faced resistance within the house. A section of representatives used to leave the chamber as soon as a debate about the hostages began, thus preventing the parliament from making decisions aimed at ending the crisis. A two-thirds quorum of representatives was required to vote for a bill.

The Shah died in July 1980. It was now apparent to many in the Iranian government that President Carter's action in admitting the Shah to the US had been motivated by humanitarian concern for an ill man. But by this stage, the matter had become much more complicated, especially as a result of freezing Iran's assets by President Carter and subsequent claims against those assets.

While the *Majlis* moved slowly on the hostage issue, Sadeq Tabatabai, Ahmad Khomeini's brother-in-law and with the purported concent of the Revolution's Leader, volunteered to contact the Americans through the German government in an attempt to resolve the issue. Ayatollah

Khomeini had four conditions for any settlement: the US to return the Shah's wealth to Iran; cancellation of all US claims against Iran; a guarantee of no future US military or political intervention in Iran; and the unfreezing of all Iranian funds by the US.

Tabatabai met with Warren Christopher, then Deputy Secretary of State, in Bonn in mid-September 1980. During a lengthy meeting, Tabatabai presented Ayatollah Khomeini's demands. Christopher said that the demand about non-intervention was acceptable. Regarding the unfreezing of Iranian assets, Christopher maintained that there were outstanding claims against Iran which were in the legal process and the US administration could not intervene with them. He did say that approximately $5.5 billion could be released immediately after the hostages were freed. With regard to voiding all legal claims against Iran, Christopher declared that this would not be possible, but that the US would accept international arbitration to bring all existing lawsuits to a mutual settlement.

With regard to returning the Shah's wealth, there existed two problems. First, Christopher maintained that the Shah could not have had a huge amount of money in the US. Iran's claim that billions of dollars existed was a fantasy. Second, even if the Shah had that kind of money, US law would not allow the government to confiscate assets without a court ruling. He pronounced that the US could only facilitate suits by the Iranian government to make its claims in the US courts.

Tabatabai was scheduled to return to Iran on September 22 and report to Ayatollah Khomeini about the progress of his talks. While he was at the airport, he realized that the flight was delayed and no explanation seemed to be forthcoming as to why. He was finally told that they could not fly to Tehran because Iraq had bombed Mehrabad Airport. Thus began the eight-year Iran–Iraq War.

Iran perceived from the onset of the War that Saddam Hussein would not have commenced the conflict without US support, and anti-American sentiment inevitably intensified. Carter wrote later that "Typically the Iranians accused me of planning and supporting the invasion."[37] The factor of mistrust was activated again. "Death to Carter" chants were now heard from inside the compound of the American Embassy to Iran's *Majlis*. Meanwhile, Iraq's invasion took precedence over the hostages' issue.

In early October, Tabatabai returned to Bonn with hope of closing the hostages' issue if the US would agree to the supply of military hardware and spare aircraft parts. What he got was a proposal covering $150 million worth of materiel for which the Shah's regime had previously paid. Tabatabai returned to Tehran to consult with Iran's leadership. While the Americans waited in anticipation to hear from Tabatabai, the *Majlis* and the government of Prime Minister Mohammad Ali Rajaei assumed responsibility for the matter. Tabatabai suddenly disappeared from the scene.

On November 2, Iran's *Majlis* finally passed a resolution to free the hostages based on the four conditions set by Ayatollah Khomeini in September, but it was too late to save Carter's presidency. "If the hostages were released," Carter wrote, "I was convinced my reelection would be assured; if the expectations of the American people were dashed again, there was little chance I could win."[38] Two days later, Ronald Reagan defeated Carter in a landslide victory.

Gary Sick, my friend and an Iran expert who served on the US National Security Council at the time, wrote a book called *October Surprise*, in which he accused Reagan allies William (Bill) Casey, who would later become the CIA Director during Reagan's presidency, and George H. W. Bush, Reagan's running mate in the election, of holding secret negotiations in Europe with Iranian officials. He claimed that they struck a deal with Iranian officials and interlocutors not to release the hostages before the US presidential election. I have no first-hand knowledge about those dealings.

In any event, on November 3, the Americans were informed that Iran had asked Algeria to serve as a mediator in the hostage negotiations. In fact, this was Rajaie's administration's initiative to take control of the hostages' affair rather than leave it to an unofficial channel, namely Sadeq Tabatabai. For the next two and a half months, the Iranians worked with the Algerians and the Carter administration, headed by Warren Christopher, regarding the details of a deal between Iran and the US. On several occasions, the negotiations almost collapsed, and between November 3, 1980 and January 19, 1981, when the final agreement was signed under the Algiers Accords[39] (or Declaration of Algiers), numerous proposals and counter-proposals had been exchanged.

Iran's stance was suddenly and significantly softened on January 16, four days before Reagan's inauguration. Iranians wanted to finalize the deal, as Christopher convincingly argues, with "the devil that they knew," that is, the Carter administration, and then concentrate on the war with Iraq and obtain the military hardware that they desperately needed for that purpose. The hostages were freed minutes after President Reagan's inauguration ceremony.

Any supposition that Iran made little or no effort to resolve the 444-day ordeal would be far from the truth. While there were clearly political forces inside Iran that sabotaged progress towards a resolution of the crisis, to claim that the hostage crisis was simply about the rooting out of one Iranian political faction by another, *rather than* reflecting the deep-rooted hostility towards and mistrust of the American government, would be a misjudgment. The aforementioned developments clearly illustrate that, over time, the crisis became increasingly complicated by a chain of actions by the US. These actions, such as the freezing of Iranian assets and the imposition of sanctions, not only intensified hostility in Tehran but also created new, sometimes massive, obstacles which took on a life independent of the hostage issue itself.

As indicated earlier, hostage-taking in Tehran had a negative impact on the American society and politics. In addition to hurt feelings, the US believed that taking hostages was an outrageous violation of international law, violating the sanctity of diplomatic immunity and protection of the Embassy premises.

Even though the American hostage crisis led to a complete breakdown in Iran–US diplomatic ties, it also provided the first opportunity for both nations to conduct meaningful discussions and hammer out their differences and disputes through bilateral negotiations brokered by Algeria. The Algiers Accords in this respect was a landmark event. While it focused primarily on the US Embassy hostage crisis, it also addressed concerns of the Iranians and led to a mutually acceptable resolution of the crisis. The agreement provided for the immediate release of the hostages by Iran, while in return "The United States pledges that it is and from now on will be the policy of the United States not to intervene, directly or indirectly, politically or militarily, in Iran's internal affairs."

Other provisions of the Algiers Accords were mainly concerned with matters of finance.[40] Subsequently, the US partially revoked sanctions against Iran and began the process of returning billions of dollars' worth of frozen assets to Iran. The Iran–United States Claims Tribunal, located in The Hague, was created in an effort to determine the claims of United States nationals against Iran and of Iranian nationals against the United States. Iran could also put forward claims in the American courts against the Shah's assets.

The US commitment to the Algiers Accords was relatively short-lived. According to reports, it was not long before President Reagan and CIA Director William Casey began funding operations aimed at undermining the Iranian government, involving various exiled groups, including the Shah's former naval commander, separatist organizations, and also the Shah's son.[41] This interference in the domestic affairs of Iran was a blatant violation of the Algiers Accords. Instead of laying the foundations for new relations based on the Accords, the US never really reversed its course of cutting relations with Tehran. America's support for Saddam Hussein's invasion of Iran essentially killed the Algiers Accords. The legacy of that agreement between the two countries might have been a future relationship based on mutual respect, cooperation, and non-interference. Instead, the failure of the US to follow through on its commitments and the counterproductive policy it adopted and pursued once again took animosity and mistrust to new levels.

Chapter 3

THE DECADE OF WAR AND CONSOLIDATION OF THE REVOLUTION: 1980–9

Joining the Revolution

I was born in 1957 into an affluent, religious family in Kashan, a city 220 kilometers south of the capital, Tehran. Kashan is internationally known for its rugs with unique shades in dazzling designs of artistic brilliance. My father was a major producer and trader of carpets. After completing high school in 1975, my mother insisted that I should study in the US. So, after a few months dedicated to learning English, I went to Sacramento, California, for my undergraduate studies at Sacramento City College and Sacramento State University. I began a four-year undergraduate degree program in engineering.

Due to my religious background, I got involved with the Muslim Students Association (MSA) of Europe and North America. Shortly thereafter, I assumed a leading role in the MSA, Sacramento State University branch. Many Iranian students who were members of the MSA later assume important roles in the post-revolutionary government. Mohammad Hashemi Rafsanjani (members of the MSA used call him "Father"), the younger brother of Akbar Hashemi Rafsanjani, one of the most influential figures in the Islamic Republic, and some ministers of Rouhani's cabinet, such as Foreign Minister Javad Zarif and Minister of Communications Mahmoud Vaezi, were among the leading MSA activists.

During my senior year at undergraduate studies at Sacramento State University, Iran was gripped by a revolutionary mood. Millions poured onto the streets, demonstrations turned bloody, workers went on strike, and state buildings were vandalized and burned. Like many other revolutionaries, as a young man of only 20 years, my understanding of politics was very limited. I had no idea about revolution and the consequences of a regime change. I did not know whether I should continue my studies or join the people inside Iran who struggled for the victory of the revolution. In October 1978, following restrictions placed on his political and religious activities by the Iraqi government, Ayatollah Khomeini, the leader of the revolutionary movement, left Iraq for Paris. In France he chose to reside in a village outside Paris called Neauphle-le-Château.

In order to resolve my dilemma of whether to stay in the US or go back to Iran, one day I called Ayatollah Khomeini's residence in France. I introduced myself to Ayatollah Khomeini's secretary and asked, "What is my duty? Should I stay and continue my studies, or return to Iran and serve the revolution?" The secretary told me he would talk to Imam (Khomeini) and I could call back the next day to obtain his answer. "If you are convinced that you can help the revolution effectively, you should come back. Otherwise you may stay and continue your studies," he told me when I called back the next day. I informed the MSA of the answer I had received, and deliberated over it for two days. I finally concluded that I would be able to assist the revolution. Without informing my parents, I returned to Iran, leaving my university program unfinished. I could wait no longer to join the revolution.

The first day after my arrival, and for a few days afterwards, I took to the streets and joined the demonstrators. Then one day I asked myself, "Am I playing an effective role in the revolution?" The answer a decided "No." But it appeared to me that 99 percent of the people who chanted "Death to Shah, Death to America" were as confused and ignorant as myself about the revolution's direction, unsure of what was supposed to happen next. Within a few days, the Shah left the country and he appointed Shahpour Bakhtiar, a politician of liberal persuasion of the Mossadegh era, as prime minister. While daily demonstrations continued across the country, I left Tehran for my home town of Kashan. My parents were shocked to see me back, having left my school in the US for such a dangerous situation at home. My younger brother, Abbas, introduced me to members of a militant group who were prepared to fight against the Shah's regime. They took me to the deserts around Kashan for a three-day training program. However, less than a month after Shah left Iran, his military apparatus, the most powerful in the region, collapsed in the face of millions of unarmed revolutionaries, and the revolution stunningly succeeded with no need for a guerrilla war.

A few months after the victory of the Revolution, the Islamic Republic Party was formed by five prominent clerics: Dr. Seyyed Mohammad Hosseini Beheshti, Mohammad Javad Bahonar, Akbar Hashemi Rafsanjani, Seyyed Ali Khamenei, and Abdolkarim Mousavi-Ardabili, all students of Ayatollah Khomeini before his exile in 1964.

The goal of the Party's founders was to mobilize popular support for the Islamic Republic which they thought was in an unstable condition, threatened by armed and unarmed opposition groups inside the country, as well as by foreign powers.

The Party was led by Ayatollah Dr. Beheshti, one of the main architects of the Islamic Republic of Iran's new Constitution and the head of Iran's judiciary in the early 1980s. He was arguably the second most powerful and influential man in Iran, after Ayatollah Khomeini. In my meeting with him a month after the victory of the Revolution, he told me that the new Iran should have multiple political parties in order to establish a real democracy.

During my next meeting with him in Kashan, in March 1981, he appointed me as editor-in-chief of the leading English daily, the *Tehran Times*. He indicated in our discussions that if he had known about the seizure of the American Embassy in advance, he would have halted the plans before it ever happened. "That was not in our hand, but to rebuild healthy relations with the US based on non-interference and mutual respect *is* in our hand. We should do our utmost to get there." At the end of the meeting, he asked me to meet with him after three months to present a report about the *Tehran Times*.

Due to his influence, Dr. Beheshti was undoubtedly the political figure most targeted by opposition groups, primarily by communist groups and the People's Mujahedin of Iran or the Mojahedin-e-Khalq (MEK), inside and outside of Iran. They intended to discredit him and by association the system. Nevertheless, he was extremely patient and considered the actions of his opponents as the inevitable outcome of the freedom that had suddenly emerged in the aftermath of the Revolution. He said that political groups who had been silenced and oppressed during the Shah's regime needed a way to express their accumulated grievances.

The MEK was founded in 1965 by a group of university students with a hybrid ideology comprised of Islam and Marxism, and devoted to armed struggle against the Shah. After the victory of the Revolution and the death of the original leaders at the hands of the Shah's security apparatus, the new leaders who were freed from prison demanded a share in power.

After the MEK's decisive loss in the first parliamentary elections in May 1980, and once it became clear that they had failed to secure a position in the new system's political structure, their approach and outlook became increasingly belligerent toward the government. They primarily targeted leaders of the Islamic Republic Party which had won that election by a landslide.

Tensions between the MEK and the Islamic Republic Party intensified after Abolhassan Bani Sadr, the first President of the Islamic
Republic, was impeached by the Majlis. The MEK threw its support
behind Bani Sadr and later, in June 1981, they declared commitment to
a military phase and armed struggle against the standing government.
On the evening of June 28, 1981, a day prior to my scheduled
meeting with Dr. Beheshti in Tehran, my wife called, crying hysteri-
cally, and implored me to come home immediately as there had been
a major bomb blast nearby. I got to my father-in-law's home, which
was attached to the headquarters building of the Islamic Republic
Party, as quickly as possible. Two large bombs had exploded inside
the conference hall of the same building where Beheshti had been
addressing dozens of high-ranking members of the Party. The scene
inside was a carnage.

I joined hundreds of citizens and rescue teams to search amongst
the rubble for survivors until the early hours of the morning. After
removing the bodies of the dead and trying to save those still alive,
the identity of the victims began to emerge. Dr. Beheshti, four cabinet
ministers, 24 members of the Parliament (*Majlis*), and 43 others,
including several government officials, had been assassinated.

In an interview years later, Saeed Shahsavandi, a former member of
the MEK's Central Committee, gave details of the terrorist operation.[1]
According to Shahsavandi, the person who carried out the operation
was Mohammad Reza Kolahi, a freshman in Electrical Engineering at
the University of Science and Technology. He had infiltrated the Party
and secured a job as the organizer of its meetings and conferences.

That evening, Kolahi's unfettered access to the conference hall
enabled him to plant two bombs: one under the podium and one
underneath a column. A few minutes before the explosion, he left the
conference hall. At approximately 9.00 in the evening, Dr. Beheshti
started his opening remarks and the two bombs went off, one after the
other. Due to the magnitude of the explosions, the conference hall's roof
collapsed directly on the participants, causing the immediate death of
nearly all of the victims. According to Shahsavandi, within a span of
six months, ten thousand people who worked for the government or
supported it were assassinated by the MEK.[2]

The bombing at the Islamic Republic Party's headquarters changed
the political climate in Iran. Parties were first restricted, and then they
were gradually banned altogether. Plain-clothes radical groups made
life difficult for any opposition to raise its voice. By this time, we were
almost a full year into the Iran–Iraq War. Some maintain that the

government used the assassinations and the War as a pretext to silence any opposition challenging its authority. The government, however, argued that it could not allow everyday street protests and a state of chaos while it was fighting to liberate the territories captured by Iraq. A sizeable part of the Province of Khuzestan, the heart of Iran's oil resources, and part of the western provinces had been captured by the Iraqi army in the early days of the invasion.

Dr. Beheshti, despite the image that the opposition groups used to present of him as a despot and a monopolist, wholeheartedly advocated freedom of opinion and expression. He advocated and participated in televised debates with Marxist theorists. His absence was a blow to moderate thinking in Iran and changed the balance in favor of radicalism. Shahsavandi says that after the bombing, the MEK eavesdropped on the police and revolutionary committees only to make sure that Beheshti was dead.[3]

A few weeks later, in July 1981, I was returning from my work at the *Tehran Times*. It was around 9.00 p.m. when I mounted my motorcycle and began my journey home. I soon realized that another motorcycle was tailing me so I attempted to lose them by taking side streets, but to no avail. As I accelerated, so did they, and it was clear that they were after me. I remember maneuvering at high speed through narrow streets, taking every step I could to reach safety. I finally turned down my father-in-law's street in a last-ditch effort to save my life. As I sped towards the house, remarkably the gates to the yard were open. I rode my bike straight through them as the motorists behind me fired shots in my direction. The bullets barely missed and I escaped without harm. If the door to the house had been closed, the time it would have taken me to open it would have cost me my life. This was the reality we faced in the aftermath of the Revolution: countless terrorist acts by the MEK aimed at disrupting every aspect of life in the society.

Another major terror attack occurred two months later, on August 30, 1981. A MEK operative, Massoud Kashmiri, had infiltrated the central command of the Islamic leadership and placed a bomb underneath the table at the cabinet meeting in the office of the newly elected President Rajai and Prime Minister Mohammad-Javad Bahonar.

I was in my office at the *Tehran Times*, approximately two miles from the office of the President, when the explosion occurred. It was so loud that it shook our building. I could see smoke rising from the government building and I raced to the scene. When I arrived, ambulances and a large crowd had already gathered. As the editor-in-chief of the *Tehran Times*, I was given access to the government building. There, I saw the burned bodies of both Rajai and Bahonar brought out from the rubble.

Over the next ten years, while working for the *Tehran Times*, I also served in other positions. Between 1981 and 1983, I worked as the Vice President of the Islamic Propagation Organization, headed by Ayatollah Ahmad Jannati was the president of the organization.[4] In 1983, I offered to set up the Parliament's administrative department, then Speaker of the Parliament (*Majlis*), and was subsequently appointed as its head.

In 1985, while still serving at the Parliament, a Samsonite briefcase was left at the front door of my home. On arriving home, I was suspicious of what might be inside it. Without approaching, I called the police station, which was two blocks from my home. The police arrived immediately and removed the briefcase to their station for further investigation. They deactivated the bomb which was placed inside the briefcase. I was told that it would have detonated upon my opening it. I had once again eluded assassination.

After the police took the briefcase, they permitted me to enter my house. Immediately after I walked in, the telephone rang and when I answered, there was an unknown person who addressed me by my first and last name, but I did not recognize the voice. A few seconds later, a third person interjected on the line. This interruption was by the Iranian Intelligence Ministry, who informed me, while the first voice continued speaking, that "On the other side of the line is a MEK terrorist from camp Ashraf in Iraq and you should hang up the phone immediately." The MEK was following up to see whether I was alive or dead. I hung up the phone. The phone rang again. I picked it up and it was the Intelligence Ministry once again. They told me, "Mr. Mousavian, we have credible evidence that you are on the hit list of the MEK and we implore you to relocate to an unknown location for a while." At the time, my wife and I had three young daughters, and to ensure everyone's safety we moved to a small apartment on Tehran's periphery and resided there for three months. In 1986, Muslim radicals within the ruling currents secured a majority in the *Majlis*. During several discussions with Rafsanjani, I informed him that due to differences in views between the radicals and myself, I could no longer serve as head of the Parliament's administration. In this period, the radicals espoused an anti-West/American posture, were opposed to the free market economy, and supported the hostage-taking move. In response to my request, Rafsanjani introduced me to the Minister of Foreign Affairs, Dr. Ali Akbar Velayati, after which I started my political and diplomatic career as the Director General for the West Europe Department of the Ministry.

During my career, "terrorism" remained one of the issues at the core of the conflict between Iran and the US and the West. Following its deadly terrorist attacks within Iran, the MEK moved its headquarters to Iraq in 1986 and allied itself with Saddam Hussein in the War against Iran—the MEK was financially and militarily backed by the Iraqi dictator until his fall in 2003.[5] The group was used by Saddam to provide intelligence and to fight against Iran. They also assisted Saddam in the bloody crackdown on the Iraqi Shia and Kurdish communities.[6]

A brief look at history would as well serve clarify the bigger picture. During the 1970s, MEK engaged in armed struggle against the Shah's regime and was responsible for assassinating a number of US military personnel in Iran. During the reign of the Shah, the MEK was responsible for attacks that killed US civilians and military personnel in Iran. Finally, on October 8, 1997, the US State Department added the MEK to its Foreign Terrorist Organization (FTO) list.[7]

Since 2010, four nuclear scientists have been assassinated in Iran. A February 2012 NBC News report claimed that, according to US officials, the deadly attacks were carried out by the MEK which had been "trained and armed by Israel's secret service."[8] The report also suggested that the statements by US officials confirmed the same "charges leveled by Iran's leaders."

Notwithstanding the evidence, in September 2012, the United States removed the MEK from the US Foreign Terrorist Organization list. This move involved the flow of millions of dollars to members of Congress, Washington lobby groups, and former top US officials.[9] What is amazing is that while the MEK was on the terrorist list, US officials received funds to support the group. It was reported that an investigation was under way by the US Treasury Department to determine whether some of the funds were provided in breach of the law relating to "material support for a terrorist group."[10] In cases involving links to other banned organizations, "such as Hamas and Hezbollah, individuals have received long jail sentences for indirect financial support."[11]

According to some reports the list of the officials who received funds is a long one, but prominent among them is Ileana Ros-Lehtinen, Chair of the House Foreign Relations Subcommittee on the Middle East and North Africa.[12] Interestingly, after a June 2013 hearing before the Subcommittee, Ros-Lehtinen was asked if she was convinced by the experts' advice, who almost unanimously agreed that the US should give the new Iranian President, Hassan Rowhani, time to change the direction of Iran's foreign policy. She replied: "Not at all. We need to continue our sanctions policy and help our allies to see the light that a nuclear Iran will destroy the United States and will destroy Israel."[13]

It is disheartening that members of the Congress should support imposing more sanctions on Iran because this position reaps a payoff by satisfying lobby groups.[14] There is now a rock-solid perception in Tehran that the US Congress is heavily influenced by lobby groups and that that personal interests of its legislators significantly impact, if not determine, its foreign policy. These lobby groups, like the MEK, are not satisfied with less than regime change, and the MEK is viewed by part of the US policy community as a viable instrument to achieve it. Congressman Ted Poe, who received thousands of dollars from the head of a pro-MEK organization, described the group as the "ticket for regime change in Iran."[15]

The problems between Iran and the US, as discussed earlier, primarily arise from deep mistrust. Removing the MEK from the terrorist organizations list could be detrimental to the efforts of many people like me who try to build bridges between the two governments. In my conversation with a high-ranking Iranian official, I was informed that "the move strengthened the position of Iran's government, saying that the United States' policy toward Iran is based on regime change at all cost—including support for terrorist organizations that do Washington's bidding in its effort."

Shortly before Iran's June 2013 presidential election, chess grand master and human rights activist Garry Kasparov launched a "virtual election" under the banner "We Choose," to provide a free and fair vote in Iran. News of his initiative gained widespread coverage in the West. According to We Choose, "The final results ... show that Iranian reformist candidates are the big winners of this global initiative."[16] Reformist candidates received 67 percent of the votes cast.

More interesting is the number of votes for Mrs. Maryam Rajavi who officially heads the MEK. It was logically assumed that the MEK would mobilize its supporters to actively participate in the voting, yet Rajavi received only 0.9 percent of the total votes.[17] This raises the question as to how a considerable number of American officials concluded that the MEK had enough popular support to actualize regime change in Iran and how it could be an alternative to the current Iranian system.

The continued misanalysis of Iran's politics and society by American officials only heightens mistrust and hostilities, further complicating the relationship between Iran and the US and providing no concrete benefit for the American government.

Iraq Attacks Iran

On September 22, 1980, Saddam Hussein, the Iraqi dictator, shocked Iranians by starting an all-out war against the country, the results of which were devastating. This war would rage for eight bloody years, costing the lives of a million people on both sides and hundreds of billions of dollars' worth of damage. That doesn't even include years of adverse effects on socio-economic development in both countries.

There have been multiple reasons suggested for Saddam's action. Some argue that Iran's "exporting revolution" slogan was seen as a major threat to Saddam's rule, particularly because the majority of Iraqis, that is, the Shias, had a religious affinity with the new leadership in Iran, as it was the first Islamic republic to be based on Shia ideology. Proponents of this argument maintain that Saddam's desire was to stifle the threat and block the expansion of an Islamic government into Iraq. This factor may indeed have played a role in Saddam's decision to invade.

However, this argument ignores historical realities and Saddam's personal, endless greed for power and domination. If Saddam's attack on Iran was due to the Iranians' "exporting revolution" mantra and the sense of being threatened by the aggressive revolutionary language of the Iranian government, then how does one make sense of the Iraqi invasion of Kuwait, a Sunni Arab country, only two years after the end of Iran–Iraq War? Besides, during the eight-year war between Iran and Iraq, Kuwait unwaveringly *supported* Iraq, pumping billions of dollars into Saddam Hussein's war machine.

History illustrates that Saddam Hussein's ambitions and his desire for expansion dated back to the Shah's era. However, the Shah's military power far surpassed other Persian Gulf nations, thanks to a sudden increase in Iran's petrodollars due to rocketing oil prices in 1973 when the Arab OPEC countries embargoed their oil exports in response to the Arab–Israeli October War. In this context, Saddam had no choice but to sign the 1975 Algiers agreement which settled Iraq's existing border disputes with Iran. In doing so, he gave up Iraq's claim to the oil-rich Iranian province of Khuzestan, while the Shatt-al-Arab waterway (called *Arvand Rood* in Iran) remained under the equal control of the two states. After the Revolution, Iran adhered firmly to the 1975 Treaty.

Iraqi provocations dated back to April and May 1979, almost a year and a half before the all-out invasion of Iran. In May 1979, Iraq bombarded the town of Mehran and some other Iranian border villages. This was only three months after the victory of the Revolution and just a month after the Islamic Republic's formation. The Iranian Foreign Ministry protested and the Iraqi government said in response that the 1975 Treaty had been imposed on Iraq under duress.[18] The reality was that Saddam sought to destroy the only power in the Persian Gulf that stood in the way of his regional domination.

In 1980, Iran was preoccupied with the hostage crisis, and still entangled with the post-revolutionary upheaval. Additionally, they were entangled in a post-revolution upheaval. With their army all but disintegrated, Saddam was conscious of Iran's significantly weakened defense position. He therefore seized this opportunity in the hope of annexing the oil-rich province of Khuzestan and crushing Iran as a regional rival once and for all.

In a televised broadcast, on September 17, 1980, Saddam tore up a copy of the "1975 Treaty concerning the Frontier and Neighborly Relations between Iran and Iraq," proclaiming the formal abrogation of agreements with Iran. Five days later, the Iraqi army invaded Iran, whose principal target was the occupation of the Province of Khuzestan.

Iraq attacked Iran on such a large scale that, from the onset, Iranians viewed the invasion as complementary to the United States' aim of overthrowing the regime and the disintegration of Iran. It was incomprehensible to Iran's leadership that Saddam would dare launch such an attack without America's green light. The evidence and events that followed would confirm this suspicion.

Although in his memoir, Jimmy Carter denies that the US gave a "green light" to Saddam, a confidential "talking points" memo written by Alexander Haig, Reagan's first Secretary of State, claimed otherwise. Investigative reporter Robert Perry revealed that in this memo Haig referred to a meeting with the Saudi Prince Fahd in April 1981 in which he learned that "President Carter gave the Iraqis a green light to launch the war against Iran through Fahd."[19] Others, however, discount Haig's story as a fabrication.

In any case, Iran's assessment was based on what they witnessed, not any knowledge of secret talks. To them, the fact that the US government did not condemn Iraq's invasion, recognize it as a breach of international law and an act of aggression, nor call for the evacuation of Iraqi troops from occupied lands in Iran was clear proof that the Americans backed Iraq's invasion.

In February 1982, the United States removed Saddam's regime from the State Department's Sponsors of Terrorism list. This move facilitated Iraq's entry into the international arms market and purchase of arms from the US, a fact that did not go unnoticed in Iran. In two operations, during March and May of 1982, to the surprise of observers and American policy-makers alike, Iranians engaged in a series of bloody battles, breaking the Iraqi line and separating its units in northern and southern Khuzestan. In late May, Iran finally regained the strategic city of Khorramshahr in Khuzestan. From this point onwards, Iran decided to push into Iraq and overthrow Saddam Hussein.

In the wake of these developments, the US suddenly decided to break its silence on the War. In a formal statement, White House Deputy Press Secretary Larry Speakes confirmed American "opposition to the seizure of any territory by force."[20] This statement did not come as a surprise to Iran's leaders. Not a single high-ranking Iranian official missed the fact that when Iraq occupied in September 1980 substantial parts of three Iranian western provinces, the US government said nothing. But when Iran went on the offensive, US leaders were outraged. Iran's leaders were under no illusions about America's real intentions despite their officially neutral position.

What motivated the Reagan administration to take such a stance is debatable. The hostage crisis, as many commentators maintain, might have played a role. As a result of the protracted crisis, the Iranian government was viewed as an irrational, uncompromising, and cruel entity. In their eyes, Saddam Hussein was the lesser of two evils.

Another reason could have been that Americans perceived revolutionary Iran as a threat to their interests and decided/resolved to prevent Iran gaining control of arguably the richest region in oil reserves in the world. The Director of the National Intelligence Council wrote that "an Iranian defeat of Iraq would set into motion forces for accommodation with anti-Western goals—whether by overthrow of existing regimes or accommodation by them."[21]

On the other hand, it is remarkable that top US policy-makers did not see Saddam as an imminent threat to the region's oil countries, despite his known ambitions of gaining supremacy in the region. His occupation of Kuwait in 1990 illustrated that the Americans had miscalculated by investing in Saddam's regime.

The Reagan administration lacked unbiased advisors who were familiar with Iranian politics and culture. Additionally, policy-makers were trapped in a Cold War mentality. Both of these facts caused the US failure to grasp two important realities. First, all that the new Iranian government and its grassroots supporters demanded from the US was recognition of their identity and a non-interventionist non-patron–client relationship. Slogans like "exporting of revolution" were, in essence, about establishing an identity which the West had refused to recognize since the Shah's era. It was about establishing a different culture and urging the West to accept it. Second, after a revolution on such large scale, it was impossible for a standard army to defeat the highly motivated, religious, nationalist, revolutionary youth who were ready to give up their lives for their cause. They would undoubtedly defend the Revolution and their country's sovereignty and independence. This sentiment was shared by Iranians from all walks of life. For example, conventional wisdom dictates that wealthy people seldom risk their lives by going to fight for their beliefs. My brother, however, who came from an affluent family, was among many young Iranians who volunteered, fought, and was martyred, in November 1983. He lost his life in the front lines on the outskirts of Kermanshah, western Iran, and his funeral was held without his body.

Less than two years after Iraq's invasion of Iran, Israel invaded Lebanon on June 6, 1982, deploying a force of 76,000 troops, 800 tanks, 1,500 armored personnel carriers, and 634 airplanes, leading to the deaths of an estimated 17,825 Lebanese soldiers, 9,797 Syrian and PLO fighters, and 675 Israelis. Between September 16 and 18, 1982, the Israeli Defense Minister, Ariel Sharon, allowed Christian Phalangist militiamen to massacre over 800 Palestinian civilians in the refugee camps of Sabra and Shatila.[22] The 1982 invasion of Lebanon had far-reaching security implications, including consequences for the US in its support of the two aggressors: Israel and Iraq.

The car bombing in Beirut in October 1983 which killed 241 American servicemen made the Americans more hostile towards Iran. American intervention in Lebanon's civil wars in favor of the Christian dominated Lebanese army against the Muslim community clearly contradicted its claim to be neutral in the conflict. Colonel Timothy J. Geraghty, the commander of the US Marines in Beirut at the time of the incident, wrote years later: "It is noteworthy that the United States provided direct naval gunfire support—which I strongly opposed—for a week to the Lebanese Army [who was fighting against Muslims] at a mountain village called Suq-al-Garb ... American support removed any lingering doubts of our neutrality."[23]

However, as stated, the bombing had a detrimental effect on the US view of Iran. Americans linked the terrorist act to Hezbollah (although Hezbollah did not exist at the time, but some elements who later founded Hezbollah were seen as organizers of the suicide attack) and, by association, to Iran, which supported and originally organized the militant Shia group. Iran denied the accusations.[24] Nevertheless, the bombing increased US hostility toward and mistrust of Iran.

The US and Iran are both victims of terrorism but the two countries have accused each other of supporting and/or organizing terrorist and militant groups to harm each other. Logically, the two countries, as victims of terrorism, should cooperate with each other to combat terrorism, rather than engage in finger pointing, name calling, and inciting hatred toward each other. The beneficiaries of this state of affairs are those who would wish to sabotage Iran–US relations inside Iran and the United States, as well as outside the two states—those who are inspired by personal, political, and ideological motivations to prevent normalization of relations between them.

While the perpetrator of the bombing in Beirut has not been identified with certainty, nonetheless, three issues about responsibility for terrorism should be noted. First, US policy-makers perceive that whatever actions are carried out by groups such as Hezbollah and Hamas are checked and coordinated with the Iranian government in advance. That is simply not the case. Second, the possible role of rogue or spy elements inside Iran, with respect to terrorist attacks, should not be ignored. Third, generally speaking, false flag terrorism, or terrorist activities that are organized by external actors, again aiming to deepen mistrust between Iran and the US, must be factored in as a distinct possibility in considering who is responsible for terrorist attacks.

Around 1983, Iranian intelligence warned the country's leaders that the Americans were providing the Iraqis with satellite images that revealed Iran's military deployment activities along the border. Declassified documents revealed later that Donald Rumsfeld, then Special Envoy for President Reagan, secretly visited Tariq Aziz, the Iraqi Foreign Minister and Deputy Prime Minister, in Iraq in December 1983. The "talking points" of Rumsfeld's meeting included assurances to Aziz that the US "would regard any major reversal of Iraq's fortune as a strategic defeat for the west."[25]

A few months later, in 1984, Tariq Aziz met with President Reagan at the White House. Following this meeting, the two sides agreed to restore diplomatic relations. A *New York Times* headline declared "U.S. restores full ties with Iraq but cites neutrality in Gulf War."[26] Secretary of State George Shultz later wrote in his memoir that "While the United States basically adhered to the policy of not supplying arms to either side, our support for Iraq increased in rough proportion to Iran's military success, plain and simple."[27]

Even without the evidence that surfaced later, Iranian decision-makers were certain that the United States would help Saddam, either directly or indirectly through other Western and Arab countries in the region. Iran blamed Washington, as a supporter of Saddam, for inciting one of the most devastating wars in Iran's history. Hostility filled the minds and hearts of not only the elite but also grassroots supporters of the Islamic Republic. After all, many of their youth lost their lives or were paralyzed or suffered permanent psychological damage, which was called *mowji* (related to wave), meaning they had lost their psychological balance as a result of waves of explosions on the battlefield.

These developments reaffirmed for Iranians that the Americans' strategic goal was regime change and if possible disintegration of Iran, and that any offer for reconciliation would be purely tactical. Iranian hardliners posited that Americans were Americans, and that there was no difference between hardliners and centrists. This mirrored the false notion of some American scholars and policy-makers who claimed that there were no moderates in Iran.

Needless to say, the obvious conflict between the formal US stance of neutrality in relation to the War, and its perceived support of Saddam, convinced many Iranian policy-makers of the US government duplicity. As a result, mistrust of the United States escalated. But the most notable conclusion drawn from the Iran–Iraq War was that Iran could not rely on the friendship of *any* country, or according to the famous Persian saying: "Go get strong if you desire comfort in the world, for in the state of nature, the weak is trampled".

Mutual Hostility and Suspicion in the Persian Gulf

The United States' grand strategy in the Middle East is driven primarily by two elements: security of energy resources and the safety of sea-lanes for the steady flow of oil; and the security of Israel. Energy resources in the region have both security and economic significance for the US. The security of the oil supply has been seen as vital to the US national interest since the presidency of Franklin Roosevelt (1933–45).

As argued by some analysts, the US reliance on the Persian Gulf's oil is considerably reduced.[28] Further, they claim that having discovered oil shale around the world, including major deposits in the United States, the Persian Gulf oil supply will soon become irrelevant[29] as a driving force behind America's grand strategy in the Middle East. Therefore, they conclude that the region will gradually lose its relevance to the US foreign policy.

But this argument is flawed. Indeed, any instability in oil supplies from the Persian Gulf region affects oil prices throughout the world. Thus, it follows that the world's economy, including that of the US, is affected, regardless of where the US purchases or produces its oil.

Energy economist James Hamilton[30] has reviewed four different events that led to oil supply disruptions.[31] In reverse chronological order, these were the 1990 Second Gulf War, the 1980 Iran–Iraq War, the 1978–79 Iranian Revolution, and the 1973 OPEC embargo. He concluded from his research that "each of these events was ... followed by a recession in the United States." Hamilton also deduced from his findings that "at their peak disruptions, these events took out 4–7 percent of net world production and were associated with oil price increases of 25–70 percent."[32]

Another significant factor to consider is that of speculation in the oil markets. The oil markets are propelled by more than just supply and demand, which was not the case historically. Political economist Professor Robert B. Reich[33] stated in 2012 that "Financial speculators historically accounted for about 30 percent of oil contracts, producers and end users for about 70 percent. But today, speculators account for 64 percent of all contracts."[34] Reich's analysis was that when there is an uncertain outlook for supply, speculation abounds, causing market prices to surge.

Furthermore, leaders in the US protect the interests of other capitalist nations that are strategically important to them, especially Japan and the EU. For example, about 87 percent of Japan's crude oil imports come from the Persian Gulf region. For the global capitalist system to thrive, no single power must be allowed to gain control of the Middle East region. The emergence of a dominant state in the Middle East could potentially disrupt oil supplies to the rest of the World.

To conclude, any instability in the Persian Gulf region increases the price of oil, and this dynamic will affect the US economy regardless of their source of oil, domestic or foreign. Considering this, any tension between Iran and its Arab neighbors can potentially destabilize the region, therefore running contrary to US national interests. Hence, relations between Iran and its Persian Gulf neighbors will remain significant to the United States for the foreseeable future.

There exists a deep-rooted sense of mistrust between Iran and the Arab countries in the Persian Gulf; members of the Gulf Cooperation Council—Saudi Arabia, Bahrain, Kuwait, Oman, Qatar and the United Arab Emirates (UAE). Historically, it dates back to the Arab Muslim invasion of Iran some 1,400 years ago, and has had lasting effects on a people who have a deep cultural memory.

Iran is the only non-Arab country in the Persian Gulf. Its language is Persian, not Arabic, and it is not a member of the League of Arab States. However, Iran is rich in history, a history that is older and more varied than that of the GCC. Historically, since ancient times, Iran has been a key player in the Persian Gulf and the Middle East, as it is today.

Bahrain, a small island country situated near the western shores of the Persian Gulf with a population of 1.2 million, used to be Iran's fourteenth province, with a seat in the Iranian parliament dating back to the early 1900s. In 1970, the Shah of Iran agreed to the independence of Bahrain. In return, the British recognized the Greater and Lesser Tunb Islands and Abu Musa as a long-standing part of Iranian territory. The continued territorial dispute over these islands between Iran and UAE has been a major issue of dispute and tension between Iran and the GCC. These islands are close to the Strait of Hormuz, a point of strategic significance in the region. The oil that flowed through the Strait in 2011 accounted for "roughly 35 percent of all seaborne traded oil, or almost 20 percent of oil traded worldwide."[35]

Due to the Shah's military ambition to become the region's dominant power, relations between Iran and its Arab neighbors in the Persian Gulf were strained. Later, during the Iraqi invasion of Iran, the Arab countries in the Persian Gulf region gave their full support to the aggressor, as a result of which the relationship between Iran and its neighbors entered one of its most tumultuous phases.

At the heart of dissension between Arab governments in the region and the newly established Islamic Republic was the so-called "exporting of revolution" slogan that Iran adopted shortly after the Revolution.[36] The emergence of tension pushed Iran's Arab neighbors in the Persian Gulf, including Saudi Arabia and five smaller states, to form the Gulf Cooperation Council in 1981. A year later, the GCC established a joint military force called the "Peninsula Shield Force" (PSF). The PSF was originally supposed to be deployed in case a member state was threatened by a foreign power. However, Iran believed that the PSF was formed primarily to confront it.

The GCC had serious concerns about the religious and revolutionary nature of Iran's governance structure and the dynamics of its political system. Meanwhile, a centuries-old rift between the Shia and Sunni communities continued to play its role in exacerbating hostile relations. Ultra-orthodox religious scholars and elements on both sides never ceased to fan the flames of controversy. The largest Saudi oil fields are in the Eastern Province, home to most of the Saudi Shia population who possess the potential to threaten the Saudi kingdom and had a prior history of sporadic episodes of unrest. The Shia community comprises 10–15 percent of the Saudi population. Bahrain, another GCC member that also happens to host the US Navy's 5th Fleet, has a population with a Shia majority that has challenged that country's sunni-dominated establishment on many occasions.

Moreover, Iran is influential in the Muslim world and in Arab nations such as Iraq, Yemen, Lebanon, Bahrain, and Palestine. This Iranian popularity is generally attributed to its unrelenting support for the Palestinian cause, providing vital political, social, and economic backing for resistance movements such as Hamas and Hezbollah. This is yet another point of concern for the GCC leaders, because support in other countries has the potential to disrupt the balance of power in favor of Iran. The reasoning is that this popularity could inspire revolution in the GCC member states. As argued by many analysts, Arabs and others, these factors led to the GCC's full support for Saddam during the Iran–Iraq War. Suspicions and mistrust were exacerbated by an attempted coup in Bahrain in 1981, in which many believed Iran was involved.

Another serious point of contention revolved around the annual demonstrations by Iranians against Israel and the United States during the *hajj* pilgrimage. The Saudi government viewed these demonstrations as incitement of Muslims and Saudi Arabia's Shia minority against its superpower ally, the United States. After 1982, when the tables turned in the Iran–Iraq War and Iran went on the offensive, Arabs were decidedly frightened and relations went from bad to worse. While astronomical amounts of money went from the GCC to Iraq in support of Saddam, the war of words and name calling between Iran and Saudi Arabia reached its peak.

Another major element of Iran's conflict with the GCC was the latter's strategic alliance with Western powers, specifically the US. Iran fiercely opposed the US presence in the region, while members of the GCC hosted the American military and their bases. Iran viewed American domination of the GCC countries as humiliating to Muslims. Obviously, the GCC leaders viewed Iran's opposition as interference in their internal affairs.

From Iran's perspective, the security and stability of the Persian Gulf has been determined by Western powers for over a century, with no major part played by regional countries. Iran has always emphasized that countries in the Persian Gulf must assume a more prominent role in the security and stability of the region. This view contrasts sharply with that of the GCC members, who seek to preserve security and stability through political, military, and security alliances with the US and other Western powers. Iran maintains that during much of the past half-century, Western powers have blocked the independence of Muslim countries by supporting traditional systems of governance in the region and preventing development in the Persian Gulf.

Iraq's invasion of Iran and its use of chemical weapons cost Iran hundreds of billions of dollars and hundreds of thousands of lives. The GCC chose to ignore Saddam's criminal conduct, including use of chemical weapons. According to the Iraq Survey Group's Final Report, Iraq received $40 billion of financial support from the GCC during the war against Iran.[37] When Saddam proclaimed Khuzestan Province to be part of Iraq's territory and called it *Arabistan*, the GCC supported the claim, leading Iranians to conclude that the GCC sought the complete disintegration of Iran. Then in the 1987 clashes between the Iranian Hajj pilgrims and the Saudi security forces led to the death of 403 people—among them 275 Iranians—and 2,000 injured.[38] There had never before been such intense hostility between Iran and Saudi Arabia.

The end of the Iran–Iraq War (1988), followed by Saddam Hussein's invasion of Kuwait (1990), coincided with the presidency of Akbar Hashemi Rafsanjani. Rafsanjani's efforts focused on the normalization of relations between Iran and the West as well as with its Arab neighbors.

Iran–Contra Scandal

During the summer of 1985, President Reagan and the Speaker of the Iranian Parliament (*Majlis*), Rafsanjani, attempted a détente between Iran and the US through signaling mutual goodwill. The plan was for Iran to use its influence over Hezbollah in Lebanon to free seven American hostages and for the US to deliver arms to Iran. In essence, selling arms to Iran was an illegal move on the part of the US because there had been an embargo since January 1984 when Iran was designated as a State Sponsor of Terrorism.

The supply of TOW and Hawk missiles started in August 1985. After the covert operations were revealed, Attorney General Edwin Meese learned that part of the $30 million that Iran had paid for the weapons had not reached the US government vault. Then Lieutenant Colonel Oliver North, a member of the US National Security Council staff, confessed that the discrepancy was because part of the proceeds of the arms sales to Iran had been diverted to the Contras, right-wing guerillas in Nicaragua who were fighting against the revolutionary leftist and democratically-elected Sandinista government. In the aftershock of the revelations, the National Security Advisor to President Reagan, Admiral John Poindexter, resigned, and Oliver North was dismissed.

There were two views in Iran (as there were in the US) about what motivated President Reagan to support the arms sales initiative. First, Reagan was thought to be obsessed with freeing the hostages in Lebanon. The other view was that Reagan and his administration sought to open the door to better relations with Iran—détente—and maybe eventually normalization of relations. This is the view that President Reagan would present as the motif of the deal with Iran. "My purpose," Reagan said in an address to the nation, "was … to send a signal that the United States was prepared to replace the animosity between [the US and Iran] with a new relationship … The most significant step which Iran could take, we indicated, would be to use its influence in Lebanon to secure the release of all hostages held there."[39] Rafsanjani told me that this was his objective, too. He told me that he had received positive messages for "détente" from Washington and that he was prepared to give it a chance.

Robert McFarlane's trip to Iran occurred after a number of messages have been exchanged between the two governments through mediating channels. A delegation of six, headed by McFarlane, arrived in Tehran on May 25, 1986 to discuss arrangements for a possible deal.

No senior Iranian official met the Americans. According to the Iranians, McFarlane appeared unaware of the arrangements to which the Iranians had agreed through the mediators prior to their May 25 meeting. A member of the Iranian delegation told me that they were shocked to discover that an Israeli was among the US delegation. That had not been discussed or agreed beforehand. Hadi Najafabadi, a Majlis deputy MP who later became Iranian ambassador to UAE and Saudi Arabia, and Fereidoun Vardinejad, from the Revolutionary Guards who later became Iranian ambassador to China, went to the Tehran Airport to receive the American delegation. The Americans were told that Tehran would never be able to have direct negotiations with the US if Israel were a party to the talks. Nevertheless, the Iranians informed McFarlane that they would try to facilitate the release of American hostages in Lebanon and make the deal happen.

McFarlane insisted on meeting with a senior Iranian official, saying that he wanted to discuss issues beyond arms and a hostage deal. The Iranians perceived that McFarlane sought to discuss Iran–US relations and explore ways to improve those relations. Rafsanjani told me later in a private exchange that he had already briefed Ayatollah Khomeini about the exchange of messages with Reagan prior to McFarlane's trip to Tehran. However, Tehran opposed talks with the Americans once it became aware that Israel was involved. Rafsanjani, then the second most powerful man after Ayatollah Khomeini, supported negotiations and normalization of relations with the US. He viewed the state of "non-negotiation, no-relationship with America, unsustainable," as he wrote in a hand-written letter to Ayatollah Khomeini.[40] In his memoir, Rafsanjani writes that he was informed that McFarlane, as a special envoy of President Reagan, had brought with him a pistol and a cake as presents and "asked to meet with the leaders [of Iran] … It was decided not to accept the presents and not to meet [them] and to keep the negotiations … limited to the issue of hostages in Lebanon and providing Hawk [spare] parts and some other weapons. They [McFarlane and his team] are more interested to talk about general and political issues [rather than simply the deal].[41]

Americans were truly looking for a way to reduce tensions and move toward more friendly relations with Iran. However, Washington made a fatal mistake by involving the Israelis at the outset of a rapprochement effort with Tehran. Détente with the US during a war in which Washington was supporting the aggressor, Saddam Hussein, was already a very big political risk for Rafsanjani. Involvement of the Israelis would have been political suicide for him. Ultimately, McFarlane's mission failed because Hezbollah had imposed conditions for releasing the American hostages which the Americans were unable to meet at that point. The hostage takers demanded Israeli withdrawal from the Golan Heights and the release of 17 prisoners held by Kuwait who belonged to the Dawa Party which waged an armed struggle against Saddam's regime.

On October 15 and 16, 1986, a leaflet was circulated in Tehran which revealed the Americans' trip to Tehran five months earlier. The person behind this sabotage was Mehdi Hashemi, a radical, and brother to the son-in-law of Ayatollah Hossein Ali Montazeri. Ayatollah Montazeri had been chosen in November 1985 as the successor to Ayatollah Khomeini. More importantly, Mehdi Hashemi was the Director of the Office for Islamic Liberation of the Revolutionary Guards (IRGC). Mehdi Hashemi, by using Ayatollah Montazeri's office, bypassed the entire government and maintained relations and contacts with revolutionary Islamic groups in several Asian and African countries. It is noteworthy that Ayatollah Montazeri who later became a leading opposition figures to radical polices in Iran was the one who initiated and promoted the slogan of "Death to America" in Friday Prayers in the early days of the Revolution while his son, Mohammad Montazeri, was one of the first officers and founders of the IRGC. In any case, Mehdi Hashemi was the first rogue element inside the Islamic Republic establishment, someone who created problems in foreign relations. He obviously had close contacts in Lebanon. Mehdi Hashemi was not only a radical anti-American, but also subscribed to a conspiratorial mentality. According to a video[42] of his confessions, before the Revolution, he had murdered Ayatollah Shamsabadi, intending to frame the Shah's security service in order to provoke rage among conservatives in Iran.[43]

In any case, almost two weeks later, on November 3, 1986, through Mehdi's links in Lebanon, McFarlane's secret trip to Tehran and the dealings between Iran and the US were disclosed in the Lebanese magazine *Ash Shiraa* (or Al-Shiraa). Mehdi Hashemi was arrested on charges of murder and illegal activities in relation to foreign revolutionary groups, and subsequently executed. The office for Islamic Liberation was closed indefinitely. Whether Mehdi Hashemi's elimination and closure of the office for Islamic Liberation could be considered a political statement—that exporting of revolution should be confined to words, and not involve deeds—remains an open question. Moreover, given his radical worldview and his close relationship with radical elements in Lebanon, the question of whether Hashemi was involved in the Beirut bombings also remains unanswered. However, a member of the Iranian team dealing with the McFarlane episode told me a different story. He said that the Israelis were involved in the revelation of the McFarlane visit to Tehran, with the purpose of creating a domestic crisis for Rafsanjani as the leading moderate figure in Iran.

With the revelation of McFarlane's mission to Tehran, the so called Iran–Contra scandal—the diversion of the proceeds of the US arms sales to Iran to Contra guerillas in Nicaragua—became so big that the sincerity and integrity of Reagan and his administration was called into question. The US administration had violated its own laws by dealing with the Hezbollah, a group designated by the same administration as terrorists.

This revelation also angered the Arab countries. To Arab countries in the Persian Gulf, the US appeared as hypocritical, duplicitous, and markedly unreliable. In Iran's perception, as a result of the public revelations, Reagan and the US administration assumed a much more hostile position toward Iran in order to restore their credibility domestically as well as internationally.

The Undeclared US War against Iran

The removal of Iraq from the State Department's list of countries sponsoring terrorism in 1982 could only have been due to the desire to assist Saddam Hussein dismantle the Iranian Revolution in Iran. This assumption was confirmed when the US crept into the War.

The Tanker War started in 1984 when Iraq attacked Iranian tankers as well as Kharg Island's oil terminal in the southern part of Iran in the Persian Gulf. This event marked the beginning of numerous tit-for-tat attacks on oil tankers from both sides. Iranians also viewed Kuwait as being "at war" with them, given that Kuwait was the second largest financial supporter of Iraq, after Saudi Arabia, and so Iranians began to attack Kuwaiti tankers as well. During four years of naval confrontations, hundreds of commercial vessels were sunk or damaged.

In response to Kuwait's support of Saddam, invasion of Iran, in 1986, Iran launched additional major attacks against Kuwaiti vessels. Following the attacks, Kuwait sought help from the international community to protect its ships. The United States offered to fly the US flag on Kuwaiti tankers, thus committing itself to the protection of these tankers against Iran's attacks. Iranians viewed Kuwait's petition as a US design and part of its broader plan to become actively involved in the war against Iran. In effect, this was an undeclared war by the US against Iran.

In October 1987, Iran attacked a Kuwaiti tanker flying the US flag. In response, the United States Navy attacked two Iranian oil fields and destroyed them. In April 1988, a US destroyer was badly damaged by the Iranian mines, and the American Navy again responded by attacking Iranian oil platforms as part of Operation Praying Mantis, which destroyed the Sassan and Sirri oil platforms and a number of Iranian vessels, and left scores of Iranian sailors dead.

Despite losing its suit against the United States for reparations at the International Court of Justice, the official statement that was issued clearly sympathized with Iran's case:

> The Court thus concludes from the foregoing that the actions carried out by United States forces against Iranian oil installations on 19 October 1987 and 18 April 1988 cannot be justified, under Article XX, paragraph 1 (d), of the 1955 Treaty, as being measures necessary to protect the essential security interests of the United States"[44]

At the height of these confrontations came a horrific tragedy. On July 3, 1988, the USS *Vincennes* guided missile cruiser shot down a civilian Iranian aircraft. Iran Air Flight 655 departed from Iran and was destined for the United Arab Emirates, a flight that takes 30 minutes from the Iranian port of Bandar Abbass, the plane's final stop-over. According to American officials, the captain of the *Vincennes* misidentified the airplane as a F–14 fighter and ordered the firing of two missiles at it.[45] Flight 655 was destroyed, and all 290 passengers and crew, including 66 children, perished—indeed one of the worst tragedies in aviation history.

On September 8, 1988, the results of an investigation conducted by the US Central Command on the downing of Flight 655 were presented to the US Senate's Armed Services Committee. The investigation had been headed by US Central Command Director of Policy and Plans, Rear Admiral William M. Fogarty. He confirmed in his testimony that the Iranian plane *was* civilian. He stated: "After an exhaustive reconstruction of the event, we now know that Iran Air Flight 655 was in fact always ascending in altitude and squawked only a Mode III signal on IFF, which is characteristic of a civilian aircraft. Iran Air 655 always flew inside the commercial airway."[46]

Making matters worse, another nearby US warship, the USS *Sides*, had issued a message to the USS *Vincennes* confirming that the airplane in question was indeed civilian.[47] With all the technical equipment aboard pointing to the identification of Flight 655 as a civilian airliner, the USS *Vincennes* ignored the evidence and fired upon the airplane. In the face of all the contrary evidence, there seems to be no reasonable answer as to why the crew of the USS *Vincennes* was so certain that Flight 655 was a military plane and posed an imminent threat to the US warship.

A simple comparison between the US reaction to the Pan Am passenger plane attacked by the Libyans at Lockerbie,[48] and the US attack on the Iranian civilian airplane demonstrates the US double standards. The US government never published a complete report of the investigations, failing even to condemn the killing of 290 innocent civilians.[49] In hearings before the US Senate, Admiral Robert Kelly, from the Joint Chiefs of Staff, asserted that Iran "must share some responsibility for this tragedy"![50]

Years later, Rafsanjani told me that he perceived the attack as a signal that the United States would officially enter the War on the side of Iraq. "I was certain Iran could not prevail in a war against both Iraq *and* the United States, while they have no shame to use chemical weapons and attack civilian airplanes." More than a quarter of a century later, the US Airbus attack, coupled with the use of chemical weapons against Iran, and the international community's indifference to those crimes, still shape the strategic thinking of the Iranian military leadership. To them, it appears that when it comes to Iran, no one would hesitate to break international law and codes of conduct, in their aim to hurt Iran. For many Iranians, these events reminded them how defenseless they were against foreign aggression, a position that forced Iran to build up a powerful military and defense system.

Open Wounds

The Iraqi invasion occurred while Iran was still embroiled with the United States over the hostage crisis. While feeling deeply hurt and humiliated by the Embassy crisis, the US also viewed Iranians as irrational and dangerous, hence, very difficult with to side with. It is also true that the Iraqi government had a strained relationship with the US, but that was much less serious than the head-on confrontation with Iran had with the US over hostage taking.

The US may also have been anxious about the Iranian official discourse of "exporting of revolution." Moreover, the establishment of a revolutionary, religion-based political system in the most geostrategic region of the world—the Persian Gulf—and possibly to be emulated by others, was perceived as a threat to US interests and security.

As discussed earlier, the situation became more sensitive in 1982 when Iran pushed back Iraq and went on the offensive. Conventional wisdom dictated that, given the majority Shia population of Iraq and Iran's close relations with the Iraqi Shia rebels who were prepared to challenge Saddam's rule,[51] if Saddam were to be overthrown and a Shia-based government established, Iran would use the alliance of the two governments as a springboard to thwart the US hegemony in the region as well as to destabilize other regimes.

Furthermore, the prospect of trouble in the Strait of Hormuz and disruption in the oil supply by a hostile regional power was a nightmare scenario for America's struggling economy in the early 1980s. In 1982, US unemployment exceeded 10 percent for the first time in forty years.[52] A year before the downing of Flight 655, Richard W. Murphy, Assistant Secretary of State for Near Eastern, told the Congress in a testimony: "We would suffer a major strategic defeat should a power hostile to the United States sharply increase its power and influence in the region."[53]

Hostage taking and terrorist activities in Lebanon against American assets, and the inclusion of Iran in the list of countries supporting terrorism, also came to make it more difficult for the US adminis-tration—already hurt because of the botched secret dealings—to adopt a conciliatory approach towards Iran.

The rivalry between the USSR and the US also impacted on relations between Iran and the US. During the Cold War years, the US embraced the opportunity to establish a good relationship with Saddam Hussein who had warm relations with the Soviet Union, with a view to distancing him from the Soviet Union and ultimately using him as an instrument to confront Soviet expansionism.

As discussed previously, the US initial acquiescent posture towards the Iraqi invasion of Iran and subsequent change of position once Iran went on the offensive as of summer 1982, appear to have convinced Iranians of US evil intentions, including the ultimate goal of toppling the Iranian system.

A revelation in the *New York Times* confirmed the Iranians view that the United States' official position of neutrality was a deception. The report read:

> The United States and other Western countries are therefore engaged in clandestine operations. The United States is financing Iranian exiles in paramilitary units in eastern Turkey near Iran, although Turkey denies this. The United States is also financing Iranian exile networks in and out of Iran and an exile radio station that broadcasts propaganda about Iran's Government."[54]

There is also extensive evidence from observers who have conducted research into the US role in supporting Iraq in waging war against

Iran. Alan Friedman's investigative book, *The Secret History of How the White House Illegally Armed Iraq*, drawing on 60 pages of declassified documents and numerous interviews, is an example in point.[55] Details of the US activities in supporting Iraq are beyond the scope of this book, but one piece of information worth highlighting is Howard Teicher's declassified affidavit[56] in 1995. Teicher served as Director of Political-Military Affairs on the National Security Council from 1982 to 1987. In his affidavit, he stated that he traveled with Donald Rumsfeld to Baghdad in 1983 when Rumsfeld met with Saddam Hussein and Tariq Aziz. Teicher recounted:

> CIA Director Casey personally spearheaded the effort to ensure that Iraq had sufficient military weapons, ammunition and vehicles to avoid losing the Iran–Iraq war. Pursuant to the secret NSDD [National Security Decision Directive], the United States actively supported the Iraqi war effort by supplying the Iraqis with billions of dollars of credits, by providing U.S. military intelligence and advice to the Iraqis, and by closely monitoring third country arms sales to Iraq to make sure that Iraq had the military weaponry required. The United States also provided strategic operational advice to the Iraqis to better use their assets in combat. For example, in 1986, President Reagan sent a secret message to Saddam Hussein telling him that Iraq should step up its air war and bombing of Iran. This message was delivered by Vice President Bush who communicated it to Egyptian President Mubarak, who in turn passed the message to Saddam Hussein. Similar strategic operational military advice was passed to Saddam Hussein through various meetings with European and Middle Eastern heads of state.[57]

Was Iran's assessment that the US would encourage Saddam to bomb Iran's cities and civilians correct or was it just based on their mistrust of the US and their conspiratorial mindset? Evidence such as Teicher's sworn declaration points to the former.

One of the most troubling aspects of this whole affair was that Iran firmly believed that without US knowledge and consent, it would have been impossible for the Iraqi government to gain access to chemical weapons. A 1994 report by Donald Riegle, Chairman of the Senate Banking, Housing, and Urban Affairs Committee, stated that:

> U.N. inspectors had identified many United States manufactured items that had been exported from the United States to Iraq under

licenses issued by the Department of Commerce, and [established] that these items were used to further Iraq's chemical and nuclear weapons development and its missile delivery system development programs ... The executive branch of our government approved 771 different export licenses for sale of dual-use technology to Iraq. I think that is a devastating record.[58]

Iran sought condemnation from the international community by tabling a draft resolution at the United Nations Security Council (UNSC) in 1984. In response, the US delegation was instructed by the State Department to lobby other countries, ensuring that the resolution would not amount to anything substantive. The official US position was outlined in a Department of State telegram: "USDEL [US Delegation to the United Nations] should work to develop general Western position in support of a motion to take 'no decision' on Iranian draft resolution on use of chemical weapons by Iraq."[59]

Satellite imagery and its interpretation by US advisors allowed Iranian military positions and its troop deployment to be assessed, in effect exposing the Iranians as sitting ducks—waiting for the inevitable assault against them. According to Allan Friedman, "At times, thanks to the White House's secret backing for the intelligence-sharing, U.S. intelligence officers were actually sent to Baghdad to help interpret the satellite information."[60]

Downing of the Iran Air passenger flight created a scar that to date has not been healed. Iranians were left in no doubt that the attack was intentional, confirmed by awarding the *Vincennes* crew with Combat Action Ribbons. Scott Lustig, the ship's weapons and combat systems officer, received the Navy Commendation Medal. And the USS *Vincennes* Captain, William C. Rogers was awarded the Legion of Merit "for exceptionally meritorious conduct in the performance of outstanding service as commanding officer ... from April 1987 to May 1989."[61]

Navy officials said the medals were awarded to the crew for their "contributions to the USS *Vincennes* over their entire tour on board."[62] But in a climate filled with hostility and mistrust, the granting of awards to the *Vincennes* crew could have only one meaning for the Iranian leadership—that the crew and their commanders were to be commended for their heroic action in killing the 290 passengers on Iran Air flight 655. The US government never apologized for the horrific act. They only expressed regret.[63]

Chalice of Poison

In July 1987 the UN Security Council passed Resolution 598 calling upon Iran and Iraq to establish a ceasefire. Iran rejected the resolution. Ayatollah Khomeini's intention was to fight until Saddam Hussein was toppled. He viewed Saddam as a permanent potential threat to the security of Iran and the region, especially when his expansionism was supported by the entire West, and in particular, the United States. Furthermore, Ayatollah Khomeini believed that Saddam's overthrow would liberate the majority Shias in Iraq, a development that would enhance Iran's position in the region.

At the time, any allusion in Iran to ceasefire was equated with treachery. Around January 1988, I was invited to visit Japan by the Japanese government. Although my trip to Japan was in my capacity as editor-in-chief of the *Tehran Times*, it was also known that I had a close relationship with Rafsanjani in my capacity as the head of the Majlis administrative department. An unpublicized meeting was arranged with a high-level diplomat at Japan's Foreign Ministry. At the time, Rafsanjani was Speaker of the Majlis of the parliament and had also been appointed acting Commander-in-Chief of the armed forces by Ayatollah Khomeini.

In the course of our exchange, the Japanese diplomat asked me, "Can we do something? You present all the Iranians' reasons that Iran should not accept the ceasefire and I will tell you my reasons why you should. Then put all the debate together and present it to Iranian decision makers. Will you do it?" I agreed, and a heated debate ensued. But the most interesting part came at the conclusion of our meeting. I was told: "Listen, Mr. Mousavian. While Iraq has failed to defeat Iran, the US and other great powers have made their decision not to let a winner emerge from this War. They would not let Iran win this War. You are wasting your resources, human lives, and time." I found that blunt statement profoundly shocking.

Upon my return to Tehran, I provided a full written account of the exchange to Rafsanjani. I showed him the whole back-and-forth argument between me and the Japanese official. But I also revealed the conclusion of the meeting, which was not recorded in the written account. "He had a message for you!" I told him what the Japanese official had said, and Rafsanjani replied: "Now what do you want to do?" I told him that I wanted to publish the conversation with no comments. He said: "I am very much agreeable." I was stunned. "To me it sounds that you are also for a ceasefire," I said to Rafsanjani.

"Yes" was his simple reply. He added that he was looking for a face-saving solution to end the War. This position was at variance with Iran's official stance, which was that Iran would fight on until the Ba'athist regime in Baghdad fell.

I published the explosive interview in two parts. It was the first time that the media had addressed the ceasefire question—for which I was summoned to the Foreign Ministry and strongly criticized. "This article advocates a ceasefire while Iran has opposed the resolution 598," said one high-level official.

The debate over a ceasefire gradually emerged in the government's inner circles. By spring 1988, that debate had grown much louder. In the month of June, Rafsanjani, in his position as acting Commander-in-Chief of the armed forces, told me that he had asked the Iran Revolutionary Guard Corps (IRGC) Commander, Mohsen Rezaie, what was necessary to conclude the War. Rezaie had responded with the view that Baghdad should be seized and Saddam should be toppled. Rafsanjani then had asked him to document what he needed to achieve that goal. In a letter to Rafsanjani, Rezaie had listed his requirements for the capture of Baghdad: a huge amount of arms and artillery and a considerable expansion of the armed forces, including a 700 percent increase in IRGC forces and a 150 percent expansion of the regular army. According to a plan prepared by the IRGC and presented to Rafsanjani, the IRGC required 1,500 battalions to attack three targets: Basra in the south with 500 battalions; Kirkuk in the north with 400 battalions; and Baghdad with 600 battalions. The operation would take one and a half years.

Rezaie's letter to Rafsanjani was taken to Ayatollah Khomeini. Meanwhile, Prime Minister Mir Hossein Mousavi and his Minister of Economy and Director of the Budget and Planning Organization had informed Ayatollah Khomeini, in writing, that financially, the system (*nezam*) was in the red. Ultimately, however, the person who convinced Ayatollah Khomeini to stop the War was Hashemi Rafsanjani. The reality is that nobody was in a position to talk to Ayatollah Khomeini about such a painful decision. However, Rafsanjani's friends and foes both acknowledge that Rafsanjani played a major role in convincing the Ayatollah to accept the ceasefire. In a public statement on July 20, 1988, Ayatollah Khomeini accepted the ceasefire and stated: "Happy are those who have lost their lives in this convoy of light … unhappy am I that I survive and have drunk the Chalice of Poison." It is also interesting to note that a few days after Iran's acceptance of ceasefire under the resolution 598, MEK, fully supported by the Iraqi army, launched a major offensive into Iran, with the declared objective of reaching Tehran in a matter of days. The onslaught was swiftly defeated through a well-coordinated heavy counter-offensive by the Iranian military forces and popular resistance. Ceasefire went into effect, due to increased international pressure on Iraq, in early August 1988.

I believe that Rafsanjani's pragmatism served Iran's best interests, although some in Iran's establishment continue to disagree, arguing that Iran should have fought to the end. Those who disagree also maintain that Rafsanjani imposed the decision on the Leader of the Revolution by exaggerating the struggle ahead and painting a grim picture of the economy.

From my perspective, events at that point were on a trajectory toward an all-out war between Iran and the United States. Such a war might have ended in the destruction of Iran's infrastructure and US assets in the region and beyond. And, as former Defense Secretary Robert Gates once put it, bombing Iran would "create generations of jihadists."[64] A US attack on Iran could not have been confined within the borders of Iran. The result would have been to "consume the Middle East in a confrontation and a conflict" that Americans "would regret," according to former US Secretary of Defense Leon Panetta.[65]

Ayatollah Khomeini's move has become the basis of a policy-shaping argument in the West; that is, once the survival of the system (*nezam*) hits the danger zone, it retreats. This is the primary rationale behind the current tough sanctions imposed on Iran to force it to halt its nuclear program. However, it is true that Ayatollah Khomeini finally consented to a ceasefire with Iran—an act of political compromise in the War—but in doing so, his country did not surrender any territory, and he did not compromise his country's independence. That is why on January 31, 2014, I told the Iranian news agency, ISNA, that resolution 598 was not a Chalice of Poison.[66] The ceasefire, in fact, helped the Iranian government to further consolidate its authority, and as will be discussed later, as a prelude to rebuilding the country after eight years of bloody war and destruction. From another angle, the ceasefire also allowed Saddam to survive as a leader, and as a man. But certainly it was not that Iran entered into a ceasefire with Iraq, was about standing down rather than giving up. And it certainly was not a matter of surrendering to a perceived strategic enemy and "global arrogance."[67]

Chapter 4

A PRAGMATIST ASSUMES THE PRESIDENCY: 1989-97

The Rise of Ayatollah Khamenei

Ayatollah Khomeini died at 10.00 p.m. June 2, 1989, but the news broke the day after. Millions of Iranians spilled onto the streets across the country to mourn the death of the Revolution's charismatic Leader. The death of Iran's Leader coincided with major challenges and concerns domestically and internationally. Although Iran and Iraq had accepted the terms of a ceasefire, peace was not yet established. When Ayatollah Khomeini died, the situation on the borders with Iraq was still uneasy and uncertain. Meanwhile, due to the Ayatollah Khomeini's *fatwa* against Salman Rushdie for the publication of his book, *The Satanic Verses*, Iran's relations with Europe were tense and confrontational. Domestically, the death of the Revolution's Leader, without a designated successor, could have plunged the country into anarchy. A major part of the country was war-torn, millions were displaced, some two million Afghan refugees were still living in Iran, and the economy was in shambles as a result of the 8-year War.

It was against this backdrop that the Assembly of Leadership Experts met on June 4, 1989 to decide who was to succeed Ayatollah Khomeini. There was heated debate over whether the position of Supreme Leader (*vali-e faqih*) should be filled by one figure, or a three- or five-person council. Interestingly, both Ayatollahs Khamenei and Rafsanjani supported the idea of electing a Council of Leadership as opposed to one single person/individual as Supreme Leader. They reasoned that there was no single individual of sufficient capacity and calibre to fill Ayatollah Khomeini's position. The idea was voted on but not approved.

The question became one of identifying a candidate capable of becoming Iran's next Supreme Leader. According to the Constitution, the Supreme Leader had to be a *Marja-e Taqlid* (Source of Emulation), but the Assembly did not find anyone in Qom politically qualified for the task. In April 1989, two months before his death, Ayatollah Khomeini had established a 25-man Council for Revision of the Constitution. One of the major amendments the ailing Ayatollah had asked the Council to consider was a law to change the conditions regarding the qualifications of the Supreme Leader—specifically that his successor would not need to be a *Marja-e Taqlid* as long as he was qualified as a *mujtahid*, a level below *Marja-e Taqlid*, a jurist who is qualified to interpret Islamic law and to generate independent judgment and decisions. Ayatollah Khomeini's concern was that the Constitution would limit the options of the Assembly of Leadership Experts to just a few, and therefore after his death the election of the new Supreme Leader could end up in a stalemate. Yet, the constitutional amendment had to be legalized through a referendum.

The meeting of the Assembly of Leadership Experts on June 4, 1989, was interrupted by Hassan Rouhani who informed Rafsanjani that the Iraqis were mobilizing their forces on the western front. This news encouraged the Assembly to expedite the decision-making process. The suggestion was raised by some members of the Assembly that since Ayatollah Khomeini had approved the idea of a *mujtahid* being qualified for the Supreme Leadership, then from a religious point of view, there was no obstacle to electing a non-*marja* as leader. However, they had to wait for the outcome of the referendum. So the decision was made to elect a *mujtahid* as the Supreme Leader but wait for the completion of the legal process.

After Grand Ayatollah Golpayegani was named as a candidate, but did not win the majority of the votes, the focus was turned to Ayatollah Khamenei. Ayatollah Rafsanjani's testimony played a major role in his election of Ayatollah Khamenei. Rafsanjani said that after the resignation of Ayatollah Montazeri as the designated successor of Ayatollah Khomeini, in March, he and a number of high-ranking officials, including Ayatollah Khamenei who was President at the time, met with the ailing Ayatollah Khomeini. He said that concern was expressed about a possible vacuum in the absence of the Ayatollah, to which he responded: "There won't be a vacuum. You have people [who can fill in]." When the Ayatollah was asked who he had in mind he said: "This Mr. Khamenei."[1] Rafsanjani also told the Assembly that on another occasion when he had met Ayatollah Khomeini alone, he had again asked: "Given the current situation [of a lack of any successor for you] what should we do about leadership?" He quoted Ayatollah Khomeini as replying: "Why are you hesitant while [a person like] Mr. Khamenei exists?"[2]

The deal was sealed. On that hot and fateful day of June 4, 1989, members of the Assembly of Leadership of Experts cast their ballots to choose Ayatollah Khamenei. He received an overwhelmingly endorsement, with 60 out of 74 votes in his favor. In his televised remarks, Ayatollah Khamenei said: "We hope temporarily to fill the leadership while the terms of the new Constitution are under review."[3] He added that the vacuum had to be filled but whether that would be temporary or permanent depended on the approval of the amendments to the Constitution.

The referendum was held on July 28th, alongside with the presidential elections, and the amendments were approved by the electorate. This eliminated the need for the Supreme Leader to be a *Marja-e Taqlid*, abolished the office of prime minister, and created the Supreme National Security Council (SNSC).

Ayatollah Khamenei's statement after his election contains interesting points which reflected his view about his election:

I did not expect, even for a second in my life, the outcome of the process which ended in my election as the new leader and the responsibility that was put on my shoulder as a humble weak servant of Allah. If someone thinks that it occurred to me even for a second at the time of struggle [against the Shah], later during the Revolution, or during my term of presidency that this responsibility would be delegated to me, he is wrong. I always considered my level [of qualifications] too low for this highly significant and crucial post but also even much lower posts like the presidency and other posts, which I have held since the Revolution.

Once I told Imam ... that sometimes my name is cited among some gentlemen while I am like common people. I did not say it as a matter of courtesy. Now, I maintain the same position. Therefore, this event was not imaginable at all. Of course, we had very sensitive hours, the most serious hours of our lives [during the Assembly meeting]. Allah knows what we experienced that night and the Saturday morning. To fulfill their duty, brothers were strenuously thinking and working to tidy up the affairs. Frequently, they talked about me as a member of [the] leadership council although I rejected it in my mind. However, it was possible that they would delegate it to me.

Then I sought refuge unto Allah. The next day, before the Assembly of Experts started its work, I cried and supplicated to Allah earnestly, "My Lord, you plan and predestine the affairs. I may become responsible as a member of the leadership council. I implore you, in case this post is going to be a little bit harmful for my religion and for me on the Day of Judgment, to prevent its realization." Really, from the bottom of my heart, I wanted not to take this responsibility.

Finally, after some debates and discussions in the Assembly of Experts, they voted for me. There I tried, debated, and reasoned to prevent the vote but they voted. Even now, I consider myself as a common religious student without any outstanding feature of special advantage, not only for this great office of significant responsibility—as I said sincerely—but also for much less important ones like the presidency, etc. delegated to me during the last ten years [since the Revolution]. However, now that they have voted for me to bear its burden and responsibility, I accept it with vigor just as Allah advised His prophets: "Take it with vigor."[4]

Beginning of a New Era

Ayatollahs Khamenei and Rafsanjani had different views on the United States.[5] However, both Ayatollahs were actively involved in anti-Shah activities and both were imprisoned during the Shah's reign.

In his hand-written will prepared in 1963, Mr. Khamenei, then a young cleric, listed the people he owed money to. He wrote: "The most money that I owed … was to Mr. Hashemi [Rafsanjani]. For he was well-off and we would borrow from him."[6] Rafsanjani believed that the two men had to and would stay united because they both were committed to protecting the Revolution. This was also what their mentor, Ayatollah Khomeini, expected and sought from them. Three days before his death, Ayatollah Khomeini, in broken words, hold told Rafsanjani: "If you stay united, the Revolution will progress. Especially you and Mr. Khamenei—do not let the wicked provoke enmity between you."[7]

During his presidency (1989–97), Rafsanjani advocated and pursued reconciliation with the West—specifically, but indirectly, with the United States—based on mutual respect, non-interference in domestic affairs, and promotion of mutual interests. This political paradigm took into account the severity of animosity between the two countries and the historical grievances each held, yet persisted in its optimism about the possibility of achieving normalization in relations based on both sides' national interests.

President Hashemi Rafsanjani, a prominent Iranian politician best characterized as a centrist, advanced a free-market economic policy, favoring privatization of state-owned industries, and a moderate posture internationally. While Ayatollah Khamenei, then newly appointed as Supreme Leader, agreed in principle with the objective of improving relations with the West, he reiterated that the United States would remain as a rival. From the Supreme Leader's point of view, as Rafsanjani informed me, any direct negotiation with the US was prohibited. Ayatollah Khamenei has reaffirmed this position in his public statements: "I am against negotiations with the United States, and it is impossible for the Islamic Republic administration to enter into any form of negotiations without my permission ... the relations with the US is a red line, one which no one can cross."[8] He has further expounded: "Of course we reject relations with the US, because the US is arrogant, [an] aggressor and [an] oppressive power ... those who believe we should negotiate with the US are either naïve or intimidated, because the US primary goal has been from the beginning of the Islamic Revolution to annihilate us."[9]

On this particular issue/aspect, I should write that the Supreme Leader's position posed a major obstacle to any attempt at détente with the US. At the time, I was Director-General for European Affairs at the Foreign Ministry, where we believed it would be possible to normalize relations with the West, despite Iran–US hostility. We in the Foreign Ministry proposed to President Rafsanjani that détente with the West was a package, which also included the United States. In our analysis/ view, removing hostilities and tensions with the West could make headway toward rapprochement with Washington. Rafsanjani agreed with us.

Rafsanjani placed great importance on normalizing relations with the West, as this would also serve Iran's national interest—a point he made clear to me as I contemplated the next steps of my career. In late September 1990, the Iranian Foreign Ministry offered me the option of becoming Iranian ambassador to China or Germany. Faced with the choice to go East or West, I sought consultation with Rafsanjani, who advised me to take the German ambassadorship. In a meeting on October 4 of that year, he told me:

> You could solve some of our major problems with Europe during the last two or three years. [As the Director-General for European Affairs at the Foreign Ministry] you were under tremendous domestic pressure [from the hardliners who reject improvement of

relations with the West] for working to resolve our problems with Europe. But you resisted those pressures and resolved some major issues in our bilateral relations with European countries.[10] Your presence in Europe is important for us; you are close to us and we trust you. Germany is a major element in Europe's power nucleus and we want you to be the pillar of reconciling our relations with Europe.

He further referred to the Supreme Leader's doctrine on the relations with the West—the "West minus the United States"—and noted that we would pursue improved relations with all other Western countries, except the United States, because the Leader was convinced that the US sought regime change and not a normal relationship based on mutual respect. He asserted, however:

> Through appropriate channels, you should make the Americans comprehend that if they are sincere in improving relations with us, the only way is to show goodwill such as releasing our assets. Return of assets would enable us to begin the process of détente with the Americans, while the process of securing the release of the Western hostages has already begun. They should be patient for a year after releasing our assets and they should also assist with the release of Sheik Obeid [Lebanese Shia leader] and other Lebanese hostages [held by the Israelis]. If they do this, we will be able to help them resolve their problems [with regard to the hostages] in Lebanon. On my behalf, tell the German President and Chancellor that Iran is ready to be a reliable partner for Europe to advance peace, security, and stability in the Middle East.

I left Rafsanjani's office with the following deductions. First, despite restrictions placed by Ayatollah Khamenei on reviving relations and negotiations with the US, we should initiate the normalization of relations with Europe while continuing efforts for a decrease in tensions with the United States. Second, Germany could be the means of cementing Iran's relations with Europe. Third, Rafsanjani would be in a position to convince the Supreme Leader to pursue détente with the US if the Americans showed their readiness for a relationship based on mutual respect, and made gestures of practical goodwill such as the release of Iran's assets. In other words, he recognized the Leader's deep mistrust of the US but did not view his position as something written in the stone. In Rafsanjani's assessment, peace was possible with the Americans if they showed a genuine willingness to change their hostile policies toward Iran. Fourth, the release of Western hostages, coupled with the liberation of Sheik Obeid and other Lebanese hostages kept by the Israelis, could be a beginning that would lead to further confidence-building measures between Iran and the West/US, also—albeit graducally—to broader regional cooperation in the Middle East.

I decided to go to Bonn. I arrived there a few days after the reunification of the country. I was the first foreign ambassador to the reunited Germany, a position I held until 1997.

Meanwhile, in Iran, the hardliner strategy was to attack moderates led by Rafsanjani and accuse anyone who supported better relations with the United States of being "anti-Guardianship of the Jurist" (*zedd-e valayat-e faqih*). Adopting radical slogans, the hardliners attacked centrists and moderates and attempted to force them to withdraw from their posture and policies—which, as discussed, enjoyed the Supreme Leader's overall sympathy and support. While he did not strictly forbid Rafsanjani from pursuing his reconciliatory policies toward the US, he did not publically betray any sign of softening his tough position.

Throughout his presidency, Rafsanjani faced huge pressure from hardliners for seeking a constructive and proactive diplomacy with the West, and for providing sufficient opportunity and assistance in a variety of areas for the West to cooperate and advance bilateral relations. Regrettably, the West—more importantly, Washington— failed to recognize the real intentions of Rafsanjani's pragmatic foreign policy, which, in essence, aimed at reaching agreement with the United States through different channels and the use of every instrument at his disposal. Instead, the lack of reciprocity toward Tehran's overtures ensured that radicalism remained relevant in the Iranian politics to derail any hopes of rapprochement with the West and the United States.

Broken Promises and the Failure of Rafsanjani

In early 1989 the release of Western hostages held in Lebanon was a critical issue for the United States and European countries.[11] Meanwhile, the War between Iran and Iraq had ended, leaving Iran's economy in ruins and in desperate need of resources for a reconstruction effort. President Rafsanjani's foreign policy was based on détente with regional countries and the international community in order to attract the resources needed to revive the Iranian economy. One of the most complicated foreign policy dilemmas at the time was how to engage with the West.

During this period, Iran received encouraging messages that "goodwill begets goodwill" from Washington. In his inaugural address on January 20, 1989, President George H. Bush gave the first indications that the US would welcome and reciprocate any form of assistance from Iran on the hostage crisis:

> There are today Americans who are held against their will in foreign lands, and Americans who are unaccounted for. Assistance can be shown here, and will be long remembered. Good will begets good will. Good faith can be a spiral that endlessly moves on.[12]

Furthermore, President Bush acknowledged US correspondence with Iran regarding the liberation of eight American hostages:

> I am open-minded to talk and to exercise every diplomatic channel I can to free these Americans[13] ... We have exercised every diplomatic channel that I can think of—some personal, some through our Secretary of State and our National Security Adviser [Brent Scowcroft].[14]

President Rafsanjani and Foreign Minister Ali Akbar Velayati[15] directed/ instructed Deputy Foreign Minister for US and European Affairs Mahmoud Vaezi[16] and myself to manage the release of hostages in Lebanon. Mr. Rafsanjani made certain that the security apparatus was properly briefed to cooperate with the two of us in this effort. The key contact person between the Americans and Iran was Giandomenico Picco, United Nations Assistant Secretary General for Political Affairs,[17] who liaised with Javad Zarif,[18] Iran's Deputy Permanent Representative to the United Nations.

Rafsanjani believed that a period of "goodwill for goodwill" would be a good starting point for bridging the gaps of the past and establishing confidence-building measures, leading toward a permanent reconciliation with the United States. However, Ayatollah Khamenei had reservations about the true intentions of the Americans and believed that Iran should assist with the release of the Western hostages purely on the grounds of moral principles and as a humanitarian gesture. As such, Ayatollah Khamenei cautioned against naively trusting and expecting the United States to respond appropriately following the efforts undertaken by Iran to free the hostages. In a 1990 speech regarding the matter, he asserted:

> Of course we announced from the beginning that we would help free the hostages to the best of our ability. We are not the superiors of the hostage-takers; they are a group of oppressed people who have for various reasons taken these hostages. The extent to which our words carry weight, we will help [release the hostages], but for our values, principles and humanitarian efforts and not for [dealing with] the US. Furthermore, suppose someone is going to do it for [dealing] with the US, what would be the American response?[19]

Before proceeding further with our endeavor, I need to make this point of clarification on the nature of the relationship between Iran and the Hezbollah. I grant that there exists quite a strong misperception in the West in this regard. It is true there is a misperception in the West with regard to the nature of the relationship between Hezbollah and the Iranian government. It is true that Hezbollah was founded with the assistance of Iran and that Iran has supported the group throughout the years of its existence. It is also true that the strategic vision of Hezbollah, which is opposed to the aggressive policies of Israel and US domination in the region, coincides with Iran's. However, I can speak with confidence that in many cases the two operate quite independently.

In any case, Ayatollah Khamenei did not want to associate the issue of the hostages in Lebanon with the release of Iran's assets by the Americans because he was convinced that the American would not reciprocate Iranian goodwill. He saw it as the right of the nation to have its assets restored and not something to be bargained for. "The Americans owe us. Our assets are frozen there and they should return it [*sic*]. This is their debt to us and our right, which has nothing to do with political issues. The assets should be returned to its owner."[20]

The course of action to be taken in response to the Americans' offer of "goodwill for goodwill" caused a divergence between the schools of thought led by Ayatollahs Khamenei and Rafsanjani. In meetings I had with Rafsanjani on the hostages issue, he reaffirmed that there was no difference between him and the Supreme Leader on the need for Iran to assist with the release of the hostages. However, he added that Ayatollah Khamenei did not like proceeding with this initiative based on President Bush's proposal of "goodwill for goodwill," for he doubted that the US administration would deliver. Nonetheless, he reiterated that our grand strategy for détente with the West required removing the hostility between Tehran and Washington with a gradual move toward normal relations.

Before leaving Tehran for Bonn, I utilized my position as editor-in-chief of the *Tehran Times* to disseminate and highlight developments on the hostage crisis. Hence the paper became known to the international community and Western media as the most reliable source of information inside Iran on the issue.[21]

In contrast to Ayatollah Khamenei, Rafsanjani was highly motivated to respond to President Bush's conciliatory words. Based on the message President Bush to President Rafsanjani (as reflected in his 1990 Memoir—in Persian[22]), the crux of the deal would be Iran's demonstration of its goodwill by assisting with the release of American and Western hostages in Lebanon. Rafsanjani's expectation was that in exchange for the release of the hostages, Iranian assets worth billions of dollars would be unfrozen and returned. The funds from the assets, once released, would be critical for Rafsanjani's gigantic reconstruction plan and facilitate a much-needed revival of Iran's economy. Meanwhile, in order to convince Hezbollah to cooperate, Rafsanjani would ask the Americans to push Israel to free Lebanese hostages, primarily Sheikh Obeid. Obeid was a senior Hezbollah cleric and a military commander of the Islamic Resistance who was abducted by Israeli forces on July 28, 1989.

A few days after the abduction of Obeid, footage was released showing the hanging of the US Marine Lt. Col. William Higgins. The footage caused a storm in the US media. In the same footage, hostage-takers threatened that they would kill a second hostage. Bush then implicitly threatened to use military force against Iran.[23] Rafsanjani responded by saying that "One cannot solve the problem with such bullying ways, with arrogant confrontations and tyranny. Come along wisely; we then will help you to solve the problems."[24]

Several days later we reported in the *Tehran Times* that indirect talks would commence in a few days. The report read: "The talks would be conducted through a third country, probably Pakistan, and likely would involve Pakistani Foreign Minister Sahabzada Yaqub Khan."[25] Following this report, the Islamic Republic News Agency (IRNA) reported that Iran was "ready to use its maximum influence for the release of all hostages" if the US released Iranian assets worth billions of dollars it had frozen ten years earlier.[26] But Ayatollah Khamenei reacted negatively to the reports: "Next to the usurper regime ruling over occupied Palestine, you [Americans] are the most cursed government in the eyes of the Iranian people. No one in the Islamic Republic will hold talks with you." These developments occurred in August 1989, shortly after Rafsanjani was sworn in as President.

Toward the end of August 1989, Giandomenico Picco delivered a message to Rafsanjani. He said that the Americans demanded that the hostages be released first before they could consider a positive response to Iranian demands. Rafsanjani countered that he perceived an "attitude of talking from above/talking from a superior position" in America's posture. Therefore he now required that certain conditions be met before Iran would take any action: Sheikh Obeid had to be freed; Iran's assets should be released; and the US had to help Iran clarify the fate of the Iranian hostages in Lebanon. In June 1982, four Iranian diplomats, Ahmad Motavasselian, Mohammed-Taghi Rastegar Moghadam, Mohsen Musavi (*chargé d'affaires* at the Iranian Embassy) and Kazem Akhavan, a photographer, were abducted and later "disappeared."[27]

However, Rafsanjani conveyed his deep disappointment that Iran had been linked to the killing of Higgins, an act from which Iran would clearly not benefit other than to provoke more US hostility.

Three weeks later, Iran offered something that had the potential being/becoming a game changer. Through Picco, Velayati sent a message to the UN Secretary General, Javier Pérez de Cuéllar, that the process of releasing the hostages could begin if the Americans would release 10 percent of the frozen assets and pay compensation for the victims of the passenger plane that had been downed by the Americans. Iran thought that this could be a face-saving solution to begin the process. Iran, via Pérez de Cuéllar, was told that Washington would consider the offer, not necessarily indicating acceptance.

Meanwhile, Tehran and Washington had an unwritten under-standing that the official and public position on the release of hostages ought to be based on humanitarian principles and not a deal. To that extent, the US State Department spokeswoman Margaret Tutwiler asserted: "The hostage issue is a humanitarian one and is not linked to other issues ... we will not make deals and we will not reward hostage takers."[28]

While we were clear on our expectations, we decided to leave no room for error by going public with them. Thus, President Rafsanjani held a press conference on October 24, 1989 where more than 100 reporters and television crews attended. Following the press conference, the *Los Angeles Times* reported on the "goodwill for goodwill" initiative:

"[Rafsanjani] repeated specifically his demand that the United States demonstrate 'good will' by releasing impounded Iranian assets ...

Rafsanjani repeated a second demand: release of three Iranians taken hostage in Lebanon in 1982."[29] The President also drew attention to the disregard for the value of the Iranian hostages and emphasized: "You have to have the same feelings and sentiments toward other people as you do to people in the West."[30]

It was my understanding that Americans might have been disappointed by these statements because they did not want the release of hostages to be associated with "a deal." This was what had already damaged Reagan's credibility during the Iran–Contra scandal. But on the other hand, what would "goodwill begets goodwill" mean if Iran was not to receive reciprocity? The Bush administration's cautious approach was understandable. He was the third consecutive President of the United States who had faced the hostages challenge. Tehran, however, chose to ignore that fact.

Throughout the process, the Iranians ensured that their major demands were not sidelined in the "goodwill for goodwill" initiative, clearly expecting reciprocity. After Frank Herbert Reed's[31] release in Beirut, the *New York Times* writes: "The *Tehran Times*, considered the mouthpiece of President Hashemi Rafsanjani of Iran, said, 'Now the ball is in the court of the U.S. and the Western countries.'"[32]

The role of Iran in the freeing of the Western hostages in Lebanon was highlighted in the international media following the release of Americans Robert Polhill on April 23,[33] and Frank Reed on April 30, 1990.[34] In his memoir Rafsanjani says, "Mr. Mousavian from the Ministry of Foreign Affairs came [to see me]. He said that the Swiss ambassador, Protector of the US interests in Iran, has brought a message from George Bush, the US President. [According to Mousavian] he [President Bush] had privately thanked us for the release of [Robert] Polhill, the American hostage, and had said that Hafez Assad, the Syrian President, had informed him that Iran's assistance had been instrumental in that respect. And he [Bush] had said that based on the US intelligence, the Iranian hostages captured by the Maronites [in Lebanon] had been killed the very first days...I said [to Mousavian] to verbally let them know that if the Lebanese prisoners are not released from Israel the issue of the hostages [and the release of the rest of them] would become more complicated."[35] The Americans, through the Swiss, were told that Iran expected an appropriate gesture from George Bush in response. Rafsanjani hoped to capitalize on any such gesture, silence those who opposed his policy of détente, and give momentum to the process of reconciliation. While Tehran awaited conciliatory news from Americans/from the US, President Bush's response was "When a step is taken that goes toward that day when all the hostages are released, I should say thank you."[36]

Following my visit to Dublin a few months earlier, Brian Keenan, an Irish hostage, was also released on August 24, 1990.[37] Finally Terry Anderson, the last American hostage in Lebanon, was freed on December 4, 1991 after Iranian intervention.[38] "Incomprehensible" was how we characterized President Bush's reaction the next day:

> I don't consider the chapter closed because I think of Robin Higgins, a young Marine whose husband was apparently killed. And I'd like to see the remains of Colonel Higgins, who was serving under the UN banner, returned. And so this chapter, this ugly chapter, albeit nearly closed, is not yet closed. And so we we'll wait and see when that is all finalized.[39]

Did that mean that there would not be a single step of reciprocation by the US in line with his own earlier suggestion? Weeks later, the remains of Col. Higgins were also returned.

In his memoir *Man Without A Gun*, Giandomenico Picco has detailed the urgency for the Americans to reciprocate Iran's goodwill since "it was nearly four months since Terry Anderson, the last of the American hostages in Beirut, had been freed, and the Iranians were growing restless. It was time for Washington to deliver its part of the implied quid pro quo."[40] He continued:

> [US National Security Advisor] Scowcroft had intimated at our first two meetings that the United States might have some difficulty living up to its "promise" of three years earlier. Even so, I held out hope that the administration would give me something I could take to the Iranians. Perhaps I was in denial: The idea that a word given would not be kept was unacceptable to me, since my credibility had been essential to the success of my work.[41]

Picco's frustration with the US administration for not living up to their promise paled in comparison to what Rafsanjani had to endure back in Tehran. Picco expressed his regret for the failure of the deal and for not letting the Iranians know sooner of the fact that no deal was imminent, particularly since "Scowcroft made it official in April [1992] that there would be no gesture toward Iran anytime soon ... Whatever the reasons, a three-year operation in Beirut built on a foundation of trust had suddenly turned to sand. Unwittingly—naively, as it turned out—I had misled an entire [Iranian] government."[42]

The effect was devastating for the credibility of all involved, including the *Iranian pragmatists*, who had taken an immense risk with the hope that the US would keep its word. The US behavior had inevitably not only significantly reduced the prospects of rapprochement but had also damaged the hand of proponents of Rafsanjani's school of thought, thereby strengthening the position taken by hardliners always stressing the unreliability of the US government. The extent of the political risk taken by Rafsanjani and his supporters and the degree to which they had put their credibility on the line was illustrated in Picco's own experience:

> My failure to deliver the American side of the deal with the Iranians essentially rendered me a liar … Going to Tehran was exactly what I had to do. I had to look into the eyes of President Akbar Hashemi Rafsanjani and acknowledge my inadvertent deception. Nothing less would do.[43]

Picco described his subsequent meeting with Rafsanjani in some detail:

> [Javad] Zarif took me to see Rafsanjani. It was our first meeting since all the American hostages had returned home from Lebanon … [I told Rafsanjani] that I had come to Tehran with news of broken promises. I explained that although the hostage operation had been based on the assumption that a goodwill gesture from America would be offered, I had been informed by Washington that no reciprocity would be forthcoming.[44] Rafsanjani, confused and dismayed, points to the Iranian overtures and the great deal of political capital invested in having the hostages released and the internal disputes that were fought to allow such measures to take place, stating: "We have assisted you in Lebanon out of respect for the United Nations Secretary General. We have taken many political risks in our cooperation with you. Not everybody was in favor of such cooperation. Nevertheless, we went ahead. Since we engaged in this effort, we have listened carefully to what you told us, including all the various assurances. You understand, Mr. Picco, that you are putting me in a very difficult position. In fact, it may be a very difficult position for both of us … The first thing I could do here is to decide never to let you leave Tehran … I am sad to hear that this is the reason you came. I think it is best if you leave Tehran very, very

quickly. The news of what you have told me will travel fast to other quarters, and they may decide not to let you go."[45]

The US, by failing to deliver on its end of the bargain, had effectively derailed a unique opportunity to engage seriously with Tehran toward rapprochement. This missed opportunity had not only strengthened the view in Tehran that the US was not only not really interested in a constructive dialogue but also that it could not be trusted. The failure to produce reciprocity from the US for Iranian goodwill had also weakened—maybe not in terms of numbers, but influence—those in the Iranian government who advocated better relations with the US, particularly the camp led and represented by Rafsanjani.

Two Men, Two Views

Since the death of Ayatollah Khomeini, two visions have dominated Iran's consideration of relations with the United States. The two visions have some common features. They both reject US dominance of, and its interference in, Iran's politics. They both support relations that would not threaten the security of the system (*nezam*) and are based on equal footing and mutual respect. They are also both opposed to the US policies of unconditional support for Israel which invariably results in a one-sided and humiliating approach toward the Islamic world in general and Iran in particular.

The Supreme Leader's school of thought is extremely suspicious about the real intentions of the US toward Iran. He believes that paramount in US strategy is the objetivce of regime change, and that any conciliatory move by American leaders is intended to mislead the Iranian government, bringing the Americans closer to achieving their long-term goal. The Supreme Leader contends that "Any relations [with the US] would provide the possibility to the Americans to infiltrate Iran and would pave the way for their intelligence and spy agents."[46] The concern is that official diplomatic relations would facilitate the creation of covert links between the US and those Iranians who are prepared to cooperate with the Americans to undermine the Iranian system.

Rafsanjani's school of thought, however, does not deny that the US holds hostile intentions toward Iran, but as a pragmatic centrist, he has consistently argued that there are sufficient common interests between Iran and the US that a fair deal through sustained dialogue is achievable. He knows from experience, as we have seen, that neither of the two countries will benefit from tit-for-tat policies, and that prudence dictates that these two enemies can and should, ultimately, become friends.

Both countries seek stability and security in the Persian Gulf region as the number one priority of Iran–US relations. Rafsanjani argues that this would not be achievable as long as the two remain hostile toward each other. He believes that Iran and the US have a common enemy in the extremists who fight both countries under the banner of Salafism, Al-Qaeda, and more recently, ISIS, terrorism. Iran has been in conflict with these forces since the 1990s, when the Taliban seized power in Afghanistan. Cooperation between Iran and the US would be the most effective way to rebuff extremist Salafis that threaten the interests of both countries and the stability of the region as a whole. Hostility between Iran and the US only enables the extremists to challenge the security interests of both countries. If there is any chance of countering these destructive forces, it would manifest itself through close cooperation between Iran and the US.

More common ground between Iran and the US, in the eyes of Rafsanjani, is the economic benefit that both sides would reap if they normalized their relations. Rafsanjani, who had been involved in private business activity prior to the Revolution, is a business-minded person who pursued economic growth during his presidency. He believes that hostile Iran–US relations present a serious obstacle to the development of Iran's economy, which is heavily dependent on foreign investment in its infrastructure, including the oil and gas industry. Rafsanjani views Iran as a tremendous opportunity for American investment. Indeed, in 1995, while he was president, he awarded a major oil contract to the US firm Conoco.

Disappointment Continues

After the US refusal to reciprocate Iran's efforts in securing the release of Western hostages in Lebanon, it was extremely difficult for Rafsanjani to initiate another overture toward the US. However, he made every effort to convince the SNSC and the Supreme Leader to examine a new path of détente with the US through opening economic relations. Despite his profound pessimism and mistrust, the Supreme Leader agreed with Rafsanjani's argument for opening economic and technical relations with the US. To begin, Rafsanjani chose the energy sector, which was of significant interest to the Americans. To that end,

Iran invited the US Conoco Oil Company to tender for the development of the Sirri oil field project. At that time, the project was the largest oil field development in Iran's history. This would fit perfectly with President Clinton's new approach to foreign policy. Clinton asserted that with the end of the Cold War emphasis should be placed on economic rather than military instruments to advance foreign policy goals, such as the promotion of democracy, which he believed America had ignored.[47]

Rafsanjani, with the approval of Ayatollah Khamenei, moved to sign the deal with Conoco with the added aim of significantly increasing Iran's economic relations with the US. As a result, Conoco was offered a billion-dollar contract to develop two offshore oil fields. Finally, in March 1995, Iran announced that a contract had been signed and thus an olive branch had been extended to the US.[48]

The Clinton administration, however, not only failed to share the same perspective but also went against its own foreign policy orientation with emphasis on economic relations. Shortly after Iran's announcement on the Conoco contract, the US government announced that it would obstruct the contract, calling it a "threat to national security."[49] Clinton went further, signing an executive order that placed an embargo on US investment in Iran's energy sector. Foreign companies intent on developing Iran's energy sector were threatened with American sanctions, thus further deterring investment in the sector.[50]

Clinton did not stop there. He signed another executive order banning any economic relations, including financial and commercial transactions, with Iran. He accused Iran of seeking nuclear technology "in order to develop its capacity to build nuclear weapons."[51]

Iran's olive branch was once again rejected, with Rafsanjani noting the missed opportunity for rapprochement: "This was a message to the United States which was not correctly understood," adding that his government had had to surmount "a lot of difficulty" to sign the deal with Conoco.[52]

In an interview with CNN on July 2, 1995, Rafsanjani stated that the Conoco deal was aimed at demonstrating Iran's readiness to open economic and technical relations with the US. But he added that Americans "have situated themselves within a framework of Zionist propaganda and hence their minds are poisoned with such propaganda and they are pulled by such propaganda to make decisions that are not wise."[53] The role of Israel, its supporters, and its lobby in derailing Clinton's foreign policy toward Iran is confirmed by many observers.[54]

In the same interview, Rafsanjani denied the Americans' accusations that Iran was pursuing nuclear weaponization, saying "We really hate the atomic bomb and its purpose ... Islam has prevented us from undertaking such adventurism."

In my discussions with Rafsanjani, I vividly recall his frustration with Washington overturning the Conoco deal. He told me: "We had taken so many risks and overcome serious internal opposition to bring establishing commercial relations with Washington to the table, starting with the Conoco contract. We first had to get the SNSC to approve it and subsequently the Supreme Leaders' approval." Rafsanjani went on to describe the difficulties he faced in convincing the Supreme Leader to approve a resumption of commercial relations with the US. Ayatollah Khamenei had warned Rafsanjani not to trust the Americans. Rafsanjani did ultimately receive his approval.

The reaction from Washington was seen as a slap in the face, especially given Rafsanjani's real motivation behind the Conoco deal. In a private exchange with me, he emphasized that "We had the intention to begin economic relations with the US and as a major first step, we chose to show our commitment to rapprochement by allowing a major energy deal to proceed. We had hoped that this would lead to the beginning of wide ranging cooperation with the US at a political level." Rafsanjani lamented: "I am so disappointed with the administration in Washington for blocking this deal. There is so much at stake!"

The US, as it appeared under the influence of pro-Israel sentiments, was not interested in major rapprochement at the time. Washington proceeded to further punish Iran and signaled the start of sanctions directly on Iran's major economic resource. On September 8, 1995, Senator Alfonse D'Amato introduced the Iran Foreign Oil Sanctions Bill to block the export of energy technology to Iran by foreign firms. Eventually reaching the statute book as the Iran–Libya Sanctions Act (ILSA), on December 18, 1995, the legislation imposed sanctions on foreign investment in Iran's energy sector.[57] According to this Act, the US would impose sanctions on foreign companies that invested more than $20 million in Iran's oil industry. A few days later, on December 31, 1995, Congress passed, as part of the Intelligence Authorization Act for Fiscal Year 1996, provisions which included $18 to $20 million to support covert operations against the Iranian government.[58]

Overall, Ayatollah Khamenei remained unconvinced that cooperation with the US would ever occur. Nevertheless, Rafsanjani has on numerous occasions emphasized the significance of the normalization of relations between Iran and the United States, including in his letter to the Leader of the Revolution while he was alive. As recalled in 2013, Rafsanjani took the unprecedented step of raising the "taboo" issue of relations with the US with the late Ayatollah. In his words:

I wrote a letter to Imam [Khomeini] in the last years of his life. I even didn't type it. As I preferred no one to read my letter, I gave it to Imam personally. I discussed about seven issues in the letter and I told him it was better to resolve those issues as long as he was alive, otherwise those issues might become a barrier against the country's development in the future. [I said] that if you don't help us remove them, it would be difficult to remove them after you [pass away] ... one of those issues was the relations with America. I wrote the style that we have adopted now, not to talk or have any relations with America is not sustainable ... Having relations doesn't mean that we submit to their will. We can negotiate, if they accept our positions, we accept theirs, that's it.[59]

In his interview with Arman newspaper in March 2014 Rafsanjani revealed interesting information with regard the mindset of Ayatollah Khomeini. He said that Ayatollah Khomeini disapproved of the slogan "Death to America,"[60] especially on Iranian state radio and TV. Furthermore, Rafsanjani told me in the course of our private exchanges: "I was commander of armed forces. Imam told me that it is not right to walk over the US flag in the military parades. Then I ordered the armed forces to stop walking over the US flag in their parades."[61]

In contrast to Ayatollah Khomeini's hostile stance against the United States during the Iran–Iraq War, there are numerous indications that he did not want relations to remain severed permanently. Mohsen Rafqdoost, former Minister of the IRGC (later re-named Ministry of Defense and Armed Forces Logistics), says that when he was appointed as the minister "in 1983 or 1984," he went to Ayatollah Khomeini's residence to get his permission to set up his office in the American Embassy. Ayatollah Khomeini asked: "Why do you want to go there? Are we going to be in conflict with America a thousand years? Don't go there."[62]

Despite the differences in approach and policies toward the US, both schools of thought (in Iran) invariably believe that the relationship between Iran and the US should be one of non-intervention and mutual respect. It should also be noted that neither of the Ayatollahs were involved in the seizure of the American Embassy. It was not their will that the Embassy should be invaded, let alone hostages to be taken or kept for so long.

Many politicians, as well as analysts in the US, argue that the real problem lies with the process of foreign policy making in Iran. They argue that no one, including the presidents, can shape Iran's foreign policy because the Supreme Leader is the ultimate decision-maker. In an interview before his election, President Rouhani presented an interesting argument. In response to a reporter who argued that as president, Rouhani would not be in a position to effect any changes in Iran's foreign policy, Rouhani drew attention to significant differences between the foreign policy of the governments of Rafsanjani, Khatami, and Ahmadinejad. In his view, such differences provided clear evidence that Iran's presidents are influential in foreign policy decision-making despite the fact that the final say lies with Ayatollah Khamenei. Noting that while the Leader has remined the same during all four presidencies, Rouhani posed the question: "If presidents are a non-factor, then, how could you explain differing foreign policies from one administration to another?" In the following section I will try to shed light on the process of foreign policy decision-making in Iran.

The Process of Foreign Policy Decision-Making

As in the US, Iran's Supreme National Security Council (SNSC) is a major element in shaping security-related foreign policy, while the Ministry of Foreign Affairs is in charge of foreign relations and diplomacy and accountable to *Majlis*. Iran–US relations and the nuclear issue are two matters that fall within the remit of the SNSC. As indicated earlier, the Council was established during the 1989 revision of the Constitution, which defined its responsibilities as follows:

- Determining the defense and national security policies within the framework of general policies set by the Supreme Leader;
- Coordination of activities in areas relating to politics, intelligence, social, cultural, and economic fields with regard to general defense and security policies; and
- Exploitation of material and intellectual resources of the country for facing internal and external threats.

The council is headed by the President, who appoints its Secretary. The decisions of the SNSC become enforceable with the Supreme Leader's approval. The Council's membership consists of the President as head of the executive branch, Speaker of Majlis, head of the Judiciary, chief of the supreme command council of the armed forces, chief commanders of the regular armed forces and the IRGC, head of the budget and planning, ministers of foreign affairs, interior, intelligence, and two representatives of the Supreme Leader. Depending on the Council's agenda, other ministers would also be invited to attend the meetings.

Based on its wide-ranging responsibilities, as just alluded, the Council would address and deliberate on all foreign policy and security issues, whether raised within the Council or brought to its attention by other governmental institutions, including the Foreign Ministry or even the Supreme Leader's Office. In each and every case, the issue is referred to the Foreign Relations Committee of the SNSC. The committee, in the course of its research and deliberation, might interview other officials outside of the Council, including Iranian ambassadors stationed abroad. The Committee's report, as per practice, would outline different options and the pros and cons of each. Final reports are ultimately submitted to the Secretary of the Council who determines whether more discussion within the SNSC is warranted, or whether it will be sent directly to the Supreme Leader's Office. Even when reports are sent back to the SNSC, they are ultimately sent to the Office of the Supreme Leader.

In some cases, upon receipt of a SNSC report, the Supreme Leader may call the members of the SNSC and sometimes even invite more people, including his advisors, for brainstorming on the case. Based on my personal experience as head of the SNSC Foreign Relations Committee, in the overwhelming majority of cases, Ayatollah Khamenei consents with the proposals suggested by the Council. Undoubtedly, like many countries, there is competition between factions within the government in order to impact the final outcome of the process. This is similar to bureaucratic competition between departments in the United States' government intended to influence its foreign policy.[63]

Because Rafsajani was so influential in Iran's politics, the role of the SNSC was not so visible. During Mohammad Khatami's presidency, however, the SNSC acquired a much higher profile in steering foreign policy.

While Ayatollah Khamenei is indeed the one who makes final decisions on Iran's foreign policy, he too possesses the inescapable human trait of being influenced by others around him, particularly a President who has been elected through a popular vote. This also demonstrates why Iran was able to adopt a more moderate, tolerant foreign policy under Khatami as President. And it explains why, despite

Ayatollah Khamenei's ultimate authority, Iran was seen as belligerent in foreign policy under Ahmadinejad's agenda.

Launching Dialogue with the West

As the head of the Western European Affairs at the Foreign Ministry, during a visit to Dublin in May 1990 I proposed dialogue on an array of issues with our European counterparts as a step toward resolving tensions with the West. At the time, Ireland held the presidency of the European Community (EC) Council, where I met with the directors general of the European troika, consisting of Ireland, France, and Italy. In the meeting, I voiced Tehran's readiness to do its utmost to facilitate the release of European hostages in Lebanon, while also proposing to establish an Iran–Europe dialogue to discuss the critical issues of both parties as a way to revive relations.[64] This meeting was the first such gathering since the 1979 Revolution, and our European counterparts responded positively to my initiative on an Iran–Europe dialogue.[65] The *Times Daily* quoted the Irish officials as confirming talks focused on improving relations and the release of European hostages in Lebanon.[66]

Based on the agreement with the EEC foreign ministers, "Critical Dialogue" would take place at a biannual gathering of Iranian and European officials at the level of deputy foreign ministers of foreign affairs in various European capitals. These meetings continued until the end of President Rafsanjani's tenure in 1997, where my colleague and friend Mr. Vaezi represented Iran. Through this initiative, the foundation of an Iran–Europe dialogue was established, while we continued to look for a way to open the door to Iran–US relations.

During the "Critical Dialogue" meetings with the Europeans, Iran proposed practical measures, such as joint working groups, to define concerns and the ways and means of cooperation. One such initiative included cooperation on curbing regional and international drug trafficking. The issue was of mutual interest as it affected both Iranians and European citizens. Other prominent areas considered were Iran's commitment to the success of the international community's grand agenda on elimination of weapons of mass destruction (WMDs) in the region and the fight against terrorism. These were matters of great importance as they could contribute significantly to international peace and security, while addressing the main areas of dispute between Iran and the West and facilitating Iran's agenda for the formation of a regional cooperation system. However, these initiatives made little progress due to the US pressure on the Europeans to the contrary/in the opposite direction.

Although this security package was discussed within the framework of the Iran–EEC "Critical Dialogue," I placed great emphasis on having the Germans play a more prominent role in advancing the package. I believed that German cooperation on this initiative would accelerate the revival of Iran–West relations and serve as an avenue to US rapprochement.

While we were trying to engage our European counterparts on combating terrorism, on April 5, 1992, the MEK conducted a near-simultaneous attack on Iranian diplomatic missions in 13 countries, including the Iranian Mission to the United Nations in New York.[67] At that time, I was the Iranian ambassador to Germany and our embassy and consulates in Bonn, Hamburg, and Munich were attacked. Much to our dismay, in the aftermath of the attacks, the West did not provide any serious condemnation.

Iran's endeavor to improve cooperation with the West endured and we continued to press the Germans to take the lead in this initiative. However, constant obstacles were set up in an attempt to derail the initiative. On July 14, 1992, Reinhard Schlagintweit, Political Director General of the German Foreign Ministry, informed me that the US had started to focus on WMD and the nuclear issue. Meanwhile, and due to positive developments in Iran–EU relations, Washington appeared to pursue the passage of a resolution at the next G7 Summit to apply further pressure on Iran. Even with this revelation and countless other obstacles, the Iranian government continued to provide ample opportunities for the West to improve relations with Iran.

One such overture was a meeting between the Iranian Secretary of the Supreme National Security Council, Hassan Rouhani, and German Foreign Minister Klaus Kinkel on April 28, 1993. Rouhani expressed Tehran's readiness to lay a framework with Europe for cooperation on the WMDs issue. The initiative would entail acceptance of all international non-proliferation conventions, openness and transparency with the International Atomic Energy Agency (IAEA) on nuclear issues, support of a WMD free zone in the Middle East, and the conversion of some military factories to civil production as a step towards demilitarization and durable peace in the Persian Gulf region. Rouhani made the same offer to Fritz Wittmann,[68] Chairman of the Bundestag Defense Committee, and Bernd Schmidbauer, the Minister of State in the Chancellor's office, on April 29, 1993. However, Rouhani also conveyed that cooperation between Iran and the West on drug trafficking was probably the easiest and most achievable matter to begin with.

Tehran had invested tremendous political capital to engage with the West, but some proponents of rapprochement began to grow uncertain of the outcome. Another setback to our efforts came in my meeting with the Director General of the German Economics Ministry, Lorenz Schomerus, on May 3, 1993, when he informed me: "Your ideas on tackling WMD, terrorism, drug trafficking, and human rights could be very helpful to resolve Iran–West relations, but unfortunately the US does not buy the moderate and constructive offers Tehran raised in Bonn."

The Iranians placed great importance on this initiative. During high-level talks at various stages of the process we brought up our offer of Iran–West cooperation in areas of mutual interest, including at the meeting between Iranian Foreign Minister Dr. Ali Akbar Velayati and Chancellor Kohl on June 13, 1994 and a subsequent meeting with German Foreign Minister Klaus Kinkel. President Rafsanjani proposed the offer in his letter to Chancellor Kohl and even went on to say that Iran and Europe could, in cooperation, could fight terrorism bilaterally, regionally, and internationally.

By this point, the EEC had transformed itself into the European Union (EU), but the EU could not advance the initiative since the US would not support it. Kinkel told Velayati that he agreed in principle with what Iran was proposing, but needed to figure out how it could be managed internationally. Ultimately our efforts proved futile. In my discussion with the Political Director of the German Foreign Ministry, Hans-Wilhelm Theodor Wallau,[69] on October 24, 1994, he informed me that Kinkel had reviewed the Iranian initiative with the EU Commission and they had rejected it. The simple fact was that there was no chance of progress as long as Washington was opposed—and it became apparent to me that the Americans were fundamentally opposed to serious cooperation between Iran and Europe.

As far as Iran was concerned, the only explanation for the US behavior was that they did not want Iran to act as a sovereign state capable of shaping its foreign policy independently, and did not want Europe to recognize Iran as such. Yet, if Washington had proceeded to play a more constructive role, Tehran was prepared to expand cooperation to include the US and make substantive progress on countering terrorism, halting the production and spread of WMD in the region, and curbing drug trafficking.

We also pursued another track in relation to building friendly relations with the West. Peace and stability in the Persian Gulf region was of vital concern to Iran, regional Arab countries, and the West. Therefore, a durable, regional, and cooperative system for peace, stability, and security in the Persian Gulf would not only secure the national interests of all parties involved but also significantly contribute to reducing tensions between Iran and the West, in particular the United States. That is why, once the Iran–Iraq War had ended, one of Tehran's foreign policy goals was to create a workable framework of cooperation between Iran, the countries in the region, and the West.

In 1990, the restoration of relations with Europe was a firm commitment by the Supreme Leader, President Rafsanjani, and the SNSC. Rafsanjani first conveyed this strategy to me when he elaborated on my mandate as the Iranian ambassador to Germany, stating: "You have to realize that our aim of better relations with Europe and the West is through the doorway of Germany followed by France."

The day after I arrived in Bonn on October 9, 1990 as the first Iranian ambassador to a reunited Germany, I was received by the German Foreign Minister, Hans-Dietrich Genscher. It was my understanding that the issue of Persian Gulf security could appeal to the US and the West. Therefore, if we could form a cooperative structure with Europe aimed at the security of the region, we might kill two birds with one stone. I decided that no time should be wasted. During my initial meeting with Genscher, I offered the German Foreign Minister the initiative of cooperation between Iran, our Arab neighbors, and Europe for security, stability, and peace in the Persian Gulf. Mr. Genscher was extremely enthusiastic and welcomed the proposed initiative. He authorized the Political Director General of the German Foreign Ministry Reinhard Schlagintweit[70] to continue the discussion on the details of the initiative with me. Schlagintweit was known to be supportive of fostering Iran–West relations—to such an extent that his nickname in political circles in Bonn was "Ayatollah Schlagintweit." During a series of meetings, I discussed the following issues with Schlagintweit:

- Establishment of a Regional Cooperation System with the participation of Iran and the Gulf Cooperation Council (GCC)[71] for security, stability, and peace in the Persian Gulf;
- Granting assurance to the international community for the safe transit of energy from the Persian Gulf through this Regional Cooperation System;
- Cooperation of this regional organization with all countries having an interest in the security and stability of the Persian Gulf;

- Regional cooperation to also include combating terrorism, weapons of mass destruction, drug trafficking, and organized crime.

To build momentum and strengthen the initiative, Mr. Genscher arrived in Tehran on May 6, 1991 to meet with Rafsanjani and focus on the mechanisms to establish the system. President Rafsanjani gave his full backing to the initiative. Genscher was excited by Rafsanjani's strong support for such an important policy that could guarantee a sustainable stability and peace in the region.

Following the meetings in Tehran, I arranged for Genscher to visit refugee camps in western Iran which housed Iraqi and Kuwaiti refugees from Iraq's invasion of Kuwait. Germany was the only Western country that played a constructive role in assisting with the humanitarian crisis resulting from that conflict. During the visit, Genscher also met with the German aid workers in the area. Moreover, it is worth mentioning that through major internal discussions and negotiations, the Iranian military establishment gave the green light for (for the first time since the 1979 Revolution) a German military contingent to assist with the humanitarian efforts.

While traveling with Genscher in the plane from Tehran to Kermanshah (western Iran), I saw him gazing out of the window, for over twenty minutes. I approached and addressed him—which in fact startled him—and asked what held him in such deep thought. In response, Genscher confessed that he was contemplating "why a country with such a rich history, natural beauty, and strategic location—being at the heart of the world with a skilled population— could not be on par with the developed nations?" I did not respond to his question, but rather asked for his own personal opinion, to which he replied jokingly, "If I tell you what I think, once we are off the plane, you would send the message to Tehran." I assured him that I would not. He then elaborated:

> I have been thinking of the reasons and I thought since Iran has an incredibly smart and educated population, it has to be the country's management that is responsible for Iran's slowed pace of development. However, after meeting with Rafsanjani for a few hours, I am baffled since, if not the most, he is one of the most competent and smart leaders I have ever met in the 16 years serving as a foreign minister of Germany … Keep in mind I have met all important leaders of the East and West. So if it is not the people in charge of Iran's management, then what? While I was thinking about it on the

plane, I came to the conclusion that it is due to the level of tensions between Iran and the United States—these tensions need to be resolved.

I responded by saying that a starting point would be the initiative we had discussed with Rafsanjani on regional cooperation and issues related to terrorism, WMD, and drug trafficking. I also added that there were many other initiatives Iran was prepared to bring to the table. Genscher told me that he was enthusiastic about examining the initiative on the Persian Gulf security and cooperation with Washington.

Genscher was known to spend his summer vacations in a castle in the Alps, during which time he would not receive any foreign visitors. I, however, was privileged to share a meeting with him during his vacation on August 5, 1991 to discuss the regional cooperation initiative. Mr. Genscher was clearly disappointed and frustrated to have to report that Washington would not support the initiative. I could not comprehend why that was the case.

Regardless of the pessimistic response I received from Mr. Genscher, for the next three years I strove to develop the initiative, as I was confident it would be in line with the common interests of all stakeholders, namely Iran, the US, the West, the region, and the international community. Mr. Javad Larijani,[72] my predecessor as the head of the SNSC Foreign Relation Committee, who led the Iran–Germany Parliamentary Friendship Group at the time, met with German officials on January 18, 1994 to confirm Iran's willingness to develop cooperation with the EU/West for peace, stability, and security in Central Asia, the Caucasus, and the Persian Gulf. The proposal would require the construction of a regional cooperation system in the Persian Gulf to provide all the necessary international guarantees for security and peace, meeting the concerns of the West. In the meeting with German Foreign Minister Klaus Kinkel,[73] Larijani told him: "Iran had been working on the initiative for three years and the Supreme National Security Council of Iran (SNSC) has approved it. However, the US is preventing our Arab neighbors to come forward [sic]. Iran would welcome UN involvement to realize this initiative." While our Foreign Minister Dr. Velayati had already showed Iran's willingness to forward the initiative, Mr. Kinkel regrettably advised that Washington did not welcome the initiative, as had been conveyed to him in his meeting with US Secretary of State Warren Christopher.

The Iranian regional cooperation initiative could have paved the way forward for increased stability and security in the region, but more importantly for Iranians, it would have been a monumental leap toward friendship with the West and obviously the United States. Yet once again, the US government blocked those efforts. I am confident that had that system of cooperation been established, we could be living in a different world today.

Mediation at the Highest Level

In April 2011, a critical oral history conference was held in Musgrove, Florida. The participants were a group of American, American-Iranian, and Iranian scholars and former politicians and diplomats, including Thomas Pickering and myself. The purpose of the conference was to contrast opposing views on "Haunted efforts to improve Iran–US relations" and delve into the issue of "Was it the United States or Iran who was responsible for missing the opportunities and bringing the relations between the two parties to a deadlock?" The conference was provocative, at times confrontational, the participants regularly interrupting the speakers to raise objections.

I asserted that Iran had made gesture after gesture in an effort to break through to the Americans, but that the US only responded with increased hostility. This was in contrast to the prevailing US view, that the Islamic Republic basically did not desire good relations with the West, or at best, only wanted rapprochement on their own terms, which the West was not prepared to accept.

My American friends were stunned when they heard from me that contrary to common belief in the US political circles, the best chance for reconciliation between Iran and the US was not presented under the reformist President Mohammad Khatami but during the presidency of Hashemi Rafsanjani. At the first session of the conference I revealed the German Chancellor's efforts to mediate between Iran and the US. I could see from the body language that most of the participants did not believe my story and others doubting its accuracy.

Bruce Riedel, a former senior member of the US National Security Council and advisor to four US presidents, told the participants just before the second session began that he found "Mousavian's entirely credible story" to be astounding. His astonishment was understandable, considering that my account was completely at variance with what he and the other Americans at the table believed at the time. Nevertheless, they indicated that they were now beginning to see the other side of the conflict—through the eyes of an Iranian.

I presented a summary of my dealings with the Germans to the members of the conference. One of my earliest meetings during my ambassadorship to Germany (1990–7), regarding German facilitation of a rapprochement between Iran and United States, was with Minister of State Bernd Schmidbauer[74] on June 30, 1992. I asked Schmidbauer to confirm with the Americans whether they were serious about mending relations and if they agreed to Germany playing a mediating role. Schmidbauer promised to convey my message to Washington, and in the coming months, in close cooperation with German officials in the office of the Chancellor and the Foreign Ministry, we laid the foundations for German facilitation of Iran–US reconciliation to take shape.

Once I received the news of Chancellor Kohl's willingness to assist with Iran–US rapprochement, I informed Rafsanjani in a meeting on August 2, 1992, where he told me he would discuss the matter with Ayatollah Khamenei. A positive response from the Supreme Leader was essential to furthering this initiative. On August 22, 1992, President Rafsanjani informed me that he had discussed the matter with the Supreme Leader, and while the Leader maintained his pessimism about American goodwill, he would not block the initiative. The main caveat was for Washington to show goodwill in return for Iran's facilitation of the release of the Western hostages, the story described earlier.

As a first step toward improving relations, the US would need to release Iranian frozen assets, in the spirit of President Bush's "goodwill begets goodwill" suggestion. Subsequently, on August 27, 1992, in a meeting with Minister of State Bernd Schmidbauer, I was informed that the US President was looking to improve relations with Iran. Schmidbauer requested that the Iranians take proactive steps in this regard and said: "To go [on a] honeymoon with Europe while there are hostilities with the US would not be [productive]." We agreed to follow up the issue of improving relations between Tehran and Washington.

In order to discuss Tehran's position, expectations, and strategy to revive Iran–US relations, I met with Schmidbauer on September 9, 1992. I emphasized that Iran expected its frozen assets to be released in recognition of Iran's efforts to free the Western hostages, while Tehran would also embark on a plan to remove hostility and revive good relations by improving "nation to nation" links in the academic, economic, and tourism fields. During the same meeting, Mr. Schmidbauer informed me that Kohl had discussed his role as a facilitator with Washington and was told that due to the upcoming presidential election, the US would not be able to take any steps until that matter was out of the way.

The development of Bonn–Tehran relations had become a worrying point for Washington, an issue that Schmidbauer mentioned in our meeting at his home in Heidelberg on December 20, 1992. He further noted that during his meetings in Washington, the Americans had focused on two major issues: WMD and terrorism. In response, I proposed establishing a joint Iran–EEC working group to cooperate on combating terrorism and work on WMD non-proliferation. Meanwhile, I suggested that we could discuss issues of mutual concern, engage in dialogue to remove suspicions, and include the US at a later phases.

George Bush lost the election and Bill Clinton was sworn in as the 42nd President of the United States on January 20, 1993. A month later, on February 10, 1993, President Rafsanjani sent a letter addressed to Chancellor Kohl and other European heads of state via Iranian Deputy Foreign Minister Mahmoud Vaezi, announcing Iran's readiness to cooperate with the EEC on delicate issues such as WMD, terrorism, and human rights. While Rafsanjani criticized the West's double standards on these issues, he emphasized that *Iran's commitment would be based on international rules and norms.*

Subsequently, Chancellor Kohl visited Washington and held a number of meetings with US officials, where he mentioned Iran's willingness to cooperate on these issues of WMD, terrorism, and human rights. I was astounded to learn from Mr. Schmidbauer on March 25, 1993, two months into Bill Clinton's presidency, that Washington was not ready to get involved with Iran's initiative, but instead was requesting that Kohl sever his ties with Tehran. Schmidbauer further advised me that the United States was mobilizing the international community against Iran on WMD, nuclear issue, human rights, and terrorism. Later on the same day, Mr. Schlagintweit,[75] Political Director General of the German Foreign Ministry, confirmed the US position during a farewell ceremony for the Qatari ambassador to Germany. Schlagintweit informed me that while Chancellor Kohl was in the US, the White House had asked him to cut his ties with Iran. This had come against the backdrop of Israeli Prime Minister Yitzhak Rabin's visit to Washington where, in a joint press conference on March 15, 1993, President Clinton stated that Israel and the US had reached a common strategic understanding on Iran.[76] I have to confess that at the time I found it difficult to comprehend the extent of the Israeli influence on the US foreign policy.

The pressure was mounting from Washington on the Europeans—in particular the Germans—to sever ties with Tehran. Schmidbauer and I discussed this in a meeting on April 6, 1993, where he informed me that the dispute between the US and Germany over Iran was heating up, as the Germans believed in cooperation with Rafsanjani's government while the US wanted none of it. It was in this highly-charged atmosphere, on May 4, 1993, that I delivered Chancellor Kohl's response to President Rafsanjani's letter of February 10, 1993. The Chancellor's letter outlined Germany's support for Iran's proposal for regional cooperation, including the Persian Gulf states, while suggesting that Iran also raise the idea of Iran–EU cooperation in the Caspian Sea and in the Economic Cooperation Organization (ECO),[77] with a guarantee of German backing. To strengthen Iran–EU relations, the Chancellor indicated that Germany was prepared to work with Iran in international organizations focused on issues relating to WMD non-proliferation, combating terrorism, and drug trafficking. The Chancellor's letter was the most positive message from a Western leader to an Iranian President since the 1979 Revolution.

Mohammad Hashemi Rafsanjani,[78] the President's brother, delivered Mr. Rafsanjani's response to Chancellor's Kohl's letter on September 10, 1993 in a meeting with Kohl. President Rafsanjani offered suggestions to end over two decades of animosity between Iran and the West, especially the United States. Chancellor Kohl appreciated Rafsanjani's message and said that he would discuss it with President Clinton, emphasizing that isolation of Iran would not assist peace, security, and stability in the region. He also praised Iran as a great country with an important role in the region, a point that he had made to President Clinton on more than one occasion, according to him. On his role as a mediator for better relations between Iran and the US, Kohl stated: "I would talk with President Clinton again with great interest. I am neither your nor the Americans' representative or attorney, but I would convey the message to Washington and the European heads of state. I have told Washington very clearly that tensions in Iran–US relations should be reduced. While Iran is ready, why should not the Americans be as well?" I also conveyed a message to Bonn from President Rafsanjani which stated that Tehran had not extended an official mandate for Chancellor Kohl to mediate on their behalf, but that Iran would cooperate and advance its own initiative to improve relations.

To further develop Iran's readiness for full cooperation on WMD, terrorism, and rapprochement with the US, I held a meeting with Dr. Rudolf Dolzer,[79] Director General of the Office of the Chancellor, on December 2, 1993. By that time, the European Union (EU) had officially come into existence. He told me that he had discussed the package with Martin Indyk[80] in the White House, and that Indyk had been stunned at the level of cooperation Iran had offered, and did not know how to respond. I told him that if the White House were receptive, Chancellor Kohl would be able to finalize a practical framework to bring President Rafsanjani and President Clinton together. I also raised the likelihood of resolving the Salman Rushdie[81] problem through a commitment to respect international norms and not interfere in the internal affairs of the United Kingdom (UK).

In a follow-up discussion with Dr. Dolzer on December 6, 1993, he offered his explanation for America's unwillingness to cooperate with Germany to resolve Iran–US tension. He cited Iran's non-recognition of Israel as the main obstacle for the US to engage with Iran as a step towards rapprochement. I was surprised by such a gross double standard. Of over 50 members of the Organization of Islamic Conference (renamed in recent years Organization of Islamic Cooperation), only a handful recognized Israel. Saudi Arabia and Pakistan, considered to be US allies, had not (and still have not in 2014) recognized Israel. How could that be an obstacle to reconciliation with Tehran? Subsequently, in a meeting with Dr. Dolzer on December 17, 1993, he told me that Washington had informed Bonn that Tehran could raise any issue related to bilateral relations through the Swiss ambassador in Tehran— in essence, a diplomatic way to tell the Germans to mind their own business. I told Dr. Dolzer that this clearly meant that Washington had rejected Kohl's mediation and that the Americans were not serious about resolving their dispute with Iran, since there was no comparison between the political status and capacity of Chancellor Kohl and that of the Swiss ambassador in relation to managing such a complicated, troubled relationship. Dr. Dolzer agreed with this assessment, and was extremely angry about Washington's response. In the end, one has to concede, Ayatollah Khamenei's pessimism about the outcome of German Chancellor's mediation initiative was well warranted.

Foreign Minister Dr. Velayati met with Chancellor Kohl on June 13, 1994, where he reiterated Iran's willingness to cooperate in the international arena on the issues of terrorism, WMD, and drug trafficking. He also voiced Tehran's frustration with the US attempts to isolate Iran despite the constructive measures and gestures it had presented. In response, Chancellor Kohl reaffirmed his commitment to improving Iran–West relations:

> My strategy is not based on isolating Iran; rather I support engagement between Iran and the international community. I believe Iran–West common cooperation on combating terrorism, WMD, and drug

trafficking is the right approach and I would continue to support this initiative, despite criticism from the US and even some EU officials. I will visit Washington within a month and talk with the US president on these issues again in order to use such opportunities in opening the door on cooperation with Iran. We have enough tensions worldwide. We do not need another major crisis.

We did not hear about the outcome of Kohl's visit to Washington, until I met with German Minister of State Bernd Schmidbauer, on June 23, 1994. He informed me that during a recent visit to Bonn by President Clinton, the Chancellor had discussed the necessity of removing tensions with Tehran and improving relations. However, Clinton had repeated the necessity for Bonn to limit its relations with Tehran, and asserted that Bonn had fallen out of line with NATO and the West by improving relations with Tehran.

During my mission in Germany (1990–7), the European Union was under constant pressure from the US–Israeli position against Iran. It was clear to me that more German efforts on Iran–US rapprochement simply produced more pressure from Washington on Bonn and the EU to limit their relations with Iran. Finally, in a meeting on December 9, 1994, Dr. Dolzer stated that the EU would not be able to go forward with what had been discussed between Bonn and Tehran. In a subsequent meeting, on April 2, 1995, he added: "In the past two months I have made three visits to US, but we have not been able to convince them. The US is in favor of mounting economic sanctions and international pressure." The following month, on May 1, 1995, President Clinton announced new sanctions against Iran[82] during a speech at the American Israel Public Affairs Committee (AIPAC).[83]

In a December 1995 article in *Foreign Affairs*, Charles Lane, then the lead editor at *New Republic*, clarified the dispute between the Germans and the Americans on how best to approach relations with Iran:

The U.S. and German governments have worked together on aid to Russia, NATO expansion, nuclear nonproliferation, and Middle East peace. German Chancellor Helmut Kohl and U.S. President Bill Clinton enjoy a natural rapport. But when it comes to dealing with Iran, Germany and America have consistently been at odds. Although the two governments have assured each other that their objectives in southwest Asia are the same—to keep Iran from developing nuclear weapons, supporting terrorism, and disrupting the

Arab-Israeli peace process—they differ radically on which means
to use. The United States has tried to isolate Iran diplomatically
and strangle its economy—[while] Germany and Europe favor
engagement.

When President Clinton banned U.S. trade with, and investment
in, the Islamic Republic in May, he was trying not only to punish the
mullahs, but also to undercut the European policy, especially that
of Germany … But even after Clinton's imposition of the embargo,
Western Europe and Japan stood pat. "We do not believe that a trade
embargo is the appropriate instrument for influencing opinion in
Iran and bringing about changes there that are in our interests," said
German Economics Minister Günter Rexrodt.[84]

On Christmas Day 1995, the Secretary of the Supreme National
Security Council, Hassan Rouhani, arrived in Germany to receive
medical treatment. We spent a week together, which I found was a
great opportunity to discuss the current strategy. I explained that the
"West Minus US" approach was bound to fail and that eventually the
Europeans would give up. My theory was that in the absence of direct
negotiations with the US to improve relations, Washington would
become entrenched in hostility and ultimately determined on regime
change. Subsequently, as relations between Iran and the US deteriorated and pressure mounted, a time would come when the Europeans
would have to choose between Iran and the US. In that eventuality, they
would undoubtedly side with the US. I believed that all efforts to build
better relations with the EU would fail and result in a united Western
bloc against Iran. Such a situation would lead to a possible confrontation between Iran and the West.

Convinced, Rouhani asked me to elaborate on my analysis in
Tehran. On my subsequent visit to Tehran, I initially discussed my
views with the Deputy Minister Mahmoud Vaezi and the Director
General for Western European Affairs, Ali Ahani.[85] Coincidentally, the
Iranian ambassador to the United Nations, Kamal Kharazi,[86] was in
Tehran at the time, and I had a chance to discuss these matters with
him and Deputy Minister for International Affairs Javad Zarif. They
also agreed with my assessment. On January 1, 1996, I had the opportunity to present my analysis to Foreign Minister Velayati. I stressed
that the Foreign Ministry should make it clear to the high authorities
in Iran that Europe would not be able to indefinitely resist US pressures
and would eventually give in. Following my discussion, Velayati held
a meeting with the Foreign Relation Committee of the Parliament

(*Majlis*), reiterating my view that if the European Union reached a point where it had to choose between Iran or the US, it would obviously side with the latter, resulting in a united Western coalition against Iran.

I also presented my outlook to President Rafsanjani on January 2, 1996, after which he was wholly convinced and supportive of my reasoning. The following week, on January 8, I attended a meeting of the SNSC, at Dr. Rouhani's behest, to explain my analysis on the "West minus US" strategy. On January 13, the SNSC for the first time approved direct dialogue between Iranian MPs and US Congressmen and Senators.

During a seminar in Bonn on "Culture, Trade and Foreign Policy," on January 15, German Foreign Minister Klaus Kinkel, confided to me: "Before, the Americans were angry with us on expanding relations with Tehran, but nowadays they have become mad." I asked whether Europe would be able to resist, to which he responded negatively. Nevertheless, on January 17, I informed Professor Dolzer that Tehran was ready to start direct talks between Iranian parliamentarians and members of the American Congress. This was an unprecedented step that could help ease years of enmity and suspicion between the two countries, but could also have a significant domestic impact in terms of moderating the policy of Washington and Tehran. Two weeks later, to my regret, Dr. Dolzer informed me that the Americans refused to respond to this outreach. We could not be certain what the rationale behind America's position was, but on the surface the US seemed to be pursuing only one goal—maintaining isolation of Iran, perhaps with the ultimate goal of bringing down the Iranian system.

Mykonos and Beyond

Two major terrorist attacks significantly impacted relations between Iran and the West in the early 1990s. Here, I would like to offer my analysis on the event in Germany whose subsequent political-judicial process and repercussions engaged me for over four years.

From 1990 to 1992, bilateral relations between Bonn and Tehran expanded exponentially. During this period, more than half of cabinet members from both countries exchanged visits, joint economic and cultural commissions were established, and both heads of state were regularly in contact to discuss regional and international issues.[87] These exceptional developments had not been seen in the relations between Iran and any Western country since the Islamic Revolution.

The improved relations with Germany and France soon transcended borders and contributed to better overall relations with Europe, with other countries beginning to expand their ties with Tehran as well. It was against this backdrop that the assassination of the Shah's last prime minister, Shapour Bakhtiar, in Paris, and the Mykonos terrorist attacks in Berlin occurred.

I was serving as the Iranian ambassador to Germany at the time of the Mykonos assassinations. On September 17, 1992, three Iranian-Kurdish opposition leaders and their translator were assassinated by gunmen who attacked the Greek restaurant Mykonos in Berlin. Upon hearing the news of the assassination from my colleagues the next day, while the embassy compound was surrounded by German police, I was in disbelief and knew it would have a detrimental effect on Iranian–German relations. I sought more information from the German authorities, who informed me that at that point they were not sure who was responsible. Shortly after the incident, I left for Tehran to meet with officials there, including the Minister of Intelligence Ali Fallahian, who assured me that Iran had not been involved and that he would send his deputy, Saeed Emami, to fully cooperate with the German authorities. Furthermore, if any evidence implicated Iran, it would be thoroughly investigated in full cooperation with the Germans. Saeed Emami, however, was arrested a few years later on charges of disappearance and assassination of a number of dissident intellectuals. Mohammad Niazi, Head of the Judicial Organization of the Armed Forces, considered him as "one of the main and central elements" of the rogue cell within the Ministry of Intelligence and National Security (MOIS) responsible for the serial killings of intellectuals.[88]

Emami duly arrived in Bonn, where he held closed-door meetings with the most senior German security officials. Security officials from both countries requested that I did not attend the meetings. I learned later from a German source that Emami's position at the meeting had been that Iran was not involved in the killings. The German source revealed that Tehran's position was that a third party had been involved and assured the Germans that once any evidence materialized, Iran would cooperate in finding the culprits—and if necessary, conduct its own investigation to remove any suspicion of Iranian involvement.

I penned a letter to the judge in charge of the Mykonos case and pledged to do whatever was in my power to assist with the investigation. For the next four years (1992–6), I followed up on this issue in my meetings with German officials to get to the root of it. They repeatedly reassured me that this was not a political issue and that the German judiciary would act independently. Despite my efforts, however, relations between Iran and Germany began to deteriorate, though they were strong enough for Bonn to obstruct the issuing of a subpoena by the judiciary to bring Iranian Intelligence Minister Ali Fallahian to court.[89] A new episode, however, suddenly aggravated the already tense situation.

In March 1996, the Iranian vessel *Kolahdooz*, with a cargo destined for Munich, was impounded in Antwerp, Belgium, and a consignment of powerful mortars discovered. Germans subsequently claimed that Iran had attempted to smuggle arms into NATO territory. "This time we are talking about a security threat to NATO," a German official told me.

Belgium announced that mortar shells were discovered in a food container, bound for Munich, Germany, on a ship from Iran, and directed this information to the German government's attention. As Iran's ambassador to Germany, I was responsible for monitoring the case on Iran's behalf. I could scarcely believe my ears when a high-ranking German official informed me that the source of this intelligence had been the United States, relayed to NATO and the Belgian government in Brussels, which is also home to NATO headquarters. Based on the intelligence passed to the German government, they impounded the ship upon its arrival in Hamburg. During inspection of the ship's cargo, the consignment detailed by American intelligence down to the container and crate number were removed from the vessel. The German official with whom I spoke said: "Americans even knew the name of the individual that transferred it to the ship back in [the Iranian port of] Bandar Abbas, and provided the information to the German Government. We have a great respect for you. That's why we would not expel you from Germany. However until this case is cleared, you should play volleyball with your wife at your residence because no official would be able to receive you."

Following this incident, I immediately went to Tehran to meet with President Rafsanjani. He was surprised to see such an incident reported by the Western media and told me that he had inquired of the Supreme National Security Council as to whether they had any knowledge of the matter. Neither Iranian intelligence, nor security officials had been made aware of it, and the President said that Ayatollah Khamenei had ordered a full investigation to be carried out. President Rafsanjani requested the German government to provide any information they had on the matter so that Iran's government could investigate within its own borders. The President emphasized that this incident was critical to Iran's national security.

Only days after the incident, MEK's newsletter published photographs and specifics about the alleged contraband, begging the question as to how was it possible that a consignment of mortar shells could be discovered on an Iranian government vessel without the knowledge of Iran's president, but with the details known to the United States government and MEK.

This incident occurred a few days prior to an international anti-terrorism conference in Sharm el-Sheikh, attended by German Chancellor Kohl. Following the conference, the German government decided to lift its restrictions on the investigation of the Mykonos assassinations and subsequently issued a subpoena on the Iranian Minister of Intelligence.[90] The timing of the *Kolahdooz* affair seemed to be perfect in terms of worsening the already troubled relations between Iran and Germany following the Mykonos murders.

The German prosecutor's reasoning and the judge's justification for the subpoena related to the testimony of "Witness C," who alleged that an Iranian "Special Committee, comprised of the Supreme Leader, President, Ministers of Foreign Affairs and Intelligence had issued the order for the Mykonos murders."[91] "Witness C" was Mr. Abolghassem Mesbahi, an indebted Iranian businessman who had fled Iran and, in an effort to secure asylum in Europe, convinced French intelligence, agents that he had valuable intelligence on the Mykonos assassination. His subsequent debriefing by Western intelligence agencies eventually brought him to the German court, where his sensational entrance shielded by security personnel added to the mystery surrounding the case.

In court, the man responsible for validating Mesbahi's statements was Abulhassan Banisadr, the first President of the Islamic Republic (February 1980 to June 1981) who had quickly fallen out of favor with the Iranian leadership and fled to Paris, never to return to Iran. Though Banisadr no longer had day-to-day experience of Iranian affairs, his validation of Mesbahi's testimony and the political nature of the case eventually led the judge to consider his testimony credible.[92]

A month after the trial, *Frankfurter Allgemeine*, the leading German daily, published Mesbahi's letter in which he refuted all the allegations made in his testimony, claiming that he had been promised a residency permit and financial support in return for his "evidence."[93] Similarly, the second witness in the court testimony, "Witness B," also refuted his confession about Iran's involvement.[94] The damage, however, had been done.

Following the Mykonos assassinations court verdict in April 1997, in which the Iranian government was judged to have "inspired, supported, and supervised" the terrorist act, Iran–German relations spiraled downward, and the years of concerted effort to strengthen relations were reversed. As a result, both countries recalled their ambassadors, ministerial-level cooperation was halted, the expulsion of diplomats by both sides began, the leading German firm Euler Hermes suspended insurance credit, and the "Critical Dialogue" process was suspended. The other European countries followed suit. Every member of the EU recalled its ambassador and, in a retaliatory move, Iran withdrew its ambassadors from all EU countries.[95] Relations with Europe deteriorated, leaving Iran feeling detached from the developed world. This was not what the government of Iran had sought.

The Supreme Leader, the President, and the SNSC had all been committed to the restoration of good relations with Europe, so it does not take a detective to deduce that the terrorist activities in Europe could not have been orchestrated by prominent Iranian politicians in charge. It would have been incomprehensible for Tehran, relentlessly pursuing an improvement in relations with the West under Rafsanjani, to jeopardize such important foreign policy objectives by seemingly mindless actions. While I was Iran's ambassador to Germany, I asked Schmidtbauer the following question: "How can one reconcile Iran's dedication to expanding relations with Germany with this terrorist act?" This line of argument and exchange had initially discouraged the Germans from issuing a subpoena on Iranian officials, but the Antwerp turned out to be the straw that broke the camel's back.

Chapter 5

THE RISE OF THE REFORM MOVEMENT IN IRAN: 1997–2005

Seyyed Mohammad Khatami emerged as Iran's first reformist President in the 1997 elections. His slogan during the campaign was "Freedom, Civil Society, and *Ghanoon Madaari*" (rule of law). With a crashing victory over the traditional right, Ali Akbar Nategh Nouri, the government's left faction, returned to power for the first time since their exit in 1988. But during the eight years leading up to this victory, the left had evolved. They no longer insisted on economic justice. Their focus was on political and, to a lesser extent, social liberties. Their vision coincided with Khatami's, a reformist who believed in a tolerant interpretation of Islam which conflicted with the right's traditional interpretation.

On May 23, 1997, Khatami was elected with approximately 70 percent of the votes in an election with an 80 percent turnout. This marked the genesis of the Iranian reform movement, also known as a "2nd of Khordad Movement", referring to the date of the elections in the Iranian calendar. Intellectuals, students, women, artists, and young middle- and upper-class urbanites fiercely supported Khatami. Political parties and organizations that supported Khatami's reform plans demanded changes aimed at greater freedom and democracy.

Interestingly, as had become customary by then, the United States grossly misunderstood Iran's politics. In a Congressional hearing just before Iran's presidential election, a top US Middle East expert, David Welch, presented this analysis:

> Iran's revolution continues to evolve. Periodically there are internal voices that are raised which criticize the regime's policies ... Unfortunately, those voices are not being given a serious opportunity for expression in next month's Presidential election in Iran. The candidates in that election share a common investment in the status quo and Iran's unacceptable policies.[1]

He later asserted that "We do not subscribe to the theory that there are emerging Iranian moderates. We do not subscribe to it today. We have not before." Richard Cottam, internationally recognized as an expert on Iran, had predicted the emergence of a very conservative figure, and the administration had informed the Congress just before the elections that it did not subscribe to the theory of emerging Iranian moderates.[2] Americans then watched with surprise the victory of a candidate who would later introduce the idea of a "Dialogue among Civilizations" in response to Samuel Huntington's influential "Clash of Civilizations."

In addition to Welch's analysis, not a single report or analysis of American think tanks, or even columnists writing for credible American newspapers, saw the reform movement approaching. The United States' chronic problem of misreading Iran manifested itself once again.

Returning to my personal story, it should be interesting that, upon completion of my mission in Germany and return to Tehran in 1997—a few months before the presidential elections—I decided to abandon the world of politics altogether. Events during my ambassadorship in Germany had worn me down. Every effort I had made to normalize the relations between Iran and Europe had been nullified by destructive events such as suspicious terrorist actions. At the end I felt that, as we say in Farsi, my efforts were nothing but "pestling water in a mortar [which can never be ground or crushed]." I set a new goal for myself: I would first study politics—quite distinct from the earlier degree in mechanical engineering—and then involve myself in research, writing, and teaching. So I entered the University of Tehran and started a Master's program in International Relations.

Soon thereafter, the ever dynamic Dr. Hassan Rouhani, then Secretary of the Supreme National Security Council, called and asked me to meet with him.

My relationship with Rouhani dates back to 1983 when I was head of the Majlis administrative department and he was Chairman of the Foreign Relations Committee of the Majlis and simultaneously Rafsanjani's deputy in the war against Iraq. Rouhani, a smart politician with a pronounced moderate persuasion, founded a group of MPs called "The Wise" or "The Prudents" to promote pragmatism in domestic and foreign policy, an objective I totally concurred with. Thirty years later, when he won the presidential election of 2013, he named his administration "Prudence and Hope."

During our meeting, he proposed that I should serve as his deputy in the SNSC Foreign Relations Committee. I informed him of my decision to leave politics and the reasons why. I failed to convince him that my decision was a good one and he insisted that I should accept the job because of my extensive background in foreign relations. I told him that I would accept the job, but only temporarily until such time that he could recruit/appoint somebody else.

He acquiesced, but there never turned out to be another candidate. I remained in that position for the next eight years, while also being a member and the spokesman of Iran's nuclear negotiating team during the 2003–5 period.

In this period I played a major role in the efforts to establish a new party called Hezbe Etedal va Tose'eh, or "Moderation and Development Party" led by Rouhani. The origin of Rouhani's school of thought—moderation—dates back to the early years of Khatami's presidency in the late nineties. Organized factionalism had begun to emerge within the establishment prompting Rafsanjani to voice his concern. He believed that the emergence of factional infighting would internally weaken the system (*nezam*), ultimately threatening its stability. Rafsanjani urged members of both camps, i.e., the Reformists and the Principlists, to unite and shape a new front under the banner of "Moderates." Pursuant to Rafsanjani's call, then-Deputy Foreign Minister Mahmoud Vaezi (Minister of Communication since August 2013), Member of Parliament Mohammad Bagher Nobakht (Vice President and the Head of Budget and Policy Planning of Iran since 2013), Deputy Minister of Culture Ali Jannati (Minister of Culture since 2013) and I met with Rafsanjani to materialize the initiative. Rafsanjani told us during that meeting: "Ruling the country with one faction would be a disaster and instead, all moderates within both major factions should unite and advance economic-political development to strengthen the pillars of the Islamic Republic." That meeting resulted in the birth of the "Moderation and Development Party." Rafsanjani endorsed Rouhani as the best candidate and in 1999, Rouhani headed the Party and chaired its Central Committee. During Ahmadinejad's presidency (2005–13), the Moderation and Development Party faced immense pressure from the opposite camp but it rose from ashes again with the emergence of Rouhani as Iran's President.

Meanwhile, I continued my doctoral studies at the University of Kent in the UK, graduating in 2002. It was the beginning of a new era in my life, but one that would later end under enormous stress and exasperation.

The Europeans Come Back

As discussed earlier, in the aftermath of the Mykonos court verdict in April 1997, diplomatic relations between Iran and the Western countries came to a complete halt. Two months later, Khatami won the election. His platform of liberalization and reform immediately raised debate and consideration by European countries about restoring their relations with Iran. We heard of this through their embassies' contact with the Iranian Ministry of Foreign Affairs. The SNSC discussed the new development and finally decided that Iran should respond positively before differences deepened.

The case was taken to the Supreme Leader, Ayatollah Khamenei, and he agreed, but on one condition: the German ambassador should be the last one to return to Iran. The Supreme Leader's single condition was conveyed to the Europeans, but they rejected it outright. Six months of discussion and negotiation between the Ministry of Foreign Affairs and the Europeans ensued before an acceptable solution could be found: the German and French ambassadors would be the last ambassadors to return and both would come to Tehran aboard the same plane. With this arrangement, Iran's condition was fulfilled, while the Europeans had not completely acquiesced with Iran's demand, which had been perceived as humiliating.

In the eyes of an outsider, the whole scenario might appear childish, but behind the scenes, the history of relations between Iran and the West, especially the United States, is full of similar episodes. Actions and words may sound irrational and immature, but this is how both sides have sought to save face and image and protect their status and value systems.

Does this prove the validity of Huntington's "Clash of Civilizations?"[3] Frankly, I do not think so. Despite the differences between a faction of society in Iran and their government, what the Iranians as a whole seek is international recognition of their right to live as an independent state. This vision and sentiment of independence is woven into Iranian culture, and its nature is more nationalistic than religious, although the dominant discourse in Iran portrays the contrary. Mohammad Mossadegh, the nationalist prime minister in the early 1950s, was not a cleric and was not driven by religious sentiments and beliefs. He hailed from an aristocratic family, had graduated from a Western [Swiss] university, wore ties, and was a true modernist. But Mossadegh and the popular movement that he led also rebelled against foreign domination. He wanted the country's independence, and the West punished him with a coup.

Ayatollah Khamenei's condition on the order of the return of European ambassadors intended to drive home the point that the West could not dictate and arbitrarily change the rules of the game without regard for Iranian pride. Conversely, Europe was determined not to let him impose his will on the powerful West. It is a struggle that still persists.

Khatami's Dialogue Initiative

Khatami was a scholar and a political thinker who believed in a tolerant interpretation of Islam, as opposed to the hard-line and traditional interpretation. His priority, as far as foreign policy was concerned, was to seek better relations with the West, but based on mutual respect and interest. Khatami did not want an unbalanced and disrespectful relationship, a relationship in which, as we say in Farsi, the West would talk to Iran from a superior position. This deeply felt sentiment, as mentioned in a number of occasions previously, has bedeviled the relations between Iran and the West, and to a greater extent, between Iran and the US, regardless of which Iranian president with what tendency has been in power. They have all coveted a balanced relationship and rejected a patron–client relationship.

In my first meeting in 1997 as the head of the SNSC Foreign Relations Committee of the SNSC, Khatami told me:

> I am glad that you accepted to lead the Foreign Relations Committee of the SNSC. I need your help advancing a moderate foreign policy. My first idea was to have you as the second man of the Foreign Ministry. But I doubted whether my reformist friends, now nominated as deputy foreign ministers, would cooperate with you. We are now faced with the same problem encountered by Rafsanjani. The Supreme Leader wants America to be excluded from the agenda of direct negotiations with the West aimed at establishing friendly relations.
>
> Due to his mistrust toward the US, the Supreme Leader argues that we should first see clear signs of change in America's hostile policies before outstretching our hands toward the Americans. In his eyes, seeking reconciliation with the US before ensuring that their enmity has changed to a real desire for a mutual, respectful relationship, would ultimately end in Iran's humiliation and would be interpreted as our weakness and our fear of the Americans.

He also maintains that as we have repeatedly experienced when Americans come forward, they always hide a dagger behind them. Although I believe the US should change its behavior and show its goodwill by actions rather than words, I prefer to convey our opinion and intention of seeking friendly relations to the American people rather than using rhetoric. In this respect I am confident having you as deputy to Dr. Rouhani, we would be able to improve our foreign relations with all countries including the West and hopefully the US.

Khatami, not as pessimistic as the Supreme Leader, argued that in order to improve relations with the US, we should first crack the thick wall of mistrust that had been built between Iran and the US. He took a bold step to achieve this. A few months after his election, Khatami held his historic interview with Christiane Amanpour from CNN.

In this interview, he skillfully presented his views and the trajectory that he intended to follow in his foreign policy:

> I respect the American nation because of their great civilization. This respect is due to two reasons: the essence and pillars of the Anglo-American civilization and [to facilitate] the dialogue among the civilizations ... We feel that what we seek is what the founders of the American civilization were also pursuing four centuries ago. This is why we sense an intellectual affinity with the essence of the American civilization.[4]

But Khatami was concerned about the new thesis of the "Clash of Civilizations," which had become popular in the US political arena. In Iran, it was widely thought that this thesis could potentially give rise to conflict between the Islamic world and the West. In his interview with CNN,[5] Khatami dealt with the issue:

> One of the major flaws in the US foreign policy ... is that they continue to live with [a] Cold War mentality and try to create a perceived enemy ... After the collapse of communism, there has been an attempt by certain circles to portray Islam as the new enemy, and regrettably they are targeting progressive Islam rather than certain regressive interpretations of Islam.

It is true that Huntington, as one of the principal proponents of this school of thought, did not argue that conflict between Islam and the West was inevitable, but there were elements in his theory that could be misinterpreted or misunderstood, thus justifying a conflict between the two civilizations.

Huntington argued that "Islam's borders are bloody"[6] and warned that "the continuing and deeply conflictual relation between Islam and Christianity" will dwarf the "conflict between liberal democracy and Marxism-Leninism."[7] In addition, in a striking generalization, he asserted that "the underlying problem for the West is not Islamic fundamentalism, it is Islam..."[8] This was a controversial assertion which made little distinction between Khatami's interpretation of Islam and Bin Laden's.

That said, less attention was paid to that part of Huntington's theory regarding universalism: "Western belief in the universality of Western culture ... is false ... and it is dangerous. That it is false has been the central thesis of this book."[9] Huntington's argument against the "West" attempting to force its values on the "rest" is realistic and valuable. Specifically, with respect to Muslim countries, what the "West" sees as modernity is often at variance with many Muslims' views. Surprisingly, Huntington's stand against the West's struggle for cultural hegemony and his non-interventionist analysis on universalism is seldom referred to in Iran.

Khatami's plausible fear was that a *deterministic interpretation* of Huntington's theory regarding a clash between Islam and the "West" being inevitable could inadvertently spark the West's fear and hatred of Islam. Meanwhile, the same deterministic interpretation could be used to justify the violent actions of Islamic extremists against the "West" in Muslim societies. When it came to Iran, the real danger was that policy-makers in the West, led by the US, would take the inevitability of a clash theory to heart, abandon any efforts at reconciliation with Iran, and instead adopt an inflexible, hostile position. This would only strengthen radicalism in Iran, which was fiercely opposed to any rapprochement with the US. In fact, the ascendancy in Iran of radical conservatives in 2005, represented by Mahmoud Ahmadinejad, was primarily a reaction to George W. Bush's treatment of Iran.

After the tragic events of September 11, 2001, Bernard Lewis, the British-American thinker who coined the concept and the term "Clash of Civilizations," was invited to the White House to brief the administration on "Why Muslims hate us."[10] His explanation of the "Clash of Civilizations," that is, unaviodable conflict between two mutually exclusive worldviews, was clearly reflected in the new discourse that President George W. Bush adopted towards Iran. By including Iran in the "Axis of Evil," the US President transformed the conflict between the US and Iran into a clash between good and evil, which logically could only end with the annihilation of one side by the other.

Because of Ayatollah Khamenei's deep mistrust of the US, and thus his objection to the normalization of relations with the Americans, Khatami sought to normalize Iran's relations with the US through his newly developed thesis of "Dialogue among Civilizations." In his interview with Amanpour he expanded on the idea:

> ... nothing should prevent dialogue and understanding between two nations ... right now, I recommend the exchange of professors, writers, scholars, artists, journalists, and tourists. But the dialogue between civilizations and nations is different from political relations. There is a bulky wall of mistrust between us and the US Administration ... there must first be a crack in this wall of mistrust to prepare for a change ...

The following pages describe how a combination of complex activities and plans by forces who fiercely opposed the normalization of relations between Iran and the US, profound mutual mistrust between the two states, the uncompromising and hostile policies of the US toward Khatami's reformist government, and misperceptions of the policy-makers of Iran and the United States caused the defeat of Khatami's Dialogue project.

Bill Clinton and his Confusing Signals

Between 1997 and 2000, when Khatami and Clinton were both in office, the US pursued a push and pull policy, with offers of reconciliation followed shortly thereafter by hostile postures, pronouncements and actions. Iran did not understand this approach and found it exceedingly confusing.

The 1996 Khobar bombings in Saudi Arabia, which happened during the presidency of Rafsanjani, had a detrimental effect on the détente policies that he and Khatami pursued. The US blaming of Iran for this episode, which seemed to follow a familiar pattern in the eyes of Tehran, bolstered the claim of hardliners that the West was only interested in pursuing regime change. On the US side, a terrorist attack that had resulted in the death of 19 Americans and wounded hundreds could not be taken lightly.

US policy towards Iran was effectively taken hostage by the Khobar bombings. This event was a major reason that a unique opportunity to end the atmosphere of hostility—the concurrent presidencies of Clinton, who sought to open the door to Iran–US relations, and Khatami, who came to power with an agenda to ease tensions between the two states—was missed.

In April 1999, Bill Clinton stunned us. At an event at the White House, he admitted that Iran "has been the subject of quite a lot of abuse from various Western nations." He continued: "I think sometimes it's quite important to tell people, 'Look, you have a right to be angry at something my country or my culture or others that are generally allied with us today did to you 50 or 60 or 100 or 150 years ago.'"[11] This sounded like an apology and raised hopes in Khatami's moderate administration of a genuine effort by the Clinton administration to improve relations.

Reflecting on the evolving situation at the time, Rouhani agreed with my suggestion that a comprehensive package aimed at removing the tension and hostility between Iran and the US be developed in the SNSC Foreign Relations Committee. In my capacity as head of the Committee, of the SNSC, I organized a series of discussions on Iran–US relations that culminated in the details of the package.

The package covered the spheres of civilian diplomacy such as culture, science, tourism, academia, and the economy, and specifically, made provisions for the opening of a US Interests Section in Tehran, similar to the Iranian interest section in Washington, DC. Moreover, the package included a political component that would pave the way for parliamentary-level dialogue between the US and Iran. This unprecedented set of proposals marked a significant move towards transforming relations between Iran and the US. The package, however, did not live long.

In August 1999, President Clinton's letter to Khatami was relayed through the government of Oman.[12] The US President addressed Khatami in a cordial tone but then went on to claim that the IRGC (Revolutionary Guards), along with certain Saudis and Lebanese, "were directly involved in the planning and execution" of the Khobar bombings. Clinton asked Khatami for "a clear commitment" to "ensure an end to Iranian involvement" in terrorist activities and to "bring those in Iran responsible for the bombing to justice either in Iran or by extraditing them to Saudi Arabia."

The letter produced a negative reaction within Iran's policy circles, Khatami himself included. While Clinton intended it as an olive branch, radicals in Iran believed that it was an attempt to widen the differences between Khatami and the Leadership, and to test Khatami's will and his ability to stand against the IRGC and the Leadership by responding positively to Clinton's letter.

Clinton's timing could not have been worse. Tehran had just witnessed the most severe street protests in 18 years, since MEK had resorted to an armed struggle against the government in 1981. Khatami's priority was to calm down the domestic political environment. He was not prepared to create more tension by responding positively to Clinton's letter. He also did not believe that the Khobar bombing was the work of Iranians. Bin Laden had every motive and also the operational capability to carry out that attack. Additionally, Clinton's letter placed the Iranian administration in a difficult position as there were no suspects to hand over. Clinton should have put himself in Khatami's shoes. What was Khatami expected to do, simply based on accusations by the US? Let us not forget that the "wall of mistrust" was applicable to Khatami, too. In fact, the letter further strengthened the notion that these pulls and pushes by the US were ultimately aimed at furthering traditional US objectives in Iran.

Simultaneously with the receipt of Clinton's letter, we had already completed the preparation of the comprehensive package at the SNSC Committee. It was ready to be sent to the Office of the Supreme Leader. The US President's letter completely derailed the process. The efforts of Khatami and his followers to initiate real change in the relationship between America and Iran failed tragically because of miscommunication.

I have also drawn attention previously to the chronic problem of mutual misunderstanding between the two countries; Tehran's general lack of understanding of US politics, and Washington's lack of understanding of politics in Iran. Most of those on the Iranian side did not appreciate that even if Clinton sincerely intended to re-establish relations with Iran, he could not ignore the adverse pressure from Congress and the FBI's assertion that Iran was responsible for the bombing in Saudi Arabia. Louis Freeh, then the FBI Director, describes in his 2012 memoir how the Clinton administration sought to prevent the FBI from making the accusation. Freeh was contemptuous of the White House efforts to "save" Iran:

> [The] White House ... ordered us to stop the practice. Not a good idea, I told Madeleine Albright, who had succeeded Warren Christopher as secretary of state. 'The Iranians are complaining,' she

responded. 'Of course, they are,' I told her. 'That's the point.' … By then, I was used to it."[13]

The administration also faced similar difficulty with the Congress. As reported in a *New York Times* column in December 1999, "Although it [the administration] would like to re-establish some relations with Iran, the administration faces strong anti-Iranian sentiment in Congress."[14]

Tehran failed to see the similarity between the constraints faced by the US government and themselves. Even though the Supreme Leader had authority over the government, during Khatami's tenure the breadth of public support for the reformist President's policies was a major reason for Ayatollah Khamenei supporting Khatami. For instance, a few years later, he reluctantly accepted the government's confidence-building measures towards the US and the West, including the sensitive issue of cooperation with America in the "war on terror" in Afghanistan.

The leadership was confused. Had Iranians been realistic, Khatami could have answered the letter, explaining why he thought Al-Qaeda was involved, and not Iran. He could have offered Iran's cooperation in the investigations. Instead, everybody's mind was made up that the letter was another conspiracy or, at best, an insult. Due to a lack of understanding of the dynamics of the US political system and due to miscommunication, Clinton's letter was rejected in its entirety, and instead of a personal response from Khatami, the *government* as a whole responded to Clinton, the key sentence of the letter reading: "Such allegations are fabricated solely by those whose illegitimate objectives are jeopardized by stability and security in the region."[15]

Iran Prepares to Attack Afghanistan

The Taliban were Afghan students who studied in Pakistan's *Madrassas* (Islamic schools/seminaries). In these schools, young Afghans—poor, deprived and many of them orphans—received an ultra-orthodox Islamic education which was handled and managed by an extremist Islamic organization called *Jamiat-Ulama-e-Islam* (The Association of the Islamic Ulema/Learned).

Young Afghans who were trained in these schools were totally disconnected from the outside world. They saw the world around them through a filter of an extremist interpretation of Islam. Modernity and reform in religion was considered as heresy—a great sin. There was to be no television, no newspapers, no music or entertainment ... nothing. These homeless youth were living, learning, and growing up in these *Madrassas* and all they were taught was an interpretation of Islam which unquestionably believed that "jihad" was the only way to deal with the "infidels." The *Madrassas* would give them three meals a day, a place to sleep, blankets, and clothes. A huge budget had to be allocated for educating thousands of students in these *Madrassas*, but how? Pakistan, under Zia-ul-Haq and Benazir Bhutto, was so poor that it had to seek help from richer countries—widely believed to have been provided by Saudi Arabia and other oil-rich emirates in the Persian Gulf.

In 1992, Islamic groups overthrew Najibollah's Communist government and captured Kabul. There was no word about the Taliban up to that point. They were not part of the resistance movement and no one heard about them during the war against the Soviets. In 1994, lawlessness, chaos, and civil war swept across Afghanistan. People were killed and homes were destroyed. Thousands were left homeless and hungry. People who were tired of 20 years of unrest and war were looking for someone, a God-sent hero perhaps, to restore law and order. After 300 years, the Pashtun tribe had lost control of Kabul. Uzbeks and Tajiks, historically the Pashtuns' rivals, now controlled the capital.

In 1994, a small group of Taliban who were ethnically Pashtun, led by a Mullah named Muhammad Omar from a village near Kandahar, appeared out of nowhere. Omar had lost one eye during the resistance against the Soviets. Within two years, the Taliban grew into a military force, with tens of thousands of fighters. By 1996 they were moving in waves from south of Afghanistan to the north. In September 1996, Kabul fell and one of the most violent Islamic groups in Afghanistan seized power. Schools were closed. Girls and women were banned from work outside of the home. Sports, entertainment, or any symbol of joy and celebration, were considered a sin. Life froze in Afghanistan.

In August 1998, the Taliban stormed Mazar Sharif, a city in northern Afghanistan which was one of the strongholds of the Afghan Northern Alliance, supported by Iran. The Taliban, also sworn enemies of the Shias, carried out a massacre, mainly targeting the Hazaras, a Shia Persian-speaking ethnic group. During the mass murders, they attacked the Iranian consulate in Mazar Sharif, capturing and killing nine Iranians, eight of them diplomats.

The killings in Mazar Sharif prompted serious, even fierce, debate within the SNSC possible Iranian response options, including a military invasion of Afghanistan to root out the Taliban. The majority of the SNSC were positive about military action, and the decision was taken to call up 100,000 troops to assemble on the border with Afghanistan. Rouhani, then Secretary of the SNSC, and some others including myself, were in the minority group that argued against military intervention in Afghanistan. We did not want Iran to initiate a war against any of its neighbors, particularly as the Taliban did not represent the nation of Afghanistan, or *any* single nation. The supporters of the attack surmised that the Taliban and al-Qaeda jointly posed a serious threat to the security of Iran and the region.

The situation was extremely dangerous. With a significant military mobilization along the Afghanistan borders, we were one step away from engaging in what might be a long and bloody war. Ultimately, the final report on this situation was sent to the Supreme Leader. Based on my experience and the past established trend, I expected the Supreme Leader to express consent with the SNSC recommendation. However, in a historic decision, he ruled against military intervention in Afghanistan. Thanks to him, a bloody war was averted. Ironically, a few years later, we collaborated with the US, perceived by many in the Iranian system (*nezam*) to be our arch enemy, in toppling the brutal and fanatical Taliban.

The decision not to go to war against the Taliban and our later cooperation with the US in overthrowing them demonstrates that Iran's foreign policy is not driven purely by religious beliefs and/or sentiments. Numerous examples illustrate the fact that pragmatism clearly supersedes ideology.

Albright makes "The Boldest Attempt"

On March 17, 2000, a few days before the Iranian New Year, Secretary of State Madeleine Albright made an unprecedented, major overture to Tehran. Frankly, I have to admit that when I learned about the contents of her speech, I was impressed. The *Washington Post* rightfully called it "the boldest attempt yet by the Clinton administration" to foster better relations between Iran and the US.[16] I would go even further and describe it as the boldest attempt up to this date by the US government, in Albright's words "to plant the seeds of a new relationship" between Iran and the United States.

She began by "wishing all Iranian-Americans a Happy New Year," and said in Persian, of course with an American accent,

"Eid-e-shuma-Mubarak," meaning, "Happy New Year to You." The speech contained three significant elements. First, Albright did not explicitly apologize, but admitted that "in 1953 the United States played a significant role in orchestrating the overthrow of Iran's popular Prime Minister, Mohammed Mossadegh." She also acknowledged that "it is easy to see … why many Iranians continue to resent this intervention by America in their internal affairs."[17]

Second, Albright went on to recognize that "during the next quarter century" following the coup, the United States and the West gave sustained backing to the Shah's regime, which, "brutally repressed political dissent." And last, but not least, she quoted President Clinton, restating that "the United States must bear its fair share of responsibility for the problems that have arisen in Iranian–US relations." Mrs. Albright condemned "aspects of US policy towards Iraq, during its conflict with Iran," and characterized them "regrettably shortsighted." Albright concluded with the following hopeful appeal: "[O]n behalf of the government and the people of the United States, I call upon Iran to join us in writing a new chapter in our shared history."

After learning about the speech, I ran to Hassan Rouhani's office. I told him that based on the conciliatory tone and spirit of the speech, we could conclude that in essence the US government had apologized in front of the world for its misbehavior towards Iran in the last half a century and was saying: "Let's fix it." I suggested: "If I were a decision-maker, I would declare a national celebration and would take the opportunity to launch direct talks with the US to overcome two decades of hostilities." Rouhani agreed that this was an opportunity that we should not miss, but he was skeptical about the Supreme Leader's reaction because of the negative part of Albright's speech. Later, I said exactly the same thing to Foreign Minister Kamal Kharrazi, which he agreed with. President Khatami also shared this opinion during my subsequent private exchanges with him. We all saw the glass half full.

However, conscious of the sensitivities of the Iranian political system in general, and the fact that at that particular juncture tensions between the conservative camp and the reformists were on the rise, my fear was that some of Albright "negative" comments could overshadow the overall positive tone of her speech. At one point Albright had said that "[the US government's] grim view towards Iran is reinforced by the Iranian Government's repression at home." She had also condemned Iran's efforts to acquire nuclear weapons and its continued terrorist activities, adding that "until these policies change, fully normal ties between our governments will not be possible, and our principal sanctions will remain."

But the straw that broke the camel's back was her assertion that "despite the trend towards democracy, control over the military, judiciary, courts and police remains in unelected hands." This part of her speech was clearly directed at Ayatollah Khamenei. For Khatami and the reform movement, Albright's message could be interpreted as "We accept Khatami and the reform movement, but we don't accept the Supreme Leader and institutions under his control."

Albright's negative tone could be understandable in peculiar US political context. Any high-ranking official in the US administration, including the President, would have their own constraints when talking about Iran. For better or for worse, they simply cannot entirely disregard the Congress, which is historically pro-Israel, as well as pressure groups and lobby groups within the American political system. However, challenging the Supreme Leader was a strategic mistake.

The issue of human rights, even if pursued in a somewhat inconsistent and discriminatory manner,[18] also happens to be one of the major elements in the US foreign policy and the pronouncements of US high-ranking officials—especially when it comes to "unfriendly" state. In her speech, Albright clearly revealed the differences between the administration and the Congress with regards to Iran:

> In fact, Congress is now considering legislation that would mandate the attachment of Iranian diplomatic and other assets as compensation for acts of terrorism committed against American citizens. We are working with Congress to find a solution that will satisfy the demands of justice without setting a precedent ... that would destroy prospects for a successful dialogue with Iran.

When Albright delivered her speech, we were already one and a half years into Khatami's presidency. Unlike Rafsanjani's period in office, which was marred by some unfortunate events such as assassinations and the Antwerp affair, Khatami's presidency had witnessed no such incidents, and the rogue cell within the Ministry of Intelligence and National Security had been dismantled after the exposure of serial killings of dissident intellectuals. So Iran did not expect the controversial issue of human rights to be raised at that juncture.

While the "unelected" allusion could be interpreted as a US attempt to marginalize the Supreme Leader, and support for Khatami as an attempt to create a wedge within the system (*nezam*), the comment is in fact not accurate. Based on the Iranian Constitution, the Iranian people elect the members of the Assembly of Experts who, in turn, elect the Supreme Leader. In many European and other democratic countries, people elect the members of parliament who will then elect the chancellor or prime minister. Direct elections for the 86 members of the Assembly are held every eight years and are next due in March 2016.

In fact, the body generally criticized for its "unelected" nature and conduct is the Guardian Council, which is composed of 12 members: six experts Islamic jurisprudence (Mujtahids) appointed by the Supreme Leader himself, and another six jurists/lawyers (with expertise in constitutional law) who are elected by the *Majlis* from among the candidates nominated by the Chief of the Judiciary (who is, in turn, appointed by the Supreme Leader). The Council enjoys wide-ranging legislative and electoral authority. It must approve all bills passed by the *Majlis*, has the power to veto bills, interprets the Constitution, and is in charge of vetting all candidates for presidency, *Majlis* as well as the Assembly of Experts. The entirely unelected Expediency Council—whose members are appointed by the Supreme Leader and has been chaired by Ayatollah Heshemi Rafsanjani since its establishment in 1989—is in charge of exercising general supervisory power over the three branches of government and, in particular, resolving differences or disputes between the *Majlis* and the Guardian Council.

Aside from the reference to the so-called unelected bodies in the Iranian power structure, the problem with Secretary Albright's statement was not simply that it could be denounced as an unwarranted interference in the country's internal affairs. Rather, the bigger and the more urgent problem was that it could be manipulated by the radical faction of the reform movement as a means of taking control of Iran's foreign policy. A few days later, an influential organization within the radical faction of the reform movement, the Organization of the Mujahideen of the Islamic Revolution of Iran, referred to Albright's speech as "a kind of victory and an achievement for … Khatami's government." Supporting direct talks with the US, the Organization also asked foreign-policy-makers of Iran "to carry out a logical, calculated and wise analysis of the changes that have come about in American stances and policies."[19]

Ayatollah Khamenei, however, furiously reacted to the speech, noting the three key elements already referred to:

[M]ore than 40 years have elapsed since ... the coup d'état. It is only now that they are admitting that they were behind the coup d'état. They admit that they supported and backed the dictatorial, oppressive, corrupt and subservient regime of the Shah for 25 years. And they are now saying that they supported Saddam Hussein in his war against Iran."[20]

Rejecting the US government's overture, the Iranian Supreme Leader added:

It is not as if some people can approach America in the hope of starting a dialogue. America's animosity will not be resolved through negotiations. America is only pursuing its own interests in Iran. If ... an independent government manages Iran, then America would act with hostility towards it [anyway].

Many Western experts posit that anti-Americanism is one of the pillars that sustains the Islamic Republic of Iran. However, the reality is more complex. It is true that Iran uses hostility towards the US whenever convenient and/or necessary—as all states do in their foreign relations with the outside world—but, as discussed previously, the negative outlook and posture of the current Iranian leadership towards the US are rooted in two intimately-related and mutually-reinforcing factors: first, because of the systematic belligerent policy towards the Islamic Republic since its inception, and second, deep mistrust of the US. At the end of the day, Secretary Albright's seemingly positive overture to Iran, once negatively perceived by Iranians because of its critical elements, marked another missed opportunity for the two sides to move in the direction of reconciliation and detente.

The Rationale for the Ayatollah's Emphatic NO

What is presented here reflects my 25-year experience of Ayatollah Khamenei, including meetings with him and discussions with many of the high-ranking officials in Iran, including former Presidents Rafsanjani and Khatami, SNSC members, ministers, and ranking religious figures.

In the mid-1980s, when I was editor-in-chief of the *Tehran Times*, a group of newspaper staff and I met with Ayatollah Khamenei, President at the time. During our discussions, a question was raised seeking his opinion about relations with the United States. The Ayatollah expressed the view that we could ultimately normalize our relations based on mutual respect and non interference. Over time, and in view of US reactions to Iranian overtures, he became much more skeptical, apparently out of the concern that the ultimate US goal was regime change in Iran.

The fact that the Supreme Leader is unquestionably the most powerful figure in Iranian politics does not mean that he is immune to the influence of other forces operating in a complex, frequently changing system of conflicting political and social-cultural factions and currents. Iran has a rare political and social structure which is shaped by two popular opposing camps: modernists and traditionalists. These forces shape a clash between two civilizations *within* a civilization.

Four major, interrelated elements shape Ayatollah Khamenei's perception of the US. First, he wholeheartedly believes that regardless of all the ups and downs, pushes and pulls between Iran and the US, Washington's ultimate intention is to topple Iran's Islamic system and replace it with client state, as it did during the Shah's era after the 1953 coup. Ayatollah Khamenei maintains that the US, no matter which school of thought and party is in power or which president is in office in Tehan, intends to "wipe out the Islamic Republic" with all possible means at its disposal. The conclusion he draws from the US rhetoric, policies, and behavior is that the US will not relent in its desire for regime change unless the current government surrenders its principles, religious beliefs, political structure, and independence.

The United States' less-than-tacit support for Saddam Hussein's aggression against Iran and subsequent provision of material and logistical support, covert operations, open support for the opposition groups (including budgetary allocations), fierce opposition to Iran's enjoyment of the right to peaceful nuclear activities under the NPT, and its intrusive and paralyzing economic sanctions are all viewed by the Ayatollah as clear evidence of the US ultimate objective—"regime change".

The second element that shapes Ayatollah Khamenei's disposition towards the US is his firm belief that the US foreign policy in the Middle East, and specifically regarding Iran, is overwhelmingly dominated by the pro-Israel lobby. From his point of view, even the President of the United States does not have any authority over US foreign policy. It is a matter of surprise for him that every year the President and other high officials of the most powerful country on earth attend American Israel

Public Affairs Committee (AIPAC) gatherings and, worse still, report on their anti-Iranian policies and actions. Although there is in general a consensus within the system (*nezam*) about Israel's influence on US Middle East policy, some argue that it is the Zionists who direct the US foreign policy, and not the other way round.

The third element concerns his Supreme Leader's perception of the US is his extreme mistrust of American politics. The documents confiscated by students after seizing the US Embassy seemed to justify such a stance by many high-ranking Iranian politicians, including Ayatollah Khamenei. According to those documents, the Embassy was involved in espionage and fostering covert links with members of the new government and the armed forces.

Finally, Ayatollah Khamenei sees the American government and the system it represents as addicted to arrogance and hegemony. He feels that the US is only prepared to accept a "lord–serf" relationship with the other countries not considered a so-called "great power."

Aside from the negative outlook of the Supreme Leader—as just discussed—foreign analysts generally tend to believe that the Iranian system is solely driven by a religious impetus. That assessment is incorrect. As indicated in a number of instances previously, underneath the outward layers of religiosity, Iranians are deeply nationalistic. They see themselves as a great country, widely acclaimed as a "cradle of history," rich in culture and history dating back thousands of years, and also known for its contributions to the world in such varied fields as science, medicine, astronomy, mathematics, art, and music. All of these attributes lend themselves to a deep-seated and cherished sense of nationalism among Iranians of all walks of life.

So, when Congress or the US administration attempt to bully Iran using threats and intimidation, or try to humiliate the Iranian government by endless repetition of the "all options on the table" mantra and other similar rhetoric, Iran's strong sense of national pride is offended. Such an outlook and behavior on the part of the Americans only serve to strengthen and deepen the Ayatollah's negative view.

However, despite Ayatollah Khamenei's distrust and pessimistic view, Rafsanjani and Khatami clearly espoused reconciliation with the US. Rafsanjani fought hard to attain this objective and "emphasized that the resumption of relations with Washington 'would not be in contradiction with Iran's objectives' if American policies were 'truly corrected.'"[21] Such efforts and overtures by both Rafsanjani and Khatami have already been laid out in relative detail.

Some might argue that the overtures by Rafsanjani and Khatami meant little because the Supreme Leader could veto them. But that's pure conjecture. Both Presidents believed that if they could find a way to reduce the level of mistrust by encouraging the US to make some friendly moves, Ayatollah Khamenei would also demonstrate some flexibility. As a matter of fact, the Ayatollah, although reluctant and pessimistic, did not block those efforts at rapprochement. In fact, he continues to emphasize that he has never said that relations with the US will remain severed forever.[22]

But in practical terms, Ayatollah Khamenei argues that the US goal of engaging in talks with Iran is not motivated by a desire to resolve problems and disputes between the two countries. He feels that the US approaches such talks with the mentality to twist arms, threaten, intimidate, and ultimately withdraw, if they felt that Iran was not prepared to concede the upper hand to them. He is also concerned that America's powerful media would make the situation even worse, humiliating the Revolution and Iranians, thus damaging Iran's image and stature as the leading anti-imperialist country in the Muslim world. He therefore posits that if Iran cannot be 100 percent certain that the US position has changed, it must not risk humiliation in "bilateral" talks, the outcome of which might have been determined in advance.

Another element in the Ayatollah's negative perception concerns the security analyses that restoration of relations with the US might simply provide an opportunity for the American intelligence to infiltrate Iran—a perception created by the 1953 coup and further supported by the documents seized in November 1979 at the US Embassy. In his own words, back in a 2008 public statement, "The US waged war against Iraq while Washington had diplomatic ties with Baghdad, secondly diplomatic ties with the US would pave the way for the infiltration of US spies into the country, so diplomatic relations with Washington would not be useful to the Iranian nation."[23]

One of the less obvious hurdles to the normalization of relations between Iran and the US, in my opinion, may be the issue of "cultural intrusion" or *tahajome farhangi*, as Ayatollah Khamenei puts it. A large segment conservatives in Iran, including grassroots supporters of the institution of *velayat-e faqih* ("Guardianship of the Jurisconsult")—symbolized and represented by the person of the Supreme Leader—harbor deep feelings of animosity towards what they perceive as alien, Western or liberal social, political and moral values. They consider their religious values and beliefs to be in conflict with the Western culture that permits sexual freedom, consumption of alcohol, women wearing revealing clothes, and the separation of church (religion) and state. In addition, Ayatollah Khamenei, and his devout followers, believe that the US—West in general—promote, as a matter of deliberate policy, liberal values among the Iranian young, both to erode their religious beliefs and ultimately to undermine the influence of the current religious system.

The Iranian ruling elite, including the Supreme Leader, have no doubt that numerous Persian television stations, primarily in the United States, are directly or indirectly sponsored by the US government as a major channel of cultural aggression against the Iranian society. This notion was reinforced by the allocation of $75 million in the US 2007 budget to expand radio and television broadcasts in Iran, an action that stirred anger among Iran's conservatives.

Some argue that hostile reactions to US cultural intrusion by the ruling elite in Iran are part of a "Cold War" strategy, primarily relating to power rather than religious motives. The reality is that apart from Ayatollah Khomeini, the Leader of the 1979 Revolution, and a limited circle of his followers, the vast majority of the clergy in Iran had been apolitical until the mid-1970s, neither opposing nor supporting the Shah openly. However, the majority of the clergy eventually joined the revolutionary movement, mostly out of resentment towards what they perceived as moral-cultural decadence of the Iranian society as a result of the Shah's Westernization program.

While the Supreme Leader does not object to people-to-people relations between the two countries, some ultra-conservatives currents and quarters in the Iranian society do not even agree with such a limited level of relations. In their view, such relations will result in the expansion of trade and commerce and thus in a greater number of Iranians visiting the US and vice versa. The outcome of such exchanges, they argue, could be the rise of Westoxicated technocrats as an influential force in the future of the society, ultimately challenging the existing authority. Nonetheless, the Leader has no objection to people-to-people relations.

9/11: The End of a Short-lived Honeymoon

George W. Bush began his presidency with a controversial dispute over election results and it ended with the quagmires that he and his administration created for the US government in both Afghanistan and Iraq, as well as the financial crisis that also occurred under his watch. When Bush took office, nobody in Tehran knew what the future held for Iran and the world. In fact, the prevailing opinion was that we would see another pragmatic Bush and that there might be the possibility of reducing tension during his presidency. At the time, Iran's Parliament (Majlis) and the Executive Branch were dominated by reformists who would have embraced an improvement in relations with the US.

The first positive sign came from Colin Powell who said in his confirmation hearing: "We have important differences on matters of policy [with Iran]. But these differences need not preclude greater interaction, whether in more normal commerce or increased dialogue."[24] Also, the Khobar bombing, a bone of centention since 1996, came to a closure. The US Attorney General pronounced in his final statement in 2001 that: "Iranian government inspired, supported, and supervised" the terrorist act, adding, however, "this indictment does not name as defendants individual members of the Iranian government."[25] Under the circumstances, the damage had been minimized.

The tragic events of September 11, 2001 appeared to have opened a new chapter in Iran–US relations. Iran was among the first countries to denounce the 9/11 Twin Tower terror attacks in New York. Immediately following the condemnation, the SNSC actively began to work within the new ambiance created by the September 11 terrorist attack and the subsequent US declaration of a "war on terror." We were also concerned with the extremist Salafis and the Taliban, whose ideologies we viewed as hostile towards Shia Iran and also dangerous to the broader region.

Prior to George W. Bush assuming the presidency, a round of talks between Iran and the US began in 1998 but it was not bilateral. The UN initiated the "6+2" forum for talks on the Afghan situation, chaired by the Algerian veteran diplomat, Lakhdar Brahimi, with the participation of the six neighbors of Afghanistan—China, Pakistan, Iran, Turkmenistan, Uzbekistan, and Tajikistan—along with Russia and the United States. The groups meetings were held in New York. But in 2001, before the 9/11 attacks, and more seriously after the tragic events, there began substantive, behind-the-scenes talks between the Iranian and US governments, seeking avenues of cooperation on Afghanistan.

Ambassador Ryan Crocker, who had lived in Iran before and knew Persian, led the US team in these talks. The Iranian team consisted of ambassadors Reza Ziaran, Zargar Yaghoobi, and Mohammad Ebrahim Taherian and a member of the security establishment responsible for Afghanistan. I did not attend the meetings but was involved, as head of the SNSC Foreign Relations Committee, in crafting the framework for Iran's cooperation with the US. Meetings were held in Geneva and Paris while both parties had agreed to include German and Italian representatives in the meetings. The presence of these representatives was precautionary. In the event the meetings were leaked to the media, both Iran and the US could deny direct contacts between them. Later, the Germans and Italians disappeared and talks became one-on-one.

The meetings covered a host of issues from terrorism to drug trafficking, and even casual talks about historical issues between the two countries. Aside from the subject matter of these meetings, of even greater significance was that the two governments were talking to each other for the first time since the mid-1980, when the Iran–Contra scandal abruptly halted such a communication/such an exchange. The talks were not hidden from Ayatollah Khamenei and he did not pronounce/express an objection, provided that they were focused on Afghanistan and not Iran–US relations.

We were pursuing two objectives. First, we sought ways to unseat the Taliban and eliminate extremist terrorists, namely Al-Qaeda. Both of these groups—arch enemies of Iran and the Shia—were nestled in Afghanistan, and both were arch enemies of Shias and the government of Iran. Second, we wanted to look for ways to test cooperation with the Americans, thus decreasing the level of mistrust and tension between us. During these meetings, neither party pursued the subject of Iran–US relations. Nonetheless, we did the groundwork for significant, mutual cooperation on Afghanistan during these meetings, resulting in Iran's assistance during the attack on the Taliban. Crocker describes the atmosphere of those talks as follows:

> During those pre-attack discussions—and you'll remember the air war began in early October—the Iranian thrust was, you know, what do you need to know to knock their blocks off? You want their order of battle? Here's the map. You want to know where we think their weak points are? Here, here, and here. You want to know how we think they're going to react to an air campaign? Do you want to know how we think the Northern Alliance will behave? Ask us. We've got the answers; we've been working with those guys for years. This was an unprecedented period since the revolution of, again, a US–Iranian dialogue on a particular issue where we very much had common interest and common cause."[26]

In those meetings, the Iranian delegation promised to capture any Al-Qaeda and Taliban members who fled to Iran in the case of an invasion by the US. They also promised assistance in planning the attack, and provision of information about the Afghan society, including the roles and capabilities of different political and ethnic groups. Most importantly, the Iranian delegation promised the full cooperation of their Afghan ally, the Northern Alliance [Officially "The United Islamic Front for the Salvation of Afghanistan"] in bringing down the Taliban and rooting out the Al-Qaeda terrorism.

The IRGC (Revolutionary Guards) was actively involved in organizing the attack by the Northern Alliance to free Herat, the third largest city in Afghanistan, from the Taliban rule, and also played a role in the capture of Kabul before any American troops had arrived.

After the fall of the Taliban, Iran arrested and extradited approximately 500 Al-Qaeda members to their respective countries. Meanwhile, a parallel team started to work with the Americans in a UN-sponsored framework to create a post-Taliban government for Afghanistan. This time, the American delegation was led by Ambassador James Dobbins and the Iranian team was led by Ambassador Javad Zarif, then Deputy Foreign Minister. Javad, a close friend of mine, is one of the savviest diplomats that Iran has ever had. Zarif and Dobbins met every day before the Bonn Conference to make sure that Is were dotted and Ts were crossed. The Conference, however, proceeded quite differently than anticipated. Disputes between Afghan warlords over the distribution of ministerial positions nearly brought the Conference to a collapse.

During a fall 2012 conference in Berlin, James Dobbins told me that Hamid Karzai was the United States' favored candidate to lead the new Afghan government. "Iranians also supported us," Dobbins said. Dobbins highlighted the role of Javad Zarif in the success of the Bonn Conference and the establishment of the new Afghan government. According to a report by Michael Hirsh, Dobbins pointed out that in an interview that "Karzai was a Pashtun from the south, like the majority of the Afghan population." Tajiks from the Northern Alliance, historically rivals to the Pashtuns, led by Yunus Qanooni, tenaciously demanded the majority share in the new government "since they were the people that had captured Kabul." Hirsh further quotes Dobbins that "by 4.00 a.m., they had reached a very critical moment. Nobody was able to change Qanooni's mind. Zarif finally and authoritatively whispered in Qanooni's ear that, 'This is the best deal you can get.' And Qanooni said, 'OK.'"[27]

Even after the creation of a new Afghan government at the Bonn Conference, talks continued. But suddenly, there came a veritable bombshell. President Bush, only a few weeks after the Bonn Conference, stunned us by including Iran in the "Axis of Evil" during his January 2002 State of the Union address. Talks continued but the Iranians' appetite for cooperation was diminished. Every person involved, from Khatami down, had the same feeling—betrayed! *Namak-nashnas* (literally "un-grateful") was the word frequently used to characterize George Bush's behavior.

In the aftermath of Bush's address, Khatami told me: "I am confident that Bush put the final nail in the coffin of Iran–US relations." He further added: "I guess any improvement in relations must be ruled out, at least during my presidency." This did not mean that we would stop our efforts, but the high hopes after overthrowing the Taliban had given way to pessimism. Khatami was confident that for at least 10 years, any attempt at rapprochement bearing meaningful fruit would be impossible.

Hassan Rouhani, then Secretary of the SNSC, told me that the Americans had made a big mistake. In his view, "Afghanistan could become a model of cooperation between Iran and the US for crisis management in the whole region." He added that Ayatollah Khamenei had told him at the very beginning that "the Americans' invitation for cooperation is tactical." Using a famous Persian saying for characterizing the US behavior, Rouhani said: "As soon as their donkey passed the bridge [meaning as soon as they got what they wanted and didn't need you anymore] they will go back to their previous hostile position."

But the most interesting reaction came from Qassem Soleimani, the commander of the Quds Force, a division of the IRGC responsible for Afghan affairs, who was key in organizing the Afghan Northern Alliance in their attack on Kabul. After one of the SNSC meetings, Qassem told me, without holding back on his ill feelings toward George Bush's response to Iran's invaluable assistance, that from the very beginning of the cooperation he had suspected that the US request for our help might have been a tactical move and not intended to lead to long-term cooperation.

At the time, I viewed Iran's assistance as a no-lose proposition. If the US were sincere, we would help them topple our arch enemies, Taliban and Al-Qaeda. Then broader cooperation would be possible. Qassem jokingly responded that "in that case, the dreams of you Westoxicated diplomats would come true." Nonetheless, he agreed that even if the US were not sincere, we would still have eliminated our enemy.

Qassem posited that if the US wanted to betray us and break away from us once they were established in Afghanistan, they would become trapped like the Soviets before them. Americans were not familiar with the complexities of Afghanistan. "Americans do not know the region, Americans do not know Afghanistan, Americans do not know Iran," Qassem added. In any case, we would win, he argued, and if the Americans crossed us, they would have to leave in defeat.

Ironically, the Northern Alliance that was funded by Iran ousted the Taliban from power in Kabul with air support from the Americans. Iran had formed the backbone of foreign aid to the Northern Alliance while they actively brought numerous different ethnic groups together, shaping the resistance against the Taliban. "In the first half of 1999 alone, thirty-three cargo planes with 380 metric tons of small arms, ammo, and fuel arrived from the eastern Iranian air base of Mashhad to Tajikistan for transport to the Northern Alliance," according to David Crist, a senior historian for the US government.[28]

The Suspicious Karine A *Affair and the Axis of Evil*

On January 4, 2002, Iran was suddenly accused of complicity in smuggling a huge consignment of weapons to the Palestinians. The news captured the headlines. According to a January 4, 2002 statement by Lieutenant General Shaul Mofaz of the Israel Defense Forces (IDF), "With the break of dawn on Thursday, January 3, 2002, IDF forces took control of the ship *Karine A*, which was carrying about 50 tons of warfare and sabotage equipment, meant to be smuggled into the Palestinian Authority area." General Mofaz added that "on the *Karine A*, we found about 50 tons of varied warfare, most of it [of] Iranian origin."[29]

Weapons were stored in 80 large wooden crates, including advanced weaponry such as Katyusha rockets, rifles, mortar shells, mines and a variety of anti-tank missiles. "Senior figures in the Palestinian Authority were involved in the smuggling," according to the IDF.[30] That attempt, according to General Mofaz, "pointed directly at the close cooperation between the Palestinian Authority, Iran and other terror organizations." By *other terror organizations*, the General meant Hezbollah of Lebanon, which, according to the IDF, had been part of the team involved in loading the weapons near an Iranian island.[31]

Iran denied the accusations. The Iranian Defense Minister, Ali Shamkhani, stated: "The Islamic Republic of Iran has had no military relations with Yasir Arafat and no steps have been taken by any Iranian organization for the shipment of arms to the mentioned lands."[32] Two weeks later, the *Jerusalem Post* published a piece which declared that "some Israeli pundits warn that denials cannot be dismissed offhand, because the evidence is simply too shaky."[33]

Following the incident, Israeli hardliners pursued two goals. They aimed to nullify the Oslo Peace Accords between Israel and the Palestinians, which if remained intact, could ultimately lead to the formation of a Palestinian state. Also, the framing of Iran and Hezbollah as terrorist entities might stifle the process of reconciliation and cooperation between Iran and the US, which had gained momentum in the preceding twelve months. Israeli hardliner maneuvers succeeded.

Immediately following the interception of the *Karine A*, Benjamin Netanyahu, a future contender for prime minister of Israel and a hardliner in the Likud party, said that a Palestinian state must never be established.[34] He also asserted: "With its own independent port, such a state would receive shiploads of arms, day and night, and we would find ourselves facing a terrorist state, armed to the teeth." A day after the incident, the Israeli Ministry of Foreign Affairs issued a statement which read: "Foreign Minister Shimon Peres said that the seizing of the ship is an important turning point for the Palestinian Authority in making [a] choice. They cannot continue playing the game. They have to make a strategic decision whether they support terrorism or they are against it."[35] The statement added that "Since the ship was carrying Iranian weapons, Foreign Minister Peres will next week call upon the leaders of the international community to declare Iran as a terror-supporting state." Similar statements by Israeli officials flooded media and news outlets.

Judging by George W. Bush's reaction, Israel's tactics worked. Bush later disclosed that "Arafat sent a letter pleading his innocence. But we and the Israelis had evidence that disproved the Palestinians' claim. Arafat had lied to me. I never trusted him again. In fact, I never spoke to him again."[36]

Regarding Iran, the timing of the *Karine A* affair could not have been better for anyone seeking to undermine the prospect of cooperation between Iran and the US. The two countries were on track to solve one of the most complex and protracted international conflicts at their highest level of cooperation in the post-revolutionary era. Instead, the *Karine A* incident basically demolished everything that Iran and the US had been working on for more than a year. Three weeks later, President Bush included Iran in the "Axis of Evil." His message was clear. The status of the new relationship between the US and Iran was strikingly similar to that of a Manichean war in which the US represented the "good" and Iran represented the "evil."

Some may argue that the neoconservative administration of George Bush would not have reconciled with Iran, anyway. The US needed Iran during the attack on Afghanistan, but once it had "used" the Iranian government to advance its goal of overthrowing the Taliban and the creation of a new Afghan government, it went back to its 20-year-long hostile position. This argument is flawed on two counts.

First, secret talks and negotiations between Iran and the US started months before September 11, 2001. During the Geneva talks, both parties sought ways to convey their grievances to the other side, hoping to build a more congenial atmosphere in which to gradually resolve their disputes. Of course, after 9/11, the talks became more objective and focused on the issue of unseating the Taliban and dismantling the terrorist and fanatical Al-Qaeda organization.

Second, the negotiations continued almost a year after the "Axis of Evil" speech, albeit with less enthusiasm for cooperation on the part of Iran. Key individuals involved in those talks included the White House National Security Advisor, Hillary Mann Leverett; her Iranian counterpart; Ambassador Zarif, the Iranian ambassador to the UN; and Ambassador Reza Alborzi, the Iranian ambassador in Geneva. Yet, a few days after Bush's State of the Union address, the *Washington Post* wrote, "The discovery of Iran's role in smuggling 50 tons of weapons to the Palestinians was a body blow to the State Department's initiative to engage Iran."[37]

Hillary Leverett, who attended the meetings together with Ambassador Ryan Crocker, and sometimes alone, remembers that the Iranians "specifically" told her "time and again, they were doing this [helping the US] because they understood the impact of this attack on the U.S., and they thought that if they helped us *unconditionally*, that would be the way to change the dynamic for the first time in twenty-five years" (emphasis added).[38] She went on to say: "It was revolutionary. It could have changed the world." But she also recalls that in the first meeting following Bush's speech, "They [Iranians] said they had put their necks out to talk to us and they were taking big risks with *their careers and their families and their lives*" (emphasis added).[39]

In 2010, Hillary told me: "Although I am sorry that the US lost a big opportunity … I am happy the direct talks played an important role [in] changing my mind on Iran. That's why I believe direct talks can change many American officials' mindset about the real Iran and not artificial

Iran made by media." Ryan Crocker's account of his first meeting after the speech is no less clear about how the Iranian negotiators felt:

> I remember fairly clearly my next encounter with my Iranian colleague. Those things in life that are least pleasant stay with you the longest and with the greatest clarity. And it was not a happy encounter. That was the time—and he was gracious enough to inform me—that the Iranian government chose to export Gulbuddin Hekmatyar [anti-American Afghan warlord] back to Afghanistan … and here I am indulging in conjecture; it's great to be a free man; I can do that—this was also the point, I think, where the Iranians made a strategic decision, which is can't work with those sons-of-bitches; told you all along, can't do it … after January of 2002, although talks continued, but with increasingly less result and with increasingly less authoritative representation on the Iranian side."[40]

"The government of Iran could not have been involved in the *Karine A* affair," Khatami told me in a meeting after the event. "Reducing tensions and hostilities was what I was looking for while I kept my hope to genuinely seek rapprochement and normal relations with the Americans. We invested immoderately in that direction. Some Muslim countries blame us because of not having any sympathy towards Yasser Arafat and the so-called Palestinian Authority. Now it is funny that Israelis accuse us of strategic relations with Arafat!"

The fact is that the relationship between Iran and the Palestinian Authority was more than cold—it was positively strained. Yasser Arafat had supported Iraq during the War with Iran in the 1980s, and when Arafat signed the Oslo Accords with Israel in 1993, Iran froze all support to the PLO and accused it of treason.[41] Many radicals in Iran considered Arafat a traitor to Muslims and Palestinians, which, in my personal view, was simply unfair.

In Iran, there was a strong tendency to believe that the *Karine A* incident had been staged by Israeli hardliners. Some other Western analysts have told me in recent years that they thought it could have been the work of a rogue cell in Iran seeking to undermine Khatami's authority and the efforts in negotiations to improve relations with the US, bringing them to a deadlock. While I do not credit such an assessment, the question of "Who did it and why" has so far failed to produce a satisfactory answer. But one thing is clear: the big victims in the *Karine A* affair was first, Iran–US détente, and second, the moderate current in Iran which relentlessly worked for better relations with the United States.

A Perturbing Revelation

Shocking revelations about the existence of Iran's nuclear enrichment facilities in August 2002 began one of the most complex international conflicts in the post-Cold War era. The National Council of Resistance of Iran (NCRI), the political wing of MEK, identified Natanz as an undeclared nuclear facility responsible for "nuclear fuel production."

The pressure increased on Iran, beginning with the visit of Mohammad ElBaradei, Director General of the International Atomic Energy Agency (IAEA), to Natanz in early 2003. ElBaradei announced during his visit that Iran had now joined the nations with access to nuclear fuel production technology. The IAEA raised a number of technical concerns as part of its inspections, but found no evidence to suggest a diversion towards nuclear weapons. During intense and extensive negotiations that followed, the EU3 (the UK, France, and Germany) implored Iran to suspend its fuel production activities for its civilian nuclear power reactor, that is, enriching uranium. They reasoned that the uranium enrichment capability was key to building the material for a nuclear bomb, regardless of intent. Uranium exists naturally in underground deposits consisting of a mixture of about 0.7 percent uranium–235, which is easily fissionable, and about 99.3 percent uranium–238, which is not fissionable. For civilian nuclear power plants, the proportion of uranium–235 is enriched and increased to about 5 percent while in the case of nuclear weapons the enrichment typically is increased to 90 percent purity or more.

Iran viewed the call to suspend its uranium enrichment activity as another means of denying its "inalienable right" to nuclear technology under the Non-Proliferation Treaty (NPT).[42] The NPT allows continued technological development for peaceful purposes, specifically noting "the inalienable right of all parties to the Treaty to develop research, production and use of nuclear energy for peaceful purposes without discrimination."[43]

Nevertheless, based on the agreement signed in Tehran with the EU3 in October 2003, known as the Saadabad Agreement, we decided to suspend the enrichment for a short period, as a confidence-building and non-legally binding measure. The Agreement, as I have discussed in detail in my previous book on the nuclear issue, was in fact a major breakthrough in the negotiation process with the Europeans, and laid the foundations for substantive progress. But, for a host of reasons, most prominently, the US open opposition, it failed to proceed as expected, not only by Iranians, but also by our French and German interlocutors. Other than the US, the British, a member of the EU3, also played tough and made progress difficult. Soon after the Tehran Agreement, John Sawers, the Political Director of the British Foreign Office, proposed in a letter to his counterparts in France, Germany, and the US that "We may also need to remove one of the Iranian arguments that the suspension called for is 'voluntary.' We could do [that] by making the voluntary suspension a mandatory requirement to the Security Council."[44]

The roller-coaster nuclear talks with the three European countries continued with ups and downs throughout 2004. To resolve the seemingly irreconcilable nuclear dispute, in March 2005 Iran suggested a number of unprecedented measures based on two broad principles: first, to ensure transparency at its nuclear sites; and, second, to provide guarantees not to divert its nuclear program towards weaponization. The practical proposals included implementing the IAEA Additional Protocol to enable on-site inspections; limiting the expansion of the enrichment program; capping uranium enrichment at 5 percent, enabling its use for fuel but not weapons; and converting enriched uranium additionall to domestic needs, ensuring that there would be no reprocessing and plutonium separation at the Arak heavy water reactor—a process that could facilitate weaponization. Tehran also suggested rules to guarantee the permanent ban on developing, stock-piling, and using nuclear weapons in return for respect for its right to enrich uranium under the NPT.[45]

In response to our initiative, in August 2005, the EU3 made a new proposal—that Iran suspend uranium enrichment indefinitely. Naturally, Iran rejected the proposal, as it amounted to waiving its right to peaceful nuclear fuel technology. At this point, it was becoming clear that negotiations were being crafted to move in a certain direction that would lead to sanctions and punitive measures against Iran.

Iran conceded that the EU3 would have been within its rights in calling for more "transparency" in relation to its nuclear program— but the Western countries clearly wanted to move beyond the transparency of Iran's nuclear activities to their "suspension." Iranians did not disagree with the need to ensure maximum transparency, but only within the framework of the NPT. In any case, the EU's insistence on their position created a cycle of distrust in Iran.

Tehran believed that behind the EU3's uncompromising stance lay the US/lay the US hand. Iran became more disenchanted with the negotiations trajectory, with each round of talks followed by increased sanctions and punitive measures. The insistence on suspension of uranium enrichment further antagonized the Iranians.

As indicated earlier, while serving as the head of the SNSC Foreign Relations Committee, I was also a member of Iran's nuclear negotiating team with the EU3 and the IAEA between 2003 and 2005. During negotiating sessions, we told our EU3 interlocutors that Iran would never accept the denial of access to enrichment under the NPT, and discriminatory impositions outside the NPT, even at the cost of a war.

The issue of double standards was one of our arguments with the Europeans. The West had singled out Iran as a nuclear threat, while overlooking, even actively supporting, other countries' nuclear ambitions. The most obvious cases in point were Israel, India, and Pakistan. None of these countries had signed or ratified the NPT despite possession of large nuclear arsenals. Indeed, the US had signed strategic partnership agreements with India in the defense, security, and nuclear spheres, had pledged more than $30 billion in direct aid to Pakistan since 1948, and contributed over $130 billion in direct aid to Tel Aviv in recent decades. Paris had also provided Israel with the Dimona reactor, used for weapons development, had furnished Saddam Hussein's Iraq with a weapons-grade fuel nuclear reactor, and provided Pakistan with plutonium extraction technology. It also continued to assist India after it detonated its first nuclear weapon in 1974.

As will be described later, President Khatami's administration and his top nuclear negotiator, Hassan Rouhani, did their best to provide the West with several options to give them peace of mind while protecting Iran's rights. But the opportunity to finalize a deal was missed due to the West's unwillingness to compromise, specifically the US position of "no enrichment" in Iran.[46] Reflecting on the situation in 2013, the British Foreign Secretary Jack Straw opined: "We were getting somewhere, with respect, and then it's a complicated story, the Americans actually pulled the rug from under [President Mohammad] Khatami's feet and the Americans got what they didn't want" remarked British Foreign Secretary Jack Straw.[47]

IAEA Director General Mohamed ElBaradei confirmed this missed opportunity and expressed his disappointment:

> The Iranians were willing in 2003, but the administration of then US President George W. Bush was not ... I adhere strictly to the facts,

and part of that is that the Americans and the Europeans withheld important documents and information from us. They weren't interested in a compromise with the government in Tehran, but regime change—by any means necessary."[48]

The Americans' uncompromising stance, insisting on the suspension of Iran's fuel production cycle, brought about the failure of the negotiations with Khatami's administration and was a significant factor in the decline of Iran's reform movement—which gave rise to the emergence of Iran's brand of Newcons, represented by Mahmoud Ahmadinejad. This development complicated the dispute over Iran's nuclear program, increasing international tension, while the people of Iran also paid a big price during the eight years of Ahmadinejad's tenure.

Iran and the Pursuit of the Nuclear Program

The US perspective of the matter is that Iran's efforts for a long period to conceal its nuclear program, and some conspicuous military dimensions of it, are reason enough for the suspension of uranium enrichment activities[49] until Iran is able to convince the international community about the program's peaceful nature. As already discussed, uranium enrichment lies at the heart of the dispute over Iran's nuclear program. To that end, the US campaigned internationally to force Iran into submission. Iran, on the other hand, has systematically rejected all accusations about weaponization. The Supreme Leader, supported by an array of forces and quarters within the system (*nezam*), believes that there are in fact other reasons why the US pushes for a timeless and open-ended suspension.

I have detailed, in the preceding pages, the Supreme Leader's outlook on the US government and policies. He firmly believes that the US uncompromising opposition to Iran's possession of nuclear technology is directly linked to its arrogant nature (*khooye estekbari*), wishing to prevent Iran from achieving real independence, establishing self-sufficiency across a variety of sectors and making major technological breakthroughs. Moreover, he maintains that, based on its pattern of behavior over the previous two decades, the US, allied with Tel Aviv, intends to use the nuclear issue as a pretext to isolate and undermine—preferably "get rid of"—the only country in the Islamic world that stands against US–Israeli domination of the Middle East region.

To make a fair judgment on the current nuclear crisis, it is critical to understand the background to the Iranian nuclear program. During the reign of the Shah, the US laid the foundations of a nuclear Iran through major nuclear deals with the country. Iran's efforts to develop nuclear energy can be traced back to 1957 and the push from the Eisenhower administration. On March 5, 1957, the two countries announced a "proposed agreement for cooperation in research in the peaceful uses of atomic energy" under the auspices of Eisenhower's "Atoms for Peace" program.[50] The US built the first nuclear facility in Iran, the Tehran Research Reactor, in 1967. In 1976, President Gerald Ford issued National Security Decision Memorandum 324, supporting the Shah's ambitions and helping Iran formulate a plan to build 23 nuclear power reactors.[51]

France also cooperated with Iran on enrichment and signed a number of long-term contracts with Iran, while Germany concluded some major deals to build nuclear plants in the country. Britain, too, signed a number of contracts to supply uranium to Iran. In general, the Americans and Europeans were competing to win lucrative projects to nuclearize Iran. However, the West's attitude, in particular that of the US, suddenly turned 180 degrees after the 1979 Revolution.[52]

The Shah did not start a nuclear military program (at least there is no clear evidence that he did), but ambitious as he was, it was clear that he intended to start one. In 1974 when asked by a French journalist whether Iran would pursue building nuclear weapons, he replied: "Certainly, and sooner than one would think."[53] Americans also knew well that the Shah would build an atomic bomb. A CIA report in 1974 concluded that "If [the Shah] is alive in the mid-1980s and if other countries [particularly India] have proceeded with weapons development, we have no doubt that Iran will follow suit."[54] But the United States, despite all the signs pointing to the Shah's intentions to build nuclear weapons, turned a blind eye on the issue. Akbar Etemad, father of the Iranian nuclear program and head of Iran's Atomic Energy Organization under the Shah, has no doubt about the issue: "The Shah's plan was to build a nuclear bomb."[55] The Iranian leadership now asks, quite reasonably, "If an arms race, as a result of Iran's nuclear weaponization, wasn't a threat under the Shah's regime, why then is it a threat now?"

Throughout the last four years of my stay in the US, I have had the opportunity to meet numerous American and European foreign policy experts, as well as scholars and pundits. During conferences and private meetings in the United States and Europe, we have held discussions, some heated, over Iran's nuclear crisis. The questions have often be put to me: "Why did Iran hide its nuclear program if it were of a peaceful nature?" and "Why is Iran so adamant about pursuing its nuclear project despite suffering tremendous international pressure because of it?" Many conclude that the only logical explanation of Iran's position is the desire to acquire the capability to build a nuclear bomb. This, they also argue, is the opinion shared by the US policy-makers.

In response to the first question, it had become clear that the West sought to block Iran's nuclear development, and the only way that Iran could advance its technology was to go it alone—and secretly.

Shortly after the Revolution, Iran canceled all of the Shah's ambitious nuclear programs. They also decided to cancel enrichment and reprocessing projects including the 23 nuclear power plants proposed by the US. They only maintained the Tehran Research Reactor (TRR) which was supplied by the US in 1967, just for producing isotopes for medical purposes. Iran also intended to the finish the Bushehr Power Plant, which was already 90 percent complete and for which Germany had already received about 8 billion DM. Iran planned to procure fuel from France through their joint venture contract, on which US$1 billion had already been spent. However, in the post-1979 situation, France declined to provide fuel, terminated the nuclear cooperation between the two countries, and the joint venture company, Eurodif, was dissolved. So, at the time, Iran's plan was to outsource fuel, and had no plans to produce fuel inside the country.

From the mid-1980s to 1990s—as detailed in previous chapters—I was involved in improving Iran–Europe relations. During this period, in more than 300 meetings, I asked German officials to complete the Bushehr Power Plant for which they had already been paid. I used to tell them: "If you do not finish the work based on your contractual commitments, Iran would complete it in any way possible and have no choice but to go for self-sufficiency and even produce fuel (enrich uranium) domestically." The Germans—as we have come to know for a fact—declined due to US pressure. The US also terminated all of its agreements with Iran, including the supply of fuel rods for the Tehran Research Reactor. The UK and other Western countries followed the US lead and terminated their nuclear agreements with Iran.[56]

Argentina had signed a contract with Iran on the provision of fuel rods but then retracted it under American pressure. Finally, China was approached and a contract was drawn up and ratified, but "when China joined the Nuclear Suppliers Group in 1992, it ceased nuclear cooperation with Iran under American pressure."[57] Iran's only successful procurement of nuclear power came through Russia in 1993.

The two countries signed a contract which was limited to restoring and completing the power plant in Bushehr.

As a result of these developments, the US and the West left Iran with no option other than to establish its own nuclear program. It was apparent that US offered little prospect of concessions negotiated on their program, and everywhere Iran turned for help, a US-created obstacle emerged/propped up. The new US strategy of "no civilian nuclear power plant" and "no access to the international fuel market" for Iran was a clear violation of the NPT. Under these circumstances, if Iran wanted to have such a program, its only way foward was through a clandestine nuclear project, hidden from the eyes of the international community. The US certainly wouldn't have let it happen in the open. The bottom line is that it was the West who pushed Iran to develop its indigenous nuclear capability.

But *why* is Iran so adamant about having a nuclear capability? A quick review of the preceding developments reveals that after the Revolution, Iran had no intention of mastering nuclear fuel cycle technology. As stated before, it canceled all of the ambitious plans agreed/concluded between the Shah, the US and Western Europe. However, when the United States led the West in fierce opposition to Iran's intent to exercise its rights as stipulated in the NPT, then the problem was transformed from one of being denied access to certain technology to one of being subjected to bullying, humiliation, and blatant discrimination, tantamount to saying: "Any nation can exercise its rights under NPT to have a nuclear capability but you Iranians." Once it was clear that the US and the West intended to deal with Iran as a third-class citizen of the international community, two major socio-psychological sentiments subsumed the dispute.

First, the familiar historical element of "culture of resistance" to foreign pressure and domination by external enemies, especially once reinforced with the quite pronounced sense of victimization in the Shia thinking and rituals—which I have addressed on a number of occasions in the preceding chapters.

Second, the element of "national pride" and the corresponding strong nationalistic sentiments which are also intimately related to the first element and find their roots in the same long, eventful historical experience and rich culture and civilization. This aspect of the Iranian society and the Iranian psyche are quite known to others— non-Iranians, whether Western or otherwise—and have been well documented in the works and analyses of Iran experts and pundits. National pride is present throughout Iranian culture and discourse.

Speeches and texts on Iranian identity repeatedly emphasize Iranian pride in its culture (*farhang*) and civilization (*tamaddon*).[58]

Closely related to such a national sentiment, is the country's sensitivity to its paramount regional status—which in the eyes of Iranians, both the government and the populace, needs to be recognized by others; that is, to be respected. For better or for worse, the nuclear program has become a matter of national pride. According to a Gallup survey conducted in November 2013, "Despite the perceived economic toll, two in three (68 percent) Iranians say their country should continue to develop nuclear power despite the scale of sanctions against Iran. This higher support in the face of international pressure highlights the role Iranian nationalism plays in the nuclear standoff with the West."[59]

This leads us to the most disputed issue—the question of uranium enrichment—and the reason why Iran is determined to have it. The answer lies in Iran's past experience in dealings with foreign countries over nuclear fuel. Those countries either imposed humiliating conditions before providing it, or they did not supply it at all. In other words, if Iran cannot enrich uranium locally, it has to rely on a limited number of countries who can supply enriched uranium. That leaves Iran vulnerable to the US, and possibly others, who might "pull the plug" at any time, thus preventing Iran from accessing the fuel market.

Finally, Iran's insistence on a nuclear program reflects a widely-held view in Iran that any compromise "under coercion," such as suspending uranium enrichment under the pressure of sanctions, would open the door to more coercion and demands for concessions by the US and the allies. The rank and file of the Iranian government tend to believe—albeit to differing degrees—that as soon as the US concludes that sanctions are working, other issues such as human rights and so-called support for terrorism will be brought into the picture in pursuit of their longer term objectives.

Considering the foregoing and the impasse that had emerged in the state of talks on the nuclear imbroglio, the November 24, 2013 Joint Action Plan signed by Iran and the P5+1 was a turning point. Together with the other world powers, the US agreed that the final "comprehensive solution would involve a mutually defined enrichment program with practical limits and transparency measures to ensure the peaceful nature of the program."[60] President Obama's remark a few weeks later that "no enrichment on Iranian soil was unrealistic" reflected a sense of creeping realism and objectivity. He likened it to "a world in which Congress passed every one of my bills that I put forward."[61]

Any Substance to the US Suspicions?

Why does the US claim that Iran's intentions in pursuing its nuclear project are suspicious? Is there any validity to this US suspicion, or could it be that the US is using suspicion as a propaganda tactic to confront Iran? Actually, Iran did fail to report some nuclear activities. It also tried to conceal certain activities and dimensions of its nuclear program from the IAEA, which were subsequently discovered by inspectors from the Agency. One such activity was the introduction of a limited amount of uranium hexafluoride gas to centrifuges at the Kalaye Electric Company in order to produce enriched uranium at a low, laboratory level.

Upon their discovery, the IAEA called on Tehran to confirm the gas introduction in question. Iran denied the accusation, but samples taken at the Company site revealed the traces of enriched uranium. That episode, combined with Iran's denial of any nuclear testing, contributed to major international suspicion about the goals and nature of Tehran's nuclear program. Suspicion was one of the most important factors in bolstering the US hardline posture and position, leading to the IAEA Board of Governors' strongly worded resolution in September 2003.

Later, the discovery of highly enriched uranium particles—which can be used to build an atomic bomb—at the Natanz installations caused grave concern in Tehran. An urgent SNSC meeting was called to discuss the matter. We reached the conclusion that since Iran had only carried out peaceful nuclear activities, the discovered highly enriched uranium particles must indicate a plot by Israeli or US intelligence services. But the IAEA diffused the situation when it concluded that those traces could have been from second-hand centrifuges, contaminated prior to their importation to Iran from Pakistan.

However, there were other failures to report as well as contradictions in Iran's statements and reports. In October 2003, soon after Rouhani was appointed as Iran's top nuclear negotiator, Tehran decided to present a full report about its past and present nuclear activities, admitting that it had carried out some previously undeclared activities. Those highly controversial and previously undisclosed matters included accessing second generation, advanced P-2 centrifuges' drawings and producing polonium, which is a highly radioactive neutron source with some applications in military and non-military industries.[62]

The installations at Natanz, generally considered Iran's central enrichment facility have been at the heart of the controversy over Iran's nuclear program. The IAEA Director General, Mohamed ElBaradei, visited the Natanz site in February 2003 and was surprised that 164 centrifuges were complete and ready for operation, with 1,000 more in production and assembly at the site. But was this a gross violation of the NPT? In fact it was not.

Based on the NPT Safeguard Agreement, member states are not obliged to report on the planning, construction, import, production, and assembly of centrifuges. According to the NPT, Iran was only obliged to report installations to the IAEA 180 days before the introduction of gas, that is, the commencement of introducing enriched uranium into centrifuges. It is understandable that the West was shocked when ElBaradei visited the enrichment site at Natanz and announced that Iran was among ten countries then in possession of enrichment technology, but that did not prove any violation of Iran's obligations under the NPT. No gas had been introduced into centrifuges and no enrichment had taken place. While it was true that Iran had concealed its activities, fact of the matter was that it was not in violation of the NPT provisions. That notwithstanding, the very fact that such a huge installation had been hidden from the international community appeared to have made the Americans very nervous.[63]

It is noteworthy that the main concerns over Iran's nuclear program related to its past activities. Dennis Ross, a former senior American diplomat and also a top Obama advisor on the Middle East, remarked in 2013: "Only by coming clean to the IAEA about its past activities can Iran persuade the United States and other powers involved in nuclear negotiations that it doesn't intend to develop warheads in the future. They have to admit what they've done."[64] However, not only the IAEA but the US National Intelligence Estimate (NIE) in 2007, and again in 2010, have confirmed that Iran does not have a nuclear weaponization program. Further, they found that no decision had been made by Iranian authorities to build a nuclear bomb.[65]

The reasons for Iran's covert efforts to establish an enrichment program have already been discussed earlier in this chapter, as well as the foundations for external suspicions, including on the part of the US government. However, the US insistence in the past on "no enrichment on Iranian soil" failed to remove mistrust. If Iran intended to acquire nuclear weapons, it simply could not do so overtly. Its recognized facilities are closely monitored by the IAEA and are the focus of international monitoring and attention. No country has ever developed nuclear weapons as a signatory to the NPT. (Reference to the case of North Korea in this particular regard is not valid. Fact of the matter is that North Korea announced its withdrawal from the NPT in January

2003 and carried out its first nuclear bomb test in October 2006.) And if Iran intends to develop or acquire atomic weapons covertly, a forced shutdown of the overt operations would offer no assurances to the US or anyone else that Iran would not attempt to do so outside of regulatory oversight. That is why Peter Jenkins, the former UK ambassador to the IAEA, said that "All talk of an 'Iranian nuclear threat' is therefore premature. Consequently, the draconian measures implemented by the US and its allies to avert that threat are unreasonable and unwarranted."[66]

American and Israeli Hoopla on Iran's Nuclear Program

Although there is an international consensus that Iran should not acquire a military nuclear capability, this movement has been spearheaded by two countries: Israel and the United States. Israel argues that because Iran denies its existence, a nuclear-armed Iran poses an "existential threat" to the Jewish state.[67] Comments by some Iranians depicting Israel as a cancerous tumor which must be removed, and pledges to wipe Israel off the map, have been used by Israel to portray the Iranian government and leadership as irrational and justify its policy on Iran's nuclear program.[68]

During my tenure of public office, I have always been opposed to the use of aggressive language, such as the pronouncements attributed to the former Iranian President, Mahmoud Ahmadinejad. I believe aggressive language, even if appeasing to rank-and-file conservatives, is damaging, domestically and particularly in foreign relations. Ultimately, the conservatives themselves would also pay the price as a result of hostile foreign relations with other states. In fact, my opposition to Ahmadinejad's approach and policies and approach cost me dearly. I will write later about the espionage dossier fabricated by Ahmadinejad and his team, but now I would instead concentrate on certain misinterpretations of facts that could even precipitate a disastrous armed conflict.

The Israeli argument outlined above is flawed in a number of ways. The statement that "Israel must be wiped off the map," as attributed to Ahmadinejad, was in fact never made. According to the Iranian presidential site, what he said was:

> O dear Imam [Khomeini]! ... The *Zionist Regime* has lost its philosophy of existence/rationale for existence ... [and] faces a

complete dead-end and under God's grace your wish will soon be materialized and [it] will be wiped off the map.[69] (emphasis added)

Ahmadinejad did not refer to the people or the land of Israel, but to the regime. Many officials in the US and in Israel have, explicitly or implicitly, called for regime change in Iran, which as everybody would guess, would not be taken as the annihilation of the Iranian nation. Moreover, Ahmadinejad did not say that he or Iran intend to do that. He had expressed the hope and expectation that the Israeli regime would collapse. Confirming this interpretation, Israeli Deputy Prime Minister Dan Meridor said in an interview, in April 2012, that Iran didn't say "we'll wipe it [Israel] out," but rather "it will not survive."[70]

On this issue, Ayatollah Khamenei's view is that a referendum should determine the type of government to rule Palestine:

> We hold a fair and logical stance on the issue of Palestine. Several decades ago, Egyptian statesman Gamal Abdel Nasser, who was the most popular Arab personality, stated in his slogans that the Egyptians would throw the Jewish usurpers of Palestine into the sea. Some years later, Saddam Hussein, the most hated Arab figure, said that he would put half of the Palestinian land on fire. But we would not approve of either of these two remarks. We believe, according to our Islamic principles, that neither throwing the Jews into the sea nor putting the Palestinian land on fire is logical and reasonable.[71]

Israel's argument about Iranian irrationality is also flawed. Iran's rhetoric aside, Israel has never referred to or demonstrated objective and specific evidence or examples to prove the Iranian government's irrationality, at least in the way it is understood in the West. This is not to defend all the policies, actions, and/or approaches of the Iranian government, but reason requires that when Israel bases the argument about an "existential threat" on irrationality, they should support that argument with clear evidence in relation to the government of Iran. Indeed, the conduct of the P5+1 in pursuing a negotiated settlement of the nuclear dispute points in the opposite direction.

The sanctions imposed on Iran were clearly based on the assumption that the Iranian government is, in fact, rational. In a 2012 interview, President Obama was asked: "General Martin Dempsey, the chairman of the Joint Chiefs of Staff, referred to the Iranian leadership as 'rational.' Where do you fall on this continuum?" Obama answered as follows:

I think it's entirely legitimate to say that this is a regime that does not share our worldview or our values. I do think, and this is what General Dempsey was probably referring to, that as we look at how they operate and the decisions they've made over the past three decades, that they care about the regime's survival. They're sensitive to the opinions of the people and they are troubled by the isolation that they're experiencing. They know, for example, that when these kinds of sanctions are applied, it puts a world of hurt on them. They are able to make decisions based on trying to avoid bad outcomes from their perspective.[72]

Israel has not been able to back up its claims of irrationality on the part of the Iranian system, other than highlighting Iranians' rhetoric and slogans—sometimes misinterpreted—which are concocted for domestic consumption or as part of their policy of "threat against threat."[73]

Over the past two decades, Israel has constantly tried to convince the international community that Iran is seeking to build an atomic bomb. The following list illustrates Israel's assessment of Iran's nuclear program, intended to convince the world of Iran's threat to its existence—and to no avail:

- In October 1992, Israeli Foreign Minister Shimon Peres warned the international community that Iran would be armed with a nuclear bomb by 1999, reiterating that Iran was the greatest threat and problem in the Middle East because it sought the nuclear option.[74]
- In 1995, Prime Minister Benjamin Netanyahu wrote in his book that Iran would possess a nuclear weapon in three to five years.[75]
- In April 1996, Prime Minister Shimon Peres claimed that Iran would have a nuclear bomb in four years.[76]
- In November 1999, a senior Israeli military official said that the Islamic Republic would possess a nuclear capability within five years.[77]
- In July 2001, Defense Minister Binyamin Ben-Eliezer confirmed that Iran would have a nuclear bomb by the year 2005.[78]
- In August 2003, a high-ranking military officer told the Knesset Foreign Affairs and Defense Committee that Iran would have the materials needed to make a nuclear bomb by 2004 and have an operative nuclear weapons program by 2005.[79]
- In November 2009, General Yossi Baidatz, an Israeli military intelligence official, told an American defense official that "it would

take Iran one year to obtain a nuclear weapon and two and a half years to build an arsenal of three weapons."[80]

- In September 2010, Jeffrey Goldberg said that Israeli officials believed that Iran was, at most, one to three years away from having a nuclear capability.[81]

In reality, the main source of Israel's fear is that a nuclear-armed Iran will undermine its supremacy as the only nuclear power in the Middle East for several decades. Israel's concern is that a nuclear Iran could project its power and influence throughout the region without fear of confrontation by Israel. Iran could also support anti-Israel militant groups without fear of threats by Israel and even Israel's closest ally, the United States. Finally, Israel is worried that a nuclear-armed Iran could destabilize and even shape new regimes in Arab countries to fall in line with its worldview, without fear of being confronted. Inevitably, such a development would make the Middle East environment more hostile and more dangerous for Israel.

Americans oppose Iran's nuclear development from a different perspective. While Israel's concerns form a major part of the US calculation, Americans have their own particular concerns, mostly related to security and energy issues in the greater Middle East, and more specifically in the Persian Gulf area. This element has been paramount in the strategic thinking of the United States since at least the 1940s.

With regard to Iran's threat to the existence of Israel, it seems contradictory that, on the one hand, the US bases its policies—namely sanctions—on the rationality of Iran's government, but, on the other, seems to buy the claim that Iran might falter in judgment and take a fatal risk as to attack Israel with an atomic bomb. Iran knows well that if it attacks Israel with an atomic bomb, not Israelis but Americans, would threaten the country existentially.[82] Therefore, the overarching US concern cannot be the security of Israel, as widely espoused by US authorities, including President Obama.[83] Rather, it is the influence and power of pro-Israel forces that pushes American policy-makers to make such comments and bring the issue of Iran's threat to Israel's existence to the forefront of America's foreign policy agenda with respect to Iran. Obama made the following assessment of the situation in an interview during the 2014 AIPAC Policy Conference:

[I]f you look at Iranian behavior, they are strategic, and they're not impulsive. They have a worldview, and they see their interests, and they respond to costs and benefits. And that isn't to say that they aren't a theocracy that embraces all kinds of ideas that I find abhorrent, but they're not North Korea. They are a large, powerful country that sees itself as an important player on the world stage, and I do not think has a suicide wish, and can respond to incentives.[84]

From an American perspective, the fear is plausible that once Iran is nuclear-armed it could assert itself as the dominant power in the Middle East and destabilize oil markets at will, simply by threatening Arab oil-producing countries in the region. Americans may also fear that a nuclear Iran could assist anti-American forces in the region without fearing a US response. Another major US concern, as it is for Israel, is that Washington's Arab allies could be destabilized by Iran and their regimes toppled and reshaped through Iranian influence. An American foreign policy expert told me that the recent upheaval in the Arab countries and the collapse of US allies in the region like Mubarak in Egypt and Bin Ali in Tunisia, coupled with the complicated crises in Iraq, Afghanistan, and Syria, have convinced the US of the need for a new policy in the Middle East. Moreover America's new security strategy appears to be shifting towards Asia–Pacific area to contain China. As Hillary Clinton wrote in *Foreign Affairs*, "The future of politics will be decided in Asia, not Afghanistan or Iraq, and the United States will be right at the center of the action."[85]

Another US worry is that Iran's acquisition of an atomic weapon might spark a nuclear arms race in the volatile Middle East. Some analysts argue that, since the countries in the Middle East considered to be Iran's rivals are all pro-US/US allies, they will not seek to build an atomic bomb without US consent, but this is questionable. Pakistan was a close US ally and its army was heavily dependent on US aid when it built its nuclear weapon in 1998.

For the reasons cited, and in the absence of a cooperative relationship with Tehran, Washington *is* concerned about Iran acquiring the capability to make atomic weapons. According to revelations by the *New York Times*, we now know that shortly after President Obama took office in 2009 he ordered the expedition of a wave of cyber attacks against Iran's Natanz nuclear facility.[86] This clearly shows that, right or wrong, the US perceives Iran's nuclear capability to pose a threat to America's national interests and its security.

As already indicated, the nuclear issue became more intractable during the presidency of Mahmoud Ahmadinejad. He thought that by going on the offensive, Iran could push back the Americans. The first time that I learned about this drastic shift in Iran's policy was shortly after he took office in 2005. He invited me to a meeting in the course of which he attacked the moderate policies of Mohammad Khatami and informed me that those policies were to be abandoned.

Why did Ayatollah Khamenei Accept Suspension?

On October 21, 2003, after several hours of talks, a joint agreement was announced at Tehran's Saadabad Palace between Iran, represented by Hassan Rouhani, then Secretary of SNSC, and the foreign ministers of the EU3: British Jack Straw, German Joschka Fischer, and French Dominique de Villepin. In essence, Iran agreed to a voluntary suspension of enrichment activities "as a confidence building measure" and to sign the so-called "Additional Protocol" to the NPT which would allow the IAEA to carry out surprise visits to suspect facilities. In return, Britain, France, and Germany pledged that they would "recognize the right of Iran to the peaceful use of nuclear energy," and that the Additional Protocol was in "no way intended to undermine the sovereignty, national dignity or national security" of Iran.[87]

From the onset of the debates between Iran and the EU3 over Iran's nuclear issue, Iran argued that it made sense for the EU3 to request strict measures in order to achieve full transparency. However, transparency had nothing to do with suspension. Any measures, including short-notice and unannounced inspections were tolerable if not reasonable, but it was incomprehensible why suspension should have been insisted on. Later, we learned that the Americans were not prepared to tolerate "a single centrifuge spinning in Iran,"[88] and it was this stance that forced the EU3 to insist on suspension. In fact, during the negotiations, Joschka Fischer told me that the EU3's main aim was to engage with Iran and find a solution to the crisis, in effect, serving as a *human shield* to prevent an American or Israeli military strike.[89] ElBaradei's memoir confirms that Straw and Fischer told him the same thing.[90]

The debate on suspension was ongoing inside the Iranian government. We, as the negotiating team with the EU3, reasoned that as a goodwill, yet legally non-binding gesture, we should suspend enrichment activities temporarily, just to build confidence. Ayatollah Khamenei was reluctant to suspend enrichment. Our argument was that if we offered suspension and they still did not respect our rights, then we would have the upper hand. If we did not concede at least a temporary suspension, then we would lose our argument later in front of the international community. Led by Rouhani, the negotiating team ultimately convinced Ayatollah Khamenei to accept voluntary, legally non-binding suspension for a few months and the provisional enforcement of the Additional Protocol, which allowed intrusive inspections.

Subsequent to our agreement with the Europeans, Ayatollah Khamenei told government officials that "Iran has chosen a wise alternative to both preserve its nuclear technology and expose its nuclear activities to the world to refute false propaganda" launched by the Americans and Israelis.[91]

Following this concession, contact with the EU3 assumed a lower profile. We accepted suspension for a few months with hopes of fostering more mutually satisfactory, permanent agreements.

It might appear in retrospect that negotiating with the EU3 foreign ministers and accepting suspension was an easy decision for Iran's Leader to make. However, radicals, driven by a so-called revolutionary discourse and constituting an ideology and an influential part of the Islamic Republic's political structure, accused Khatami's administration and the nuclear negotiating team of selling out on the nation's pride and submitting to the will of the enemy. We also came under pressure from the security and intelligence community who were seriously concerned about the infiltration of foreign intelligence agents and spies among the IAEA inspectors.

Despite these objections, the Supreme Leader finally accepted the Khatami team's argument and proposed solution. The Ayatollah said: "Allegations that the recent measure was an act of submission were not compatible with the realities of the situation. He further emphasized that this was a political and diplomatic move that contained no element of submission."[92]

Despite the name calling and attacks by our political opponents, the outcome of the Saadabad negotiations was a victory for Iran, and that was what really bothered our political rivals. Based on the Saadabad Agreement, Iran's right to nuclear technology was recognized and US efforts to have Iran's nuclear case referred to the UN Security Council (UNSC) were defeated. We argued at the time that if the case were referred to the UN Security Council, then the US would succeed in pushing the Council to impose sanctions on Iran. This is what ultimately happened during the presidency of Mahmoud Ahmadinejad.

The Saadabad negotiations also provides an insight on the process of decision-making in Iran; the fact that the Supreme Leader, subject to the constant pull and push of contending political forces and currents, ultimately has to decide. And in that particular case, he agreed—even if reluctantly—with the request of the negotiating team and Khatami's reformist government.

2003 Iraq and the US Miscalculation

The contemporary history of relations between the governments of Iran and Iraq until the fall of Saddam Hussein is littered with episodes of rivalry and a quest to establish dominance in the region. Long before the Islamic Revolution in 1979, the Shah of Iran viewed Saddam as his number one regional threat, and that remained the conventional wisdom in the post-revolutionary period, especially after the 8-year War. I have already discussed in detail the dynamics of Iran-US liaison in the aftermath of 9/11 and on the Afghan situation, as well as the deep disappointment over the "Axis of Evil" issue. Given the circumstances, it was obviously difficult for Iran to cooperate, directly or indirectly, with the US in the 2003 invasion of Iraq.

During the months prior to the US military engagement in Iraq, there were three lines of thinking in Iran on this issue. One line was represented by the radical old-guard who argued that we should form a strategic alliance with Saddam against "Imperialism and Zionism" in the region, and beyond. They reasoned that Iran and Iraq possessed the most powerful armies in the Muslim world, which once joined by Syria, enjoyed the necessary potential for defeating the US in the region. They argued that a US victory in Iraq would result in the creation of a puppet regime, imposition of Western values, stripping Iraq of its Islamic identity, and exploitation of its oil and natural resources. Put simply, they believed that Iran had to resist the "Global Arrogance" that aimed to invade an Islamic country—and an important neighbor.

The second line was more pragmatic. Its advocates argued that if the US invasion was a success, American military bases would be set up in Iraq. Those bases, they asserted, would be used as a springboard for future attacks against Iran. They also made the point that despite Iran's assistance to stability and security in Afghanistan, the US had not reciprocated—instead, matters had worsened. The proponents of line questioned the rationale of providing similar assistance and cooperation again, this time to defeat Iraq.

The majority, including myself, bought into a third line of thinking, arguing that Saddam did not have any grassroots support among his people and therefore would be toppled regardless of whether or not help was given. We argued that because of the religious and ethnic divisions within the Iraqi society, the establishment of a stable government would be a very lengthy and complicated process. If the Americans declined to cooperate with Iran, they would find themselves entangled there for years before the situation could be brought under control.

But the pillar of our argument was that the US removal of Saddam meant the elimination of Iran's most lethal enemy an important gain for Iran. Moreover, since Shiites constituted the majority of the Iraqi population, Sadaam's fall would pave the way for them to gain their rightful place in the society, including a dominant position in the new emerging system. Moreover, given our close relations with the opposition Shiite groups, Iraq's new government would most likely shift the balance of power in the region in our favor. And if the US cooperated with Iran, this would be welcomed as an important confidence-building move that could pave the way to further regional cooperation and rapprochement. But, if the US rejected Iran's role and stature in Iraq and continued a negative approach and policy, they would end up at the losing end of the game—which would be our gain.

The ironic thing was that Iranians and Americans were both considering the prospects of democratization in Iraq, but drawing two contrasting conclusions. Americans viewed democratization as a prelude to the fall of the Iranian Islamic system, while Iranians predominantly viewed it as a huge game changer in their favor. The main reason that the US invaded Iraq was to strengthen its influence in and democratize Iraq in order to stimulate other regime changes, first in Iran, but more broadly throughout the Middle East.

Three weeks before the invasion, President George W. Bush described the "democratic domino theory" in which—apparently—he wholeheartedly believed. He said: "A new regime in Iraq would serve as a dramatic and inspiring example of freedom for other nations in the region."[93] But Tehran was suspicious about the "US democratic theory" because according to the democratic peace theory, *democracies never go to war with each other*, a point duly noted in President Bush's speech: "The world has a clear interest in the spread of democratic values, because stable and free nations do not breed the ideologies of murder."

Natan Sharansky, a Russian-born Israeli political activist, argues in his book entitled *The Case for Democracy* that democracy is the best insurance against aggression. His thesis was so embraced by George W. Bush that in an interview with reporters, he wondered if they had read

The Case for Democracy. "If you want a glimpse of how I think about foreign policy, read Natan Sharansky's book. It will help explain a lot of the decisions that you'll see being made, you've seen made and will continue to see made," he remarked.[94]

Iranians, however, believed that the US would only accept new democracies if those who came to power fell in line with US policies and helped Americans interests, pointing to the US opposition to democratically-elected leaders such as Salvador Allende in Chile and Mohammad Mossadegh in Iran. In addition, US support for past and present dictators from Latin America to the Middle East was another reason why Iranians were skeptical about America's commitment to the democratization project.

Paul Wolfowitz, then the US Deputy Defense Secretary and one of the architects of the Iraq invasion, also said that Iraq could be "the first Arab democracy" that would "cast a very large shadow, starting with Syria and Iran, but across the whole Arab world."[95]

Looking back, the problem with the Bush doctrine was that it simply failed to materialize in Iraq, let alone its possible expected impact on Iran and others in the region. In fact, contrary to the US expectations, Iran's influence in Iraq, and consequently in the region, became ever stronger over time. Americans miscalculated the outcome of their attack of Iraq by ignoring two major factors. First, they failed to realize the role and influence of Islam, and the way it had forged strong ties between the two societies. Iran, unlike Iraq, is not an Arab country but both are Shia dominated and have engaged in constant cultural exchange for the past 14 centuries. Iranian pilgrims regularly visit the holy cities of Najaf, Karbala and Sammara, home to the shrines of Shia Imams.

Moreover, Najaf in Iraq and Qom in Iran are home to the two most important seminaries in the Shia world. Top Shia ulama (*Marja-e Taqlid*/Sources of Emulation) have constantly lived in and moved between the two countries, including late Ayatollah Khomeini who resided and lectured in Najaf during his 14-year exile in Iraq. Presently, the highest ranking Shia *Marja*, Grand Ayatollah Ali al-Sistani, 83, who was born in the holy city of Mashhad, Iran, lives in Najaf. Interestingly, after living in Iraq for more than six decades, he still carries an Iranian passport.

Another indication of the connection between the two countries is the fact that many high-ranking Iranian officials in the post-revolutionary era are Iraq-born. These include Ayatollah Mahmoud Hashemi Shahroudi, former head of Iran's judiciary; Ali Akbar Salehi, former

Foreign Minister and current head of the Atomic Energy Organization; Ali Larijani, Speaker of the Majlis since 2008; and Mohammad Reza Naghdi, commander of the Basij militia. These deep religious and historical ties between Iran and Iraq have created a natural and mutual influence between the two countries, something American planners did not consider in calculating the consequences of the invasion of Iraq.

Second, the US ignored the political influence that Iran had gained in Iraq over the two decades preceding the US invasion. The only organized, well trained, and equipped opposition groups to Saddam who could play a stabilizing role in the post-Saddam era were the Iranian-backed Shia political and militant groups. Iran had made a major investment in such groups, providing them with financial assistance, training, weapons, and accommodation. These facts, along with ideological commonalities, established a strong relationship between Iraqi Shiites and the Iranian system (*nezam*). Those groups included the Supreme Council of the Islamic Revolution of Iraq (SCIRI), with its militant branch, the Badr Brigade; the Islamic Dawa Party (Islamic Call Party); the Kurdish forces, both Barzani and Talebani groups; and even the Iraqi National Congress (INC), led by Ahmad Chalabi, who was also close to the American intelligence community and State Department. The INC had an office in Tehran through the 1990s and maintained close relations with Iran's intelligence apparatus. Indeed in the aftermath of America's invasion of Iraq, there were whispers in the corridors of power in Tehran that Iranian intelligence had used the INC to feed disinformation to the Americans regarding Saddam's possession of weapons of mass destruction. Ahmad Chalabi was the main source of this information and the closest figure to the US government among the Iraqi opposition to Saddam Hussein. In a nutshell, no country in the world, including the Arabs, had such a presence and influence in Iraq as did Iran—which afforded Iran a unique position and opportunity to exercise its influence in the post-Saddam era.

The entire Iranian leadership and foreign policy apparatus, including those of us at the SNSC, did not believe at all that the invasion of Iraq was because of the so-called weapons of mass destruction. Instead, we believed that oil and other geostrategic considerations lay behind the US decision to invade and occupy Iraq. We analyzed at the time that the emergence of a pro-Western government and a free market economy would allow Iraq to increase its oil production and guarantee a steady supply of oil from the Persian Gulf area and stabilize global oil markets. Additionally, mega construction projects in relation to Iraq's infrastructure would provide American and European contractors with long-term, lucrative business.

As the war drums got louder, Tehran gave the green light to Iran-backed groups to cooperate with a US invasion of Iraq to topple Saddam. Major General Qassem Soleimani's constructive role on matters pertaining to Afghanistan in 2001, and then Iraq in 2003, was crucial in orchestrating Iran's field strategy.

After successfully cooperating in Afghanistan, Iraq was an incredible opportunity for the US and Iran to test cooperation on regional stability and security. However, mistrust and divergence soon replaced convergence and cooperation. Fearing Iran's rising influence in the post-Saddam Iraq, the US assumed an aggressive posture and policy to contain it. Iran, on its part, responded by pushing to expand its influence through its own ways, outlets, and networks. While increasing violence raged in Iraq, Iran and the US blamed each other. This further increased tensions within the Iranian government, and cost those who favored rapprochement with the US a great deal of political capital and reputation.

In retrospect, the US invasion of Iraq paradoxically advanced Iran's regional position by freeing the Shiite majority from the Ba'athist rule. This irony was summed up by Iranian expert Vali Nasr: "The Shi'a ascendancy in Iraq is supported by and is in turn bolstering another important development in the Middle East: the emergence of Iran as a regional power."[96]

Iran's Proposal: "Too Good to Be True?"

In late April 2003, a few weeks after the US invasion of Iraq, the SNSC received a draft outline of a road map for improving relations between Iran and the United States. The initiative was managed by Sadeq Kharrazi, Iran's ambassador to France, in cooperation with Tim Guldimann, the Swiss ambassador to Tehran. Since May 1980, Iran–US relations had been severed and the Swiss Embassy in Tehran acted as the protecting power of the US in Iran. According to my information, Guldimann had initiated the new effort. After the initial draft was prepared by Kharrazi and Guldimann, it was given to Foreign Minister Kamal Kharrazi. Kharrazi then invited his top diplomats, such as Javad Zarif, Iran's ambassador to the UN, to assist in editing the draft[97] and crafting the final version.

The draft presented an outline of the aims and expectations of each of the two governments, and it identified three steps required for the two sides to reach a grand bargain.[98] In essence, the proposal was a practical roadmap to end hostilities between the two states. Iran would address US concerns with respect to terrorism, weapons of mass destruction, Iran's opposition to the peace process between Israel and the Palestinians, and Hezbollah of Lebanon. In exchange, the US would end its hostility towards Iran by lifting sanctions and abandoning its quest for regime change. The totally unprecedented part of the proposal was the focus on Iran's position on the peace process and Arab-Israeli conflict, which had been very much in line with other Muslim states and members of the Organization of Islamic Cooperation.

On May 4, 2003, Tim Guldimann attached a cover letter[99] to the proposal and faxed it to the US State Department.[100]Apparently trying hard to convince the Americans that the deal was authentic, Guldimann quoted Sadeq Kharrazi as saying: "The leader uttered some reservations as [to] some points … [but] they [meaning above all, the Leader] agree with 85% to 90% of the non paper. But everything can be negotiated." According to Guldimann, Kharrazi added, "But everything can be negotiated." I have some reservations about the accuracy of these statements, especially that the Supreme Leader had seen the draft.

The draft was discussed in the Foreign Ministry. The Secretariat of the SNSC and the President were informed. According to the discussions I had, Khatami, Rouhani, and Foreign Minister Kamal Kharrazi all strongly believed that as long as there was no willingness on the part of the United States to respond positively to the "road map," we should not make it an official proposal and offer it to Ayatollah Khamenei. Time and time again, he had blamed us for being naive about the American government's true intentions towards Iran. Khatami argued that a "grand deal" proposal should only be presented to the Supreme Leader if the Americans were receptive and indicated interest in such an initiative. There was also a consensus among us that since the proposal was unofficial, we could always deny its authenticity if the Americans publicized it and attempted to humiliate us.

I met Sadeq Kharazi in April 2014 in New York. He had been struggling with cancer for the previous two years. He had his 11th surgery in New York to treat his cancer. I reviewed with him my take on the 2003 proposal. "I was authorized by Tehran. Tim [Guldimann] sent me the first draft. We made some changes. I sent it to my contact in the US State Department. We exchanged the draft two or three times with the State Department. However, the State Department never responded to the final draft. Therefore there was no need to raise the issue with the Leader," Sadeq told me in New York.

Richard Armitage, the US Deputy Secretary of State, was one of the influential people in the White House who rejected and buried the offer. His rationale, as explained in an interview, was: "It didn't fit with some of the other things ... that we'd been hearing from Iran."[101] When asked to elaborate, he responded:

> After the terrible devastation of the earthquake in Bam [in December 2003] ... completely as a humanitarian and not as a political matter [we offered the Iranian government] assistance and earthquake relief [but we got no signal]. If there had been a desire on the Iranian side to seek a better relationship, it would have been an ideal time afterward to send that signal.

Let us examine the facts. The US earthquake relief was offered in December 2003, so it was only a few months after the US rejected Iran's unprecedented offer for reconciliation. Why would Iran have thought that the relief offer was intended as an overture? Also, on behalf of the US administration, Armitage offered relief but at the same time emphasized that it was completely humanitarian in nature. He explicitly stated that it had nothing to do with politics. To place Armitage's words in the context of 2003, the US administration was clearly saying: "Despite our offer of humanitarian assistance, we are not interested in changing the political status quo." Considered together, and in relation to the circumstances of Iran's natural disaster, it is hard to fathom that Armitage expected Iran to send another positive signal aimed at better relations.

Some analysts[102] question the validity of the proposal based on the fact that in 2003, Iran's UN ambassador, Javad Zarif, had met with US diplomats Zalmay Khalilzad and Ryan Crocker in Paris and Geneva but had never raised the issue of Iran's readiness for all-encompassing negotiations with the US. They also emphasize the fact that Khalilzad had met Zarif the day before Guldimann delivered the grand bargain fax. They say/inquire: "Why didn't Zarif say a word about Iran's offer to Khalilzad?" A plausible diplomatic explanation could be: Switzerland was the initiator and mediator and the case should have been followed through them. Opening a new and parallel channel wouldn't have sat well with them.

Also, at that time we were seeking a normalization of relations with Europe. However, the Iran–US conflict was a major obstacle in that respect, and the Europeans constantly blamed us for taking an uncompromising stance towards improving relations with the US. It was critically important for us to demonstrate to them that we were ready to deal with all the issues in dispute between Iran and the US, and that if there were an obstacle, it wasn't on our part. Switzerland, as the protector of US interests in Iran, was perfectly placed to act as witness to Iran's reconciliation efforts and to provide an objective judgment on the whole process to the European community.

Furthermore, nobody in Khatami's administration was mandated or authorized to talk directly to the Americans about resolving disputes. After the big failure with Afghanistan, the Khatami administration scoffed at such a broad proposal for cooperation through any direct channel because they were highly unsure about its outcome. The administration did not trust the Americans and felt it was a real possibility that the US might use the proposal against us by leaking it to the media. The Khatami administration wanted to leave room for denial in case the overture was revealed. Also, Zalmay Khalilzad, a staunch neoconservative who was fundamentally against the Iranian system, would not have been the right channel, even if the Iranians had wanted to make such a move.

Some notable commentators have speculated that this offer of a grand bargain so soon after the US attack on Iraq arose out of fear that Iran would also be attacked.[103] As argued on a number of occasions previously, the wrong impression among Americans that threats and intimidation would elicit favorable response from Tehran accounts for the current state of relations between the two countries. The very fact that Iran's cooperation with the US in Afghanistan occurred while there was no threat of attack on Iran disproves such a seemingly entrenched impression. The same line of thinking also applies to the nuclear issue.

As someone who has been closely involved with the foreign policy apparatus, I can say with certitude that US threats have never been *the key* factor in Iran's foreign policy decision-making, while, of course, they are never totally ignored, as is expected in the rational calculation of a modern state. What makes the difference in the extant political system is the rather peculiar mix of traditional Iranian nationalism and post-revolutionary Islamic fervor. Resisting external pressure has been—and continues to be—a matter of preserving national and ideological identity.

Moreover, given that Iran's proposal was made a few weeks after the US invasion of Iraq, the so-called threat of military attack against Iran was simply out of question. The US had already a full plate in Iraq. So, offering the grand bargain proposal at that juncture would not have been due to imminent security fears.

Finally, the real reason why Bush's administration rejected the proposal was *not* because it was "too good to be true," as US officials maintained.[104] Common sense dictates that sending a positive signal would have easily verified the proposal's authenticity. Based on our assessment, the real reason that the offer was spurned was that the neoconservatives, led by Vice President Dick Cheney and Secretary of Defense Donald Rumsfeld, sought regime change in Iran and did not *want* any solution to the Iran-US problem. At the same time, their swift victory in Iraq had made the Americans overconfident, and their expectation was that it would not take long before, with a little bit of a push from outside, the democratic domino theory would take effect and claim Iran's government.

The perplexing nature of the relationship between Iran and the US manifested itself once again in the spring of 2004. Hassan Rouhani, still the SNSC Secretary at the time, recounted the following story to me:

> After a visit to Washington, ElBaradei, the Head of the IAEA, called me and said: "I need to see you immediately." Within a couple of days, he was in Tehran. I thought he conveyed a message from Washington with regard to the nuclear issue. But he divulged to me that he wanted to speak privately about an important issue. In the meeting, he confided: "I was in Washington a few days ago. I met with George Bush. I told him, 'Why don't you talk directly with the Iranians and together find a solution to this nuclear dilemma?' Bush replied, 'Why just the nuclear issue? Why not talk about all issues disputed between the two countries and solve them all at once? I propose that someone with full authority come from Tehran, sit with me personally, negotiate, and find a blanket solution to all mutual problems.'" ElBaradei maintained that it was an excellent opportunity now that [the] Americans have volunteered to reconcile.

There was no need to hear how the story ended. At that point, I knew Iran's Supreme Leader had put on hold any such talks and negotiations. The wounds of humiliation had not yet been healed.

As the present narrative shows, the history of relations between Iran and the United States is full of similar disappointments. When Iran was ready to reconcile, the US was not, and when the US stretched out its hands, Iran would step back. Chances were missed, one after another.

I was Right and John Sawers was Not

Between the announcement of the Saadabad Agreement in October 2003 and October 2004, a full year, Iran carried on substantive negotiations with the EU3 and also the IAEA while uranium enrichment was halted. These negotiations were intended to reach a long-term agreement within the framework of which, under the NPT regulations and inspections, Iran could run the full cycle of a peaceful nuclear project.

Our nuclear negotiation team was under pressure from two sides. The Europeans demanded that uranium enrichment suspension should be extended for a longer term while the US insisted on an indefinite halt. On the other hand, the Iranian leadership was growing impatient and pushed us to bring the open-ended process to its conclusion.

During the entire negotiation process, the whole time negotiations were taking place, we sought to use the nuclear issue as leverage towards a major settlement with the West. We hoped that a nuclear agreement would ultimately prepare the ground for better relations with the West, including United States. In October 2004, I said in an interview:

> Besides inviting the West's main exporters of nuclear plants to take a "substantial part" in Iran's nuclear projects, Tehran is also ready to offer them a "golden package" that would include full cooperation in fighting international terrorism and restoring peace and security in the region, as well as in trade and investment.[105]

In November 2004, the so-called Paris Agreement was concluded between Iran and the EU3. The negotiations leading to this outcome were amongst the toughest that I ever experienced during my career, including the highly sensitive talks on the Salman Rushdie affair, humanitarian exchanges between Hezbollah and Israel, release of European and American hostages in Lebanon, and also cooperation with the US in Afghanistan.

In Paris, the two sides agreed to form three working groups, in nuclear, political and economic fields, to negotiate for three months on finding a framework within which Iran would provide "objective guarantees" regarding non-diversion from peaceful nuclear activities. In exchange, the EU would recognize Iran's right to peaceful nuclear technology under the NPT. Additionally, the EU would commit to long-term strategic political, economic, and security cooperation with Iran. Again, the Agreement would emphasize that enrichment suspension was temporary, voluntary, non-legally binding, and a confidence-building measure to last during the negotiations of the working groups. Happy and satisfied after finalizing the Paris agreement, the nuclear team went to Vienna to participate in an IAEA Board of Governors' session. While we were there, shocking news came from Tehran—Ayatollah Khamenei had rejected the Agreement.

While we were all in a state of shock, Khatami, Rouhani, and Rafsanjani rushed to meet with the Supreme Leader. Dr. Rouhani explained the tasks of the three Paris working groups to the Leader. He told Ayatollah Khamenei that after reaching a long-term agreement in three months, Iran's file at the IAEA would be normalized, and having given the necessary assurances on non diversion, Iran would be able to resume enrichment, and a new era of relations between Iran and the EU would commence.

Thanks to Rafsanjani's mediation, Ayatollah Khamenei indicated that he would accept the framework of the Paris settlement, but with one condition: suspension should not last more than three months. We informed the Europeans about the developments in Tehran. Under this arrangement, the end of that three-month period would mark 15 months since the Saadabad Agreement and the beginning of the enrichment resumption.

During the following months, we argued that the implementation of the NPT safeguards, Subsidiary Arrangement Code 3.1, and additional protocols[106] should be sufficient as "objective guarantees" for non-diversion. As a matter of fact, there are no international regulations on the transparency of a nuclear program of a member state of NPT beyond these three measures, just referred to, but the Europeans seemed to lack the authority and confidence to accept this offer. What was the obstacle? The United States. Later, in 2006, when no longer in charge of the nuclear negotiating team, Dr. Rouhani told me that Joschka Fisher, former German Foreign Minister, had told him that "[the] EU3 and Iran could have reached a compromise but the United States prevented it from happening."

By March 2005, the talks came to almost a complete halt. On May 25, Rouhani met in Geneva with the foreign ministers of the EU3— the last chance to save the talks. The Europeans asked for three more months to come up with their final offer. After the negotiating team came back to Tehran and after intense deliberations, it was decided to agree with a two-month extension. I notified the EU3 ambassadors of Iran's final decision.

Knowing the atmosphere in Tehran, and with the aim of convincing the Europeans that it was the last chance, I planned an unofficial visit to Europe to talk to my German, French, and British interlocutors. First I met my German counterpart, Michael Schaefer, on a Sunday, in a Berlin pizzeria. During a three-hour meeting, I told him that Iran would never compromise on its legitimate right to a uranium enrichment program and that no change should be expected in Iran's position after the upcoming Iranian elections, set for June 2005. I also pointed out that regardless of who the next president might be, Iran would restart its uranium enrichment activities if the present negotiations failed.

Unofficially, I disclosed to Schaefer a proposal to escape a possible crisis and save the talks. The Isfahan uranium conversion facility, at which yellowcake (uranium concentrate powder) is converted into uranium hexafluoride (which is then introduced to centrifuges at the Natanz facility for the purpose of enrichment), would restart its processing but would export its output to South Africa and in return, import an equivalent amount of yellow cake from South Africa. The Natanz enrichment facility would restart, but only work at the level of a pilot plant. Meanwhile, negotiations could continue for a maximum of one year, allowing both sides to secure objective guarantees that would ensure non-diversion in Iran's nuclear program in exchange for guarantees of nuclear, technological, and economic cooperation between Iran and the EU3. Schaefer was receptive to my proposal, and encouraged me to talk to Paris and London.

The next day, I was in Paris. Sadeq Kharrazi, the Iranian ambassador to France, joined me in my talks with the French Foreign Ministry's Political Director, Stanislas Lefebvre de Laboulaye. After repeating what I had told my German counterpart, I perceived his position to be lukewarm. What I read between the lines was: "If London accepts the plan, we would too." So, everything ultimately depended upon the outcome of my discussions with the British Foreign Office. The UK negotiator was none other than Sir John Sawers, then Director General for Political Affairs at the Foreign Office and later head of MI6—which I heard about in 2009.

The news about his appointment as head of the MI6 shocked me, and conjured up in my mind a number of past episodes. Of all the European negotiators, Sawers was the one who appeared most determined to achieve a long term suspension of the enrichment program. I recalled at least three or four occasions when the British Foreign Secretary, Jack Straw, showed signs of flexibility and seemed ready to compromise, but would suddenly reverse his position and become as rigid as a rock after Sawers whispered something in his ear. These flashbacks, coupled with the news of his appointment as MI6 supremo, led me to believe that in reality Sawers was more than a Director General during the negotiations. After a few meetings with the EU3 ministers or their teams over the 2003–5 period, Dr. Rouhani remarked more than once to me: "Hossein! John Sawers is extremely mysterious with a sophisticated personality [*pichideh*], and is the most influential in EU3 team."

In any event, I endured a tough, two-hour meeting with John Sawers. He told me point blank that Washington would not tolerate even one centrifuge spinning in Iran, and added that my proposal about letting a pilot plant operate in Natanz would not make much difference: "Don't forget that we [British] built an atomic bomb with only 16 centrifuges running." However, he also indicated that he was prepared to talk further after the Iranian elections. Once again, the delaying tactic was in play.

I told him: "Listen, John, the system (*nezam*) has made its decision. There will be no more extension after the two-month period is over. Iran will start enrichment even at the cost of war." He replied that if Iran restarted enrichment, then we should expect a US attack. When I said goodbye that day, I felt that Sawers thought I was bluffing. Interestingly, I also thought that by threatening a US attack, he was bluffing. What transpired after that spring day in 2005 showed that he was indeed bluffing and that I was not. Again, however, an opportunity had been missed.

Fast forward two months: Iran had a new President and a sea change was under way. The EU3 ambassadors in Tehran delivered the EU3 package in early August 2005. Subsequent to that, I met with them at my SNSC office in Tehran. I quickly reviewed the package, and it is fair to say that it was attractive from a political, economic, technological, and even nuclear cooperation prespective. However, all the positive content was undone by the fact that it again sought "suspension of uranium enrichment for the period of negotiations." I was totally deflated. Looking at the three ambassadors, I asked "Can you tell me if we can decide together and specify a period for the negotiations?" They looked at each other, paused for a while, and finally Richard Dalton, the UK ambassador replied: "Unfortunately not."

Dalton's reply was hesitant, seeming to confirm my own observation that his personal position was different from John Sawers—Dalton was far more realistic than his bosses in London. I followed up by asking: "So does it mean that it can be one year, three years, five years?" Dalton replied: "Perhaps ten years would be needed for negotiations to build confidence." I continued with the question: "Should I convey to the higher authorities that the EU3 is asking for indefinite suspension?" They confirmed this to be the case, on which I observed: "If this is the EU position, then our good times are over. Tehran will restart enrichment regardless of the consequences; be it referral to the UN Security Council, imposing sanctions, or even war."

I was sure that the three ambassadors did not agree with their superiors and had sympathy toward my view. During a private meeting in summer 2005, François Nicoullaud, the French ambassador and a good friend of mine, told me: "The EU3 is more flexible but for the US, the enrichment in Iran is a red line which the EU cannot cross."[107] In the end, due to the US position of "no enrichment in Iran," Ayatollah Khamenei instructed Rouhani to restart Isfahan nuclear facility. The talks collapsed and thus began the tumultuous years in Iran–US relations.

Chapter 6

SIXTEEN YEARS OF MODERATION COME TO AN END: 2005‑12

Emergence of the Principalists

Ahmadinejad came to power in August 2005 at a time when negotiations between the EU3 and Iran, under the presidency of Khatami, had almost hit a dead end. Further complicating matters, there were no more individuals like Khatami, Rouhani, and Rafsanjani to simultaneously negotiate with the Supreme Leader and the West in pursuit of a halfway solution. For the first time in the Islamic Republic's history, in addition to the three branches of government, military, and security and intelligence establishments were all in the hands of conservatives, calling themselves *Principalists*.

Although there were two distinct factions, one more moderate than the other, within this camp, the dominant one shared the Supreme Leader's level of mistrust of the West. However, this faction also believed that the antagonism between the Islamic Republic and the West had its origin deep in their respective natures and worldviews, and so it would be impossible to secure Iran's right to enrichment only through negotiation. They argued that the only way forward was to resist the bullying policies of the West and adopt an aggressive stance until the West recognized Iran's rights and retreated. As a result, Iran's position dramatically shifted to one of non-compromise and inflexibility.

Ahmadinejad won the election by campaigning for social and economic justice, and war against corruption. He promised that he would bring the corrupt mafia that monopolized power and wealth to justice, yet, as is now widely known, many of the worst corruption cases in the history of the Islamic Republic, involving high-ranking public officials, governmental bankers and businessmen, occurred during his 8-year term of office. However, he used "anti-corruption platform" as a populist tactic—promising to fight corruption—to buy popularity and marginalize his political rivals; specifically, moderates and reformists.

In July 2005, the office of then-President-elect Mahmoud Ahmadinejad called and invited me to meet with him. I hardly knew him, having met only once at an informal occasion years earlier. On July 19, 2005 at 5.00 p.m., I met the new President in his temporary office. The meeting was scheduled for 20 minutes but ran for more than two hours. Mojtaba Hashemi Samareh, Ahmadinejad's close friend and confidant, was also present at the meeting. My encounter with Ahmadinejad shed light on the profound differences ahead between him, the representative of the Principalists, and the moderate-reformist current within Iran's establishment that his administration was about to replace.

Ahmadinejad wore slippers and no jacket. As I entered his office he hugged me and greeted me by my first name. "How are you doing, Hossein Agha [Mr. Hossein]? Have you had lunch?" I told him that I had already had lunch. He went to his desk, grabbed a handful of pistachios, and said: "This is my lunch."

Without wasting time, Ahmadinejad continued: "You know, I view your approach [to the nuclear issue] as problematic. Why do you negotiate for your rights? Uranium enrichment is our legal right. Negotiation [over our given rights] does not make any sense." I retorted:

> It is true that uranium enrichment, within the framework of the NPT, is our right but in order to implement the Treaty, the international community has created the IAEA. Within the IAEA, the Board of Governors which represents the member states has the role of policy-making. Their decisions are binding for the members and signatories, including Iran. Now, the Board of Governors has passed a resolution demanding Iran suspend its uranium enrichment program. We have a choice, either abide by the rules and suspend Iran's enrichment program temporarily and restart after we reach an agreement with the world powers, or defy. In choosing the latter, Iran's nuclear dossier will be referred to the UN Security Council and we will face international sanctions.

Ahmadinejad fiercely opposed my argument, stating: "The IAEA does not have the right [to refer Iran's nuclear case to the UNSC]. These are all bluffs to frighten you." With an obvious critical look and words, he asked: "Why have you chosen to talk to the Europeans anyway?" I responded:

> We are talking with Europe, Russia, China and members of Non-Aligned Movement. We would have preferred to include the

United States as the key player but at that juncture that was a red line and the administration was forbidden from holding discussions with the US. Therefore, we chose the Europeans because first, they are a powerful bloc; second, to prevent referral of our case to the UNSC; and third, by improving our relations with Europe, we sought a channel to détente with the US.

Ahmadinejad would not give way. "America and Europe cannot do a damn thing," he asserted, and added: "We should continue enrichment and not be frightened by the West's bluffs."

I described for him the likely consequences of acting on his stated position. I told him that the case *would be* referred to the UNSC and that this was not a bluff. I told him that Iran's nuclear program would be categorized as a threat to international security under Chapter 7 of the United Nations Charter, adding: "In that case, Iran would be subject to punishment including imposition of sanctions and even military action." Ahmadinejad was not daunted: "Neither America, nor the UNSC can do a damn thing. You committed suicide out of fear of death [during Khatami's presidency]."

After two fruitless hours of argument, I was still unclear as to why I had been invited to that meeting. Finally, he said: "The reason I asked you to meet with me is that I have five candidates in mind for the Foreign Ministry. You are the first one I decided to talk to. Mojtaba [Hashemi Samareh] told me that you have been our best ambassador since the Revolution." I thanked him and Mojtaba for their consideration and confidence, but declined the offer. "We have been talking about Iran's foreign policy for two hours and we haven't had a single common view on any issue," I said. "Also, I come from a wealthy family. You campaigned as a president for the poor, having been raised in a disadvantaged family yourself. But I have no idea about their pain and suffering. I am not suitable for your cabinet." Ahmadinejad insisted that we could work with each other but I already knew that was impossible. By the time I left, it was clear that no goodwill existed between us.

From Ahmadinejad's office, I went directly to Rouhani's office. As soon as I saw him, I told him, in so many words, that: "Iran's foreign policy was going to face dramatic changes, in fact that foreign relations would soon be turned upside down. Neither of us would be able to work with the new President. We should resign." The next day, we left Tehran for London to participate in a farewell meeting with our EU3 counterparts. It was a bitter day, knowing that this meeting represented the end of 16 years of efforts under Rafsanjani and Khatami to reduce tensions with the West.

Rouhani met Ahmadinejad on August 9, 2005. After his meeting, Rouhani told me that he had cautioned Ahmadinejad about the potential consequences of the referral of Iran's file to the UNSC. Ahmadinejad had told the president that a major share of the IAEA's budget was provided by the Western countries and therefore they controlled the outcome of decisions made by the IAEA. Ahmadinejad had commented in return: "Call ElBaradei right now and tell him Iran will pay the IAEA's full budget."

Rouhani was stunned. He told Ahmadinejad: "First of all, such a decision has to go through the *Majlis* and, secondly, international organizations have their own rules and structures. Iran cannot individually dictate such matters." Rouhani told me that Ahmadinejad fired back in an angry tone: "I am instructing you and you should obey." Rouhani's patience had come to an end, saying: "You should nominate another person to follow such instructions. I resign as of this moment." And he did. Rouhani resigned as Secretary of the Supreme National Security Council and the head of Iran's nuclear negotiating team on August 20, 2005. It was plain to see that Iran's foreign policy, particularly with respect to the nuclear issue, would change from one of engagment and cooperation to one of confrontation and disagreement.

Ali Larijani, who later became the Speaker of the Majlis, was chosen to succeed Rouhani. Soon after his appointment, he invited me to meet with him. Larijani insisted on offering me a position. Since I had worked together in the SNSC during the Rouhani period, I agreed to work with him, but only in the capacity of "Foreign Policy Advisor."

During Hassan Rouhani's tenure as Secretary of the SNSC, we had two red lines with regard to the nuclear issue. First, we insisted on recognition of our rights under the NPT, and second, we sought to avoid referral of Iran's nuclear file to the UNSC. In the first meeting after Larijani's appointment as the new Secretary I met with a group of individuals, the majority of whom I did not know. At the end of a long discussion, Larijani concluded the meeting by saying that the new nuclear policy would abandon the strategy of "two red lines" and assume only one, our nuclear rights under the NPT. The reason for such a decision was first their deep mistrust toward the West and second their disappointment with two years of negotiations with EU3. In the course of the discussion, I wrote a note to Larijani:

> By adopting such a strategy, Iran's nuclear file will definitely be referred to the UNSC and a perfect storm targeting Iran is in the

making. I don't want to be part of this historical shame. Therefore, I will not participate in nuclear meetings any more but in case you want to consult with me I will be at your disposal.

Ten years of confidence-building efforts with the West, several agreements on mutual economic and political cooperation with the Europeans, and preparation of the ground for joining the World Trade Organization had gone out the window, practically overnight.

Following these developments, Rouhani became the head of the Center for Strategic Research, a think tank associated with the Expediency Council, headed by Rafsanjani. The Center also serves as a consultative arm to the Office of the Supreme Leader. In September 2005, Rouhani appointed me as his deputy for international affairs. I worked in that position until I was arrested in April 2007.

The Hardliners' Platform

As already indicated, by 2005, the moderates and reformists became almost completely irrelevant, and the so-called Principalists dominated all branches of government. During the 16 years of their tenure (1989–2005), moderates under Rafsanjani and reformers under Khatami had sought to resolve the conflict with the West, despite unyielding opposition and sabotage by the conservatives. Regrettably, the United States increased sanctions and toughened its stance toward Iran without regard for the rapprochement efforts made by the Rafsanjani and Khatami administrations.

The Principalists argued that Khatami's conciliatory policies begat increasingly aggressive behavior by the United States under President George W. Bush. They insisted that Europe would follow the US, the difference being that Europe wanted to sell their products, but sought no serious or long-term political relationship with, or economic investment in, Iran. The Principalists also argued that while the US supported and maintained warm relations with dictatorships across the region, it castigated Iran as undemocratic—despite Iran's political system being clearly more similar to that of Western democracies.

The Principalists specifically questioned the outcome of Khatami's conciliatory policies, which they argued to have led to more pressure and humiliation for the nation during the nuclear negotiations. They argued that while Iran was a party to every international convention related to the non-proliferation of nuclear, chemical, and biological weapons, it continued to be accused of their breach. Principalists pointed out that even though Pakistan and India had not signed the NPT *but had* developed atomic bombs, they were not subject to any sanctions or pressure by the West. On the other hand, Iran had cooperated with the West for 20 consecutive months between 2003 and 2005 had even opened some of its military facilities to the IAEA inspectors, though not required under the NPT. And "although the IAEA repeatedly reported a lack of evidence of any military diversion in Iran's nuclear program, the EU3 had demanded that Iran suspend its uranium enrichment program in August 2005. So, what was the point of your cooperative policies and what did you gain, other than another humiliation?" the Principalists uses to question us.

Having effectively marginalized moderates and driven them off the political stage by 2005, the conservatives turned Iran's foreign policy around 180 degrees by ignoring Western demands and those of the international institutions. The conservatives' rationale was that by defying the demands of the West, and the US in particular, Iran's opponents would eventually be forced to accept Iran's position on the nuclear issue and recognize our rights. They also believed that this approach would yield another significant benefit, arguing that if Iran were to spearhead resistance against the US and adopt an aggressive posture against Israel, ordinary Muslims across the Islamic world would rally to its support. This, they believed, would place Iran in a stronger position in relation to the United States in the Middle East region and significantly increase the cost of any likely Western military action against the country.

Iran: An Aggressive Foreign Policy Discourse

Ahmadinejad was determined from the very beginning of his term to alter the trajectory of Iran's conciliatory efforts with the West. Before he took office, the reformist President, Mohammad Khatami, had worked closely with his Secretary of the Supreme National Security Council, Hassan Rouhani. But in 2007, Iran's Ministry of Foreign Affairs drafted a paper[1] that attacked the conciliatory nature of Iran's "Critical Dialogue" with the West under President Hashemi Rafsanjani's direction between 1989 and 1997. The paper proclaimed a change in strategy in Iran's foreign policy position, from "the accused [who has to convince the accuser of not being guilty] to the accuser." In effect, with this paper,

Ahmadinejad announced to the world that Iran now subscribed to the notion of "the best defense is a strong offense."

And Ahmadinejad *did* go on the offensive, with a verbal attack on the credibility of mainstream historical accounts of the Holocaust. His team believed that by raising doubts about the accuracy of conventional wisdom on the Holocaust—fully known highly sensitive issue in Israel, the US and the entire West—they might also encourage the world to question the need for Israel to exist. As observed by one of Ahmadinejad's advisors in 2007, "by raising the issue of the Holocaust we closed [Iran's] nuclear file."[2]

It has been discussed in previous pages that the controversy created by this tactic, along with the mistranslation of Ahmadinejad's statement about "wiping Israel off the map" and other inflammatory remarks, did serious damage to Iran's standing with the West. Israeli hardliners and pro-Israel lobbyists in the US used the public position of Ahmadinejad's government to turn the rest of the world against Iran. Ahmadinejad's statements at the same time dashed any hopes of negotiations between the US and Iran. As publicly perceived in the US at the time, the mere suggestion of engaging with Iran simply seemed outlandish and damaging to the US world standing.

Another consequence of this new policy was that the propaganda war between Ian and Israel became more heated, sharpening in turn the state of dispute between Iran and the US, and the West in general.

Ahmadinejad's emergence came on the heel of two major developments that facilitated the creation of an offensive foreign policy. First, Iran's two arch enemies, the Taliban to the east, and Saddam Hussein to the west, had already left the scene—in 2001 and 2003 respectively. Both had served, even if inadvertently, Iran's regional position and posture, particularly in Iraq—which I have discussed in relative detail. Second, the sudden increase in the price of oil, reaching record levels after 2005, generated a surge in oil revenues for Iran, which allowed the adoption and perusal of increasingly aggressive policies geared to challenging the US hegemony in the region.

Ahmadinejad's nuclear policy was basically one of substantial expansion of the nuclear program as a response to Western pressure. The rationale for the policies and measures in this field by Ahmadinejad's administration was rooted in three flawed calculations. First, they did not believe that any sanctions could be imposed. Their calculation was that the IAEA would *not* refer Iran's nuclear file to the UN for the imposition of sanctions—that talk of sanctions "was all a Western bluff and would not happen." Second, they believed that even if sanctions were imposed, they would not be effective. And third, they were convinced that they only needed to master the complete nuclear fuel cycle, by which time the matter would be a fait accompli and the US would have no choice but to back down from its bluffs and threats. It is unfortunate, though, that in the end, that Iranian posture and policy proved to be mistaken—and costly.

In a remarkably short time, the Ahmadinejad administration's ignorance and inexperience cost Iran almost all of the international goodwill that it had accrued. They had very little capacity for effective diplomatic relations, yet they exuded an abundance of overconfidence, reinforcing their own strategic assumptions amongst each another, but far removed from the realm of practical politics. Ahmadinejad ostensibly departed from the solemn conduct traditionally expected from heads of state, and instead engaged in belligerent and provocative postures that only served to damage Iran.

Where did Ahmadinejad Stand?

Ahmadinejad rose to power in 2005 almost out of nowhere. His rise was primarily attributed to the widespread support from the Principalists (conservatives) loyal to the Supreme Leader, not only within the establishment but also their grassroots conservative supporters. Additionally, his populist pro-justice slogans and so-called "anti-corruption" drive also attracted substantial segments of disenchanted middle-class urbanites in his early years. That seemingly strong base of support came to lose its initial lustre gradually and once the campaign promises failed to materialize, and rising oil revenues were either spent on non-economic projects, ostentatious waste, increased corruption, and costly foreign adventures. His once unquestioningly solid political base within the conservative bloc—Principalists—also came to erode after the controversial 2009 elections, especially since April 2011 when a major rift emerged between him and the mainstream Principalists. The latent problem flared up when the Minister of Intelligence, Heydar Moslehi, was forced to resign by Ahmadinejad. However, Ayatollah Khamenei intervened and reinstated Moslehi.

To my understanding, Mahmoud Ahmadinejad was never a Principalist, hardliner or conservative. His main agenda was to grab power and then stay in power. In pursuit of this goal, he embarked on a multi-dimensional plan. Domestically, he attacked Rafsanjani and

Khatami who represented the moderate and reformist currents respectively. By doing so, he sought to eliminate his most threatening rivals, but at the same time buy the support of hardliners and the Supreme Leader who, although not considered a hardliner, *had* sought a tougher foreign policy and *also* did not believe in Rafsanjani and Khatami's conciliatory foreign policy.

With respect to foreign policy, Ahmadinejad pursued a dual approach. His vitriolic language against the US and Israel aimed to win the support of the conservatives inside the country and also among the masses in the Islamic world as well as in the developing countries. He wanted to acquire enough political clout internationally so that the US could not ignore him. At the same time, he made overt but veiled suggestions regarding rapprochement. Covertly, he intended to take much more significant strides toward rapprochement with the United States. The logic behind this strategy was that if Ahmadinejad could covertly strike a deal with the United States, he would then proclaim the success publicly. In the wake of such a revelation, he would launch a propaganda campaign claiming that the deal was due to his courageous and aggressive stance, and that the US had finally come to settle for Iran's "regional and even international paramountcy"—as he so often stated in his public pronouncements. Ahmadinejad's announcement of a deal with the US was perceived—by himself and his people—to further discredit moderates and reformists, galvanize the support of conservatives, and, most importantly, make Ahmadinejad a national hero who had been able to force the US into retreat. A legendary Ahmadinejad then would be in a position to craft a Medvedev–Putin-type political model at the end of his second term by placing one of his "confidants" in the office for four years, only to regain the position afterwards—as had happened in Moscow.

Ahmadinejad wasted little time, sending messages to the US indicating his willingness to talk even though this ran counter to his public belligerence toward the United States. Barbara Slavin, the well-known American journalist and Iran expert, quotes Condoleezza Rice to have told her in 2006: "We were getting pinged in a lot of places, from the United Nations, to Baghdad and the Afghan Capital, Kabul, with messages saying the Iranians wanted to talk."[3]

When those messages went unanswered, Ahmadinejad wrote a letter to President George W. Bush. A former American politician told me that "the letter was a reflection of an unstable mind." President Bush's response was that Iran's President was "a very strange man."[4] And indeed he was. According to a former US foreign policy official—and also a close friend—Ahmadinejad made two mistakes. His first mistake was presenting himself as an "unstable and unpredictable" man. Ahmadinejad lost respect and credibility as a result of his actions. A glaring example of such a conduct, as seen by my friend, was his UN speeches, where he condemned "rapacious capitalism" and predicted the collapse of the "American empire."[5] Ahmadinejad's second mistake was his belief that by denying the Holocaust, he would put the US and the West on the defensive. But, on the contrary, this tactic simply provoked a more aggressive Western policy toward Iran. Apart from anything else, it became politically difficult, if not impossible, for a US sitting President to talk to a leader who denied that the Holocaust ever took place.

Ahmadinejad's unprecedented, congratulatory letter to President Obama also went unanswered. Instead, Obama wrote a letter to the Supreme Leader, completely ignoring Ahmadinejad. In his interview with Larry King in September 2010, Ahmadinejad said that he was ready to meet with Obama during the UN General Assembly.[6] But a couple of days later, in his UN speech, he proclaimed that the US was behind the 9/11 attacks![7]

In 2012, an American member of the Iran–US Track II[8] (simply called Track II) told me that Mashaei, Ahmadinejad's senior aide and mentor, had met with former US officials to discuss the possibility of opening direct talks. Earlier, in January 2011, another American member of Track II told me that Iran, through its ambassador to the UN, had asked the State Department to introduce a representative for "serious and comprehensive" talks. "The State Department's response was disappointing," my Track II friend said. "They are ready to meet with the Iranians but they will only listen, not talk." He also told me that in an effort to arrange a meeting between the Iranian and American officials, he had been in contact with an Iranian ambassador in Europe. The ambassador had told him that everything was set from Iran's side—Esfandiar Mashaie and Mojtaba Hashemi Samareh were going to attend the meeting. "[The] meeting will be held in Berlin," the Iranian ambassador told my American friend. He responded:

> But the White House said "no." They said that they did not want to engage with the Iranians outside of the P5+1 framework. The White House maintained that if they [other members of P5+1] realize that we have been engaged in secret talks behind their back, it would cause a deep sense of mistrust of the US government.

Two Track II members (one of them a former US official) contacted me a month and a half later and said that they had met Mostafa Dowlatyar, then Director General for the Institute for International and Political Studies (IPIS), associated with the Foreign Ministry, in Stockholm. Dowlatyar, a former classmate and close friend of Saeed Jalili—then Secretary of the SNSC—is reported to have proposed to extend an invitation to Marc Grossman, US special envoy to Afghanistan, to officially travel to Tehran and meet with Foreign Ministry officials. The two Track II team members said that on their return to Washington, they met with and conveyed the message to Hillary Clinton. They were later told that Grossman would not go to Iran, but Iranian and American ambassadors in Kabul can meet there.

In March 2011, an American official told me at a conference that the US regularly received messages from Mashaei claiming that Tehran was eager to talk and establish relations with the US. He said that "Ahmadinejad's administration constantly sends the US messages. The channels that convey these messages are so numerous that we don't know which one to choose. We are just confused. We did not answer for we were not sure if those messages had Ayatollah Khamenei's backing."

While Ahmadinejad attacked Obama publicly, claiming that "he cannot even write his own name" (a Persian saying alluding to a perfect illiterate), he relentlessly pursued the Americans seeking talks with himself or his representatives. Another Track II friend told me: "I have met Mashaei eight times. In all meetings Tehran is seeking an opening to talks and relations with the US."

On September 25, 2011, during his visit to New York, Ahmadinejad stated: "The Islamic Republic is ready to reconsider its negative view toward the US." Implying that Iran and the US should talk bilaterally rather than within the framework of P5+1 (which at the time was completely out of his control and was supervised by the Supreme Leader directly), Ahmadinejad added "This issue is between Iran and the US ... I believe we must resolve it through different means other than the nuclear negotiations."[9]

In fall 2011, Professor Frank Von Hippel and I were teaching a class at Princeton University on the Iranian nuclear crisis. The university had arranged for students to meet with German and French authorities who had been involved in the nuclear talks with Iran. During the visit, a German official whom I knew told me "Mashaei had a secret meeting with Christoph Heusgen, National Advisor on Foreign and Security Policy to Chancellor Angela Merkel. The meeting took place in the residence of a former German deputy foreign minister.

Mashaei had asked the Germans to inform Washington that Tehran was ready to re-establish relations, and was even ready to "contribute to Obama's campaign in the next elections." According to my friend, the Americans' response to the Germans was: "Don't get involved in the issue."

A few months before the end of his second term, during his last appearance in New York in September 2012, Ahmadinejad announced: "Iran recognizes the United States and believes that we can have relations with each other."[10] He went on to add "The Islamic Republic of Iran is prepared to expedite [the re-establishment of the] relations between the two countries." He was clearly not worried about the prospect of domestic attacks by the hardliners at that juncture. Dr. Velayati, former Foreign Minister and advisor to the Supreme Leader, swiftly reacted to the statement and observed: "Iran's general policy with respect to relations with the US has not changed and no decision has been made in this regard."[11]

Beleaguered and struggling for his political life, Ahmadinejad did not let go of his agenda. It is my understanding that he knew that his advocacy of better relations with the US would not get anywhere, except that he considered in the last attempt by him to remain politically relevant. During his final New York visit, he repeated the proposal on no fewer than five different occasions, intending to demonstrate his commitment and sincerity by restating the message. After all his negative rhetoric, it appears that he wanted to convince the world and the Iranian people that he was the man who sought to bring the Iran–US conflict to an end, with all that it implied, but his opponents prevented him from doing so. Judging from his words and conduct, it appears that he espoused the hope until the very end of his presidency that he could still maintain his earlier grassroots support for an eventual comeback.

George W. Bush vs. Mahmoud Ahmadinejad

President Bush's second term coincided with Mahmoud Ahmadinejad's election in Iran. In 2006, Iran's nuclear dossier was referred to the UNSC by the IAEA for punitive action. This was primarily the consequence of failed talks with the EU3 and failure to fulfill the IAEA demands. The Board of Governors' resolution cited the "absence of confidence that Iran's nuclear program is exclusively for peaceful purposes resulting from the history of concealment."[12] Iran was therefore implored to "re-establish full and sustained suspension of all" enrichment activities.

The second US National Security Strategy under George W. Bush was unveiled on March 16, 2006. "We may face no greater challenge from a single country than from Iran," the report read.[13] The very same day, Ali Larijani, Iran's new Secretary of the SNSC, announced that Iran was willing to talk to the United States, but it was clear that the Americans had decided to get tough on Iran and that they would even consider launching a pre-emptive military strike against it. As Tehran sent messages through numerous channels requesting direct talks, it was shocked by Condoleezza Rice's request for an additional $75 million to promote democracy in Iran.[14] "Now regime change is the official policy of the United States," I was told by an Iranian official.

Shortly thereafter, the State Department announced the opening of a new Iran Desk in Dubai, and added staff and training for more Farsi-speaking officers, all assigned to watch Tehran.[15] To the Iranian government, it was apparent that the purpose of the station was to organize an espionage network for possible sabotage inside Iran. Undersecretary Nicholas Burns compared the new Dubai outpost to the Riga station in Latvia where the American diplomat, George Kennan, had laid the foundations of the Cold War against the Soviet Union in the 1930s with the strategic aim of bringing down the communist system.[16] While rumors about a broad air campaign were all over the news every day, I was told by an Iranian official that Iran's intelligence had discovered evidence that the Americans were in contact with minority groups to use them for organizing terrorist operations inside the country. A horrific story revealed in the *Telegraph* added to the anxiety in Tehran. It claimed that Britain was holding secret talks at the highest levels of government "to discuss possible military strikes against Iran."[17] It was against this backdrop that, for the first time in 27 years, Iran's President, Mahmoud Ahmadinejad, initiated communication with his American counterpart.

In his 18-page letter to George W. Bush, Ahmadinejad covered many subjects. These included regional and international concerns such as the misguided war that the US waged in Iraq and Afghanistan, destabilizing the region; Palestinian rights; strong US support for Israel; research and development in science; and even the reasons for the September 11, 2001 attacks. He listed Iran's grievances with the US, namely the 1953 coup; US support for Saddam; downing of the Iranian passenger plane; freezing of Iranian assets; and the attempts to block Iran's programs and projects. He brought in numerous references to religion and an affinity with God. The letter also included a number of exhortations and ultimatums that anyone familiar with a Western political culture would have recognized as irrelevant, if not insulting. Many of my American friends, scholars, and politicians considered the letter inquisitive, insulting, and naïve. But regardless of its content, the fact that for the first time an Iranian President wrote an official letter to the US President was highly significant. I believe that the letter was intended to open the doors to bilateral dialogue. As I mentioned earlier, for personal reasons, Ahmadinejad was determined to resolve the conflict between Iran and the US. During his first term in particular, he enjoyed the wholehearted trust of the system (*nezam*) and could have possibly struck a deal with the US. In any event, George Bush did not respond to the letter.

A few months later, in July 2006, in response to the abduction of two Israeli soldiers and the killing of eight others by Hezbollah militants, war broke out between Israel and Hezbollah. Kidnapping the Israeli soldiers was in retaliation for Prime Minister Ariel Sharon's reneging on his agreement with Hezbollah to release all Hezbollah prisoners during the last prisoners' exchange.

Israel initiated heavy air and ground operations, bombarding Lebanon's major highways and ports, with the ultimate stated objective of decapitating Hezbollah's military and political organization. At the end of the first week, Israel expanded its air attacks against civilian centers, including schools, community centers, and mosques. They believed that Hezbollah hid its military assets inside those civilian centers. The result of this assessment and action was the tragedy of Qana.[18] The US and other Western powers stood by as spectators, hoping that Israel would root out Hezbollah's military capability. Secretary of State Condoleezza Rice describing the bloody confrontation as "The birth pangs of a new Middle East."[19]

Through the fourth week, it became apparent that Israel and the Western governments had miscalculated Hezbollah's strength, as it withstood the invasion and Israel was forced to retreat. The Israeli army's failure to accomplish its goal marked the first significant Israeli defeat in a full-fledged war against any Arab force. The conflict was referred to as the 33-Day War in Iran, and it established a mindset within the Iranian military-intelligence establishment that despite its highly-advanced army, Israel was not invincible. But another significant outcome of the conflict was that Iran's emergence as a regional force which could successfully wage a proxy war against Israel, something that tilted the balance of power in Iran's favor.

Meanwhile, in Iraq, IEDs (improvised explosive devices) or roadside bombs were explicitly targeting US troops. The US government accused Iran of supplying IEDs to the insurgents—which Iran denied. Some reports claimed that IEDs were responsible for three out of five conflict-related deaths in Iraq.[20] As discussed in detail previously, Iran's position in Iraq steadily grew in the aftermath of the 2003 US invasion and the fall of the Ba'athist regime. With the passage of time, it appeared that Iran was becoming, more and more, indispensable to the restoration of stability in Iraq. As stated by Dr. Vali Nasr, a prominent Iran expert, in 2007, "an endgame in Iraq," but there was "no endgame without involving Iran."[21]

By late 2006, the picture was very different and Washington's early victories seemed a long time ago, as the US was now bogged down in Iraq and faced increased sectarian violence and mounting US casualties. To assess the situation in Iraq and identify mechanisms to protect the US interests, Congress formed the bi-partisan Baker–Hamilton Iraq Study Group. The Group's panelists met, interviewed, or consulted hundreds of high-ranking current and former officials, senior military officers, non-governmental organization leaders, and academics.[22] James Baker, a leading member of the Group, had a long meeting with Iran's UN ambassador, Javad Zarif, at his New York residence.

The Group's report produced a great stir in policy circles in the US as it prescribed bold moves to address the worsening conditions in Iraq. With regard to Iran–US relations, the report recommended that "Given the ability of Iran and Syria to influence events within Iraq and their interest in avoiding chaos in Iraq, the United States should try to engage them constructively."[23] President Bush, however, did not agree with the much-anticipated outcome of this initiative. His view was that "Iran is promoting an extreme form of religion ... Iran's a destabilizing force."[24] Even Admiral Fallon, head of the US Central Command, recommended US engagement with Iran, but he was overruled by Bush. At a White House meeting on Iran, Admiral Fallon said: "I think we need to do something to get engaged with these guys."[25] Using a very derogatory term for the Iranians, Bush rejected Fallon's suggestion. "Fallon was stunned. Declaring them '...' was not a strategy."[26]

The deteriorating situation in Iraq left the Bush administration with no choice but to give the green light to the US ambassador in Iraq, Ryan Crocker, to hold talks with his counterpart, Ambassador Hassan Kazemi-Qomi, in trilateral meetings hosted by the Iraqi government that would focus on Iraq's stability.[27] The Baghdad talks, held on May

28, 2007, marked the first official meeting between the US and Iran since the Algiers Accords of January 1981.[28] Following the first round of talks, there was cautious optimism, with the US ambassador stating:

> The Iranians, as well as ourselves, laid out the principles that guide our respective policies toward Iraq. There was pretty good congruence right down the line: support for a secure, stable, democratic, federal Iraq, in control of its own security, at peace with its neighbors.[29]

Meanwhile, his Iranian counterpart provided concrete steps for cooperation: "Iran is willing to train and equip Iraqi security forces to create a new military and security structure."[30] There were three rounds of talks in total, taking place in May, June, and August of 2007 during which both countries discussed ways to mitigate the violence in Iraq and pave the way for its stability.[31] While the talks were restricted to topics pertaining to Iraq's stability, the mere fact that both sides were at the same table was an important step towards dialogue and understanding. But the talks stuttered, with Americans claiming that Iran was playing an increasingly destabilizing role in Iraq by supplying weaponry, training, and finance to insurgents that had conducted attacks on US and the coalition forces—a charge denied by Iran.[32] Ambassador Crocker acknowledged that during the talks, he "laid out before the Iranians a number of direct, specific concerns about their behavior in Iraq—their support for militias that are fighting both the Iraqi security forces and the coalition forces." He went on to add "The fact [is] that a lot of explosives and ammunitions used by these groups are coming from Iran ... The Iranians did not respond directly to that, they did again emphasize that their policy is support of the [Iraqi] government."[33] The Iranians also voiced their grievances with America, demanding an explanation for groups that were committing "infiltration and sabotage in western, central and south-western areas of the country" at the behest of the US and UK to heighten ethnic tensions in western Iran as a means of pressing Tehran on other issues such as the contentious nuclear program.[34]

Mutual accusations on both sides hampered the talks. The fact that the Iranian leadership permitted talks between Iran and US to take place at all was an indication of their willingness on the part of Iran to build upon areas of mutual interest. However, leading figures in the Iranian government were skeptical about striking a deal with Washington and expected that the US would not respond in kind. Given the circumstances, the US could have welcomed the Iranian delegation's offer to establish a "trilateral mechanism" to coordinate security matters in Iraq and make a concerted effort to stabilize that country, rooting out the al-Qaeda network and operatives.[35] But the Bush administration's natural inclination at the time was to turn their backs on cooperation with the Iranians.

Tehran identified two clear motives for the Bush administration's behavior. First, neo-conservatives appeared committed to military and forceful solutions, including "deterring or, when needed ... compelling regional foes to act in ways that protect American interests and principle."[36] For them, foes were foes and to make friends with them was off the table. Second, the Israel lobby now had unprecedented influence with the American government, pursuing a hardline with Iran.

The book *The Israel Lobby and U.S. Foreign Policy*, the first of its kind in the academic sphere, authored by Stephen Walt (Harvard University) and John Mearsheimer (University of Chicago), was an indication of the lobby's increased influence in US foreign policy. Mearsheimer and Walt argued that Iran's nuclear ambition did not pose a threat to the US, but *did* pose a threat to the security of Israel. They posited that "the overall thrust of U.S. policy in the [Middle East] region is due almost entirely to U.S. domestic politics and especially to the activities of the Israel lobby."[37] After examining the issue of the Israeli lobby, they concluded that neither strategic interests nor moral imperatives explained the "unconditional support" for Israel. They therefore argued that the policies of the US in the Middle East were influenced by the "unmatched power of the Israel lobby" actively working "to shape US foreign policy in a pro-Israel direction."[38] David Miller, scholar and former American official, remarked: "Today you cannot be successful in American politics and not be good on Israel. And AIPAC plays a key role in making that happen."[39] According to Jeffrey Goldberg, a well-known American journalist, AIPAC is a "leviathan among lobbies."[40] The sad fact was that Ahmadinejad's rhetoric, e.g., denial of the Holocaust, was a major factor in increasing the influence of Israel and its lobby on US policy toward Iran.

In December 2007 the National Intelligence Estimate (NIE) was released. It stunned the US administration, Israel, and Western countries. The report maintained "with high confidence" that Iran had suspended its military nuclear program in 2003 and that there was no conclusive evidence of its revival. The report dealt a serious blow to the consistent US assertion that Iran was in the process of building an atomic bomb. The most shocking revelation connected with this matter came much later, however, when President Bush revealed in his memoir that the unexpected NIE assessment had "tied my hands on the military side."[41] This statement could explain why the Bush administration did not want to engage in serious talks and cooperation with Iran.

Confusion in the Bush administration became ever more apparent in July 2008. Despite their firm position against talks unless enrichment ended by July 2008, William Burns, Nicholas Burns' successor, joined the European Union Foreign Policy Chief, Javier Solana, and Saiid Jalili, Iran's nuclear negotiator, in a meeting in Geneva. However, a few days later, President Bush once again spoke of his regime change in front of an audience.

> Even now, change is stirring in places like Havana and Damascus and Tehran. The people of these nations dream of a free future, hope for a free future, and believe that a free future will come. And it will. May God be with them in their struggle. America always will be.[42]

All said, the outcome of the escalating tension from 2005 to 2009 between the two countries was to convince Iran, more than in the past, that the US aim was "regime change." Iranian mistrust of the US intensified even further, leading to the conclusion that the only way to deal with hostile US policies was to resist and damage US interests in the Middle East. As things stood, Iran resolved to do this, on the one hand, spreading anti-Americanism, and on the other, by strengthening its military, primarily missile capability.

The Espionage Dossier

After ending my relationship with Ahmadinejad's team in 2005, I began a new career at the Center for Strategic Research, as Rouhani's deputy for international affairs. The Center works on policy issues as an advisory think tank for the Expediency Council. Hassan Rouhani had already been appointed as the head of the Center, and I worked as his deputy of international affairs. My stand-off with Ahmadinejad's confrontational policies on nuclear and foreign issues started here, as I regularly prepared policy papers criticizing those policies, sending them to hundreds of high-ranking officials, including ministers, Majlis deputies, provincial governors, and others. In those papers I predicted the consequences of Ahmadinejad's policies, including escalation of sanctions. Interestingly, every time I warned the system (*nezam*) of a new set of sanctions, Ahmadinejad and his administration showed defiance. The sanctions, however, happened the way I analyzed and predicted in those papers. In one case, after the sanction resolution 1373 had been passed by the UNSC, I held a press conference at Mehr News Agency and explained to the public how detrimental the sanctions could be, both economically and politically. Ahmadinejad could not tolerate this stance, especially as I belonged to his rival camp. Finally, on April 30, 2007, I was arrested and charged with actions against Iran's national security and revealing secret documents to Western officials.

Ahmadinejad accused me in his public speeches of espionage for the West, while neither the interrogators nor the judge made such an accusation. Ahmadinejad called me a "lackey for the West" and a traitor. From April 30 to May 10 I was in a solitary cell under interrogation.

The day after I was released, I met with Rafsanjani in his home. He told me that some reliable sources had informed him that a series of arrests targeting the moderates and reformists had been planned after my arrest. He said that Ahmadinejad's camp wanted me to confess to the charges that had been leveled against me, and then, based on that confession, they would launch a huge propaganda campaign to discredit Rafsanjani, Khatami, and Hassan Rouhani, portraying the former nuclear negotiating team as traitors, and follow this up with a new series of arrests. Also, by meting lengthy jail sentences, they planned to eliminate moderates from the Iranian political arena. In addition, because I regularly attended international conferences and was considered a de facto spokesman of the moderates, they intended to send a message to the West showing how weak and irrelevant we were as a group inside Iran. According to Rafsanjani, to eliminate both moderates and even their rivals in the Principalists' camp, they planned to collect documents to use against prominent figures considered as rivals in the next parliamentary elections (March 2012). He confided: "I am convinced their main target is the Supreme Leader but they need to eliminate me first."

The pro-Ahmadinejad media published 13 accusations and charges against me, such as spying, communicating with foreign embassies, revealing secret documents, encouraging the world powers to pass sanction resolutions against Iran, meeting with American diplomats, and others. I was stunned because not even one of those charges existed in my case file, nor were they raised during interrogations. The interrogators and the judge never raised any of the 13 charges published in media. Later I discovered that the list of charges had been prepared prior to my arrest and that they anticipated that I would confess to those charges under pressure during interrogation.

I met with the judge and the representative of the security establishment supervising my case. I asked them why they let the pro-Ahmadinejad media make totally fabricated accusations against me. Their response was curt and simple: "We cannot do anything about it." Ahmadinejad took every opportunity to attack me and label me a spy. After my arrest, a number of top politicians, from the Principalists to moderates and reformists, met with the Supreme Leader and complained about the "espionage" propaganda against me. They included former Presidents Rafsanjani and Khatami; Nategh Nouri, former Majilis Speaker and head of the Inspection Office of the Supreme Leader; Mehdi Karroubi, another former Majilis Speaker; Emami Kashani, Tehran Interim Friday Prayers Leader; and even Hashemi Shahroudi, head of the Judiciary. They informed me that based on a report from the head of the Judiciary, the Supreme Leader did not believe the charges on espionage, and regretted the action taken against me, but did not want to interfere in judicial matters. Rouhani told me that Ayatollah Khamenei had once privately criticized Ahmadinejad for his public accusations on espionage, but to no avail.

My case was investigated by three judges in the span of a year. All of the judges found me "not guilty" on espionage charges, but one of them maintained that while I was in jail and during my defence at the court, I had confessed to my opposition to Ahmadinejad's nuclear and foreign policy. Therefore, I was guilty of challenging Ahmadinejad as President and head of SNSC, thus jeopardizing national security. Finally on March 20, 2008, prior to court hearing, I was informed by Mortazavi, the Prosecutor General of Tehran, that I would receive a two-year suspended jail sentence and a five-year ban on holding any diplomatic position. I told him: "I would not accept any diplomatic post, nor would Ahmadinejad offer me one. However, this mean that Ahmadinejad plans to have another term and my ban would run concurrent to his term—for that period, I would be out of a diplomatic job." He smiled at me and said "You are very clever."

On September 15, 2008, Ahmad Tavakoli, a prominent parliamentary figure from the Principalist camp and head of the Majlis Research Center—and also manager of an influential political website called Alef (letter A in Persian)—publicly stated that all the accusations against me were "completely fabricated." In a letter that appeared on his website, Tavakoli explained:

Almost all the news in this regard was either direct quotes from state officials such as the President, government spokesperson, Minister of Intelligence, spokesperson for the Majlis Foreign Relations Committee, or other such sources. Defense attorneys for the accused asserted that most of the charges against their client that appeared in the media were false and neither the Ministry of Intelligence nor the Attorney General had reported them in their documents. After four months of investigation including meetings with relevant authorities and reading many documents, I came to the conclusion that Mousavian is right and all accusations are baseless.[43]

Tavakoli listed all 13 accusations and apologized for them, asking my family and me to forgive him.[44]

In response, I wrote him in a letter: "Until now, I have remained silent in the interests of the country, and I want to continue this. I am confident that after studying relevant documents and speaking with appropriate officials, you now understand the secret of my silence."[45]

Nevertheless, Ahmadinejad remained defiant. Responding to a question about my arrest on March 20, 2009, he said: "If this had happened anywhere else it would have been punished with death."[46]

In addition to Ahmad Tavakkoli, some other important media outlets, including those close to the Principalist camp, apologized to me a few months after publishing the initial accusations. Dr. Emad Afroogh, a sociologist and a prominent Principalist Majlis deputy, wrote to me, noting that I was a "victim of misunderstandings, connections and the usual political and factional bickering which of course are contrary to moral and spiritual values espoused by society and the Islamic Revolution." However, after the court final verdict was issued in April 2008, referred to above, Ahmadinejad once again called for the death penalty and criticized the way the Judiciary had handled the case.[47]

Under the circumstances, I took the advice of my friends, both moderate and Principalist, to stay in Iran until the next election, planned for June 2009.

The Biggest Domestic Crisis since the Revolution

The June 2009 election turned out to be the biggest internal crisis since the Islamic Republic's inception. Soon after the announcement of Ahmadinejad's victory on public TV and radio stations, protestors poured onto the streets of Tehran. They claimed that the election had been rigged and that the actual winner was Mir Hossein Mousavi, the reformist candidate (former prime minister in the 1980s). Massive demonstrations were held in Tehran and other large cities. The protests turned bloody. Security forces deployed an excessive use of force to counter the protestors. As the waves of arrests and bloody confrontations continued unabated, I hastened to meet top politicians such as Rafsanjani, Velayati, Rouhani, and Nateq Nouri. I sought their advice on whether I should stay or leave the country. With the exception of Rouhani, they all agreed that in the circumstances I would better advised to pursue postdoctoral research and studies abroad.

My absence did not stop Ahmadinejad from attacking me. In a private meeting in the holy city of Mashhad, he is reported to have said: "If Mousavian's file would have been managed properly he would have received a death sentence."

In June 2013, the landslide victory of Rouhani, a moderate mid-ranking cleric, put an end to the eight-year rule of Ahmadinejad. Not surprisingly, his farewell was preceded by months of humiliating public attacks from all political persuasions, from Principalists to moderates and reformists.[48] Before the 2013 presidential elections, some of Ahmedinejad's close allies were accused variously of financial corruption,[49] sorcery,[50] or espionage.[51] Following Rouhani's victory, of the moderate cleric Hassan Rouhani, Ahmadinejad was summoned to a criminal court in Tehran to answer unspecified charges.[52]

Wrong Analyses abound in Tehran and Washington

During his presidential election campaign, Obama had advocated US engagement with Iran without preconditions. So, logically, his election victory was a major boon to all those in Iran hoping for a genuine opportunity to improve relations with the US. However, by that time, the moderates had already been pushed to the margins and the Principalists were in full control. Probably the Iranian most pleased with the election result was Mahmoud Ahmadinejad. As I have already discussed, he viewed Obama's election as an opportunity to resolve the dispute between the two countries and leave a lasting legacy in the history of the Islamic Republic. On November 6, 2008 he became the first Iranian President since the 1979 Revolution to send a complimentary letter to his US counterpart. The letter opened with "I would like to offer my congratulations on your election by the majority of the American voters."[53]

The letter was written in a conciliatory tone, encouraged "fundamental change in the American government's policies", and went on to state that "Iran would welcome major, fair and real changes, in policies and actions, especially in [the Middle East] region."[54] He further added that there was a genuine hope that Obama would reverse "[US] unjust actions of the past 60 years ... to a policy encouraging full rights for all nations, especially the oppressed nations of Palestine, Iraq and Afghanistan ... and that the enormous damage done in the past would be somewhat diminished." While the White House confirmed receipt of the letter it was never replied to.

Ahmadinejad was oblivious to the fact that his past actions and pronouncements, including his ostentatious lecturing of the leaders of the developed countries, repeated harping on the imminent collapse of the "decadent" West, and also his self-promoting hollow claim of having designs for "global management",[55] had earned him a reputation as an unstable figure, not to be taken seriously. The tremendous cost to Iran and Iranians as a result of his anti-Holocaust rhetoric has been addressed before.

Then came Nowruz, the Iranian New Year. On March 20, 2009, Obama sent a congratulatory televised message to the Iranians.[56] In that unprecedented broadcast, he addressed the "Iranian leaders" and "the Islamic Republic" as opposed to the "Iranian regime," which had been the descriptive term traditionally used by his predecessors in office. Obama offered a "new beginning," but also cautioned the Iranian government against supporting "terror" and attempting to build "arms." To those not familiar with the importance of pride in Iranian psyche and politics, these references might not appear significant, but to Iranians they touched a raw nerve.

Ayatollah Khamenei immediately attacked Obama, alluding to "a velvet glove" concealing a "cast iron hand." He went on: "[T]hey congratulate the Iranian New Year, but, at the same time, accuse Iran of supporting terrorism and efforts to gain access to nuclear weapons ... Our nation ... hates [the policy of] threat and enticement."[57]

Notwithstanding, Ahmadinejad made a second attempt. Mohamed ElBaradei revealed in his memoir that Ahmadinejad sent a message through him in 2009 offering Obama Iran's readiness "to engage in bilateral negotiations, without conditions, on the basis of mutual respect."[58] He also held out the prospect of "helping the US in Afghanistan and elsewhere." This overture met with the same fate as the first one.

President Obama, blatantly ignoring Ahmadinejad, wrote[59] a letter to Ayatollah Khamenei. I heard from reliable sources that Obama informed the Iranian Supreme Leader of his willingness to engage in bilateral talks aimed at improving relations between their two countries, fostering regional cooperation, and in search of a resolution of the dispute over Iran's nuclear program. The message was passed to the Iranian Foreign Ministry by the Swiss Embassy.

A former US diplomat told me that the "White House was surprised that Ayatollah Khamenei responded in a respectful tone. However, the Supreme Leader described the grievances of Iran and criticized American policies, not only toward Iran but toward the entire Islamic world, but he positively responded to Obama's offer for détente based on mutual respect and mutual interest."

In the backdrop of decades-old mistrust between the two countries, the Supreme Leader said, in a 2013 public speech, that he was "not a diplomat but a revolutionary,"[60] hoping to convey to Washington that he was a straightforward person who did not use diplomatic language. As argued previously in the book, lack of understanding between Iranians and Americans has played its negative role. Only a few senior Iranian officials have lived in the West, and quite a few have studied politics or related subjects. Diplomacy with the US, therefore, is certainly not one of Iran's strongest suits. There is a similar shortage of knowledge about Iran's society, culture, and politics among American analysts and policy-makers. Very few analysts and policy-makers are fluent in Persian, and barely any Iranian-American analyst has resided in Iran for any extended time period. To make matters worse, most of them do not relate and have not related to ordinary Iranians, and even fewer work with or have ever worked with Iran's influential clergy, ruling elite, or high-ranking officials, something that would have provided them with an insight in/into Iran's perceptions and motivations. Moreover, some of the former Iranian officials and experts who have left the country since 1979 either follow an oppositional line or align themselves with a Western/US view of politics in Iran.

In any case, the fact that Ayatollah Khamenei replied to President Obama's letter was enough for Obama to send a second one.[61] As an informed former US diplomat reliably disclosed to me, President Obama took this opportunity to introduce two representatives— William Burns from the State Department, and Puneet Talwar from the White House—to talk with Iranian representatives of Ayatollah Khamenei's choice. The letter arrived only days prior to Iran's June 2009 presidential elections. An informed Iranian diplomat told me that "Ayatollah Khamenei was ready to respond positively again." In his words: "Tehran was even working on the draft of the letter. But in the aftermath of the 2009 presidential elections, protests took the streets of Tehran by storm and the US sided with the demonstrators, making the Leader doubtful about the real intentions of the US. That was why he did not respond to the second letter."

Three hours after the polls closed, Mir Hossein Mousavi rushed to claim at a late night press conference that "I am the definite winner of this presidential election."[62] His claim, it appears, was based on the results he had received from the yet-unfinished counts from the Tehran polling stations. He called on his supporters to celebrate the following day.

Reviewing the slogans, pronouncements, and demands of protestors following the June election, it was apparent that despite the economic hardships that many Iranians were experiencing, economic demands did not feature in their list of expectations. While many intellectuals, writers, artists, and academics were among the protestors, however, it was the middle- and upper-class youth who formed the bulk of the protest movement. The fact that the backbone of the so-called Green Movement was shaped by the middle- and upper-middle class explains why the movement was focused on civil rights and posed no economic demands during and after the protests. In other words, the Green Movement mainly reflected the *will* and demands of a particular, albeit not insignificant, liberal segment of society. To see the Green Movement as the will of *the* people of Iran is a misperception. It was no surprise that in Tehran and Shemiranat, the northern part of Tehran, where upper- and middle-class residents live, Mousavi beat Ahmadinejad. It also may explain why the protests varied in size and lingered in Tehran in comparison to other large cities. Moreover, Ahmadinejad's attitude towards those that did not want to see him as president for another term was offensive, insulting, and extremely disrespectful—which further infuriated the protestors and made the situation more difficult. This had produced disdain for him among a large faction of young urbanites.

During Friday prayers a week after the election, Ayatollah Khamenei gave his support to Ahmadinejad against Rafsanjani. Alluding to past—and continuing—differences between Rafsanjani and Ahmadinejad, he went on to emphasize: "Of course, Mr. President's [Ahmadinejad's] views are closer to mine."[63] During the same sermon, he dismissed the idea of election fraud. Two weeks after this sermon, the Guardian Council pronounced that "The vote tally affected by such matters as the cast votes surpassing the number of eligible voters could be just over 3 million, and would not noticeably affect the outcome of the election."[64]

In its detailed report, the Council gave unequivocal approval of the result of the election: "[T]he Guardian Council discussed all issues in various meetings and decided that complaints and objections raised about the tenth presidential election were not valid."[65]

Addressing the street protests, Ayatollah Khamenei said in his sermon: "I want everyone to end this sort of action. If they do not stop, then the consequences of this rest with them ... Please note, it is a wrong impression that some people have, thinking that through illegal street gatherings, they can create a lever of pressure against the system (*nezam*)." Mousavi was placed in a difficult position. Nevertheless, he remained defiant and seriously questioned the impartiality of the Guardian Council—which in turn helped to sustain the protests. Meanwhile, Ahmadinejad had his own agenda which did not exactly coincide with that of the Supreme Leader. Many leading Principalist politicians also underestimated the strength of ill feeling toward Ahmadinejad amongst a large segment of the Iranian society. Furthermore, the protests had done significant damage to the image and credibility of the system (*nezam*)—a development that could be exploited by outside forces, especially the United States. As it came to pass, there was a heavy price to be paid for supporting Ahmadinejad, who ultimately turned against the Principalists in his second term.

The post-election tumult caused a sudden shift in the West's approach toward Tehran, especially that of the US. Obama, who had already written his second letter to the Supreme Leader only a few days before the elections, condemned the heavy-handed crackdown on protestors and said:

> I strongly condemn these unjust actions ... I've made it clear that the United States respects the sovereignty of the Islamic Republic of Iran and is not interfering with Iran's affairs. But we must also bear witness to the courage and the dignity of the Iranian people, and to a remarkable opening within Iranian society. And we deplore the violence against innocent civilians anywhere that it takes place ... Those who stand up for justice are always on the right side of history.[66]

Obama's remarks elicited an angry response from the Ayatollah. Referring—implicitly—to the letter, he said in his post-election sermon: "On the one hand, they write a letter to us to express their respect for the Islamic Republic and for re-establishment of ties, and on the other hand they make these remarks."[67]

The clashes between the Iranian security forces and protestors were widely reported in the West. The US support for the protests convinced an already-suspicious Iranian leadership that the Green Movement was guided from Washington, which sought to organize a "color revolution" on the model developed in a number of states of the former Soviet Union and in the Balkans. Secretary of State Hillary Clinton's statement seemed to confirm this assessment: "Now, behind the scenes, we were doing a lot. We were doing a lot to really empower the protestors without getting in the way. And we're continuing to speak out and support the opposition."[68]

The US support for Iran's newly born civil rights movement, the Green Movement, was seen by the Iranian leadership as clear evidence of the US interference in Iran's internal affairs. Many observers posited that the US had to support and empower the Green Movement,[69] based on the logic that "The only thing standing between the mullahs and the bomb is the Green Movement."[70] Simultaneously, Voice of America provided unprecedented air time and coverage to various opposition figures and activists, who advocated, among others, practical suggestions for civil disobedience and street action. The participants in the program suggested ways for people inside Iran to engage in anti-government protests and other forms of civil disobedience. Michael Posner, Assistant Secretary of State, told the US Senate:

> We have increased the scope of our efforts aimed at challenging the Iranian government's deplorable human rights violations. [Among other plans] we also continue to work quietly with civil society organizations in Iran to give them the tools they need to expand political space and hold their government accountable.[71]

Believing that one further push might be enough to bring down the Iranian government, a foreign policy expert asserted that: "if the United States … supports the aspirations of the Iranian people, it could inspire young non-ideological Iranians … to confront [the] security forces in the hope of overthrowing the regime."[72] Richard Haass, a noted American foreign policy expert and President of the Council on Foreign Relations, wrote in an article titled "Regime Change Is the Only Way to Stop Iran" that "I've changed my mind. The nuclear talks are going nowhere... Outsiders should act to strengthen the opposition and to deepen rifts among the rulers. This process is underway, and while it will take time, it promises the first good chance in decades to bring about an Iran than, even if less than a model country, would nonetheless act considerably better at home and abroad. Even a realist should recognize that it's an opportunity not to be missed."[73]

It might be of interest that the website of Mir Hossein Mousavi's campaign claimed that the actual distribution of votes in the 2009 election was 21.3 million for Mousavi and only 10.5 million for Ahmadinejad.[74] Even if this source might not be considered objectives, but taking these figures at face value, the conservatives, at the time represented by Ahmadinejad, had a minimum of over 10 million supporters. Also, considering Mousavi's popularity among rank and file supporters of the Islamic Republic, many conservatives ("Principalists") might as well have voted for him.

The debate about who really won the 2009 election is beyond the scope of this book.[75] However, it could be safely concluded that, despite the large number of protestors on the street, a substantial segment of the populace also supported the sitting President and his team and policies. All in all, the 2009 post-election protest movement was not directed against the system (*nezam*), rather a manifestation and revival of the hundred-year-old struggle—which Ramin Jahanbegloo, an Iranian professor of philosophy, refers to as a continuous tension— between tradition and modernity.[76]

By misreading the situation in Iran, the US government therefore adopted policies that did not help them achieve their stated objective of "promoting democracy" in Iran, let alone "regime change." But it *did* justify the hardliners' negative reaction to the US approach. In line with the argument in this book, I drew attention to such a misunder- standing in a June 2010 interview with the *Wall Street Journal*: "Regime change is not part of Iran's outlook in the near future, Iran is not in a pre-revolutionary state. What is happening on the streets of Iran is an internal challenge wherein the final result will greatly impact Iran's domestic and foreign policies." Along the same line of thinking and analysis,I emphasized in the same interview[77] on the need for the US to engage with Iran—to shape a comprehensive dialogue with Iran based on shared interests in stabilizing Iraq and Afghanistan. While emphasizing the merits of constructive cooperation between Tehran and Washington, including in developing a broad security plan for the Persian Gulf region, I deliberately down-played the prospects of any quick change in the Iranian system. I also underlined, in the interview, that a move toward democracy in Iran could only come from inside. Instead, I implored Washington to adopt a patient foreign policy toward Iran, understanding that progress in improving Iran–US relations would take years, not months.[78]

It is also interesting to note that the interview titled "Iranian Diplomat in U.S. Opens Window on Tehran"[79]—which was intended to dispel then prevailing misperceptions in the US about the stability of the Iranian government—was used by the pro-Ahmadinejad media to launch a new round of personal attacks against me. At the time, many in the US thought that the Green Movement would bring regime change in Tehran. My interview was aimed at dispelling such misperceptions. However, the pro-Ahmadinejad media in Iran used the title of the *Wall Street Journal* article to launch a new round of attacks on me. For example, *Kayhan*, the hardline newspaper, mistranslated the title, commenting that "Mousavian has opened a window of information for Americans"—leading to further baseless accusations of espionage against me. Here again, domestic rivalry in Iran contributed to more misanalysis and a further escalation of hostility between Iran and the United States.

Chapter 7

TWO OPPOSING VIEWS ON MAJOR ISSUES

Terrorism

The issue of terrorism has been one of the major elements of Iran–US dispute since the 1979 Islamic Revolution. Iran has been labeled as a "State sponsor of terrorism" by the US government since January 19, 1984.[1] Washington's primary claim is that Iran has provided material, political, and logistical support to militant groups in the Middle East. Tehran continues its support for militant groups battling Israel, including the Palestinian Hamas and Islamic Jihad and the Lebanese Hezbollah. Iran considers these Palestinian groups to be freedom fighters for the liberation of Palestine, and whose struggles are viewed as a legitimate means to liberate their lands, and Hezbollah as a group fighting to preserve Lebanon's territorial integrity against Israeli military threats.

Blaming Iran for supporting "terrorism" has in turn prompted Tehran to not only reject such a labeling but also to reciprocate and use the same designation for the United States and its policies and conduct. Accusations going back and forth have not only derailed attempts at rapprochement but also sidelined the areas where both countries see eye to eye. Mutual recrimination has negated the fact that Tehran and Washington share the same goals/objectives in the fight against global terrorism, including rooting out the most extreme terrorist groups such as Al-Qaeda, the Taliban, and other extremist Salafi groups such as ISIS/IS. As indicated earlier in the introductory chapter, given the present book's goal of providing a better understanding of the Iranian side, Iran's outlook and positions on "terrorism" will be explored more fully.

The American/Western view of Iran's role in terrorism

The West, particularly the United States, has long accused Tehran of masterminding terrorist acts, and has branded it as the leading state sponsor of terrorism mainly due to its support such militant groups as Hamas, Hezbollah, and Islamic Jihad.[2] Since the 1979 Revolution in Iran, American Presidents and high-ranking officials have invariably at various times referred to Iran as a "rogue state,"[3] a member of the "Axis of Evil,"[4] a "pariah state,"[5] and a "state sponsor of terrorism."[6]

The following is a list of the major charges levied against Iran in this regard.

Beirut military barracks bombing
On October 23, 1983 twin truck-bombings occurred in Beirut, Lebanon, targeting the US and French military barracks, with a total casualty of 299 people, among them 241 US military personnel. The US accused Iran of aiding the bombing.[7] Hezbollah[8] and Iran both denied any involvement, with Foreign Minister Velayati stating: "We deny any involvement and we think this allegation is another propaganda plot against us."[9]

Khobar Tower bombing
The US accused Hezbollah and Iran of the June 25, 1996 bombing of the Khobar Towers in Saudi Arabia that killed 19 US Air Force personnel and injured 372 others. Iran maintained its innocence.[10]

Killings of dissidents in Europe
In the late 1980s and early 1990s, a slew of killings in Europe of Iranian dissident figures placed considerable pressure on Iran–Europe relations since all the assassinations were attributed to the Iranian government. The most prominent of these killings were the assassination of the leader of the Kurdish opposition group Abdolrahman Qassemlou in Vienna on July 13, 1989; the assassination of the Shah's last prime minister, Shapour Bakhtiar, in Paris on August 6, 1991. The most serious assassination incident was the killing of Iranian Kurdish opposition leaders at the Greek restaurant Mykonos, in Germany, on September 17, 1992. The eventual Berlin court verdict on April 17, 1997 accused factions within the Iranian government of responsibility for the murders.

Support for militant groups in Lebanon and Palestine
The West, specifically the US, has blamed Iran for providing support for militant organizations such as Hamas, Islamic Jihad and Hezbollah. All three groups are designated by the US State Department and as Foreign

Terrorist Organizations (FTO) as such constitute part of the "war on terror."[11] Iran has never denied its support for these groups.

Suicide bombings in Israel

The 1979 Revolution led to the severance of Iran's ties with Israel, followed by unequivocal condemnation of the Israeli occupation of Palestine as unjust. Post-revolutionary Iran—the Islamic Republic—was therefore committed to support resistance movements dedicated to the liberation of Palestine. Yet by adopting such a policy, Tehran came under tremendous pressure from the United States, Tel Aviv's main supporter and ally. With respect to suicide bombings in Israel, the following story is enlightening.

During my tenure as Iranian ambassador to Germany (1990–7) I learned that many German politicians believed that, from a broader geopolitical perspective, reduction in tensions between Iran and Israel would be conducive Iran–US rapprochement. To that end, in a March 1996 meeting with senior members of the German Chancellor Kohl's office, I was told that an initiative by Iran to manage a humanitarian exchange between Hezbollah and Israel would facilitate a positive change in relation to the perceived position of Iran in the Middle East peace process, and would also reduce Tel Aviv's grievances and fears. Furthermore, it was conveyed that such an initiative would facilitate rapprochement between Iran and the United States, to be mediated by Chancellor Kohl. The Germans were indeed confident that the US would come to the table if Iran were to take this step.

A subsequent visit to Tehran and meetings with senior Iranian officials, followed by my meeting with the leader of Hezbollah, Hassan Nasrallah, in Damascus, bore fruit. Our efforts were focused on securing the bodies of two Israeli soldiers and Antoine Lahad's South Lebanese Army (SLA)[12] militiamen held prisoner in Lebanon in exchange for the bodies of Lebanese soldiers, and the release of Lebanese and Palestinian prisoners. In a lengthy meeting with Hassan Nasrullah in Damascus, we finally agreed on the exchange and its details. I left immediately for Bonn to make the final arrangements with the German Chancellery. While my focus was on negotiations between Tehran and Hezbollah, the Germans assisted with coordination with the Israelis, eventually leading to one of the largest humanitarian exchanges between Hezbollah and Israel on July 21, 1996. It goes without saying that one of my main objectives in this process was to facilitate the mediation efforts of Chancellor Kohl between Tehran and Washington. This initiative included a comprehensive package covering major issues such as terrorism, the peace process, and WMD, with Chancellor Kohl mediating the details between Presidents Rafsanjani and Clinton, while I served as the main contact point.

It was at this critical point in the rapprochement effort that numerous suicide bombings took place across Israel, including Tel Aviv.[13] Iran was accused[14] of backing these terrorist acts. However, the timing of these bombings—in the midst of Iran's efforts to reduce tensions with Israel and consequently with the United States—clearly illustrates that a charge of Iranian involvement made no sense, since it was contrary to these efforts. Nevertheless, those bombings practically derailed the initiative and rendered it futile.

Support for extremist groups in Afghanistan and Iraq
Iranians have been accused of complicity in providing extremists in Afghanistan and Iraq with the lethal weapons and training they needed to carry out attacks on US and Allied forces.[15] These accusations followed Iran's comprehensive cooperation with the United States to oust the Taliban from Afghanistan and subsequent assistance with the overthrow of Iraq's Saddam Hussein—two ardent enemies of both Tehran and Washington. Yet, according to the State Department annual Country Report on Terrorism 2011, "Iran continued to provide lethal support, including weapons, training, funding, and guidance to Iraqi Shia militant groups targeting U.S. and Iraqi forces, as well as civilians." In Afghanistan, the Report writes: "They provided the training to the Taliban on small unit tactics, small arms, explosives, and indirect fire weapons, such as mortars, artillery, and rockets."[16] The former US Director of National Intelligence, Michael McConnell, commented in June 2007 that "the evidence is overwhelming in the Iraq situation support [for terrorists by Iran], and it's very plain and, to me, compelling in Afghanistan.[17] Iran has repeatedly denied involvement in attacks on U.S. forces in Iraq and Afghanistan.[18]

Assassination attempt on US soil
In October 2011, the US government accused Iran of masterminding an assassination attempt on the Saudi Arabian ambassador to the US, Adel Al-Jubeir. It was alleged that Iranian-American Mansour Arbabsiar, a used car salesman nicknamed "Jack" by his friends because of his love of Jack Daniel's whiskey, had recruited Mexican drug traffickers to kill the Saudi ambassador.[19] Iran categorically denied the accusations, and "the US version of events" was met with skepticism "both from

sympathisers of the Iranian regime and its opponents."[20] Professor Juan Cole, a Middle East and Iran expert, wrote:

> 1.5 million dollars is the claimed price for killing the ambassador of the biggest petroleum reserve on the planet in the capital of the world's largest weapons manufacturer along with ubiquitous and innocent doll faced Americans in a "fictional restaurant" serving pork chops with freedom fries. But wait a minute, what else can 1.5 million dollars buy? Well it can buy you a medium sized apartment in Tehran or a Bugatti supercar, the kind that drug dealers buy for their girlfriends, or perhaps a nice European painting by an obscure artist.
>
> Any self-respecting drug dealing gang makes more than a million dollars a week on any busy street in a big city. The gang at the center of this controversy, the Zetas, are estimated to have an annual revenue of over 40 billion dollars ... And the 100,000 dollar down payment means just one minute of their usual time ... One wonders why would these guys even talk to an Iranian moron who cannot wear matching socks, loses his cellphone in public toilets, is high on whiskey all the time, smokes cheap pot, and is basically a fat 56 year old guy who is broke and has not killed anyone in his life and has no useful skill set.[21]

It's rather quizzical that these events occurred at a time when Iran had made major overtures in relation to its dispute with the West on the nuclear dossier and also in an attempt to revive rapprochement efforts with Washington. Some months prior to the assassination plot, five significant developments occurred during Ahmadinejad's presidency: 1) in February 2011, Iran invited the US Representative in Afghanistan, Marc Grossman, for talks on cooperation in Afghanistan; 2) in July 2011, Iran welcomed the "Russian Step by Step Plan" on the nuclear dossier which addressed all of the West's concerns about Iran's nuclear activities; 3) in August 2011, Tehran offered the IAEA full supervision of its nuclear program for five years; 4) in September 2011, Iran freed the American hikers who had crossed into Iran from Iraq and been charged with espionage; and 5) in September 2011, Tehran offered to halt its enrichment of uranium to 20 percent and limit its future uranium enrichment to 5 percent, if provided with fuel rods for the Tehran Research Reactor.[22]

These overtures, unprecedented since 2005, occurred during a short span of time and coincided with headway being made on the nuclear dossier with the P5+1 and the IAEA. The alleged assassination plot against the Saudi ambassador did in fact ruin the possible positive impact of these measures. What could Iran have gained by committing such a gross act of terrorism, other than more international isolation and increased hostility from the United States and Saudi Arabia? The only rational explanation is that either a) the whole episode was a fabrication to isolate Iran even further or b) it was a false flag operation by the ultimate beneficiaries of such a terror plot.

The Iranian point of view

The history of terrorism has left a major mark on the psyche of Americans, especially following the 9/11 events, yet for decades Iranians have had to face a heavy toll from terrorism in their country. Some of the groups involved in this activity—according to internal reports prepared by the Iranian security and intelligence services as well as Western media revelations[23]—were supported by the US government. Surprisingly, the issue was even raised in Congress. During a Congressional hearing in April 2006, former US Congressman Dennis Kucinich stated: "There are reports that the US is fomenting opposition and supporting military operations in Iran among insurgents groups and Iranian minority ethnic groups, some of whom are operating from Iraq. The Party for a Free Life in Kurdistan, PJAK, is one such group, and the other group is called the MEK, the Mujahedin-e Khalq. It is an Iranian anti-government group, which was listed as a terrorist group by the State Department from 1997–2012."[24] Additionally, according to a *New Yorker* report, US intelligence sources have indicated US financial, equipment, and tactical support for the PJAK, with the aim of placing internal pressure on the Iranian government, the same sources also claiming that the group was provided with "a list of targets inside Iran of interest to the US."[25]

Furthermore, the Baluchi militant Salafi group Jundullah, aligned with the Taliban and Al-Qaeda thinking, has conducted targeting civilians and key political figures. Examples of Jundullah terrorist attacks include the bombing of a school for girls in the city of Zahedan in 2007[26] and a deadly bombing that killed around 40 Iranians during the Ashura commemoration of the martyrdom of Imam Hussein in the city of Chabahar in 2010.[27] Abdolmalek Rigi, the leader of Jundullah, was eventually arrested in February 2010. Subsequently, Iranian authorities provided extensive evidence of foreign intelligence agencies' cooperation with Rigi in carrying out terrorist acts within Iran. In a detailed confession released by the Iranian media, Rigi divulged: "One of the CIA officers said that it was too difficult for us to attack Iran militarily, but we plan to give aid and support to all anti-Iran groups that have the capability to wage war and create difficulty for the Iranian system."[28] Further reports revealed that the CIA gave support and supplied money to Jundullah, which conducted raids into Iran from bases in Pakistan.[29] As reported in a January 2012 *Foreign Policy* article, Israeli Mossad operatives had posed as CIA agents when attempting to recruit members of Jundallah for attacks against Iran.[30]

Terrorism in Iran has claimed the lives of thousands of civilians and more than 200 members of government, including a former president and prime minister, members of parliament, and military officials. Others, such as the current Supreme Leader Ayatollah Khamenei and former President and Majlis Speaker Hashemi Rafsanjani, have suffered injury at the hands of terrorists. Iranians therefore know all too well the meaning and impact of terrorism. And as is widely known, the Iranian government was the first in the Islamic world to extend its condolences to the US following the 9/11 attacks, with President Mohammad Khatami stating: "On behalf of the Iranian people and the Islamic Republic, I denounce the terrorist measures, which led to the killing of defenseless people, and I express my deep sorrow and sympathy with the American people."[31]

US covert support for separatist groups inside Iran was detailed in a 2008 *New Yorker* report by Seymour Hersh, exposing the involvement of the CIA, the Defense Intelligence Agency (DIA), and Special Forces. Hersh claimed that the United States was supporting several groups engaged in acts of violence inside Iran:

> The use of Baluchi elements, for example, is problematic; Robert Baer, a former C.I.A. clandestine officer who worked for nearly two decades in South Asia and the Middle East, told me, "The Baluchis are Sunni fundamentalists who hate the regime in Tehran, but you can also describe them as Al Qaeda."[32]

Hersh added that other groups, such as the Jundallah, the Party for a Free Life in Kurdistan (PJAK), and the MEK had been or were currently supported by the United States.[33] According to another Hersh article, the MEK had been provided with training and access to covert military operational knowledge inside the US, at Department of Energy sites in the State of Nevada.[34]

The policy of covert operations and support for opposition groups did not change during President Obama's tenure; in fact, at times it even accelerated, as revealed in an investigative report by David Sanger of the *New York Times*: "From his first months in office, President Obama secretly ordered increasingly sophisticated attacks on the computer systems that run Iran's main nuclear enrichment facilities, significantly expanding America's first sustained use of cyber weapons."[35] The same report uncovered the close cooperation between the US and Israeli intelligence agencies in using covert operations against Iranian targets: "[T]he N.S.A. [National Security Agency], and a secret Israeli unit respected by American intelligence officials for its cyber skills, set to work developing the enormously complex computer worm that would become the attacker from within."

The Islamic Republic also maintains that Israeli and US agents have co-opted terrorist groups such as the MEK to conduct a series of attacks on Iranian scientists and bombings of Iranian military and industrial sites. To date, four Iranian nuclear scientists have been assassinated, with the former head of the Atomic Energy Organization of Iran (AEOI), Fereydoun Abbasi-Davani, also injured.[36]

Anti-Israel movements

The Iranian government has supported the Palestinians' struggle against Israeli occupation, and, in response to the Israeli aggression against Lebanon, has also supported Hezbollah since its foundation in the 1980s. While both Hamas[37] and Hezbollah[38] enjoy widespread support within their constituencies—winning elections and participating fully in the politics of their respective countries[39]—Iran has played a major role in transforming these groups into more inclusive socio-political movements eager to engage in the political process. However, instead of welcoming the willingness of the two groups to embrace non-violent political activities, the US maintained its hostile stance. The US could change the political environment in both Lebanon and Palestine by recognizing the democratically expressed will of the people, thus helping to consolidate the position of the two groups within the democratic process. Instead, US foreign policy in the Middle East region, characterized by unconditional support for Israel, has only made matters more complicated.

No doubt Hamas and Hezbollah have military wings that conduct operations against Israel and to date are in fact the only groups that have successfully resisted Israel's military apparatus. The acts of state violence against civilians in Palestine and Lebanon by the Israelis have provided further justification for Tehran's resolute support for both Hamas and Hezbollah, a situation that is likely to continue in the future. There is therefore the need for a more pragmatic approach to dealing with groups that have extensive support and are elected representatives and seen as advocates of the Palestinian cause. American backing of Tel Aviv, regardless of the international outcry at the atrocities committed by the Israelis, has alienated the US in the region and contributed to the perception that Israel and the United States pose the biggest threat to peace and security. This conclusion is reinforced by the results of a January 2012 poll conducted in the Middle East by the Arab Center for Research and Policy Studies, involving 12 Arab countries that account for 84 percent of the region's population—the biggest-ever survey of its kind. The poll found that 73 percent of respondents considered Israel and the US to be the biggest threat in the region, with Israel seen as a greater threat than Iran by a ratio of 15 to 1.[40]

The Secret Mission to Jeddah and the Khobar Bombing

The Khobar terrorist attack occurred in 1996, the final year of Rafsanjani's second term. Iran was accused of complicity in the incident by the US. But the bombing happened at a time when Iran had made major progress on bilateral relations with Saudi Arabia, not seen since the 1979 Revolution. I was involved in that rapprochement effort, and what follows is an account of my secret mission to Saudi Arabia.

After the Iran–Iraq War, relations between Iran and Saudi Arabia were deeply troubled due to the enormous financial assistance that the Saudis had given Saddam Hussein between 1980 and 1988. In a meeting in the mid-1990s, Rafsanjani told me about his meeting a few years back, at a meeting of the Organization of the Islamic Conference (OIC), with the Saudi Crown Prince Abdullah, subsequently King Abdullah as of 2005 (who died in January 2015). Rafsanjani, recalled the encounter:

> Ignoring all the formal protocols, Amir Abdullah followed me to my car and sat down inside. He then followed me to my room where we had a long, cordial talk. I realized that he was sincerely looking for friendly relations with Iran. During our discussions, Amir Abdullah asked me to send a representative to Saudi Arabia with enough authority, to solve the problems between our two countries.

Rafsanjani decided to send me as his representative to Saudi Arabia. The trip was informal and not intended to be publicized. I told him that I knew little about the Arab countries and that Iran would be better served by another diplomat more experienced in Arab affairs. He countered strongly and added: "That's exactly why you should go!" His fear, as he explained, was that a seemingly more appropriate diplomat would get wrapped up in the details with the Saudis and derail what should amount to a broad, general discussion, thus preventing any meaningful outcome. "What I need," he said, "is first, a grand agreement, and then we'll get into the details. I will send Mehdi, my son, with you as a signal of my full trust in you/as a signal of full confidence."

The person that Amir Abdullah introduced as his representative contacted me and asked me to meet directly with Amir Abdullah in Casablanca, Morocco. Surprised, I asked: "Why Casablanca?" He replied: "Amir is on his summer holidays and wants to see you there." I told him that I did not have a visa and asked: "What shall I say I am doing there when I arrive in Casablanca?" He responded: "Just get a flight and come to Casablanca. Leave the rest to us." I flew to Frankfurt, and from there to Casablanca. Upon landing, cars waited for us by the plane. Nobody checked my passport and we went directly to Amir Abdullah's palace, no more than five minutes' drive away.

Abdullah was waiting for me in a vast hall. He was very welcoming. We talked for almost four hours about the history of grievances between our two countries, about the region's general political situation and its future, and grounds for cooperation. But primarily, this was a review of the previous 15 years of bitterness. At the end of our meeting, he told me that our talk was informal. "I just wanted to test your level of knowledge and your vision." He then said that our formal talks would take place in Jeddah, Saudi Arabia. He said: "Bring your wife to Jeddah, too. You are my guests."

A month later, I again went with Mehdi to Jeddah. We flew from Germany and upon arrival, were put up in a super-luxury room in a top-notch hotel. That night we rested and the next morning, after breakfast, we readied ourselves to hear from the Crown Prince. Strangely enough, we heard nothing until the evening. After such hospitality in Casablanca, I was surprised and felt somehow insulted not to have heard from anyone until 9:00 p.m., when someone called and told me to be ready in two hours. We were completely confused by the timing of this meeting. We expected to have a brief courtesy meeting to get reacquainted that day, and that we would start the talks the following day. They told me on the phone that we were going to Amir Abdullah's residence.

It was spring 1996. Abdullah wore casual dress and told me that he was ready to conduct talks. We talked until 4.00 a.m. After the exchange, I asked our contact why we had not started until 11.00 p.m. and he informed me that when the weather gets very hot, they rest during the day and work at night.

We talked about all dimensions of the relations between Iran and Saudi Arabia, including security, economic, political, and cultural concerns. I soon realized that his biggest concern was that of security; in particular the allegation that Iran was involved with the Shias inhabiting the eastern oil-rich province, a situation that could potentially threaten the stability of the Saudi regime. In response, I shared Iran's concerns about the alleged involvement of Saudi Arabia in the Sunni regions of Kurdistan, Baluchistan, and the oil-rich Khuzistan where Arabs inhabit. I told him that "Our intelligence has concluded that you fund our enemies to destabilize the country," which he denied.

I proposed that we make a grand bargain to address all of our concerns within the framework of a cooperative security committee comprising a delegation from both countries. The committee would meet every six months or on an annual basis and any concerns could be presented in a documented manner by one party to the other— and it was the obligation of the accused side to consider the case and take necessary remedial measures. I told Abdullah that this type of cooperation could ultimately become the foundation for a security pact between our two countries. I also suggested that the respective foreign ministers should meet every six months and that the heads of state should meet every two years until relations were normalized. I further proposed that investors be empowered to secure work permits and invest in each other's country. This had not happened before, even under the Shah. Abdullah was extremely amenable to the plan, so we proceeded to prepare a draft preliminary agreement covering 15 areas.

Amir Abdullah told me to meet Nayef Bin Abdulaziz, Saudi Arabia's Minister of Interior, to discuss the security aspect of the agreement in greater depth, and also proposed a short meeting with King Fahd, during which I could outline our agreement. Then he said: "Afterwards, the ball is in Ayatollah Khamenei's, Ayatollah Rafsanjani's, and your court." My next task then was to present the draft agreement to Tehran and convince them of its merits.

Following my meeting with Amir Abdullah, I met with Nayef. The meeting was extremely challenging, as there was a night-and-day difference between the approach of the Saudi Crown Prince and the Minister of Interior. Amir Abdullah had been extremely cooperative and receptive, whereas Nayef was staunch, detail-oriented, and from his body language, appeared highly cautious and distrustful, if not disinterested. I found him to be quite radical but because of my agreement with Abdullah, I had the impression that ultimately Nayef could not stand in the way.

Finally, I met with King Fahd, with seven or eight people from the King's court also in attendance. I presented a brief review of the agreement with the Crown Prince, and then King Fahd spoke:

> Mr. Ambassador, anything you have agreed with Amir is acceptable to me. The future of this region depends on relations between the main pillars: Iran, Saudi Arabia, and Iraq—three regional powers. With Saddam, we both have problems at this point. But Amir Abdullah has my full support to restore relations with Iran.

During that last meeting, Amir Abdullah called me by my first name. He said to me: "You are a Hashemite, you are a son of the Prophet.[41] I trust you like *my* son." I asked him: "Why don't you pay a visit to Iran?" He replied: "Let me tell you something privately. Buy a piece of land for me by the Caspian Sea.[42] I will build a palace there. I will also marry a Shirazi girl,[43] all of this to show that I want Iran to become my second home." He added: "Any price you tell me for the land, I trust you 100 percent. I will immediately send you the money." I thanked him for his trust and told him that what he had said led me to believe that he wholeheartedly desired the restoration of Saudi Arabia's relations with Iran.

Upon my return to Tehran, I met with President Rafsanjani and Foreign Minister Velayati. I briefed them about my trip to Jeddah, and Rafsanjani said he agreed 100 percent with the points that I had discussed and agreed on with Amir Abdullah. He also agreed that Amir Abdullah's closing words held the same significance for him as they did for me with regard to restoring and improving relations between Saudi Arabia and Iran. Rafsanjani said he would discuss the agreement with Ayatollah Khamenei. Two days later, he informed me that the Ayatollah had agreed with all the 15 areas agreed with Amir Abdullah. I then informed the Saudis about our plan's positive reception by Iran's leaders.

After receiving Tehran's seal of approval, both countries agreed to revive relations. The package that I finalized with Amir Abdullah not only encompassed reviving bilateral relations, but also covered regional and international issues pertaining to the entire Islamic world. There is no doubt that such an agreement would have contributed enormously to regional peace, security, and stability. Furthermore, in the months that followed, Amir Abdullah and I agreed that our two countries would also cooperate in the Organization of Petroleum Exporting Countries (OPEC) to ensure stability of the oil market and also security of passage at oil transit points. As the two leading Islamic countries representing the Shia and Sunni communities, our partnership also had the prospect of contributing to the reduction of sectarian tensions in the Islamic world. It was against this backdrop that the Khobar bombings occurred.

On June 25, 1996, a massive truck bomb exploded at a housing complex in the city of Khobar, Saudi Arabia, located near the Dhahran headquarters of the national oil company (Saudi Aramco). The bomb killed 19 and injured 372 Americans,[44] along with several other nationals. The US accused Iran of involvement in the terrorist attack[45]—which kept being repeated afterwards for a number of years. Looking back, and considering the concrete progress we had achieved towards normalizing relations with Saudi Arabia, it would be absolutely unthinkable that Iran would have been involved in such a deadly terrorist act.

In 1997, while I was head of the Foreign Relations Committee of the Supreme National Security Council, the Iranian intelligence assessment pointed to the role of Al-Qaeda and other radical Salafi groups in the Khobar bombings, with a number of simultaneous anti-American, anti-Iranian, and anti-Shia objectives. The intelligence findings also hinted that an imminent deal between Amir Abdullah and the representatives of the Shia community in Saudi Arabia would have paved the way for improvement in their situation, including in the economic field. If concluded, the deal would have permitted the Shia population to participate in economic activities from which they had previously been barred, including involvement in the lucrative oil industry. There were also reports that Saudi authorities had been engaged in private talks with their Iranian counterparts, expressing their dissatisfaction with the US position of implicating Iran in the bombing.

According to intelligence assessments at the time, Bin Laden, already at war with the US, had the motivation as well as the operational capability to carry out the attack. He was clearly at war with the US. In November 1995, only months before the Khobar bombing, a car bomb was detonated at the Office of the Program Manager of the

Saudi National Guard (OPM SANG)[46] in Riyadh. Members of the Saudi National Guard were trained at that location by the Americans—five of whom were killed that day.

During an interview published in *al Quds al Arabi* on November 29, 1996, Bin Laden said: "We had thought that the Riyadh and Khobar blasts were a sufficient signal to sensible U.S. decision-makers to avert a real battle between the Islamic nation and U.S. forces, but it seems that they did not understand the signal."[47]

Fast forward to 2007—*Reuters* reported that former Defense Secretary William Perry "says he now believes al-Qaida rather than Iran was behind a 1996 truck bombing" in Khobar. "We probably should have been more concerned about it at the time than we were but in the first term we did not see Osama bin Laden and al-Qaida as a major factor, or one that we were concerned with," Perry said.[48]

The Khobar terrorist attack significantly affected the relationship between Iran and the US for several years. It marked the point of failure for rapprochement efforts made by both sides throughout Bill Clinton's second term as President, a period that coincided with the emergence of Mohammad Khatami's reformist government. The period appeared to offer a golden opportunity to make real progress in bilateral relations, but it was lost again amidst American misanalysis of the situation.

The Mother of all Disputes: Iran–Israel Conflict

During the presidency of Rafsanjani, the issue of the Middle East Peace Process was of primary concern to the US and played an important part in the continuation of its dispute with Iran. The US has viewed Iran's support for militant Palestinian groups—Hamas and Islamic Jihad—unacceptable in its essentially anti-Israeli drive and also as undermining the peace process between Israel and the Palestinian Authority.

Any analysis of this situation first requires an answer to the question "Why *is* the Iranian system (*nezam*) hostile towards Israel?" In this respect, the following points should be considered:

• Israel is a non-Muslim state that has taken over Muslim lands by force, with the support of world powers. Neither the Palestinians, nor the Arabs and Muslims as a whole, bear any responsibility for the mass murders carried out by the Nazi regime in Germany against the Jews, gypsies, communists and others during the Second World War. The responsibility for those horrible crimes against humanity that took place in Europe lies with their perpetrators. Iran's government considers it unjust that Palestinians should be uprooted from their homeland and nation in order to compensate the victims of Nazi atrocities. The creation of millions of new victims in Palestine, as a compensation for the past crimes committed by others in Europe, runs counter to reason and morality.

- As an Islamic state, the Iranian government's hostile position toward Israel is also rooted in two major religious factors. First, the Quran teaches that Muslims may resort to armed struggle when they are compelled to leave their homes, as illustrated in the following verse: "Permission to take up arms is hereby given to those who are attacked because they have been oppressed—Allah indeed has power to grant them victory—those who have been unjustly driven from their homes, only because they said: 'Our Lord is Allah'" (22.39–40).

  Despite the fact that millions of Palestinians are scattered throughout the Middle East and around the globe, Israel denies Palestinians the right to return to their homeland. In contrast, the official policy of the Israeli government has been to encourage Jewish immigration from all over the world, offering financial incentives, job placements, and housing grants. The Israeli Law of Return grants every Jew, wherever he or she may be, the right to come to Israel as an *oleh* (a Jew immigrating to Israel) and become an Israeli citizen—effective on the day of arrival in the country.[49]

  The second religious factor in the dispute between Iran and Israel is the occupation of Al-Quds (Jerusalem). Jerusalem is considered the holy city for all Abrahamic religions—Christianity, Judaism, *and* Islam. For Muslims, Al-Quds, and the Al-Aqsa Mosque in particular, carry major significance. Muslims, based on Qur'anic verses, believe that Prophet Mohammad (PBUH) ascended to Heaven from the Al-Aqsa Mosque and returned there in his night journey. In addition, Muslims initially prayed in the direction of this Mosque, later changed towards Kaaba in Mecca, Saudi Arabia.

- During the pre-revolutionary period, Israel maintained very close and warm relations with the Shah's regime. Israeli interests in Iran, as a non-Arab state, became prominent as of early 1950s when Mossad cooperated with the CIA in establishing Iran's brutal secret service, the SAVAK. A 1979 CIA report noted that "The main purpose of the Israeli relationship with Iran was the development of a pro-Israel and anti-Arab policy on the part of the Iranian officials. Mossad has engaged in joint operations with SAVAK over the years since the late 1950s."[50]

The close cooperation between Israel and the Shah's regime was deeply offensive to the religious establishment in Iran. Ayatollah Khomeini's June 3, 1963 speech with a pronounced anti-Israeli, anti-American orientation is widely considered as the event that ignited the first widespread, religious-political movement that led to the 1979 Revolution in Iran, sparked three days of serious rioting in Tehran and a number of other major cities. The theme of the speech was "The Shah and Israel; the root of people's suffering in Iran." In part of the speech in Qom, the Ayatollah said:

> I was informed today that a number of preachers were taken to the offices of SAVAK and were told that they could speak about anything they chose other than three subjects: they were not to say anything bad about the Shah; not to attack Israel; and not to say that Islam is endangered … Israel does not wish the Qur'an to exist in this country. Israel does not wish the *ulama* [high ranking clergy] to exist in this country. Israel does not wish to see Islamic precepts in this country. It was Israel that assaulted the *Madrasa*[51] [the Seminary] by means of its sinister agents. It [Israel] wishes to seize your economy, to destroy your trade and agriculture and to appropriate your wealth. Anything which proves to be a barrier, or blocks its path, is to be removed by means of its agents. The Qur'an is blocking its path; it must be removed. The religious establishment is blocking its path; it too must be removed; *Fayziya* [*Madrasa*/Seminary] is blocking its path; it must be destroyed. The religious students might later prove to be barriers; they must be flung from the roof and their arms and necks broken. We are affronted by our very government, which assists Israel in achieving its objectives by obeying its command.[52]

The Iranian leadership is firmly of the belief that Israel's long-term goal is to subdue the Muslim countries in the region, and the Islamic world in general, creating a resistance-free environment conductive for its aggressive expansionism.

• One of the primary objectives of Ayatollah Khomeini and his followers, both before and especially after the Revolution and ascendancy to power, has been to revive "Islam's dignity." Israel's aggressive policies toward the Palestinians and not-so-hidden general disrespect for Muslims has fostered a hatred of the Israeli government, especially its hardline factions and elements. Under such circumstances, the long-established policy of the United States to give Israel unquestioning and unconditional support makes anti-Israeli and anti-American sentiments among Muslims more entrenched. Within this overall framework, the Iranian government's view of Israel could be summarized as follows: "After more than six decades of occupation; demolition of people's homes in Jerusalem, the West Bank, and the Gaza Strip; and the humiliation and oppression of the Palestinians, who played no role in the atrocities against the Jewish people, the US government—under the influence of Israel—exhibits no sign of sympathy toward the Palestinian people and their plight. Instead, the US steadfastly supports any action of the Israeli government." Such a view of Israel and the US is not peculiar to the Iranian system (*nezam*). It is even shared by Americans, including, among others, Stephen Waltz:

> The protracted failure of U.S. policy on the Israel–Palestine issue [goes] back several decades. That's not news, of course. What has changed in the past few years is that the [Israel] lobby's operations and its harmful influence are now out in the open for all to see, which makes it almost impossible to make the old arguments that Israel is a "vital strategic asset" or a country that "shares our values" with a straight face, or to convince anyone who's not already in agreement … The United States has backed Israel no matter what it did because AIPAC and the other groups in the lobby have enormous influence inside the Beltway [i.e. Washington] and use that political muscle to defend Israel whenever its government's policies clash with America's interests.[53]

The US position, as described, has served only to intensify the degree of hostility between Iran and the US on the one hand, and Iran and Israel on the other. Contrary to the American calculation, its own policy has in fact become a major obstacle to peace and stability in the Middle East. Unqualified and consistent support for Israel is undoubtedly a major reason for the growth of anti-American sentiment and Islamic extremism throughout the region. As long as this dynamic remains unchanged, hardliners in Iran will remain relevant and more effectively be able to plead their case for non-compromise and non-cooperation with the US.

In the majority of UN Security Council resolutions relating to Israel, the United States has been Israel's lone supporter. Resolutions considered critical of Israel and its policies—many relating to Israel's military actions, anti-Palestinian settlement policies, or even humanitarian issues—have been blocked (vetoed) by the US. A quick look at the history of US vetoes in favor of Israel, from 1972 to 2011, confirms that Washington's support for Israel supersedes any consideration of humanitarian needs. The following provides a few examples in this regard:[54]

- 1985 UNSC draft resolution condemning Israeli action against civilians in Lebanon.[55]
- 1985 UNSC draft resolution condemning repressive measures by Israel against the Arab population.[56]
- 1988 UNSC draft resolution urging Israel to abide by the Fourth Geneva Convention, by rescinding the order to deport Palestinian civilians, and condemning the policies and practices of Israel that violate the human rights of the Palestinian people in the occupied territories.[57]
- 1997 UNSC draft resolution demanding that Israel halt illegal settlement construction in east Jerusalem and throughout the occupied territories.[58]
- 2006 UNSC draft resolution demanding that Israel stop the bombing of Gaza and its associated military operation.[59]
- 2011 UNSC draft resolution condemning all Israeli settlements established since 1967 as illegal and calling for an immediate halt to all settlement building.[60]

On June 14, 1994, Foreign Minister Velayati met with the German Foreign Minister, Klaus Kinkel, to discuss the Middle East Peace Process in detail. Kinkel told Velayati that the peace process was in its final stages and that the only country opposing it was Iran, but also noted that Iran's support was critical to the success of the process. In response, Velayati said that the Europeans did not fully comprehend the realities of the region and that Iran was not the main obstacle to the success of the peace process. Velayati said that Iran would not impede the peace process but wanted to express its viewpoint. From Iran's perspective, the so-called "Middle East Peace Process" was far more complex than was implied by the West's "silver bullet" approach to peace and security in the region—but if the West did indeed believe that peace was imminent, then, Velayati promised, Iran would not obstruct it, but would respect whatever the Palestinians decided. Two decades later, the Israeli government is widely believed, even in the US, to be the main stumbling block on the way to any possible "Peace Process" with the Palestinians.

The Obama administration also tried its hand in the Middle East peace process, advocating direct talks between the Palestinians and Israelis.[61] President Obama's efforts thus far have failed, but there are signs that this administration is adopting a more critical stance towards Israeli Prime Minister Benjamin Netanyahu's flouting of international law. In response to the Israeli government stepping up its illegal settlement-building program in the West Bank, in November 2011 the Obama administration publicly expressed its dismay at Tel Aviv's actions:

> We are deeply disappointed by [the] announcement about accelerated housing construction in Jerusalem and the West Bank ... Unilateral actions work against efforts to resume direct negotiations and they do not advance the goal of a reasonable and necessary agreement between the parties.[62]

Secretary of State John Kerry reinforced that view, remarking in November 2013 that "We consider now, and have always considered, the settlements to be illegitimate."[63] He warned Israel in November 2013 that it faced an economic boycott if it failed to reach a peace accord with the Palestinians.[64] To ignore the root cause of failure in the peace process between Palestinians and Israel, while vilifying Iran as *the* obstacle to ending the conflict, only exacerbates the situation. It ensures the endurance of the decades-old conflict between Palestine and Israel, and the continuation of turbulence in the region in general. Hoping to sweep away any prospects of an Israeli–Palestinian peace deal, Israeli Prime Minister Benjamin Netanyahu has emphasized the apocalyptic threat supposedly posed by Iran. This move is intended to divert the spotlight from Tel Aviv's ever more aggressive actions against the Palestinians, as more land is seized and settlements established.

As declared by the Palestinian Authority President, Mahmoud Abbas: "The peace process is clinically dead and Israel bears full responsibility."[65] This sentiment is shared by much of the international community, in view of the Israeli government's acceleration of settlement construction and disregard for its commitments and obligations under international law and other conventions.[66]

The Islamic Republic's position on the question of a durable peace was outlined by Ayatollah Khamenei in his address to the 16th Non-Aligned Movement (NAM) Summit in Tehran on August 30, 2012:

> We have put forth a just and entirely democratic solution. All the Palestinians—current citizens of Palestine and those who have been forced to emigrate to other countries but have preserved their Palestinian identity, including Muslims, Christians and Jews—should take part in a carefully supervised and confidence-building referendum and choose the political system of their country, and all the Palestinians who have suffered from years of exile should return to their country and take part in this referendum and then help draft a constitution and hold elections. Peace will then be established.[67]

Cooperation, non-interference, and peace

If the international community wishes to achieve a long-lasting solution to the Palestinian–Israeli conflict, it needs to be just and acceptable to Palestinians. In this respect there is a role for Iran to play, especially in relation to its influence with militant anti-Israeli groups. The US could concurrently exert meaningful pressure on Israel. Cooperation between the US and Iran therefore holds great potential for progress in the Middle East Peace Process.

Iran has often indicated its willingness to refrain from interference that might adversely affect the peace process. During high-level talks with the Germans, including the Political Director General of the German Foreign Ministry, Reinhard Schlagintweit, I repeatedly confirmed Iran's readiness to support any possible solution acceptable to the Palestinians. Similarly, the Iranian Deputy Foreign Minister, Mahmoud Vaezi, offered the same assurance to his counterparts in the "Critical Dialogue" meetings between Iran and the EU Troika which were held semi-annually in the 1990s. In fact, the Iranian Supreme Leader publically has confirmed that Iran would not impede any settlement which would be acceptable to the Palestinians.

Let's Talk About Human Rights

Human rights violations and lack of democratic values in Iran have been a constant theme in the criticisms leveled at the Iranian government by the West, particularly the US. The Iranian government, in turn, has underlined the politicization of the issue and pointed to the West's dismal human rights track record, especially in the Middle East. Both sides also claim to be champions of universal values, justice, equality, and dignity. In the absence of cordial relations between Iran and the United States and the wider West, the issues of human rights and democracy have become entangled in the web of bilateral disputes.

Inside Iran, there has been a debate amongst political decision-makers on how to address the issue of human rights. There are some who adamantly believe that the West seeks to impose their own version of human rights at the expense of Islamic values. Proponents of this view are reluctant to accommodate a Western interpretation of human rights—specifically on such Sharia-related issues as women's "hijab" and corporal punishment. Another school of thought recognizes the innate differences between Islamic and Western values. However, adherents to this view advocate religious coexistence through inter-faith dialogue that would produce a better understanding of cultures, religions, and values, and thereby reduce the existing gap between Islam and the West. By identifying common ground and addressing differences, their aim is to align themselves with the United Nations Universal Declaration on Human Rights (UDHR). Despite differences of view in certain areas and issues, there exist agreement on important areas relating to respect for civil and political rights, including illegality of torture, legal representation and independence of the judiciary. Where differences remain, the focus is on seeking to understand and accommodate such cultural variety.

The latter school of thought was dominant during Rafsanjani's presidency (1989–97), when the government, judiciary, and Foreign Ministry supported international cooperation on human rights issues. Moreover, the Supreme Leader backed increased cooperation with the United Nations Human Rights Commission. The UN Special Representative for Iran from 1986 to 1995, Reynaldo Galindo Pohl, was permitted to visit Iran, first in 1990 and on two subsequent occasions during his tenure of office. His visit to Iran from January 21 to 28, 1990 was coordinated with the Iranian government and provided him with access to prisons and prisoners, judiciary representatives and senior government officials. Following his visit, Pohl's report on the human rights situation in Iran was presented to the United Nations General Assembly.[68] The report detailed the concerns of the international community in relation to human rights violations in Iran, with emphasis on the penal code, corporal punishment, lack of legal representation, confessions under duress, and women's rights.[69]

While serving as the Iranian ambassador to Germany, I organized several seminars on Islam, human rights, and the West. Participants included officials, lawyers, religious figures, media representatives, and academics from both Iran and Western countries. These seminars, intended to develop a better mutual understanding between the two sides, had a significant impact on both Iranians and the Western participants. However, certain interest groups in the West were opposed to this type of dialogue, and applied tremendous pressure to halt the process, particularly following the Mykonos assassinations and similar incidents in Europe. Such incidents hampered our efforts to forge close cooperation on matters of religion, human rights, and other issues of mutual concern.

On June 8, 1992 we finalized plans for a seminar following my meeting with Lothar Wittmann,[70] Director General for Cultural Policy at the German Foreign Ministry. That seminar, on Human Rights in Islam and Christianity, took place in Hamburg and was attended by more than 50 high-level officials and scholars from Germany and Iran. The discussions were enlightening on the legal, religious, and political aspects of Islam and Christianity, showing the similarities and differences, and advancing cooperation and tolerance between and among religions.

Following the success of this seminar, there was a clearly expressed desire from both Germany and Iran to continue the inter-religious dialogue. This led to a number of joint seminars in the following years, with a wider scope of topics and participants not only from Germany but also from other European countries. These seminars also facilitated the participation of high-level Iranian religious figures, politicians, and scholars. Up to the end of my ambassadorship in Germany in 1997, five major inter-religious seminars were held in Germany and Iran.[71]

On April 27, 1993, Rouhani, Secretary of the Supreme National Security Council and the head of the Majlis Foreign Affairs Committee, of the parliament, proposed bilateral cooperation on human rights to German officials. Rouhani also reassured Germany that Iran would never send commandos to kill Salman Rushdie[72] and would respect international norms in this matter.

Rouhani also brought forward the need for inter-faith dialogue between Christians and Muslims on human rights issues in order to advance peace, security and stability in the Middle East.

During President Rafsanjani's era, Dr. Rajaee Khorasani's,[73] head of the Majlis Human Rights Subcommittee, made a four-day visit to Bonn in May 1994, during which he engaged in extensive discussions on human rights issues in the Bundestag, the German Foreign Ministry, and the Interior Ministry. In these discussions, Khorasani's primary focus was on the need to depoliticize the human rights issue, but he also expressed the need for the West to correct their double-standard policy on human rights. He exemplified the latter point by noting the West's inaction on human rights violations in countries such as Egypt, Yemen, and Saudi Arabia because they were US allies, while the West had also stayed silent on the mass violations of human rights under the Shah—a US ally. Dr. Khorasani contrasted the West's attack on Saddam for launching a few missiles against Israel, while taking no action to prevent him from launching 1,800 scud missiles and chemical weapons against Iran, killing and injuring tens of thousands of Iranian civilians. The West had even supported Saddam in this gruesome act by supplying him with weapons. Dr. Khorasani concluded by saying that the West's behavior had convinced Iranians that the West was not genuinely concerned with promoting human rights but only using it as a foreign policy instrument to further its own interests.

During the same period, Foreign Minister Velayati had also indicated to me that Iran was keen to establish a forum for dialogue and cooperation with the European Union on human rights issues, as well as on terrorism, WMD, and drug trafficking. I relayed this proposal to the Political Director of the German Foreign Ministry, Hans-Wilhelm Theodor Wallau[74] on October 24, 1994, but he told me that the proposal had already been considered by the EU Commission and rejected. He also revealed that German Foreign Minister Klaus Kinkel had been very positive about the initiative, but due to Washington's opposition, the EU had felt obliged to reject it.

Yet again, Washington had prevented possible progress on human rights and other matters of international concern, a trend that was continued unabated and exerted further pressure on those within Iran who had staked high political capital in an attempt to establish cooperation on these sensitive issues.

Perpetuation of such policies led the Iranian government, particularly the hardline elements and currents, that a secret hand was directing US foreign policy in the Middle East—the Israeli lobby. The interests and objectives of this political force coincided with those of the traditional hawks in the US establishment, but mainly in the US Congress. In June 2013, after Hassan Rouhani's election, a congressional staffer noted that "US legislators are partial to piling on more sanctions because it has a high political payoff in terms of satisfying lobbying groups."[75] The ultimate objective of this political dynamic, when it comes to the question of Iran, as seen by the Iranian leadership, including the Supreme Leader himself, is nothing short of regime change even if through gradual attrition. In retrospect, it appears that contrary to the once promised positive message of "goodwill begets goodwill," the actual policy has been to ensure that "hostility begets hostility". As we will see in the next chapter, even when power in Iran changes hands and the moderates gain more control over foreign policy, the traditional hawks in the United States, in tandem with the pro-Israel lobby, do their utmost to render any and all Iranian overtures towards resolving disputes and rapprochement futile. As has been discussed in the preceding parts of the book, such a pattern of US behavior has served to solidify the position of hardliners in Iran, further weakening of the position of moderates favoring reconciliation and rapprochement.

Chapter 8

ROAD MAP TO PEACE

Anatomy of the Iran–US Conflict

Iran's attempts to counter US hegemony in a region with vast energy resources and of significant importance to US national interests and security has been a major cause of tension and conflict between the two states. Iran seeks to tip the existing "balance of power" in the Middle East in its favor, thus securing a leading role in the Islamic world. But it is necessary to consider whether this aspect of Iran's foreign policy is defensive or offensive in nature. I would argue, as other analysts do,[1] that Iran's strategy is defensive and that it is in response to the security challenges emanating from aggressive US policies.

Since 1979, the US has maintained a heavy military presence close to Iran's border and regularly used the mantra that "all options are on the table" in relation to Iran. Iran sees her relationship to the United States as a quest for survival, not for expansion. Despite this defensive posture, however, Iran still seeks to secure its historical regional stature, and to be seen and respected as such—which in fact continues to drive its foreign policy. Some radical elements and quarters in Iran espouse a more active anti-American policy as long as the the US is seen to be acting contrary to Iranian interests. This outlook, however, represents a minority view and not in a position to determine the country's national security strategy. This is confirmed by the fact that under every Iranian presidency since the end of the Iran–Iraq War, Iran has made significant rapprochement efforts towards the US, which as discussed in detail previously, have all been spurned by Washington, for one reason or another.

Undoubtedly, competition over power and interests is a principal source of conflict between Iran and the US, but it does not in itself explain why the two countries have failed to engage in a meaningful dialogue in 35 years towards resolving—or at least, minimizing—their differences. Even advocates of *Machtpolitik*[2] do not rule out negotiations between adversaries. In this respect, the Iran–US relationship is unusual.

The US policy approach kept denying Iran's legitimate rights under the NPT and insisted on the suspension of Iran's uranium enrichment program delayed a nuclear deal for ten years, primarily because, in the absence of any meaningful direct dialogue, any sort of compromise was simply unattainable/out of reach. Yet, several conciliatory attempts initiated by both governments attest to the fact that both Iran and the United States have a desire for, and value, improvement in relations.

A clash of cultures,[3] or *kulturkampf* (also known as a "clash of civilizations"), might be another explanation for the conflict between the US and Iran. Some analysts argue that the core values which shape the Iranian system's ideological base (Islam), and the liberal values on which US society and its political system are based, are inherently antagonistic. According to Bernard Lewis, who coined the term "clash of civilizations," the US is "the great Satan" in the eyes of the Iranian leadership because of its role "as the preeminent power of the West and the ultimate custodian of Western values."[4] By including Iran in the "Axis of Evil," President George W. Bush defined the conflict between the US and Iran as an inevitable clash between two mutually exclusive worldviews: a clash between good and evil.

Because political leaders in the US are often seeking popular approval, American cultural values have a direct impact on American policies toward Iran. However, many of those liberal values contrast sharply with the conservative values of Iran's religious leaders. The clerical establishment, represented by the Supreme Leader (*vali-e' faqih*), as well as grassroots supporters, reject Western liberal values and view them as contrary to their own religious principles. For example, issues such as sexual freedom, alcohol consumption, women wearing revealing clothes, and the separation of religion and state are matters that clearly set Iran apart from America. Iranians look to their own history and centuries-old civilization for guidance on these and other matters.

While a clash of cultures undoubtedly plays a role in the Iran–US conflict, evidence also points to a significant level of ideological tolerance, if not flexibility, implying that the foreign policies of the two states are not solely driven by their value systems. Saudi Arabia and many other US allies in the Middle East clearly violate liberal values, but Washington has maintained strategic relations as well as long-standing economic and defense ties with them. In April 2011, days after the Saudis sent troops into Bahrain to crack down on the pro-democracy demonstrators, former US Defense Secretary Robert Gates met with King Abdullah. After the meeting, he told reporters: "It was an extremely cordial, warm meeting. I think the relationship is in a good place."[5] Gates added that he did not raise any concerns with Abdullah about the Saudi troops in Bahrain. American ideological flexibility even extends to Iran on occasion, as exemplified in the change from President Bush's "Axis of Evil" characterization to President Obama's offer to engage with the same "evil" for a "new beginning." Ironically, as Rouhani tells us, even President Bush made a rapprochement effort in 2004.[6]

A closer examination of Iranian foreign policy reveals that in many cases, pragmatism and national interest has superseded Islamic ideology. For instance, despite the fact that communism is generally viewed as the number one ideological enemy of Islam, Iran has maintained good relations with China and North Korea. Iran also has much better relations with Armenia than it does with Azerbaijan, a Muslim country with an overwhelming Shia majority. Moreover, despite cultural differences, Iran maintains diplomatic relations with European and other "non-Muslim" countries that are culturally closer to the US than to the Islamic world. Two particular episodes highlight this pragmatic approach on the part of Iran: first, in turning a blind eye to China's oppression of Uighur Muslims; and second, in its neutral position on the war between Russia and the Muslim Chechen rebels, which Iran has chosen to characterize as a Russian "internal affair".[7]

Iran has even offered cooperation on the release of American hostages in Lebanon in the 1980s ("Iran–Contra affair) and in the early 1990s (during Bush Senior presidency); provision of active intelligence and logistical support during the the US-led operations to oust the Taliban from Afghanistan; contribution at the 2001 Bonn Conference for the formation of the new Afghan government; assistance in Iraq prior to and after the fall of Saddam Hussein; and the 2003 "Grand Bargain" offer.[8] A less-noted and publicized overture from Tehran was the message that Rouhani sent to President Bush in 2004. In his memoir, ElBaradei recalled, "I had brought with me a written message … But neither Bush nor Rice seemed, at that time, open to such [a] prospect."[9]

Another explanation for the Iran–US conflict is to be found in the state of mutual hostility between Iran and Israel. While certainly a serious impediment to any improvement in Iran–US relations, but it is not necessarily a barrier to the establishment of a sustained dialogue aimed at détente. Some argue that until Iran recognizes Israel as a state, real detente between Tehran and Washington will be impossible. This argument ignores the fact that the Organization of Islamic Cooperation (OIC) has 57 members, of which only 11 have thus far recognized the state of Israel,[10] but it is also true that many of them have been less vitriolic than Iran in their public pronouncements about Israel. Saudi Arabia and Pakistan have not recognized Israel, but maintain friendly relations with the US. And let us not forget that until 2012, the United States had an embassy in, and diplomatic relations with, Syria, arguably the most hostile country toward Israel in the Arab world.

Notwithstanding ample areas for commonality in interests and concerns, it could be said with a high degree of certainty that it is unlikely the Iranian government will accept normal relations with the US in the short term.[11] On February 17, 2014, at the commencement of new round of nuclear talks between Iran and the P5+1, Iran's Supreme Leader repeated his pessimistic view about the possibility of détente with the US and a nuclear deal with the US-led West.[12] Addressing a large number of visitors from Iran's northwestern Azarbaijan province in Tehran, drawing on the bitter experiences with the US policy during the previous 80 years, he wondered: "How can one change such an ugly and criminal face when it comes to relations with the Iranian nation?" He continued: "Some statesmen in the previous and the present administrations imagined that if we negotiate with the US, the problem will be solved; [in response] I stated that I didn't have any objection to negotiation over the nuclear issue due to their insistence, but I stressed right then that I was not optimistic … even if the nuclear issue were resolved exactly the way the US wished, the Americans would seek other excuses [for pressure]."

Yet, the Leader emphasized that his words should not be interpreted as an end to the nuclear negotiations, pointing out: "What the foreign ministry and government officials have started with regard to the nuclear talks will continue and Iran will not violate what it has started, but everyone should know that the US in essence feels enmity towards the Islamic Revolution and Islam and this enmity will not end with the talks."

However, the direct talks that began in the latter part of 2013 raised hopes that some steps toward normalization might be taken if the two parties could reach a final deal on the nuclear issue. Ayatollah Khamenei has stated on various occasions, including in 2012, that when the day arrives that relations with the US are beneficial, he "will be the first one to say that relations should be established."[13]

Why is Conciliation between Iran and the US Necessary?

The current state of relations between Iran and the United States is uncertain and unsustainable. The two countries are locked in a "spiral conflict" which, if not addressed, could well end in a destructive, most-likely protracted war. Both parties constantly fuel the mutual ill feeling, based on a combination of fact and fiction.

The current deadlock reflects the respective discourse and polemics of two adversarial doctrines. Many Americans appear to have based the official policy on the assumption that Iran will surrender once sanctions threaten the Iranian government's survival.

My career experience gives me the certitude that the popular American perception of sanctions' efficacy is misjudged: *Iran will not bow to coercion.* Contrary to the claims of some US lawmakers and Israeli officials, foreign pressure and sanctions only served to produce a much expanded nuclear program and a dramatic rise in the number of operating centrifuges, as Tehran sought to demon-strate that it would not succumb to pressure. As already argued, the Iranian leadership has been of the belief that every concession made under duress will simply encourage the US to demand more conces-sions until the Islamic Republic undergoes transformation—whether through outright subversion or gradual attrition.

Meanwhile, US foreign policy on Iran, inclusive of public pronouncements by American officials, particularly on the nuclear issue, almost entirely ignore the significant influence of national pride in Iran's pattern of behavior and response. The West formulates political decisions predominantly on the basis of cost-benefit analysis, as also does Iran. This is what provides the rationale for US sanction policies, according to high-ranking US officials, including President Obama.[14] Iran has shown that it understands the cost-benefit principle, as demonstrated by its adherence to well-established policies, including that relating to the NPT, despite the immense pressure that US-led sanctions have imposed on the country. However, what US leaders have failed to appreciate is that the Iranian government's pragmatism and cost-benefit analysis recedes under intimidation, coercion, and humiliation. Traditional Iranian culture is fiercely resistant to humili-ation, regardless of the cost. This culture is seemingly incomprehensible and alien to most American analysts and policy-makers, even though Americans themselves strongly dislike being humiliated, ignored, or pressured.

In relation to the whole sanctions issue, it is perhaps instructive to study the "Joint Plan of Action" (JPOA), agreed in Geneva on November 24, 2013 between Iran and the world powers on the nuclear dossier. The ultimate goal of the Plan has been to reach a mutually acceptable, long-term, comprehensive solution to the problem of Iran's nuclear program, specifically to ensure that it would be exclusively peaceful and allow Iran to fully enjoy its right to nuclear energy, including enrichment, under the relevant articles of the NPT.

The US Congress maintains that Iran was brought to the negotiating table in fall 2013 as a result of sanctions.[15] While it is true that Iran was determined to find a way to end economically harmful sanctions, this argument is flawed because it ignores a number of factors. First, before sanctions even started, while I was a member of the Iranian nuclear negotiating team in March 2005, Iran had expressed its readiness to adopt measures similar to those specified in the November 2013 JPOA. The 2005 overture included implementation of the IAEA Additional Protocol that permits on-site snap inspections; limitation of the enrichment program, capping it at 5 percent; conversion of all the enriched uranium to fuel rods; and a guarantee that there would be no reprocessing and plutonium separation at the heavy water reactor in Arak—a process that could have facilitated weaponization. Tehran also suggested measures to guarantee the permanent ban on developing, stockpiling, and using nuclear weapons, all in exchange for respect for its right to enrich uranium under the NPT.[16]

The talks in 2005 failed as a result of the Western insistence on depriving Iran of exercising its legitimate right to enrichment. The Geneva agreement eight years later made provision for "a comprehensive solution [that] would involve a mutually defined enrichment program with practical limits and transparency measures to ensure the peaceful nature of the program." I have already discussed—in detail—that if the US and the other Western powers had not previously denied Iran a civilian nuclear power plant and access to international nuclear fuel market, there would not have been an enrichment facility in Iran. Moreover, if they had accepted this in 2003, the crisis in relations between Iran and the West, in particular the US, could have been avoided. It was the acceptance of the principle of enrichment in Iran that clinched the deal in Geneva, not years of draconian sanctions. As Mohamed ElBaradei, former Director General of the International Atomic Energy Agency (IAEA) rightly penned "It took the West a decade to realize that bare-knuckle competition for regional influence was not a viable strategy for dealing with Iran. The recent interim agreement, facilitated by Rouhani's low-key diplomacy, could have been reached 10 years ago."[17]

The key point is that after eight years of fruitless rounds of talks and ratcheting up of unilateral and multilateral sanctions, the West finally settled down for a deal similar to Iran's March 2005 proposal. While back in 2005 Iran enriched uranium below 5 percent purity, possessed 3,000 (164 operative) centrifuges and a small stockpile of enriched uranium, in 2013 it had reached the capability to enrich up to 20 percent at two sites possessing 19,000 (9,000 operative) centrifuges, possessing a stockpile of 8,000kg of enriched uranium and a more sophisticated generation of centrifuges.[18]

During the 2003–5 nuclear talks, I used to tell my European interlocutors that Iran would not comply with the will of the United States, such as halting its nuclear program, because to do so would be to destroy the authority and stature of Iran's leadership among its grassroots supporters. The cost of submission, tantamount to losing national and religious identity, would be simply too high to countenance.

Many believe that a comprehensive settlement of differences between the US and Iran is impossible, and this prophecy of failure tends to be self-fulfilling. But if the direct nuclear and diplomatic talks between Iran and the US fail, and if no comprehensive agreement between Iran and the US and the world powers is reached in a timely manner, sanctions will inch closer towards crippling the Iranian government. Then, one of two scenarios will likely occur.

The first scenario is that, as the pressure from sanctions increases over time, patience for a lengthy diplomatic process may finally wane and the US policy of imposing pressure aimed at forcing Iran's surrender may be supplanted by military confrontation. The other possible scenario is that the Iranian government will eventually perceive themselves as "backed into a corner" with nothing more to lose and their republic's survival in jeopardy. At that point, they will adopt retaliatory measures against US interests in the region, hoping to change the status quo through the endurance of temporary pain while administering pain to the other side for their own long-term gain. This will end in a calamitous, regional war—a war that in former American Secretary of Defense Leon Panetta's words will "consume the Middle East in a confrontation and a conflict that we would regret."[19]

A war between Iran and the US will most likely do serious damage to Iran's infrastructure and claim a large number of Iranian lives. On the other hand, the same war will have dire consequences for the security and interests of the US, Israel, and the entire West, the costs perhaps ten times those paid by the US in Afghanistan and Iraq.[20] Furthermore, such a war will not be confined to the territory of Iran, but will most likely cover much of what is arguably, in terms of US interests, the most important geostrategic region of the world. The security of energy resources and the safety of sea lanes for the steady flow of oil in the Persian Gulf will certainly be interrupted for a time.

Some American experts assert that Iran would be unable to close the Strait of Hormuz,[21][22][23] which is probably true. However, it is also true is that Iran would be capable of disrupting the safe and secure passage of vessels that transport nearly 40 percent of the world's seaborne oil exports. Zbigniew Brzezinski, currently a senior research professor of international relations at the School of Advanced International Studies at Johns Hopkins University, said in an interview in July 2012, "We would open it [Strait of Hormoz] by force — and we have the power to do it, and I'm fairly confident we would do it ... but let's not be simple-minded about it. We can open it up, but you can be absolutely certain that the costs of oil will skyrocket because it will still be a dangerous passage." In their book, *War With Iran: Political, Military, and Economic Consequences*,[24] Geoffrey Kemp and John Allen Gay have demonstrated how Iran can, by adopting asymmetric tactics utilizing not-so-sophisticated instruments spread out over days and weeks, destabilize Hormuz, thus causing a significant surge in oil prices.

A war between Iran and the US would most likely involve many countries in the Middle East, including the Arab states and Israel, ultimately bringing about new waves of extremism and new life to jihadists, as well as chaos and instability across the region for many years into the future. Former US Defense Secretary Robert Gates once remarked that bombing Iran would "create generations of jihadists, and our grandchildren will be battling our enemies here in America."[25]

If the US were to launch a high-intensity war on Iran, the outcome would not likely be the collapse of the Iranian government but rather Iran's withdrawal from the NPT, an acceleration of its nuclear program towards weaponization, and an unstable Middle East, including America's Arab allies, already vulnerable due to the "Arab spring."

Hypothetically, if a US attack were to bring about the fall of Iran's current system, the lack of an alternative government would cause the country's descent into chaos. This would lead to a situation not unlike that experienced in other parts of the region, such as Afghanistan, Egypt, Iraq, Libya, and Syria. Iran would become another failed state alongside all the others from Afghanistan to Lebanon, further destabilizing the entire region and becoming a home to international and regional terrorist organizations. Iran would become another refuge for organized crime, especially a major route for drug trafficking between Afghanistan and the West, as well as a center for the production of drugs. Chaos and civil war would spill into Iran's neighbors and disrupt them. And, the price of oil would skyrocket unpredictably for a lengthy period.

Hostile relations between Iran and the US have also had a significant effect on relations between Iran and its Arab neighbors in the region. Strained relations between Iran and the Arab countries has resulted in the waging of dangerous proxy wars in Syria, Iraq, and Lebanon, with no prospect of peace in sight. Ironically, extremists who are supported by conservative Arab countries are, by nature, the arch enemies of both conservative Arab rulers and the United States. Supporting these ruthless groups is, as a Persian saying has it, "tantamount to raising a snake in your own sleeve."

Another negative effect of a confrontational relationship between Iran and the US is the intensification of the hostility between Iran and Israel, which may ultimately transform from a war of words into one of military confrontation. It is true that Iran–Israel relations have been problematic at best since the Iranian Revolution, but the situation has deteriorated in response to the worsening relationship between Iran and the United States. Thus another potentially dangerous front has opened up in the Middle East. The US has made little to no effort to diffuse the Iran–Israel situation; indeed the US government's policy of unconditional support for Israel has only strengthened the position of Israeli hardliners.

The current trend in Iran–US relations will only exacerbate the hostility between Iran and Israel, possibly to an explosive point. This does not mean that if tensions between Iran and the US diminish, Israel and Iran would become friends. Rather, it means that if Iran and the US were reconciled, the spiraling conflict between the Iran and Israel would likely lose momentum. After all, it is only relatively recently—mainly since the emergence of Mahmoud Ahmadinejad in 2005—that Israel and Iran have threatened each other militarily.

Last but not least, the ever-escalating animosity between Iran and the US has strengthened radicalism in Iran which advocates "inherent, irreconcilable antagonism between Iran and the United States." For example, President George W. Bush's condemnation of Iran as part of the "axis of evil" gave Iranian radicalism the upper hand in both domestic politics and in Iran's foreign policy. President Hassan Rouhani, indeed, campaigned against "securitization of the country" during the 2013 Iranian presidential election.[26]

Hostile US policies have convinced Iran's Supreme Leader that the policy of "threat against threat" is Iran's sole option in dealing with

America. If this phenomenon continues, it may escalate the Iran–US conflict to a state of war. Taking advantage of the situation, while tension between Iran and the US heightens, hardliners are certainly capable of mobilizing their ultra-conservative grassroots supporters, known as *kafan pooshan* (those who wear a shroud as a symbol that they are ready to fight to death for their cause), for violent confrontations with the enemy both inside and outside of their country.

Conciliation between Iran and the US is the Rational Choice

The rewards of a peaceful relationship between the two states would be significant for both countries. For Iran, first and foremost, benefit, it would mean the end of US policies aimed at "regime change," removing the biggest concern of the Islamic Republic: security of the system (*nezam*).

Iran remains embroiled in tense political relations with the Western countries. Peace with the US would open the door to normalization of relations with other Western countries. If that occurs, then Iran would be ultimately relieved of the burden of sanctions imposed by the UNSC, European countries, and the US. Unemployment and inflation in Iran are rampant and economic growth is stifled. Although this situation is due in part to mismanagement during the eight-year presidency of Mahmoud Ahmadinejad, sanctions are in large part responsible for Iran's economic problems. Reconciliation between Iran and the US would give the former access to foreign investment and trade. Lack of investment in the country's oil industry not only deprives Iran of a vital source of revenue, but in the long term will make it an importer of oil, according to a senior Iranian energy official.[27] The country requires at least $200 billion in investment to upgrade and expand its run-down oil and gas industry.[28] According to Iran's former Oil Minister, the annual investment needed to save Iran's oil infrastructure is 2.5 times greater than the country's total annual development budget.[29] Peace with the United States would ultimately facilitate integration of Iran's economy into the global economy, creating opportunities for Iran to diversify both its imports and its exports and become active in the Western market.

The Iranian government wants to become a developed country. To achieve this, Iran needs to open itself to the world and receive a flow of know-how, advanced technology, capital investment, and finance from the West. Iran enjoys an astonishingly gifted faculty, students, and researchers, but this pool of talent should have access to the latest scientific and technological advancements. Sharif University of Technology, according to Bruce A. Wooley, a former chair of the Electrical Engineering Department of Stanford University, "has one of the best undergraduate Electrical Engineering programs in the world. That's no small praise given its competition: MIT, Caltech and Stanford in the United States, Tsinghua in China and Cambridge in Britain."[30] Sadly, the University is listed among the institutions sanctioned by the United States.

Some experts argue that the "enemy narrative" serves as a pretext for the Iranian government to crack down on dissent.[31] The Iranian government views the issue quite differently. They say that they are not delusional about the US strategic preference to see an end to the Islamic system (*nezam*) in Iran. As argued before, in their eyes, regime change has been a US goal since the Islamic Republic's inception. Their thinking, based on a combination of facts and fiction, is supporting internal dissent has been—and continues to be—part of the US policy aimed at changing the extant system in Iran. In any case, peace with the United States could diminish or eliminate Iran's phobia about being attacked by America, thus allowing the government to apply fresh thinking to the issue of dissent in Iran.

Iran is surrounded by the presence of American military bases and personnel from Afghanistan and Pakistan to the east, Bahrain and the United Arab Emirates in the south, Turkey in the west, and Turkmenistan and Kyrgyzstan to the north. "In addition, the US has close military partnerships with Georgia and Azerbaijan in the Caucasus [north of Iran], where US troops are involved in training missions, and where local facilities are used in moving supplies across the Caspian Sea towards Afghanistan."[32] The Iranian system (*nezam*) considers the US as its number one security threat. Reconciliation with the US would not only eliminate that threat, but also reduce the perpetual stress on the system, and ultimately strengthen its sense of legitimacy in the eyes of the Iranian people—a critical concern of the Iranian government.

Americans also can reap great benefits if they make peace with Iran. History shows that coercive US hostility towards Iran during the past 35 years, and its corresponding coercive policies and measures, have heightened existing security concerns for the Americans and even created new ones.

From an economic perspective, the current state of relations between Iran and the US do not make any sense. American companies have been left out of the Iranian market for more than three decades. Yet, under Iranian law and policy, American companies can become actively involved in important projects in various sectors of the Iranian oil, gas, and petrochemical industries. As one of the region's largest economies, Iran has lots to offer beyond oil. As the 19th largest economy in the world based on purchasing power parity,[33] Iran has a diversified economy and a broad industrial base. Iran's labor-rich economy with a developed infrastructure in transportation and telecommunications offers both potential and opportunity for foreign investment. Its large population of 77 million,[34] one of the youngest in the world, has created a huge consumer market. Its strategic location, with many neighbors, some land-locked, has afforded Iran an exceptional position for trade and transit.

Peace between Iran, as a regional power, and the US, as a global superpower, would allow two states to cooperate against their common adversary, such Salafi/Takfiri[35] groups as Al-Qaeda and ISIS/IS, primarily in Afghanistan, Iraq, and Syria, but also across the region as a whole. As things stand, Takfiri extremism, violence and terrorism have already become the number one national security threat for the countries of the Middle East, for the US, and for the world powers alike. Intelligence, military, and logistical cooperation between Iran and the US could create the backbone of a potent force to confront extremism across the region. Mending fences between the two countries would also assist in the reconstruction of Iran's relations with its Arab neighbors, including in changing the attitude and approach of the Arab countries support for Shia, anti-Iran Salafi groups.

Peace between Iran and the US will also clear the path for building a regional cooperation system geared to providing security, stability, and peace in the Persian Gulf between Iran and its neighbors, most importantly Saudi Arabia. Such a development would also secure the stable flow of oil and bring to an end the proxy wars in the region led by Iran and Saudi Arabia that could spiral out of control any moment. The US would also be able to gradually withdraw from the region, saving billions of dollars.

One of the most complicated issues in the conflict between Iran and the US relates to the question of Iran's position and posture regarding Israel, and its corollary, the Middle East Peace Process. The background and rationale for Iran's support for the Palestinian cause and hostility towards Israel since 1979 have already been adequately discussed. However, there are four major reasons for the intensification of Iran's hostile stance towards Israel in recent years: 1) the US threats against the security of the Iranian government, including the imposition of paralyzing sanctions and the US adoption and articulation of its "all options are on the table" mantra, and the Israeli role behind the coercive US policies; 2) Israel's threatening and bullying posture towards Iran's peaceful nuclear program, while Israel, despite possessing one of the largest nuclear arsenals in the world, is not accountable to any "body"; 3) the seemingly unconditional US support for Israel's stance on coercive policies against Iran; and 4) Israel's involvement in the covert war against Iran,[36] including the assassination of Iranian nuclear scientists.[37] There is enough ammunition here for hardliners and radicals in Iran to intensify the country's hostile and uncompromising posture and policy towards Israel.

There is no doubt that the Iranian leadership dislikes the Israeli government. Refusal to recognize the state of Israel (as is the case with many Muslim countries) is one thing, but an intensified "cold war" relationship that could inch, as a practical possibility, toward a regional war is quite another. While the issue of non-recognition of Israel is as old as the Islamic Republic, gradual drift towards a military conflict is a relatively new situation which developed subsequent to escalation of the crisis over Iran's nuclear program and with the emergence of Mahmoud Ahmadinejad.

It is reasonable to say that the escalation of the conflict between Iran and Israel centers on Iran's nuclear program, but is not limited to it. If a comprehensive, win-win deal between Iran and the US could be reached on the nuclear dossier and subsequently on a larger scale in bilateral relations, then tension between Iran and Israel will most likely be reduced. Furthermore, if Iran's security were guaranteed as part of a comprehensive peace package, the Iranian government would not have any active interest in opposing an Israeli-Palestinian deal if it were acceptable to the Palestinians themselves.

Critical Factors to be Considered

The preceding analysis of the Iran–US relationship presented above give us some insight into the nature of the discord, but it does not fully explain why the two states, despite expressions of interest in ending hostility toward each other on numerous occasions, are still locked in a protracted conflict spiral predominantly characterized by *non-compromise*. During the Cold War, the West and the Communist bloc employed espionage and engaged in proxy wars against each other in such places as Nicaragua, Vietnam, and Afghanistan, while at the same time maintaining diplomatic relations across the ideological divide. But in the case of the Iran–US conflict, a combination of deep mutual mistrust, prevalent misperceptions and misanalysis by policy-makers in both countries, not to mention the activities and maneuverings of the domestic hardliners and foreign opponents of rapprochement, have prevented the establishment of an enduring negotiation process between the two states. This, in turn, has caused the longevity of the state of non-compromise as well as the escalation of the conflict.

Mistrust between Iran and the US is a major factor obstructing meaningful and enduring talks between the two states. From the Iranian government's perspective, the United States' overriding objective in relation to Iran, since the formation of the Islamic Republic, has been regime change. Therefore, they believe that even when the Americans smile at Iran, they hide a dagger behind their back. This deep suspicion is not only a product of misperception, but also reflects the lessons of history of the Iran-US relations, as discussed throughout the book, but also the US international conduct.

In the eyes of the Iranian policy-makers, the West's treatment of Colonel Gadhafi is symptomatic of their real intentions. As they view the Libyan case, the US and UK found the excuse to attack Libya once Gadhafi had agreed with the total dismantling of his nuclear program. Even more compelling is the case of Iraq. They argue that Iraq, as everybody knows, was not engaged in making atomic bombs, but "What was Saddam's fate?" The answer, as relayed to me by a high-ranking Iranian official was clear: "The US invaded Iraq and removed him based on unsubstantiated claims of Saddam having WMDs." In their analysis, the US used Iraq and Saddam Hussein as long as they served American interests, including in containing the revolutionary Iran, and then found the excuse to dispose of him and the Ba'athist regime. Such an analysis and view lies at the very foundation of Iran's mistrust of the Americans, including during Obama's administration when the discrepancy between words and actions can hardly be concealed. While Obama offered Iran a "new beginning" in the early days of his administration, he later organized the most comprehensive mix of unilateral and multilateral sanctions against Iran and ordered a wave of cyber-attacks on Iran's Natanz nuclear facility.

Americans, of course, have their own grievances and reasons not to trust the Iranians. The 444-day US Embassy hostage-taking by

Iranian militants humiliated the United States in the eyes of its own people and those of the world and violated international law, leaving Americans angry and very negative about Iran. Iranians could not see how parading the blindfolded hostages before television cameras and chanting "Death to America, death to Carter" could hurt American feelings. In the words of Gary Sick, a close friend of mine, who served as Zbigniew Brzezinski's assistant during the hostage crisis, "the mirror image of Iranian depictions of the U.S. as the 'Great Satan' had its effect on the media, on the U.S. Congress, and on the public." Furthermore, aside from blaming Iran for terrorist attacks the sudden revelation of Iran's sophisticated enrichment installation in Natanz heightened the US mistrust of Iran.

Non-reciprocation is another contentious issue for Iran in relation to its view of America. As detailed previously, during my career, I was actively engaged in, and witness to, numerous diplomatic and tactical overtures toward the United States.[38] In return, the United States ratcheted up its pressures of sorts, which, among others, served to marginalize the moderates in Iran and prepared the ground for the emergence of a hardline faction with a new aggressive, confrontational foreign policy agenda—confrontation with the West and with the UN and turning to China, Russia and radical Anti-American states, particularly in Africa and Latin America.

Iranians view non-reciprocation as a sign of the American system's dishonesty. However, as relayed to me by some informed US sources, Iranian rejection of some of the outreaches by the US, specifically President Obama's second letter to the Supreme Leader, has created a decidedly negative perception among American policy-makers— occasional conciliatory moves by Tehran does not represent the real dominant, strategic perspective of the Iranian system. As seen in Washington, the essence of Iran's policy is not just a matter of non-compromise with the US, rather actively seeking to harm US interests and standing in the Middle East.

Coercive policies and the language of threat—major elements in the US approach to Iran—tend to ignore significant cultural traits in Iranian politics, particularly the deeply-entrenched element of national pride and millennial desire for independence. For the past two centuries, Iran's sovereignty, independence, and integrity have come under threat politically and militarily. The Iranian power elite, quite similar to the common folks, across the entire political spectrum—from reformist, to moderate, to hardliner—believe in resistance to bullying, pressure, and perceived humiliation.

I have argued in this book that the nuclear program, as a prominent case of dispute between Iran and the world powers, has become a symbol of national pride. As analyzed by a keen Iranian observer, "The Iranian leadership has constantly linked Iran's nuclear program to the nation's pride and dignity (*ezzat-e melli*). To surrender to pressures and suspend that program is tantamount to betrayal and abandoning the nation's dignity. In such cases, the Iranian leadership will lose its authority and stature among grassroots supporters and rank-and-file conservatives. Simply put, the *nezam* (Iran's political system) cannot afford the costs of such a decision."[39]

In the words of the same analyst, "the United States is not simply asking the Iranian government to change its policy. Rather, in the Iranian view, it is asking them, in a sense, to accept foreign domination and give up their independence under coercion. What makes the matter worse is the involvement of Israel, which wants to impose a perceived humiliating compromise on the Iranian system (*nezam*)."[40]

Misperceptions about the American system also abound in Iran. Some politicians in Iran view America as a declining power—even on the verge of collapse. Therefore, they argue that if Iranians resist, they will ultimately be the victor in this battle. Such a line of thinking, whether of genuine old-guard revolutionaries or political opportunists, does not believe in diplomatic solutions, viewing an antagonistic relationship between Iran and the US as a natural state of affairs. After nearly a decade, followers of this line of thinking still attack moderates/reformers for their confidence-building policies toward the West, particularly with respect to Iran's voluntary suspension of its uranium enrichment program in 2003.

This political current argues that the only way forward is to adopt aggressive policies. It keeps accusing the moderates/reformers of "vadadegi"—retreat in the face of threat and intimidation. They misanalyzed—underestimated—Western threats of referring Iran's nuclear dossier to the UNSC, wantonly dismissing it as a mere bluff. Similarly, they underestimated the, let alone impact, of the sanctions and the West's determination to impose a de facto oil embargo on Iran. This faction, symbolized by *Kayhan* manager Hossein Shariatmadai, views any deal or compromise with the US as a red line and contrary to the fundamentals of the Revolution. With the emergence of Mahmoud Ahmadinejad in 2005, this group became dominant in Iran's foreign policy. As a result, hostile relations between Iran and the West—in general, and with the US, in particular—intensified. The rest is history, as already discussed.

The final factor identified in this book as an obstacle to the creation of an enduring and meaningful dialogue and negotiation process between Iran and the US, and consequently the establishment of detente between them, is the role of "spoilers." These are the groups fundamentally opposed to US–Iran rapprochement, specifically the MEK, Israel, some Arab countries, and hawks in both the United States and Iran. While those in Iran hate their "unwitting" counterparts and collaborators outside the country, they have a common objective: to obstruct mending fences between Iran and the US. They are motivated materially as well as ideologically.

As discussed throughout this book, careful study of the *missed opportunities* for better Iran–US relations in the last three decades reveals an astonishing pattern of active steps taken by this motley of inchoate actors to thwart progress. They become even more active, even ferocious, whenever optimism appears on the horizon about progress in talks, let's say, on the nuclear issue, or on any other area of concili-ation between Iran and the West/US.

Creating the Road Map

After more than three decades of deeply-entrenched official mistrust and hostility, the road to peace between Iran and the US is truly a bumpy one. It is hard to cross but not impossible. It requires utmost patience and vigilance. Reconciliation can come about only through an unshakable commitment to resolving the conflict, a necessary but not sufficient condition. For in the absence of a genuine mutual desire—and will—for peace, no plan will work. I am confident that the dominant outlook within the Iranian system (*nezam*), including that of the Supreme Leader, is to end the hostilities with the US based on mutual respect, non-interference, and mutual interest. From Iran's side, there is the will to bring an end to the existing era of hostilities. What follows is based on the assumption that this necessary condition exists in the United States as well.

One of the reasons that Iran–US relations have been oscillating between hostility and short-lived positive engagement is the piecemeal approach of both sides, but, as shown in the book, mainly on the US side. This approach has repeatedly failed, simply because when a small step of engagement and cooperation is not followed by bigger, more sustainable steps, the effects of the small step quickly evaporate and are overtaken by the bigger hurdles along the way.

There are two reasons why the blame lies chiefly with the US. First, the Americans are in the driving seat, operating at the international level while Iran is at the regional level, so the onus is on the US to initiate change. Second, the US does not appear to a have a consistent comprehensive strategy regarding Iran, including how to negotiate an endgame.

American policies seem to lack coherence. For example, in 2002 President Bush included Iran in his "Axis of Evil," which seemed to elevate the state of tension between the two sides to new heights. Yet, two years later he came out with an unprecedented gesture towards Iran, emphasizing a readiness to personally engage in talks with Iran not just to deal with the nuclear problem but to "resolve all the issues" between Iran and the US. The same inconsistency has characterized American policy during the Reagan, George H. W. Bush, Bill Clinton, and Obama administrations. Each of the top three nuclear negotiators during the Khatami and Ahmadinejad administrations proposed a broad dialogue aimed at rapprochement toward the US administrations of George W. Bush and Obama, but they were rebuffed,[41] although both Presidents made conciliatory overtures to Iran.

Unless the US endgame is a reduction of tensions with Iran—and preferably a normalization of relations—then limited modus operandi on specific issues or situations will prove to remain insecure and susceptible to be be broken by one side or the other, or both. Let us assume that a final nuclear deal between Iran and the US and other world powers is reached and implemented. If the US endgame is not Iran–US détente, Congress may well pass a bill to impose new sanctions based on the pretext of human rights violations or state-sponsored terrorism. In that case, Tehran might regard the nuclear deal as simply a huge liability, offering no return, and launch retaliatory moves that would effectively end the nuclear agreement.

When it comes to the resolution of specific, individual issues or situations, the two countries should first agree on the end objective. In other words, each party should clearly know what it has to give and what it should expect to gain. This is an important factor which I have sought during the past few years to bring to the attention of US politicians and the American public through numerous lectures and articles. One of the reasons that the November 2013 nuclear interim deal in Geneva happened was that the end objective was defined. In the talks between Iran and the US during the second half of September 2013, Iranian negotiators had proposed that both parties needed to agree on the end state of a nuclear deal before seeking agreement on the initial and interim steps. William Burns, the US Deputy Secretary of State agreed. Without this measure, the talks would most likely have been another failure.

In the pre-Geneva and Geneva talks, the two sides agreed to negotiate a "phased approach" toward a "comprehensive agreement." This is the only way that the United States and Iran can deal with this diplomatic Gordian Knot covering the nuclear question, WMD, and other disputes.

Having worked for three decades on Iran–West relations within the Iranian administration and spending four years in the US talking to foreign policy practitioners and scholars on Iran–US relations, I have come to believe that Washington and Tehran can negotiate a "comprehensive package" to ensure the "end state" and then properly implement it. I have made this suggestion to Americans in hundreds of seminars, roundtables, lectures, and articles during my stay in the US.

Energizing Negotiations with Mediation

Article 33 of the UN Charter encourages the "parties to any dispute the continuance of which is likely to endanger the maintenance of international peace and security [to] seek a solution by negotiation ... mediation [or] arbitration." The conflict between Iran and the US is too important to both sides and too complex to allow it to be resolved by arbitration. Negotiation must therefore be the basic method by which the conflict is brought to a peaceful resolution. However, based on past experiences and the problems discussed earlier—primarily profound mistrust, misperceptions, and a lack of mutual understanding—negotiations have mostly been short-lived and unsuccessful. To avoid repeating the failures of the past, mediation should be introduced to the negotiation process. As one of the UN Charter-enshrined methods for resolving international conflicts or preventing their escalation, mediation has strong experiential and theoretical support. Jacob Bercovitch, widely considered to be one of the world's leading experts on international conflict resolution, defined mediation as "a process of conflict management ... where those in conflict seek the assistance of or accept an offer of help from, an outsider (whether individual, an organization, a group, or a state) to change their perception or behavior."[42] According to Bercovitch and Fretter, in the period 1945–2000 there were 300 international conflicts and more than 3,750 cases of mediation.[43] The success rate of mediation in conflict resolution has been remarkable. Based on numerous studies, Bercovich concluded that "mediation [is] an effective strategy that can deal with all types of conflicts."[44]

When it comes to the Iran–US conflict, some may argue that representatives of a superpower and a regional power can hardly be influenced by mediators. In this respect, a few points are worthy of note. First, Iran and the US, like any other adversaries, have motives to seek help from the mediators, relating to the role that the mediators would play. Mediators are catalysts, educators about the constraints and reasons behind one party's position on an issue for the other, bearers of good and bad news, and facilitators of a favorable climate for negotiation.

Mediators can make the parties understand each other's sensitivities, prevent the process of negotiation from getting stalled or falling apart, help prevent or avert misunderstandings and misanalysis of the situation, and facilitate the continuation and endurance of the negotiations. Mediators are expected, by definition, to try to keep the win-win spirit governing the negotiations, as opposed to the spirit of a zero-sum game. Mediators can help a party to save face, suggest trade-offs, and highlight the costs of non-agreement.[45] They can also help the two parties search for common ground and enhance the attraction of certain alternatives.[46]

An example of mediation in action has been the role played by Sultan Qaboos bin Said, the monarch of Oman since 1970, in facilitating the recent Iran–US talks that led to the "historic" November 2013 nuclear deal in Geneva (JPOA).[47]

Gradual Confidence-building

The June 2013 Iranian presidential election marked a profound change in attitude and approach in relation to international affairs. It reflected the desire of the nation to change course in the face of an impasse. "I'll pursue a policy of reconciliation and peace, we will also reconcile with the world," remarked Rouhani following his election. The US embraced the change, perhaps not based solely on these words, but because of Rouhani's record as a rational pragmatic politician during the 2003–5 nuclear negotiations with the EU3. In a number of secret meetings between August and October 2013, the two governments decided to tackle the impasse over Iran's nuclear program. In between, we witnessed the September 2013 telephone conversation between Obama and Rouhani, and the Zarif–Kerry talks in New York on the fringes of the UN General Assembly session/Session. These were events that marked a clear break with the era of hostility that had been prompted by the seizure of the American Embassy in Tehran in 1979.

This chain of events also paved the way for the November interim nuclear deal in Geneva between Iran and the P5+1. Although neither of the parties said so explicitly, the move could be considered as the *first step* of a phased process toward reconciliation. There are two reasons for such an assessment. First, is the matter of urgency: Iran–US relations have steadily deteriorated since 2005 over Iran's nuclear program. Since the US had based its policies on an erroneous perception that Iran would ultimately submit to pressure, it appears to have concluded that the only solution to Iran's nuclear crisis was to toughen the sanctions to the point of paralysis. This, as discussed earlier, would not work, and would most likely end in a dismal failure—in the worst scenario case, a destructive war. Logic dictates that this process be brought to a halt before the patience of one or both sides breaks and things spiral out of control.

Second, by agreeing to a comprehensive solution to the nuclear issue, a precedent has been established to allow Tehran and Washington to begin talks and strike a deal on other disputed issues. Finding a solution to the nuclear issue has required negotiation and compromise, but has demonstrated that both countries are willing to work towards a solution. In itself, this would be a significant step forward, showing that both the United States and Iran have abandoned their so-called uncompromising, maximalist positions, expectations and demands. Potential agreement on the nuclear issue, therefore, could be used as a starting point to address other areas of conflict between the two nations, specifically regional competition, security-related issues, terrorism, WMD, and human rights.

A final comprehensive agreement on the nuclear issue is quite possible if it is based on four principles: 1) full transparency of Iran's nuclear program in a verifiable manner; 2) adoption of measures to ensure there is no diversion toward weaponization; 3) Iran's right to carry out enrichment under the NPT; and 4) the lifting of sanctions imposed on Iran. Based on conversations with other nuclear negotiators from P5+1, I am convinced that they would accept these four principles if Iran and the US could agree on them. These four principles should then be implemented step by step, based on an equal application of the terms by both sides in each step.

As the *second step*, the group of Track II mediators could prepare a comprehensive package for detente/reconciliation outlining the macro demands and expectations of both parties. Once reviewed by both governments, the package could be finalized with the help of the mediators, but needs to be agreed upon by both sides. From the Iranian perspective, key requirements include American reaffirmation of its commitment from the Algiers Accords of 1981 "not to intervene, directly or indirectly, politically or militarily, in Iran's internal affairs"; respect for Iran's independence and territorial integrity; cessation of subversive or destabilizing activities aimed at attrition or regime change; and abandonment of the language of threat and intimidation, including the "all options are on the table" mantra. The two parties could immediately begin adopting measures to decrease tension and hostility, preparing the public in both countries for the move toward détente and eventual resumption of full diplomatic relations.

Iran and the United States must immediately cease hostile rhetoric, propaganda, saber rattling, and threatening each other at the official level. Neither government can, or is expected to, effectively control individuals and political currents outside their authority—such as the hardliners who are able to provoke the conservative elements and constituencies in the Iranian society, or similar political quarters or media in the American society. But, it is vital that the governments act in a responsible manner in order to diffuse any tensions that may arise. Here, the mediators will also have a crucial role to play.

Furthermore, as an acknowledgment of Iran's past gestures of goodwill, the United States could pursue the unfreezing of Iranian assets. This could be done by means of the International Court of Arbitration in The Hague or through a legal process in the US. In the case of the claims by individuals in the US courts, Iran could be permitted to file a defense against such claims.

Other practical measures that would assist rapprochement between Iran and the United States could include, inter alia, the resumption of the sale of civilian aircraft by the US to Iran (which would enhance airline safety in Iran); US support for loans from the World Bank to assist in humanitarian projects in Iran; and US support for Iran's admission to the World Trade Organization. Interdependence reduces the risk of hostile confrontations and helps prevent military conflict.

Strengthening people-to-people relations would be vital to creating an atmosphere in which the two sides can ultimately take steps toward normalizing their relations. Easing restrictions on travel for business, academic, and professional purposes would help improve relations between the countries and would be very constructive. The resumption of academic, business and professional exchanges between the two nations and cooperation between universities and professional organizations should be encouraged. The establishment of robust exchange programs, involving students, youth, think tanks, media, libraries, NGOs, business leaders, and academics, would help tremendously to rebuild trust, bring together the hitherto divided worldviews, and stabilize the reconciliation process between the two countries.

The promotion of tourism in both directions—for example, by the restoration of landing rights for commercial airlines in both Iran and the US—would help to dispel negative stereotypes and engender greater cultural awareness. Development of a a long-term, durable, inter-faith dialogue between American and Iranian religious leaders and scholars, with the objective of promoting peaceful coexistence between the two great religions of Islam and Christianity. This initiative under the banner of "Dialogue of Abrahamic religions" can create a better understanding, remove misperceptions, and revive friendship and peace between the two nations.

Cooperation on humanitarian issues such as fighting malicious diseases, especially cancer and AIDS, drug addiction, and environmental issues would not only be beneficial to both sides but also a major door opener to friendship and building trust. Among health-related information exchanges between the two countries, Iran's experience on the treatment of tens of thousands of victims of chemical weapons could be valuable to the studies on the devastating and long-term effects of the use of chemical weapons on and the horrific sufferings of the victims.

Some may argue that this step is not realistic, especially from the Iranian side, where the government and conservatives do not seek such a relationship. In April 2013 my joint op-ed with the former American ambassador to Ukraine, William Miller, came out in the *Christian Science Monitor.*[48] The focus of the piece was "civilian diplomacy," proposing both governments should lift restrictions on their citizens' travel to their respective countries. The article was widely reported in Iran, even by the most conservative newspapers and websites—and did not attract any criticism. It should be noted that this or similar steps should only be taken after a general agreement on mending fences is concluded.

Detente or Cooperation on Issues of Mutual Interest

Aside from a host of strictly bilateral issues between Iran and the US— which have remained unaddressed and unresolved since the early days of the 1979 Revolution—security-related issues, whether in the Persian Gulf or on a larger scale in the Greater Middle East, have come to be recognized as the areas of mutual interest and concern to both Iran and the US. Throughout the book, I have tried to trace, some briefly and others in relative detail, the trajectory of the respective policies of both countries over the past three and a half decades. I have looked at issues and situations where the respective policies of Iran and the US have collided or provided the opportunity for understanding and even cooperation of sorts, most notably in Afghanistan and Iraq in the post-9/11 period. Cooperation on the release of Western and American hostages in Lebanon has been another issue and area of convergence of interests.

The on-going tumult in the area, both in the immediate neighborhood of Iran—Afghanistan and Iraq—and further to the west in the Levant—most notably in Syria—provide ample opportunities for proactive Iran-US cooperation in favor of bringing peace and stability to crisis-ridden countries and situations. Syria is the verge of collapse, more in terms of its social fabric than in the formal structure of governance. Syria is on the verge of collapse. If mechanisms for a post-uprising transition are not immediately put in place through international effort, then the emergence of one of the two following scenarios is inevitable: a) an endless proxy war between the Syrian government, Iran, and Russia on one side, and the Persian Gulf Arab countries, Turkey, and West (including the US) on the other, with the potential of spiraling into a full-fledged regional war; or b) Syria descending into total chaos and becoming a failed state and thus a haven for extremist terrorist groups and organized crime. The sudden rise of the ISIS/IS (so-called Islamic State) and its spill-over into Iraq, and later developments, appears to have lent credence to the second scenario. The new situation, with all its perils for both Syria and Iraq, and to some lesser extent, Lebanon, has brought in its wake a new sense of realism—and urgency—to the parties involved; something needs to be done as a matter of priority for the Syrian crisis. Iran and the US, in the framework of a forum with the participation of the Permanent Members of the UN Security Council and the other members of what I call R5 (five regional powers: Iran, Iraq, Egypt, Turkey and Saudi Arabia), and finally S2 (representatives of the current Syrian government, as well as of the political, military, and civilian opposition inside Syria and abroad), could engage in intensive exchanges towards drafting an initiative or macro plan for the resolution of the Syrian crisis. The plan should identify concrete, pragmatic, and attainable goals relevant to both a short-term and medium-term transition from war to peace.

The plan should consist of substantive elements, such as a genuine ceasefire by all armed parties, including the Syrian government and opposition forces, fully backed and guaranteed by regional and international players; robust mechanisms for both broadening and deepening all levels of humanitarian assistance to alleviate the suffering of civilians; identification of key steps to prevent state failure, outbreak of sectarian violence, and civil war; holding of free elections overseen and administered by the UN; and a national constitutional referendum based on freedom of conscience, belief, and religious practice. The example of the cooperation between Iran, the United States, and Russia which led to the dismantling of Syria's chemical weapons in 2013 offers a possible blueprint—and hope—in this respect.[49]

Iran and the US have common interests in jointly combating drug trafficking. One of the main sources of supply for the drugs destined for Europe and the US is Afghanistan, via Iran. Joint efforts to stop this trafficking would be beneficial to both countries, and certainly to the entire international community. Cooperation on halting international organized crime through existing international organizations such as Interpol and agreements between law enforcement agencies would be a good way to build trust between the US and Iran.

Cooperation on Iraq and Afghanistan would also be mutually beneficial to the US and Iran in order to assure stability and peace following the cessation of hostilities. Iran's capabilities in terms of intelligence and logistics in this area are unmatched. Mutual cooperation between Iran, the US, and Afghanistan on combating terrorism and terrorist groups, halting the trafficking of drugs, smuggling, and other criminal activities would contribute significantly to a post-war settlement in the region. The three countries establish a committee to facilitate cooperation on political, economic, security, crime, and reconstruction matters in Afghanistan. Similarly, Iran and the United States could assist the new Iraq to develop its social infrastructure and economy and support a durable democracy reflecting the ethnic, religious, and cultural diversity of the country. As already indicated, the tumultuous and uncertain situation created in Iraq following the emergence and early military gains of the so-called Islamic State has added urgency to the acutely needed Iran-US cooperation to fight and effectively nullify the threat of the new generation of violent, extremist Salafi forces in the area. Given the importance of stability in Iraq for the entire region, Iran, Iraq and the US could also establish a committee for Iraq, similar to the committee proposed for Afghanistan.

Concluding an agreement on disputed issues such as terrorism would constitute the *third step* of the proposed process. Although the US and Iranian governments both condemn terrorism in its individual and state form, the two differ in their definition of terrorism. The US government considers terrorism as "activities that involve violent ... or life-threatening acts ... that are a violation of the criminal laws of the United States or of any State and ... appear to be intended (i) to intimidate or coerce a civilian population; (ii) to influence the policy of a government by intimidation or coercion; or (iii) to affect the conduct of a government by mass destruction, assassi-nation, or kidnapping." Iran, like many other developing countries in the "Global South", does not consider armed resistance by national liberation movements (such as Hamas and Hezbollah) as terrorism, but rather as legitimate political movements that have no choice but to resort to armed struggle in order to repel armed aggression or illegal occupation. With regard to the US government's definition of terrorism, the government of Iran maintains that if violence against innocent civilians is one manifestation of terrorism, then all states that carry out heavy bombing of civilian areas (such as Beirut and Gaza) are guilty of state terrorism. And those who provide the weaponry or the finance to purchase such weaponry are also to be considered accomplices in the crime.

Notwithstanding the serious differences at the international level on the definition of "terrorism"—and in this particular case, between Iran and the US—there exists a basis on which Tehran and Washington could agree to combat terrorism, namely UN Security Council resolu-tions, and specifically UN resolution 1373.[50] This resolution, adopted unanimously by the UN Security Council under Chapter VII of the United Nations Charter and therefore binding on all UN member states, provides the most comprehensive framework for an Iran–US agreement on terrorism. Under this umbrella, both countries would be committed to countering terrorism bilaterally, regionally, and internationally without discrimination. As a quid pro quo for Iran's cooperation in countering terrorism, the US could remove Iran from the State Department's list of state-sponsors of terrorism.

In parallel with talks over terrorism, the two capitals could establish a joint commission on human rights and democracy. Such a commission, comprising distinguished citizens nominated by each country, could jointly consider and review human rights cases raised by both sides, with recommendations then made to the two governments for further consideration and subsequent necessary action.

Having built some mutual trust through cooperation on issues of common interest, Tehran and Washington could begin to consider other, more problematic international issues, such as *weapons of mass destruction* (WMD). This matter has been on the Western agenda since the early 1990s, and there is an urgent need for Iran and the world powers to agree on a set of principles to deal with the matter. Moving beyond talks on the nuclear issue, the goal should be the establishment of a WMD-free zone (WMDFZ). The revolutionary upheaval of recent times in the Middle East has shifted the priorities of regional leaders from advancing a WMDFZ initiative to dealing with domestic issues. It appears that rising nationalism and populist sentiments, coupled with extremism and terrorism led by radical Salafists, stand in the way of progress towards WMDFZ in the Middle East.

A *comprehensive agreement* with Iran, however, could become a platform for a broader Middle East agenda, a road map for a WMD-free zone, and as a model for addressing proliferation challenges in this part of the world in the future. Within such a context, as discussed in a paper published by the International Panel on Fissile Material,[51] the world powers and Iran could agree on six principles covering the Iranian nuclear issue and a nuclear weapon free zone in the Middle East: 1) no nuclear weapons in the Middle East; 2) no production of plutonium and seperation of plutonium in the Middle East; 3) a ban on cessation of the production of highly enriched uranium, and indeed with no enrichment beyond 5 percent in the Middle East; 4) no stockpiles beyond domestic needs for nuclear civilian use; 5) establishment of a regional or international consortium for producing nuclear fuel; and 6) ensure WMD non-proliferation by creation of a regional authority responsible for regulating nuclear development and verifying its peaceful nature in the region.

Iran could reaffirm its adherence to all international conventions related to weapons of mass destruction such as a Non-Proliferation Treaty and the Chemical Weapons Convention, and ratify the Biological Weapons Convention and the Comprehensive Test Ban Treaty. It could also agree to the maximum level of verification detailed in these conventions and treaties. In return, the US could encourage UNSC member states to cooperate in peaceful technological development with Iran under the auspices of these conventions and treaties. Because a WMD free zone in the Middle East is the only sustainable long-term solution, the UNSC would be committed to pursuing the implementation of the initiative.

The Arab–Israeli conflict is another important area of dispute between Tehran and Washington. In what appeared to be a gesture of goodwill, last year Javad Zarif sent good wishes to the Jewish people for Rosh Hashanah on his Twitter page. He received a response from Christine Pelosi, daughter of US House Minority Leader Nancy Pelosi, who wrote: "The New Year would be even sweeter if you would end Iran's Holocaust denial, sir." Zarif quickly responded: "Iran never denied it. The man who was perceived to be denying it is now gone. Happy New Year."[52]

In line with historical facts, the government of Iran maintains that neither the Palestinians nor the Arabs and the Muslims, as a whole, bear no responsibility for the horrendous, systematic crimes of the Nazi Germany against Jews, gypsies, communists, socialists, democrats, nationalists, the disabled, or people with inherited disabilities. Iran believes that the victims of these horrible crimes against humanity, or the heirs of those victims, should receive due compensation from those responsible for such crimes committed in Europe. Iran considers it unjust that millions of people in another nation, in another continent, should be uprooted from their homes and dispossessed of their livelihood and possessions in order to compensate the victims of Nazi crimes. To create millions of new victims in order to compensate the victims of past crimes is contrary to reason, international law, morality, and simple common humanity.

Consequently, it is the view of the government of Iran that Palestine should be allowed to return to its previous status: that of a multi-ethnic, multi-confessional land governed by a single, democratically elected government. Given the bitterness of the past history and the existing conditions on the ground, the US maintains that the only way to achieve a durable and equitable settlement is by the creation of two separate states: one for the Palestinians, the other for the Israelis. In addition, the fear that Iran's political-military support for Hamas and Hezbollah poses "an existential threat to Israel," a close ally of the United States, needs to be addressed. Both the Iranian and US governments believe that a fair, negotiated political settlement is far more desirable than any imposed military solution. Therefore they should be able to agree on certain principles respected by the international community.

The idea that a broad framework for conciliation between Tehran and Washington, addressing Iran's security concerns, might also encompass an Iranian commitment to non-interference in the Middle

East Peace Process, provided that any solution proposed is accepted by Palestinians, is still a feasible one. In other words, in exchange for US recognition and respect for Iran's sovereignty and interests, the Iranian government would agree not to impede or undermine any agreement reached between Palestinians or the Arab countries and the Israelis. I believe that once misperceptions are removed on both sides, Washington and Tehran might be able to agree on the following principles:

- Iran and Israel would respect UN resolutions and refrain from threatening another member of the UN.
- Iran would continue to defend the legitimate rights of Palestinians and be allowed to provide financial help for humanitarian purposes.
- The government of Iran would not attempt to substitute its voice for that of the Palestinian people, and will respect any solution that is freely chosen by the majority of Palestinians.
- The US would commit itself to support the legitimate rights of Palestinians and the right of return of millions of Palestinians in diaspora to their homeland.
- The US would commit itself to support the implementation of all UN resolutions on the Israeli–Palestinians dispute.

Establishing a regional security and economic cooperation system in the Persian Gulf between Iran and its neighbors, supported by the US, would also be a useful strategy for guaranteeing a durable reconciliation and detente between Iran and the US. The US currently spends billions of dollars on maintaining a military presence in the Persian Gulf. Iran, the US, the Gulf Cooperation Council (GCC), Iraq, and the world powers could cooperate to establish a regional system among themselves for maintaining peace, security, and stability in the region. Establishment of such a regional arrangement will allow the US to reduce, and eventually withdraw, its military forces from the area, with its corollary huge economic and financial savings in the order of tens of billions a year.

A "Persian Gulf Security and Cooperation Organization" comprising the six member states of the GCC, plus Iran and Iraq, could be established in accordance with Paragraph 8 of UN Security Council resolution 598. The regional countries could establish "common security arrangements", similar to the European example of the Organization for Security and Cooperation (OSCE) and even NATO, and cooperate collectively on combating terrorism, extremism, sectarianism, organized crime, drug trafficking, and other common security concerns. The beauty and merits of a such a cooperation will, over time, manifest themselves in the gradual elimination of various barriers impeding political, economic, and cultural cooperation, and instead assisting the promotion and development of trade and commercial relations. Free trade among regional states is a realistic goal, which in turn could enhance political relations and progress towards the goal of a Middle East free of weapons of mass destruction. Resources otherwise earmarked for military and security purposes under conditions of insecurity and tension could instead be diverted to economic development and alleviation of poverty, thus reducing the risk of social unrest.

Gradual reduction in tension on the most disputed issues would open the door to business and commerce between Iran and the United States. The year before Islamic Revolution, the United States and West Germany had been Iran's main trading partners,[53] but after the Revolution, the US saw its trade with Iran decline significantly. The first round of US sanctions on Iran went into effect in 1979—which were further extended in 1995 under President Clinton. Since 2005, and following the crisis over Iran's nuclear program, the sanctions applied by the US and EU were expanded further, in both scope and depth. Yet up until 1992, before the Clinton administration toughened its sanctions, the United States remained Iran's sixth largest source of imports,[54] while for more than 15 years after the Revolution, Germany was Iran's largest trading partner, followed by Japan, Italy, and France.[55]

The imposition of US–EU unilateral and multilateral sanctions, especially after the nuclear crisis, led to a gradual decline in trade between Iran and the West, accompanied by a growth in trade between Iran and such Asian countries as China and India. Therefore, US-led sanction regimes have promoted the growth of East Asian influence in Iran, specifically that of America's main rival, China. Since 2001, Chinese exports to Iran have increased nearly sixteenfold.[56] In retrospect, it can be noted that the sanctions regime, other than hurting the Iranian economy and people, has also served to force a significant shift in Iran's foreign trade from the West to the East—also referred to as "Easternization" in the relevant literature.[57]

The European Union had more than a 50 percent share of Iran's trade in the 1990s,[58] while 40 years ago over 60 percent of Iran's foreign trade was with Europe and less than 20 percent with Asia. By 2013, Asia accounted for over 83 percent of Iran's foreign trade.[59] Trade turnover between Iran and China amounted to about $36 billion in 2012,[60] and $40 billion in 2013, close to 50 percent of Iran's annual foreign trade. Today, China is Iran's largest trading partner.[61] Moreover, in February 2014, the Iranian Finance and Economic Affairs Minister, Ali Tayyebnia, and the Chinese Commerce Minister, Gao Hucheng, signed an agreement in Tehran to double bilateral trade over the course of three years.[62] In fact, in response to the bullying policy of the West, Tehran repositioned itself in terms of commerce by adopting a trade policy of "Asianization" and "economic regionalism".[63]

Although bilateral ties between the West and Iran have been weakened dramatically, there still exists the potential to revive strategic economic links between them, including, in particular, the US. The past trends in Iranian industry and the economy as a whole stand testament to the prominence of the West in Iran's economy. Many top Iranian businessmen are Western-educated, and even today a majority of overseas Iranian students and academics study or work in the US and other Western countries. During my trips to Iran since fall 2013 I have been surprised by the fact that almost every Iranian businessman I met was eager to establish business relations with the US. This is what I call "civilian diplomacy", which I am sure can contribute to a revival of the traditional industrial and trade relationships between Iran and the West.

The opening of banks and commercial entities in each country by the other should be encouraged to facilitate the export and import of goods and services. With the risks of confrontation diminished, the US government could encourage investment in gas and oil resources and in particular the pipelines that will move Central Asian oil and gas through Iran to the Persian Gulf. Developing pipelines to carry Iranian oil and gas to Pakistan and India, as well as northward to Europe, could also be the type of mega projects in which American companies could participate.

In the long term, it would be useful to establish an implementation mechanism, such as a permanent joint commission, tasked with strengthening relations between the United States and Iran on all important issues, such as security, commerce, and cultural exchange. This permanent joint commission could be modeled on the joint commissions that were established with Russia, Ukraine, and other European Nations after the end of the Cold War.

This road map could pave the way for rapprochement and the restoration of normal diplomatic relations between Iran and the US, and bring to an end 35 years of mutual hostility. But to realize this, a historical, monumental step should to be taken by the two states; recognizing the other side's grievances followed by *mutual forgiveness*.

AFTERWORD

I am writing this short "Afterword" in the wake of the historic agreement between Iran and the world powers on April 2, 2015 in Lausanne, Switzerland. The overall political agreement on Iran's nuclear program—to be developed into a comprehensive agreement by the end of June 2015—has indeed changed the entire landscape. After more than a decade of roller-coaster talks mostly marked with failure for the bigger part of the period—for reasons I have discussed in various parts of the book—both sides have finally arrived at a formula that would, on the one hand, assure the international community of the strictly peaceful nature of Iran's nuclear activities, and on the other, terminate all unilateral and multilateral economic and financial sanctions imposed on Iran during the past years.

This historic overall understanding, whose quite complex details involving a whole lot of parameters and nuances to be negotiated and articulated in the form of legally-binding documents before the agreed deadline—has been rightly lauded by almost everybody as the framework for a diplomatic resolution of a seemingly intractable international problem, which, if left unresolved with inevitable further festering and complication, could have led to a possible new war in the Middle East with all its devastating and catastrophic consequences. President Barack Obama, in his statement right after the completion of the talks in Lausanne and in an unmistakable effort to convince the colorful doubters and opponents of the nuclear understanding of the superiority of the diplomatic recourse, clearly referred to the option of war as one of the three possible avenues for resolving the nuclear impasse.

While the agreement reflects the commitment, hard work, sound judgment, and above all, political will of all the parties involved; that is, Iran on side and the US, UK, France, Germany, Russia and China on the other, it has to be admitted that it has been the direct interaction between Iran and the United States—the main two protagonists in the on-going drama—particularly since September 2013, that has helped steer the process of negotiation towards the positive outcome in Lausanne. In my detailed discussion in the book, covering more than thirty years of deeply-felt and entrenched mutual distrust, hostility, name-calling, tension, tit-for-tat negative policies, measures and actions aimed at harming the other side, I have tried to depict an objective picture of the state of relations, or lack thereof, between the two capitals, including the numerous missed opportunities at rapprochement and ultimate détente between them. This particular aspect of the matter at hand has not escaped the attention and eyes of pundits and keen Iran observers, including William Burns who has been personally involved in the nuclear talks for a number of years.

While the drama over the nuclear talks will continue for the next three months until the comprehensive agreement is reached and goes into effect—with all its expected and inevitable complications and haggles over each side's interpretation of the practical ways and means of the implementation of the agreed provisions—we have to look at the longer horizon and how the state of interaction between Tehran and Washington will—or better to say, should—develop in the post-nuclear period.

As I have argued throughout the book, there exist ample grounds— and reasonable justification—for the two countries to overcome the unsavory history of distrust and hostility, leave the bitter past behind, and move in the direction of resolving the outstanding issues and difficulties that have kept them apart and hampered such a move. I grant that jumping the hurdle is neither easy nor can be achieved overnight. However, aside from particular bilateral issues that might either not be considered immediate or urgent, the on-going tumultuous, and in fact, ever-conflagrating situation in the Middle East and the Persian Gulf area can hardly afford the continuation of Iran-US political hostility and tension.

The long catalogue of possible areas for cooperation—similar to the 2001 and 2003 episodes in Afghanistan and Iraq—includes, and definitely not limited to, the fight against the so-called Islamic State in both Syria and Iraq, the Syrian protracted crisis, and the unfolding crisis in Yemen. Iran-US cooperation in combating extremism and terrorism and drug trafficking in the Middle East, as critical areas of serious concern to both countries as well as to the peace and security throughout the region, can also serve as practical catalysts for gradually ameliorating the state and sentiments of distrust and suspicion between the two states. The positive future-looking pronouncements by high-level officials in both capitals since the Lausanne Agreement, even if

peppered with allusions of sorts to the long and lingering shadows of
the past, appear to augur well—potentially, of course, for less-tension-
ridden days on the horizon. Gradual easing of tension between the two
countries on political and security issues, as is widely seen by experts
and analysts, both Iranian and American, can also create the necessary
ambiance for gradual expansion of trade, economic and technological
relations—which have been eagerly anticipated by the private sector,
entrepreneurs and investors in both countries. The potentials in these
fields are tremendous indeed.

As I look back at the actual track record during the past three and
a half decades—amply documented in the book—I can reckon, with
a sense of certainty, that both sides need to back words with action
and simply do not allow opportunities to be missed again. Based on
hard-won experience and insight, I believe honest commitment to
and compliance with the provisions of the framework agreement in
Lausanne by both sides, despite the grumbles and subversive activities
of the wide range of naysayers and opponents of the deal on the
nuclear issue, will ensure achievement of the comprehensive agreement
in due time. Perpetuation of the same spirit and commitment to
the full implementation of the provisions of the final deal—once it
goes into effect—will certainly help weaken the bitter feelings of the
past and promote, over time and even if in small measure, a sound
foundation for moving forward towards what I have termed all along
as 'rapprochement and détente' between Tehran and Washington. It is
not easy, but it is doable.

NOTES

Introduction

1 "Rice Talks with Journal's Editorial Board," *Wall Street Journal,* June 11, 2007, http://online.wsj.com/news/articles/SB118157691550731274

2 Kenneth Pollack and Ray Takeyh, "Doubling Down on Iran," *Washington Quarterly* 34, no. 4 (2011): 9, http://csis.org/files/publication/twq11autumnpollacktakeyh.pdf

3 Hamilton Jordan, *Crisis: The Last Year of Carter Presidency* (New York: G. P. Putnam's Sons, 1982), 129.

4 Elliot Gerson, "To Make America Great Again, We Need to Leave the Country," *Atlantic,* July 10, 2012, http://www.theatlantic.com/national/archive/2012/07/to-make-america-great-again-we-need-to-leave-the-country/259653

5 Hooshang Amirahmadi and Shahir Shahidsaless, "Avoid Repeating Mistakes toward Iran," *Washington Quarterly* 36, no. 1 (2013): 145–62, http://csis.org/files/publication/TWQ_13Winter_AmirahmadiShahidSaless.pdf

6 Ali Khamenei, "Supreme Leader's Address to Academics at Tehran Science and Technology University" (lecture in Persian, December 14, 2008), Iranian Supreme Leader's website, http://farsi.khamenei.ir/speech-content?id=4992 (accessed February 2, 2014)

7 "Khamenei Open to Direct US Talks," *United States Institute of Peace: The Iran Primer,* last modified March 24, 2013, http://iranprimer.usip.org/blog/2013/mar/24/khamenei-open-direct-us-talks

8 "Shariatmadari: America Wants Talks Just to Talk" (Persian), *Alef News,* last modified May 13, 2007, http://alef.ir/vdcg.w97rak9ynpr4a.html?8935

9 Ibid.

10 US Department of State, "Update on Iran Democracy Promotion Funding," last modified June 4, 2007, http://2001–2009.state.gov/r/pa/prs/ps/2007/jun/85971.htm

11 Seymour M. Hersh, "Our Men in Iran?," *New Yorker,* April 6, 2012, http://www.newyorker.com/online/blogs/newsdesk/2012/04/mek.html#ixzz1rfY0i96w

12 "CIA Spies Caught, Fear Execution in Middle East," *ABC News,* November 21, 2011, http://abcnews.go.com/Blotter/cia-spies-caught-fear-execution-middle-east/story?id=14994428#.T4Wc17_LxJU

13 Douglass K. Daniel, "No Security Guarantee for Iran, Rice Says," *Washington Post,* May 21, 2006, http://www.washingtonpost.com/wp-dyn/content/article/2006/05/21/AR2006052100369_pf.html

14 Shailagh Murray, "Obama Rails against Attacks from Palin, GOP," *Washington Post*, September 5, 2008, http://www.washingtonpost.com/wp-dyn/content/article/2008/09/04/AR2008090403433.html

15 "Khatami Suggests Warmer Relations with US," *CNN*, January 7, 1998, http://www.cnn.com/WORLD/9801/07/iran

16 James L. Richardson, *Crisis Diplomacy: The Great Powers Since the Mid-19th Century* (New York: Cambridge University Press, 1994), 256.

17 US Department of State, "Joint Statement on Iran Sanctions," last modified June 23, 2011, http://www.state.gov/r/pa/prs/ps/2011/06/166814.htm

18 "Rouhani Sworn In" (Persian), *Fararu News*, August 4, 2013, http://fararu.com/fa/news/158380

19 "The Impact of Sanctions on Iran's Nuclear Program," Arms Control Association, last modified March 9, 2011, http://www.armscontrol.org/events/RoleSanctionsIranNuclear

20 Barry Blechman, Daniel Brumberg, and Steven Heydmann *Engagement, Coercion, and Iran's Nuclear Challenge* (Washington, DC: United States Institute of Peace/Henry L. Stimson Center, 2010), 11.

21 Council on Foreign Relations, "Mujahadeen-e-Khalq (MEK) (aka People's Mujahedin of Iran or PMOI)," last modified July 18, 2012, http://www.cfr.org/iran/mujahadeen-e-khalq-mek-aka-peoples-mujahedin-iran-pmoi/p9158

22 Ibid., 159.

Chapter 1

1 Kamyar Ghaneabassiri, "US Foreign Policy and Persia, 1856–1921," *Iranian Studies* 35, nos. 1–3 (2002): 152.

2 Ibid., 149.

3 Mansour Bonakdarian, "US–Iranian Relations, 1911–1951" (working paper, Council on Middle East Studies, 2008), 10.

4 Ibid., 11.

5 Ibid., 16. For the text of this treaty, see *(US) Department of State Bulletin*, March 21, 1942, 249.

6 The Qajar dynasty ruled Iran from 1785 to 1925 after defeating the Zand dynasty. Until the Constitutional Revolution of 1906, the Qajars ruled as an absolute monarchy and subsequently became a constitutional monarchy. "In Memoriam: Farrokh Ghafari (1921–2006)," *University of St. Andrews*, last modified 2010, http://www.st-andrews.ac.uk/anthropology/nafa/qajar/conference

7 Ghaneabassiri, "US Foreign Policy and Persia, 1856–1921," 153.

8 Scott Peterson, *Let the Swords Encircle Me: Iran—A Journey behind the Headlines* (New York: Simon & Schuster, 2010), 47.

9 Ghaneabassiri, "US Foreign Policy and Persia, 1856–1921," 154.
10 Ibid., 156.
11 William Morgan Shuster, *The Strangling of Persia: Story of the European Diplomacy and Oriental Intrique That Resulted in the Denationalization of 12 Million Mohammedans, a Personal Narrative* (Washington, DC: Mage, 1987), 333.
12 Ibid.
13 Ghaneabassiri, "US Foreign Policy and Persia, 1856–1921," 162.
14 Bonakdarian, "US–Iranian Relations, 1911–1951," 12.
15 "Anglo-Persian Agreement of 1919," *Encyclopedia Iranica*, last modified August 5, 2011, http://www.iranicaonline.org/articles/anglo-persian-agreement-1919
16 Ghaneabassiri, "US Foreign Policy and Persia, 1856–1921," 167.
17 Bonakdarian, "US–Iranian Relations, 1911–1951," 13.
18 Reza Shah Pahlavi (1878–1944), shah of Iran (1925–1941), began his career as a soldier in the Cossack Brigade, gradually gaining a reputation for leadership. Later, he was promoted and became an army officer. He led a British-supported coup in 1921 and became the prime minister of Iran under the rule of Ahmad Shah, the last Qajar king. Virtually a dictator, he deposed Ahmad Shah in 1925 and was proclaimed shah of Iran. He chose the name Reza Shah Pahlavi, thus founding the Pahlavi dynasty. In 1935, he officially changed the name of the country from Persian to Iran. In the Second World War, Pahlavi's rapprochement with the Germans was criticized by the Allied powers, primarily the British and the Russians. In 1941, British and Russian forces invaded and occupied Iran. Forced to abdicate in favor of his son, Muhammad Reza, he died in exile in South Africa in 1944.
19 John A. DeNovo, *American Interests and Policies in the Middle East, 1900–1939* (Minneapolis: University of Minnesota Press, 1963), 281.
20 Bonakdarian, "US–Iranian Relations, 1911–1951," 14.
21 Ibid., 15.
22 "Reza Shah Pahlavi," *Encyclopedia Britannica*, last modified March 30, 2009, http://www.britannica.com/EBchecked/topic/500867/Reza-Shah-Pahlavi
23 Ibid.
24 Behrooz Moazami, *State, Religion, and Revolution in Iran, 1796 to the Present* (New York: Palgrave Macmillan, 2013), 45.
25 Bonakdarian, "US–Iranian Relations, 1911–1951," 16. For the text of this treaty, see *(US) Department of State Bulletin*, March 21, 1942, 249.
26 Bonakdarian, "US–Iranian Relations, 1911–1951," 17.
27 Ibid.
28 John P. Miglietta, *American Alliance Policy in the Middle East, 1945–1992: Iran, Israel, and Saudi Arabia* (Lanham, MD: Lexington Books, 2002), 35.

29 Bonakdarian, "US–Iranian Relations, 1911–1951," 18.
30 Jean-Charles Brotons, *US Officials and the Fall of the Shah: Some Safe Contraction Interpretations* (Lanham, MD: Lexington Books, 2010), 32.
31 Mostafa Elm, *Oil, Power, and Principle: Iran's Oil Nationalization and Its Aftermath* (Syracuse, NY: Syracuse University Press, 1992).
32 Mohammad Mossadegh (1882–1967) was born in Tehran into a prominent family of notables. His father was a senior official of the state treasury and his mother was from the Qajar dynasty. As an Iranian nationalist politician and prime minister (1951–3), Mossadegh led the movement for the nationalization of the Anglo-Iranian Oil Company. His democratically elected government was overthrown on August 19, 1953 by a coup engineered by the United States and Great Britain.
33 Elm, *Oil, Power, and Principle*.
34 Ibid.
35 Ibid., 213.
36 Stephen Kinzer, *All the Shah's Men: An American Coup and the Roots of Middle East Terror* (Hoboken, NJ: John Wiley & Sons, 2008), 3.
37 Ibid.
38 Ibid., 4.
39 Kinzer, *All the Shah's Men*, 6.
40 Ibid., 170.
41 "The Iranian History 1953 AD," last modified 2011, http://fouman.com/history/Iranian_History_1953.html
42 Nikki R. Keddie and Yann Richard, *Roots of Revolution: An Interpretive History of Modern Iran* (New Haven, CT: Yale University Press, 1981), 142.
43 James G. Blight, *Becoming Enemies: The Origins of US–Iran Enmity in the Crucible of the Iran–Iraq War, 1979–1988* (Lanham, MD: Rowman & Littlefield, 2012), 9.
44 Mark Gasiorowski, *U.S. Foreign Policy and the Shah: Building a Client State in Iran* (Ithaca: Cornell University Press, 1991) 118.
45 Khosrow Mostofi, "Iran: Wartime and Nationalization of Oil," *Encyclopedia Britannica*, last modified November 25, 2013, http://www.britannica.com/EBchecked/topic/293359/Iran/32187/Wartime-and-nationalization-of-oil
46 Public Papers of the Presidents, Jimmy Carter, XXXIX President of the United States: 1977–1981, Tehran, Iran, Toasts of the President and the Shah at a State Dinner.
47 "Chronology: US–Iran Relations, 1906–2002," *PBS Frontline*, accessed February 16, 2014, http://www.pbs.org/wgbh/pages/frontline/shows/tehran/etc/cron.html
48 Charles Kurzman, *The Unthinkable Revolution in Iran* (Cambridge, MA: Harvard University Press, 2005), 157.

49 Karen Armstrong, *The Battle for God: A History of Fundamentalism* (New York: Alfred A. Knopf, 2011), 206.

50 Secretary of State Madleine K. Albright, remarks before the American-Iranian Council, March 17, 2000, http://www.fas.org/news/ iran/2000/000317.htm

51 US Department of State, Bureau of Near Eastern Affairs, "US Relations with Iran," August 28, 2013, http://www.state.gov/r/pa/ei/bgn/5314.htm

52 From the late 1980s to mid-1990s, there were a number of suicide bombings that took place within major urban centers of Israel. The main Palestinian militant groups who claimed responsibility for the bombings were Hamas and Islamic Jihad.

53 US Department of State, Bureau of Counter Terrorism, "Foreign Terrorist Organizations," September 28, 2012, http://www.state.gov/j/ct/ rls/other/des/123085.htm

54 According to the State Department's annual *Country Report on Terrorism 2011*, "Iran continued to provide lethal support, including weapons, training, funding, and guidance, to Iraqi Shia militant groups targeting U.S. and Iraqi forces, as well as civilians," while in Afghanistan they provided "training to the Taliban on small unit tactics, small arms, explosives, and indirect fire weapons, such as mortars, artillery, and rockets."

55 In October 2011, the US government accused Iran of masterminding an assassination attempt on the Saudi Arabian ambassador to the US, Adel Al-Jubeir. The US claimed that Mansour Arbabsiar, a used-car salesman nicknamed "Jack" by his friends due to his love for Jack Daniel's whiskey, hired Mexican drug traffickers to kill the Saudi ambassador. The Iranians rejected the accusations as "yet another plot against [Iran]."

56 "Exporting Rovolution Does Not Mean Military Invasion" (Persian), *Fars News Agency*, June 8, 2009, http://www.farsnews.com/newstext. php?nn=8803181107 (accessed February 16, 2014).

57 US Department of State, "Iran," http://www.state.gov/documents/ organization/186637.pdf (accessed February 16, 2014).

58 Human Rights Council, "Report of the Special Rapporteur on the Situation of Human Rights in the Islamic Republic of Iran," United Nations General Assembly, March 8, 2012, http://www. ohchr.org/Documents/HRBodies/HRCouncil/RegularSession/ Session19/A-HRC–19–66_en.pdf

59 Ibid.

60 Kelley Beaucar Vlahos, "Capitol Hill Mulls 'Regime Change' in Iran," *Fox News*, February 4, 2005, http://www.foxnews.com/story/2005/02/04/ capitol-hill-mulls-regime-change-in-iran

61 Representative Peter King and Tyler Hicks, interview by Martha Raddatz, *This Week*, September 22, 2013, http://www.foxnews.com/ story/2005/02/04/capitol-hill-mulls-regime-change-in-iran

62 William Lowther and Colin Freeman, "US Funds Terror Groups to Sow Chaos in Iran," *Telegraph*, February 25, 2007, http://www.telegraph.co.uk/news/worldnews/1543798/US-funds-terror-groups-to-sow-chaos-in-Iran.html

63 Tim Shipman, "Bush Sanctions Black Ops against Iran," *Telegraph*, May 27, 2007, http://www.telegraph.co.uk/news/worldnews/1552784/Bush-sanctions-black-ops-against-Iran.html
    "The Secret War against Iran," *ABC News*, April 3, 2007, http://abcnews.go.com/blogs/headlines/2007/04/abc_news_exclus
    Seymour M. Hersh, "Preparing the Battlefield," *New Yorker*, July 7, 2008, http://www.newyorker.com/reporting/2008/07/07/080707fa_fact_hersh
    Shipman, "Bush Sanctions Black Ops against Iran."

64 Lowther and Freeman, "US Funds Terror Groups to Sow Chaos in Iran."

65 Shipman, "Bush Sanctions Black Ops against Iran."

66 152 Cong. Rec. 152, 7161 (2006).

67 Seymour M. Hersh, "The Next Act," *New Yorker*, November 27, 2006, http://www.newyorker.com/archive/2006/11/27/061127fa_fact

68 US Department of State, Bureau of Counter Terrorism, "Foreign Terrorist Organizations," September 28, 2012, http://www.state.gov/j/ct/rls/other/des/123085.htm

69 "Imam Did Not Issue Permission for the Terror of the Shah" (Persian), February 7, 2007, http://www.magiran.com/npview.asp?ID=1341281

70 US Department of State, "Country Reports on Terrorism 2009," August 2010, http://www.whs.mil/library/Reports/CountryReportsTerrorism2009.pdf

71 Elizabeth Rubin, "The Cult of Rajavi,"*New York Times*, July 13, 2003, http://www.nytimes.com/2003/07/13/magazine/the-cult-of-rajavi.html

72 Chris McGreal, "MEK Decision: Multi-Million-Dollar Campaign Led to Removal from Terror List," *Guardian*, September 21, 2012, http://www.guardian.co.uk/world/2012/sep/21/iran-mek-group-removed-us-terrorism-list

73 Seymour M. Hersh, "Our Men in Iran?," *New Yorker*, April 6, 2012, http://www.newyorker.com/online/blogs/newsdesk/2012/04/mek.html

74 Brian Ross and Richard Esposito, "Bush Authorizes New Covert Action against Iran," *ABC News*, May 22, 2007, http://abcnews.go.com/blogs/headlines/2007/05/bush_authorizes

75 "Investigation into the Downing of an Iranian Airliner by the USS "Vincennes,'" in *Hearings Before the Committee on Armed Services*, 100th Cong. (1988), http://homepage.ntlworld.com/jksonc/docs/ir655-sasc–19880908.html

76 *Aerial Incident of 3 July 1988* (Iran v. United States), ICJ Reports 1989, http://www.icj-cij.org/docket/files/79/6629.pdf

77 David Evans, "One Must Question the Current Value of Military Medals," *Chicago Tribune*, April 6, 1990, http://articles.chicagotribune.com/1990–04–06/news/9001280334_1_uss-vincennes-iranian-airbus-rogers

78 Robert William Love, *History of the US Navy* (Harrisburg, PA: Stackpole Books, 1992), 787.

79 *Oil Platforms* (Iran v. United States), ICJ Reports 2003, http://www.icj-cij.org/docket/index.php?sum=634&code=op&p1=3&p2=3&case=90&k=0a&p3=5

80 Committee on Banking, Housing, and Urban Affairs with Respect to Export Administration, *The Riegle Report: US Chemical and Biological Warfare Related Dual Use Exports to Iraq and Their Possible Impact on the Health Consequences of the Gulf War*, 103rd Cong. (May 25, 1994), http://www.gulfweb.org/bigdoc/report/riegle1.html

81 Ole R. Holsti, *American Public Opinion on the Iraq War* (Ann Arbor: University of Michigan Press, 2011), 14.

82 Shane Harris and Matthew M. Aid, "CIA Files Prove America Helped Saddam as He Gassed Iran," *Foreign Policy*, August 26, 2013, http://www.foreignpolicy.com/articles/2013/08/25/secret_cia_files_prove_america_helped_saddam_as_he_gassed_iran#sthash.lIzx7AkF.dpuf

83 David E. Sanger, "Obama Order Sped Up Wave of Cyberattacks against Iran," *New York Times*, June 1, 2012, http://www.nytimes.com/2012/06/01/world/middleeast/obama-ordered-wave-of-cyberattacks-against-iran.html

84 Select Comm. on Intelligence, press release, June 6, 2012, http://www.intelligence.senate.gov/press/record.cfm?id=336952

85 "Senators to Open Inquiry into 'Kill List' and Iran Security Leaks," *New York Times*, June 5, 2012, http://www.nytimes.com/2012/06/06/us/politics/senators-want-inquiry-on-national-security-leaks.html

86 "Remarks by the President," June 8, 2012, http://www.whitehouse.gov/the-press-office/2012/06/08/remarks-president

87 Erin McClam, "Successful Hacker Attack Could Cripple US Infrastructure, Experts Say," *NBC News*, February 19, 2013, http://usnews.nbcnews.com/_news/2013/02/19/17019005-successful-hacker-attack-could-cripple-us-infrastructure-experts-say

88 Peter Beaumont, "Cyberwar on Iran More Widespread Than First Thought, Say Researchers," *Guardian*, September 21, 2012, http://www.guardian.co.uk/technology/2012/sep/21/cyberwar-iran-more-sophisticated

89 Bernard Weinraub, "The US Policy on Arms Has a Life of Its Own," *New York Times*, September 18, 1977, http://news.google.com/newspapers?nid=1734&dat=19770919&id=E1AcAAAAIBAJ&sjid=i1EEAAAAIBAJ&pg=3324,1857249

90 Central Intelligence Agency, *Iran in the 1980s* (October 5, 1977), 8. Cited

in Jeffrey T. Richelson, *A Century of Spies: Intelligence in the Twentieth Century* (New York: Oxford University Press, 1995), 371.

91 Jimmy Carter, *Keeping the Faith: Memoirs of a President* (New York: Bantam Books, 1982), 438.

92 Central Intelligence Agency, *Iran: The Radicals in the Opposition* (January 12, 1979), 2.

93 Robin Wright, *The Last Great Revolution: Turmoil and Transformation in Iran* (New York: Alfred A. Knopf, 2000), xii.

94 Odd Arne Westad, *The Global Cold War: Third World Interventions and the Making of Our Times* (Cambridge: Cambridge University Press, 2005), 290.

95 Ibid.

96 Ibid.

97 The Shah–People Revolution (The White Revolution) was a series of social and economic reforms aimed at transforming Iran into a global power. The platform included abolishing feudalism, extending the right to vote to women, profit sharing for industrial workers as the main elements of that program. It was put to a national referendum on January 26, 1963.

98 The Shah's plan to modernize and Westernize Iran with the hope of bringing back Iran's ancient glamor.

99 A surreal, highly modern art festival held in Shiraz annually from 1968 to 1978. The festival included modern and avant-garde works as well as classical artists, musicians, theatre directors, etc.

100 Set of festivities and celebration of the 2,500th anniversary of the founding of the Persian Empire that took place from October 12 to October 16, 1971. The exorbitant expense of the ceremonies aroused criticism inside and outside Iran.

101 Anthony Parsons, *The Pride and the Fall: Iran, 1974–1979* (London: Butler & Tanner, 1984), 54.

102 Dilip Hiro, *Iran under the Ayatollahs* (New York: Routledge, 2013), 306.

103 William H. Sullivan, *Mission to Iran* (New York: W. W. Norton, 1981), 22.

104 Sandra MacKay, *The Iranians* (New York: Plume, 1998), 198.

105 Abbas Milani, *Eminent Persians: The Men and Women Who Made Modern Iran, 1941–1979* (Syracuse, NY: Syracuse University Press, 2008), 345.

106 Karen Armstrong, *The Battle for God: A History of Fundamentalism* (New York: Alfred A. Knopf, 2011), 130.

107 "The Role of Ayatollah Kashani in Popularizing the Nationalization of Oil Slogan" (Persian), Islamic Revolution Documents Center, accessed February 4, 2014, http://www.irdc.ir/fa/content/6242/default.aspx

108 Ervand Abrahamian, *Iran between Two Revolutions* (Princeton, NJ: Princeton University Press, 1982), 265–6.

Notes   301

109 Milani, *Eminent Persians*, 346.
110 Anna Mulrine, "How US military plans to carry out Obama's 'pivot to Asia'", *Christian Science Monitor*, February 18, 2013, http://www.csmonitor.com/USA/Foreign-Policy/2013/0218/ How-US-military-plans-to-carry-out-Obama-s-pivot-to-Asia

Chapter 2

1 William J. Daugherty, "Jimmy Carter and the 1979 Decision to Admit the Shah into the United States," *American Diplomacy*, April 1, 2003, http://www.unc.edu/depts/diplomat/archives_roll/2003_01–03/ dauherty_shah/dauherty_shah.html
2 Massoumeh Ebtekar's book titled "Takeover in Tehran: The Inside Story of the 1979 U.S. Embassy Capture" (Talonbooks, 2000) provides interesting details about the event and how it was executed. Ebtekar—then referred to as "Sister Mary"—served as an interpreter for the Embassy captors. The Book's Preface, written by Mr. Mousavi Khoeiniha, also sheds light on the rationale for the Embassy seizure.
3 "Penumbras of the Seizure of the American Embassy" (Persian), *Deutsche Welle*, March 11, 2009, http://dw.de/p/KLvy
4 Amir R. Sotoodeh and Hamid Kaviani, *444 Days Crisis in Tehran: Told and Untold Stories of the Seizure of the American Embassy* (Persian), (Tehran: Zekr, 1990), 102.
5 Mark Bowden, *Guests of the Ayatollah: The Iran Hostage Crisis* (New York: Grove Press, 2006), 548.
6 Hamilton Jordan, *Crisis: The Last Year of the Carter Presidency* (New York: Putnam Adult, 1982), 128.
7 Masour Farhang, "US Policy toward the Islamic Republic: A Case of Misperception and Reactive Behavior," in Hooshang Amirahmadi (ed.), *The United States and the Middle East: A Search for New Perspectives* (Albany, NY: SUNY Press, 1993), 155.
8 Bowden, *Guests of the Ayatollah*, 19.
9 Jimmy Carter: "The President's News Conference," February 13, 1980. Online by Gerhard Peters and John T. Woolley, The American Presidency Project, http://www.presidency.ucsb.edu/ws/?pid=32928 (accessed March 10, 2014).
10 US Department of State, "Carter's Foreign Policy," http://history.state.gov/ departmenthistory/short-history/carter (accessed February 17, 2014).
11 Mehdi Bazargan, *Revolution in Two Steps* (Persian), 5th edn (Tehran: Freedom Movement of Iran, 1984), 90.
12 "Ebrahim Asgharzadeh: Mousavi Khoeiniha Had Veto Power" (Persian), *Etemad Newspaper*, November 4, 2011, http://tarikhirani.ir/fa/news/30/ bodyView/1485

13 Herbert C. Kelman is the Richard Clarke Cabot Professor of Social Ethics, emeritus, at Harvard University and was (from 1993 to 2003) Director of the Program on International Conflict Analysis and Resolution at Harvard's Weatherhead Center for International Affairs.

14 Herbert C. Kelman, "Social-Psychological Dimensions of International Conflict," in I. William Zartman (ed.), *Peacemaking in International Conflict: Methods and Techniques*, rev. edn (Washington, DC: United States Institute of Peace Press, 2007), 64.

15 John W. Burton (1915–2010) was a senior associate and distinguished visiting Professor of Conflict Resolution and International Relations at George Mason University.

16 Burton, cited in Kelman, "Social-Psychological Dimensions of International Conflict," 65.

17 Nikki R. Keddie was a professor of Eastern, Iranian, and women's history. She retired from the University of California, Los Angeles, after 35 years of teaching.

18 Nikki R. Keddie and Yann Richard, *Roots of Revolution: An Interpretive History of Modern Iran* (New Haven, CT: Yale University Press, 1981), 275.

19 Ruhollah Khomeini, interview by Oriana Fallaci (Italian), *Corriere Della Sera*, September 26, 1979, http://www.oriana-fallaci.com/khomeini/intervista.html

20 Robert Jervis, *Perception and Misperception in International Politics* (Princeton, NJ: Princeton University Press, 1976), 277–8.

21 Rose McDermott, *Politics: Prospect Theory in American Foreign Policy* (Ann Arbor: University of Michigan Press, 2001), 86.

22 David Rockefeller, *Memoirs* (New York: Random House, 2003), 374.

23 Ibid.

24 Ahmad Ashraf, "Conspiracy Theories: A Complex of Beliefs Attributing the Course of Persian History and Politics to the Machinations of Hostile Foreign Powers and Secret Organizations," *Encyclopedia Iranica*, last modified October 28, 2011, http://www.iranicaonline.org/articles/conspiracy-theories

25 Mehrdad Mashayekhi, "Culture of Mistrust: A Sociological Analysis of Iranian Political Culture," in Ibrahim Abu-Rabi (ed.), *The Blackwell Companion to Contemporary Islamic Thought* (Oxford: Blackwell, 2006), 544.

26 Ibid., 551.

27 Gary Sick, *All Fall Down: America's Fateful Encounter with Iran* (London: I. B.Tauris, 1985), 168.

28 Anthony H. Cordesman, Bradley Bosserman, Jordan D'amato, and Andrew C. Gagel, *US and Iranian Strategic Competition: The Sanctions Game: Energy, Arms Control, and Regime Change* (Washington, DC:

Center for Strategic and International Studies, 2011), http://csis.org/files/publication/111006_Iran_Sanctions.pdf

29 Patrick Clawson, *Much Traction from Measured Steps: The Iranian Opposition, the Nuclear Issue, and the West* (Washington, DC: Washington Institute for Near East Policy, 2010), http://www.voltairenet.org/IMG/pdf/Iranian_Opposition.pdf

30 Ray Takeyh, *Guardians of the Revolution: Iran and the World in the Age of the Ayatollahs* (New York: Oxford University Press, 2011), 163.

31 Ibid.

32 Mark Landler and David E. Sanger, "US Follows Two Paths on Unrest in Iran and Bahrain," *New York Times*, February 15, 2011, http://www.nytimes.com/2011/02/16/world/middleeast/16diplomacy.html

33 Ibid.

34 Douglass K. Daniel, "No Security Guarantee for Iran, Rice Says," *Washington Post*, May 21, 2006, http://www.washingtonpost.com/wp-dyn/content/article/2006/05/21/AR2006052100369_pf.html

35 "Ebrahim Asgharzadeh."

36 Ibid.

37 Jimmy Carter, *Keeping Faith: Memoirs of a President* (Fayetteville: University of Arkansas Press, 1995), 568.

38 Ibid., 575.

39 "Algiers Accords," January 19, 1981, http://www.parstimes.com/history/algiers_accords.pdf

40 Ibid.

41 Golnoush Niknejad, "Algiers Accords: A Good Precedent?," *PBS Frontline*, February 23, 2009, http://www.pbs.org/wgbh/pages/frontline/tehranbureau/2009/02/algiers-accords-a-good-precedent.html

Chapter 3

1 "The Terror of Martyr Beheshti with the Code Allah-o-Akbar" (Persian), *Mashregh News*, July 1, 2011, http://www.mashreghnews.ir/fa/news/132325

2 Ibid.

3 Ibid.

4 Ayatollah Ahmad Jannati is a hardline Iranian cleric and Secretary of the Guardian Council (1988–present).

5 US Department of State, Office of the Coordinator for Counter Terrorism, "Country Reports on Terrorism 2009," last modified August 2010, http://www.whs.mil/library/Reports/CountryReportsTerrorism2009.pdf

6 Elizabeth Rubin, "The Cult of Rajavi," *New York Times Magazine*, July 13,

2003, http://www.nytimes.com/2003/07/13/magazine/the-cult-of-rajavi.
html

7 US Department of State, "Foreign Terrorist Organizations," September
28, 2012, http://www.state.gov/j/ct/rls/other/des/123085.htm

8 Richard Engel and Robert Windrem, "Israel Teams with Terror
Group to Kill Iran's Nuclear Scientists, US Officials Tell NBC
News," *NBC News*, February 6, 2012, http://rockcenter.nbcnews.
com/_news/2012/02/09/10354553-israel-teams-with-terror-group-to-
kill-irans-nuclear-scientists-us-officials-tell-nbc-news

9 Chris McGreal, "MEK Decision: Multi-Million-Dollar Campaign Led to
Removal from Terror List," *Guardian*, September 21, 2012, http://www.
guardian.co.uk/world/2012/sep/21/iran-mek-group-removed-us-
terrorism-list

10 Ibid.

11 Ibid.

12 Ibid.

13 Barbara Slavin, "Congress Not Won Over by Rouhani Victory in
Iran," *Al Monitor*, June 18, 2013, http://www.al-monitor.com/pulse/
originals/2013/06/congress-iran-election-rouhani-skeptical-sanctions.
html

14 Ibid.

15 McGreal, "MEK Decision."

16 "Iranian People Vote for Change in 'We Choose' Free Election," *We
Choose*, accessed February 19, 2014, http://we-choose.org/results–2

17 Ibid.

18 Pirouz Mojtahed-Zadeh, "Evolution of the Shatt al-Arab Dispute after the
1913 Protocol," in Pirouz Mojtahed-Zadeh (ed.), *Boundary Politics and
International Boundaries of Iran* (Boca Raton, FL: Universal, 2006), 154.

19 Robert Parry, "Lost History Hurts Obama's Iran Deed," *Baltimore
Chronicle*, March 26, 2009, http://baltimorechronicle.com/2009/032609
Parry.html

20 Anne Shutt, ed., "US Calls for an End to Iran–Iraq Fighting,"
Christian Science Monitor, July 15, 1982, http://www.csmonitor.
com/1982/0715/071522.html

21 Henry S. Rowen, "Memorandum for: Geoffrey Kemp, Senior Staff
National Security Council," July 20, 1982, http://www.foia.cia.gov/sites/
default/files/document_conversions/89801/DOC_0000763462.pdf

22 Spencer C. Tucker and Priscilla Mary Roberts, eds, *The Encyclopedia of
the Arab–Israeli Conflict: A Political, Social, and Military History* (Santa
Barbara: ABC-CLIO, 2008), 879.

23 Colonel Timothy J. Geraghty, "25 Years Later: We Came in Peace,"
Proceedings Magazine 134, no. 10 (2008), http://www.usni.org/
magazines/proceedings/2008–10/25-years-later-we-came-peace

24 "Iran Denies Any Involvement in Bombing of US Embassy," *New York*

Times, April 20, 1983, http://www.nytimes.com/1983/04/20/world/iran-denies-any-involvement-in-bombing-of-us-embassy.html

25 Joyce Battle, ed., *Shaking Hands with Saddam Hussein: The US Tilts toward Iraq, 1980–1984*, Electronic Briefing Book 82 (Washington, DC: National Security Archive, 2003), http://www.gwu.edu/~nsarchiv/NSAEBB/NSAEBB82

26 Bernard Gwertzman, "US Restores Full Ties with Iraq but Cites Neutrality in Gulf War," *New York Times*, November 27, 1984, http://www.nytimes.com/1984/11/27/world/us-restores-full-ties-with-iraq-but-cites-neutrality-in-gulf-war.html

27 George Shultz, *Turmoil and Triumph: My Years as Secretary of State* (New York: Scribner, 1993), 237.

28 From January to June 2013, 25 percent of the total crude oil imported was from the Persian Gulf. US Energy Information Administration, "Crude Oil Imports from Persian Gulf," last modified August 29, 2013, http://www.eia.gov/petroleum/imports/companylevel/summary.cfm

29 Victor Davis Hanson, "An Irrelevant Middle East," *National Review Online*, May 2, 2013, http://www.nationalreview.com/article/347108/irrelevant-middle-east

    Paul D. Miller, "The Fading Arab Oil Empire," *National Interest*, June 28, 2012, http://nationalinterest.org/article/the-fading-arab-oil-empire–7072?page=1

30 James "Jim" D. Hamilton is an American economist currently teaching at the University of California, San Diego. His work is especially influential in time series and energy economics. He received his PhD from the University of California, Berkeley, in 1983.

31 James D. Hamilton, "Historical Oil Shocks," National Bureau of Economic Research, February 2011, http://www.nber.org/papers/w16790

32 Ibid.

33 Robert Reich is Chancellor's Professor of Public Policy at the University of California, Berkeley.

34 Robert Reich, "The Extra Dollars You're Paying at the Pump Are Going to Wall Street Speculators," *Chicago Tribune*, February 28, 2012, http://www.chicagotribune.com/sns–201202280930--tms--amvoicesctnav-a20120228feb28,0,2500569.column

35 US Energy Information Administration, "Strait of Hormuz," last modified August 22, 2012, http://www.eia.gov/countries/regions-topics.cfm?fips=WOTC#hormuz

36 Alireza Nader, "Iran and Nuclear-Weapon-Free Middle East," Arms Control Association, last modified September 2011, http://www.armscontrol.org/print/5013

37 Hossein Asgari, *Conflicts and Wars: Their Fallout and Prevention* (New York: Palgrave Macmillan, 2012), 124.

38 John Kifner, "400 Die as Iranian Marchers Battle Saudi Police in Mecca;

Embassies Smashed in Teheran," *New York Times*, August 2, 1987, http://
www.nytimes.com/1987/08/02/world/400-die-iranian-marchers-battle-
saudi-police-mecca-embassies-smashed-teheran.html

39 Ronald Reagan, "Address to the Nation on the Iran Arms and
    Contra Aid Controversy," Ronald Reagan Presidential Library and
    Museum, November 13, 1986, http://www.reagan.utexas.edu/archives/
    speeches/1986/111386c.htm

40 "Ayatollah Hashemi: I Told Imam (Khomeini) That Not Talking to
    America and Not Having Relations Is Not Sustainable" (Persian),
    Entekhab, April 2, 2012, http://www.entekhab.ir/fa/news/57013

41 Ayatollah Akbar Hashemi Rafsanjani, "The Bitter Report of Ghalibaf and
    Ghasem Soleimani to Hashemi" (Persian), Official Website of Ayatollah
    Hashemi Rafsanjani, May 25, 1986, http://goo.gl/F4KkRg

42 "Confessions of Mehdi Hashemi on Television" (Persian), http://www.
    youtube.com/watch?=l_TMYLbCDWU (accessed February 19, 2014).

43 According to Mohsen Rafiqdoost, one of the first senior officers of
    the Islamic Revolutionary Guards, Mohammad Montazeri, the son of
    Ayatollah, was the first person who came up with the idea for this force.
    It is worthy to note that Ayatollah Montazeri was the first one who
    initiated the slogan of "Death to America." http://www.theguardian.com/
    commentisfree/2009/dec/21/iran-ayatollah-montazeri-death

44 "Summary of the Judgment of 6 November 2003," *Oil Platforms* (Iran v.
    United States), ICJ Reports 2003, http://www.icj-cij.org/docket/?sum=63
    4&code=op&p1=3&p2=3&case=90&k=0a&p3=5

45 Richard Halloran, "The Downing of Flight 655," *New York Times*, July 4,
    1988, http://www.nytimes.com/1988/07/04/world/downing-flight-655-
    us-downs-iran-airliner-mistaken-for-f-14-290-reported-dead.html

46 "Investigation into the Downing of an Iranian Airliner by the USS
    "Vincennes,'" in *Hearings Before the Committee on Armed Services*,
    100th Cong. (1988), http://homepage.ntlworld.com/jksonc/docs/
    ir655-sasc-19880908.html

47 US Department of Defense, "Formal Investigation into the
    Circumstances Surrounding the Downing of Iran Air Flight 655," July
    3, 1988, http://homepage.ntlworld.com/jksonc/docs/ir655-dod-report.
    html

48 On December 21, 1988, a suitcase bomb exploded aboard Pan Am Flight
    103, killing all 259 passengers and crew members, along with 11 people
    on the ground in Lockerbie, Scotland. A Libyan citizen was convicted
    years later with regard to the incident.

49 Ali Chenar, "Remembering Iran Air Flight 655," *PBS Frontline*, July 4,
    2010, http://www.pbs.org/wgbh/pages/frontline/tehranbureau/2010/07/
    remembering-iran-air-flight-655.html

50 Max Fisher, "What Iran Air Flight 655 says about America's Role
    in the Middle East," *Washington Post*, October 17, 2013, http://

www.washingtonpost.com/blogs/worldviews/wp/2013/10/17/
what-iran-air-flight-655-says-about-americas-role-in-the-middle-east

51 See Chapter 5 for more details.

52 "The Reagan Presidency," Ronald Reagan Presidential Library and
Museum, http://www.reagan.utexas.edu/archives/reference/pressketch.
html (accessed February 19, 2014).

53 Fisher, "What Iran Air Flight 655 says about America's Role in the
Middle East."

54 Leslie H. Gelb, "East–West Rivalry for Influence in Iran: US Has
Weak Hand," *New York Times*, March 9, 1982, http://www.nytimes.
com/1982/03/09/world/east-west-rivalry-for-influence-in-iran-us-has-
weak-hand-news-analysis.html

55 Alan Friedman, *Spider's Web: The Secret History of How the White House
Illegally Armed Iraq* (New York: Bantam Books, 1993).

56 Howard Teicher's affidavit, January 31, 1995, http://www.gwu.edu/
~nsarchiv/NSAEBB/NSAEBB82/iraq61.pdf

57 Ibid.

58 US Senate Comm. on Banking, Housing, and Urban Affairs, *Second
Staff Report on US Chemical and Biological Warfare-Related Dual-Use
Exports to Iraq and the Possible Impact on the Health Consequences of the
War*, 102nd Cong. (October 1992), http://www.gulfwarvets.com/arison/
banking.htm

59 US Department of State, "Telegram to the US Delegation to the United
Nations," June 14, 1984, http://www.gwu.edu/~nsarchiv/NSAEBB/
NSAEBB82/iraq47.pdf

60 Friedman, *Spider's Web*, 27.

61 Molly Moore, "Two Vincennes Officers Get Medals; Citations Do Not
Mention Downing of Iranian Airliner That Killed 290," *Washington Post*,
April 23, 1990.

62 Ibid.

63 Ronald Reagan, "Statement on the Destruction of an Iranian Jetliner
by the United States Navy over the Persian Gulf," American Presidency
Project, July 3, 1988, http://www.presidency.ucsb.edu/ws/?pid=36080

64 "Iran Nukes Report Toughens Case for Sanctions," *USA Today*,
November 9, 2011, http://usatoday30.usatoday.com/news/opinion/
editorials/story/2011-11-09/Iran-nukes-nuclear-sanctions/51144578/1

65 Secretary of Defense Leon E. Panetta, "Remarks at the Saban Center,"
US Department of Defense, December 2, 2011, http://www.defense.gov/
transcripts/transcript.aspx?transcriptid=4937

66 "Mousavian: Resolution 598 Was Not a Chalice of Poison" (Persian),
Iranian Students' News Agency (ISNA), February 24, 2014, http://isna.ir/
fa/news/92111107150

67 "The Supreme Leader's View of Global Arrogance," Center for
Preserving and Publishing the Works of Grand Ayatollah Sayyid Ali

Khamenei, September 10, 2009, http://english.khamenei.ir/index. php?option=com_content&task=view&id=1179

Chapter 4

1 Ayatollah Hashemi Rafsanjani, "Memoirs about the Death of Imam (Khomeini) and the Election of Ayatollah Khamenei as the Leader" (Persian), official website, June 2, 1989, http://tarikhirani.ir/fa/news/30/bodyView/2247

2 "The Death of Imam Khomeini and the Election of Ayatollah Khamenei as the Leader of the Islamic Revolution" (Persian), Institution Representing the Supreme Leader in the Universities, http://www.siasi.porsemani.ir/node/1792 (accessed February 20, 2014).

3 Michael Ross, "Death of the Ayatollah: Iran Mourns; New Leader Is Chosen: President Khamenei Takes Khomeini Spiritual Roles to Avert Power Struggle," *Los Angeles Times*, June 5, 1989, http://articles.latimes.com/1989-06-05/news/mn-1275_1_ayatollah-ruhollah-khomeini-post-khomeini-khomeini-spiritual-role

4 "Biography of Ayatollah Ali Khamenei", The Office of the Supreme Leader Sayyid Ali Khamenei, http://www.leader.ir/langs/en/index.php?p=bio

5 For details see Chapter 4 – Two Men, Two Views

6 "Hashemi Rafsanjani's Financial Situation in 1963 as Told by the Supreme Leader" (Persian), *Asr-e-Iran News*, February 4, 2010, http://www.asriran.com/fa/news/99605

7 Ayatollah Hashemi Rafsanjani, "Memoirs: 'Don't Let the Wicked Provoke Enmity between You and Mr. Khamenei" (Persian), official website, May 30, 1989, http://goo.gl/9qjyfP

8 Ayatollah Khamenei, "Speech at the Meeting with a Large Number of Teachers, Laborers, and Official of Cultural Affairs," official website, May 2, 1990, http://farsi.khamenei.ir/speech-content?id=2304

9 Ayatollah Khamenei, "Speech for the Death Anniversary of Imam Khomeini," official website, June 4, 1992, http://farsi.khamenei.ir/speech-content?id=2623

10 With the establishment of the Islamic Republic, ties with Britain were severed, and the UK Embassy in Tehran was closed. Bilateral ties remained at their lowest level throughout the Iran–Iraq War, with the UK rallying behind Saddam. In 1983, having served as the head of the Majlis administrative department under Rafsanjani, I moved to the Foreign Ministry as head of the Department for Western Europe.

I discussed the idea of re-establishing Iran–UK relations, at ambassadorial level, with Rafsanjani, and he was supportive of the idea. Once we had his blessing, we approached Prime Minister Mir Hossein

Mousavi. Dispite his generally radical outlook, and much to our surprise, he also supported the idea. The last and most important authorization sought on this matter was that of the Ayatollah Khomeini. We felt an air of anxiety as we expected the initiative to face a high degree of opposition, owing to the turbulent history of Iran–UK relations and due to British interventionist policies since the beginning of the twentieth century, which peaked in the 1953 US–UK led coup. Finally we acted, and the Director-General for Western Europe, Mahmood Vaezi, and I held a meeting with Foreign Minister Velayati and his deputy Javad Larijani. It was decided at the meeting that Larijani would raise the issue with Ahmad Khomeini, the son of Ayatollah Khomeini, and his confidant. Two days passed and I went to Larijani's office to hear the latest developments. While I was there, Larijani called Ahmad Khomeini on a secure line. The conversation was brief and I was not sure of the outcome until Larijani told me that Ahmad had brought up the issue with the Ayatollah and he had agreed. We had received the green light to proceed.

I relayed the good news to Mahmood Vaezi and Foreign Minister Velayati, who both welcomed the news, and shortly afterwards, Velayati informed us about the next move; Vaezi and I were instructed to meet with our British counterparts in a neutral location. We chose Vienna as our meeting point and the British agreed. Within days, we were heading to the Austrian capital. Upon arrival, we met with the British for a long and detailed discussion that lasted five hours. The end result was an agreement to re-establish bilateral ties at the ambassadorial level. Subsequently, bilateral relations improved, leading to the reopening of the UK Embassy in Tehran in 1988.

The broader aim of re-establishing bilateral relations with the UK was that it was seen as a means to a larger goal—the restoration of relations with the US. There was therefore a sense of optimism once relations improved with the British that we could begin to advance towards a rapprochement with the US.

11 The Western hostage crisis refers to the period 1982 to 1992, when 96 hostages, mostly from America and Western Europe, were taken hostage in Lebanon.
12 Donette Murray, *US Foreign Policy and Iran: American–Iranian Relations since the Islamic Revolution* (New York: Routledge, 2010), 67.
13 Jack Nelson, "Bush Says He's Ready for 'Maximum' Iran Dialogue: Effort for Hostages Intensifies," *Los Angeles Times*, August 9, 1989, http://articles.latimes.com/1989-08-09/news/mn-253_1_american-hostage
14 Question-and-Answer Session With Reporters on the Hostage Situation in Lebanon 1989-08-02, http://bushlibrary.tamu.edu/research/public_papers.php?id=775&year=1989&month=8 (accessed March 10, 2014).
15 Ali Akbar Velayati, a pediatrician by profession, served as Foreign

Minister from 1981 to 1997. Since leaving the Foreign Ministry, he has served as the Supreme Leader's Advisor on International Affairs.

16 Mahmood Vaezi, former Deputy Foreign Minister for US and European Affairs (1988–97), has been serving as the Minister for Telecommunications since August 2013 under President Hassan Rouhani.

17 Giandomenico Picco was an Assistant Secretary General of the United Nations. A notable achievement during his career at the United Nations from 1973 to 1992 was the effort that led to the release of the Western hostages in Lebanon.

18 Mohammad Javad Zarif, a career multilateral diplomat, served as deputy permanent representative to the UN (1988–92), Deputy Foreign Minister for International and Legal Affairs (1992–2002), and permanent representative to the UN (2002–7). He was appointed Minister of Foreign Affairs in August 2013 by President Rouhani.

19 Khamenei, "Speech at Meeting with a Large Number of Teachers, Laborers, and Official of Cultural Affairs."

20 Ayatollah Khamenei, "Speech at the Meeting with the Minister and the Employees of the Ministry of the Foreign Affairs," official website, August 21, 1989, http://farsi.khamenei.ir/speech-content?id=2167

21 "Freedom Near for Hostages, Report Says: Lebanon: A Tehran Newspaper Says One or Two Captives Could Be Released within Days," *Los Angeles Times*, December 1, 1991, http://articles.latimes.com/1991-12-01/news/mn-826_1_tehran-times
   "Hostage Release Reported Near," *New York Times*, November 17, 1991, http://www.nytimes.com/1991/11/17/world/hostage-release-reported-near.html

22 Website of Ayatollah Hashemi Rafsanjani, published May 12, 2013, http://www.hashemirafsanjani.ir/content

23 "Bush: U.S. Ready To 'Strike Back,'" Philadelphia Daily News, August 3, 1989, http://articles.philly.com/1989-08-03/news/26149274_1_tom-cicippio-cicippio-today-joseph-cicippio (accessed March 10, 2014)

24 "Excerpts from Remarks by Iranian and Bush," *New York Times*, August 5, 1989, http://www.nytimes.com/1989/08/05/world/excerpts-from-remarks-by-iranian-and-bush.html

25 Janet Cawley, "Caution Rules Comments on Hostages," *Chicago Tribune*, August 11, 1989, http://articles.chicagotribune.com/1989-08-11/news/8901030833_1_direct-talks-tehran-times-iran

26 Alan Cowell, "Iran's Top Cleric Rejects Talking to Washington," *New York Times*, August 15, 1989, http://www.nytimes.com/1989/08/15/world/iran-s-top-cleric-rejects-talking-to-washington.html

27 Amnesty International, "Israel's Forgotten Hostages: Lebanese Detainees in Israel and Khiam Detention Centre," July 1997, http://www.amnesty.

org/ar/library/asset/MDE15/018/1997/en/54eb5607-ea82–11dd-b05d–
65164b228191/mde150181997en.pdf

28 Nick B. Williams Jr., "No Reason to Get Involved, Rafsanjani Says of
    Lebanon Hostages," *Los Angeles Times*, October 24, 1989, http://articles.
    latimes.com/1989–10–24/news/mn–738_1_hostage-takers

29 Ibid.

30 Ibid.

31 Frank Herbert Reed, director of the Lebanese International School,
    was abducted on September 9, 1986 near Beirut airport. John J.
    Goldman, "'He's out!'—a Phone Call Brings Tears and Family Joy at the
    Kitchen Table," *Los Angeles Times*, May 1, 1990, http://articles.latimes.
    com/1990–05–01/news/mn–279_1_kitchen-table

32 Thomas L. Friedman, "Hostage Sleight of Hand," *New York Times*, May
    2, 1990, http://www.nytimes.com/1990/05/02/world/hostage-sleight-
    of-hand.html

33 Members of a Lebanese militia, posing as police officers on January 24,
    1987, kidnapped Robert Polhill, former Assistant Professor of Business
    Studies at Beirut University College. Youssef M. Ibrahim, "Beirut
    kidnappers Free American, 55, a Hostage 3 Years," *New York Times*, April
    23, 1990, http://www.nytimes.com/1990/04/23/world/beirut-kidnappers-
    free-american–55-a-hostage–3-years.html

34 "Ex-Hostage Reed Reunites with Mother, Makes Plea for Release of
    Other Captives," *Los Angeles Times*, May 28, 1990, http://articles.latimes.
    com/1990–05–28/news/mn–80_1_frank-reed

35 Unpublished memoir of Akbar Hashmi Rafsanjani in 1980 (Persian),
    Etemad Newspaper, Oct. 31, 2013
    http://www.aftabir.com/articles/view/politics/iran/c1_1383210366p1.php

36 George Bush, "Remarks and Exchange with Reporters Prior to a Meeting
    with Former Hostage Robert Polhill," Geroge Bush Presidential Library
    and Museum, April 30, 1990, http://bushlibrary.tamu.edu/research/
    public_papers.php?id=1828&year=1990&month=4

37 Brian Keenan, a dual citizen of Ireland and the UK was an English teacher
    at the American University of Beirut when he was abducted in April
    1986. According to the BBC, his release had been credited to negotiations
    by Iran on behalf of Ireland with the kidnappers in Lebanon. "1990:
    Irish Hostage Released in Lebanon," *BBC News*, http://news.bbc.co.uk/
    onthisday/hi/dates/stories/august/24/newsid_2511000/2511857.stm

38 Terry Anderson, Chief Middle East correspondent for the Associated
    Press in Beirut, was abducted in March 1985. His release on
    December 4, 1991 makes him the longest-held American hostage in
    Lebanon. Semira N. Nikou, "Timeline of Iran's Foreign Relations,"
    United States Institute of Peace, http://iranprimer.usip.org/resource/
    timeline-irans-foreign-relations
       Among the Western hostages taken in Lebanon between 1982 and 1992,

several were from West Germany. Even though the Germans were the closest Western nation to Iran, the release of their citizens turned out to be the most challenging. The German authorities had arrested Mohammed Ali Hamadi in 1987 and had convicted and sentenced him to life imprisonment for his involvement in the 1985 hijacking of a TWA jetliner to Beirut and the killing of a United States Navy diver who was aboard the plane. His brother, Abbas Hamadi, received a 13-year prison sentence in 1988 for his involvement in the January 1987 kidnapping of two Germans, Alfred Schmidbauer and Rudolph Cordes, who were later freed in September 1987 and 1988 respectively. In retaliation for these convictions, the Hamadi family abducted two Germans, Heinrich Strubig and Thomas Kemptner, in May 1989, while they were working in Palestinian refugee camps for the German humanitarian aid group A.S.M.E.-Humanitas.

The release of the Germans was complex, since German officials would not release the members of the Hamadi family in return for their freedom. In an attempt to broker a deal, I invited the older brother, Abdel Hadi Hamadi, to my office in Tehran in the mid-1990s, where we discussed for hours the details of the two German hostages. However, he was not persuaded and I had to follow up on the case on my return as ambassador to Germany. With close cooperation with the German officials, we got the green light to extend an amnesty to the two Hamadi brothers in exchange for the release of the German hostages, Heinrich Strubig and Thomas Kemptner, in June 1992.

The key German officials at the time, with whom I was in constant contact regarding the case, were the Foreign Ministers Hans-Dietrich Genscher and Klaus Kinkel, Chairman of the Foreign Affairs Committee of German Bundestag Hans Stercken, and the Minister of State Bernd Schmidbauer. I also facilitated and organized a private meeting between Hans Stercken and the elder brother, Abdel Hadi Hamadi, in Tehran in the early 1990s. Ultimately the two Germans were freed in June 1992 and the Hamadi brothers in 2006.

39 George Bush, "The President's News Conference," American Presidency Project, December 5, 1991, http://www.presidency.ucsb.edu/ws/?pid=20305
40 Giandomenico Picco, *Man without a Gun: One Diplomat's Secret Struggle to Free the Hostages, Fight Terrorism, and End a War* (New York: Crown, 1999), 3.
41 Ibid.
42 Ibid., 3–4.
43 Ibid., 4.
44 Ibid.
45 Ibid.
46 Karim Sadjadpour, *Reading Khamenei: The World View of Iran's Most Powerful Leader* (Washington, DC: Carnegie Endowment for

International Peace, 2009), http://www.carnegieendowment.org/files/sadjadpour_iran_final2.pdf

47 Susan Welch, John Gruhl, John Comer, Susan M. Rigdon, *Understanding American Government* (Boston: Cengage Learning, 2011), 572.

48 "Burned by Loss of Conoco Deal, Iran Says US Betrays Free Trade," *New York Times*, March 20, 1995, http://www.nytimes.com/1995/03/20/business/burned-by-loss-of-conoco-deal-iran-says-us-betrays-free-trade.html

49 Ibid.

50 Barbara Slavin, "US–Iran Relations: Catalog of Missed Opportunities," American Foreign Policy Project, June 12, 2008, http://americanforeignpolicy.org/overview-how-to-deal-with-iran/a-short-history-of-US–Iran-relations-post-revolution

51 William J. Clinton, "Remarks to the American Gathering of Jewish Holocaust Survivors in New York City," April 30, 1995, *Public Papers of the Presidents of the United States* (Washington, DC: US Government Printing Office, 1995), 1:614.

52 Robin Wright, "New US Sanctions Will Backfire, Iranians Say," *Los Angeles Times*, May 16, 1995, http://articles.latimes.com/1995–05–16/news/mn–2535_1_united-states

53 Thomas R. Mattair, *Global Security Watch—Iran: A Reference Handbook* (Westport, CT: Praeger Security International, 2008), 47.

54 Shireen Hunter, *Iran's Foreign Policy in the Post-Soviet Era: Resisting the New International Order* (Santa Barbara, CA: Praeger, 2010).
   Donette Murray, *US Foreign Policy and Iran: American–Iranian Relations since the Islamic Revolution* (New York: Routledge, 2010).
   Ali Ansari, *Confronting Iran: The Failure of American Foreign Policy and the Next Great Conflict in the Middle East* (New York: Basic Books, 2006).

55 Kenneth Katzman, "The Iran–Libya Sanctions Act (ILSA): Report for Congress," US Secretary of State, October 11, 2006, http://fpc.state.gov/documents/organization/74902.pdf

56 Dore Gold, *The Rise of Nuclear Iran: How Tehran Defies the West* (Washington, DC: Regnery, 2009), 139.

57 Ayatollah Hashemi Rafsanjani, "Severed Relations with America Not Forever" (Persian), official website, September 22, 2013, http://goo.gl/crktbz

58 Ayatollah Hashemi Rafsanjani, "Memoirs" (Persian), official website, July 5, 1984, http://www.hashemirafsanjani.ir/content

59 "Ayatollah Hashemi: Imam said that it is not right to walk over the US flag" (Persian), *Entekhab News*, March 8, 2014, http://www.entekhab.ir/fa/news/151174

60 "A New Quote from Imam Khomeini with Regard to Relations with America" (Farsi), Iran Diplomacy, October 21, 2013, http://www.irdiplomacy.ir/fa/page/1923246

61 Christopher Hill, *The Changing Politics of Foreign Policy* (Basingstoke: Palgrave Macmillan, 2003), 72–95.

62 The European hostages consisted of 16 French, 12 British, seven Swiss, and seven West Germans.

63 "Meeting Raises Hope for Hostages," *TimesDaily*, May 17, 1990, http://news.google.com/newspapers?nid=1842&dat=19900517&id=jVkeAAAA IBAJ&sjid=Z8gEAAAAIBAJ&pg=5740,2771720

64 Ibid.

65 "US Terrorism Report: MEK and Jundallah," United States Institute of Peace, August 23, 2011, http://iranprimer.usip.org/blog/2011/aug/23/us-terrorism-report-mek-and-jundallah

66 Fritz Wittmann was the Chairman of the Defense Committee of the Bundestag, the lower house of Germany's parliament. He was a member of the Bundestag from 1971 to 1994 and from 1996 to 1998.

67 Hans Wilhelm Theodor Wallau, former German diplomat and ambassador to a number of countries.

68 Reinhard Schlagintweit is a politician and diplomat. He served as the Political Director General of the German Foreign Ministry from 1993 to 1999. He joined Foreign Service in 1952 and was assigned to Ankara, Kabul, and Bangkok, and then served as ambassador in Jeddah.

69 The Gulf Cooperation Council (GCC) is a political and economic union of the six Arab states in the Persian Gulf, namely Bahrain, Kuwait, Oman, Qatar, Saudi Arabia, and the United Arab Emirates.

70 Mohammad Javad Ardashir Larijani, former Deputy Foreign Minister (1986–1988), Majlis deputy during the 4th and 5th Majlis, has been serving as the Secretary of the Headquarters for Human Rights at the Judiciary.

71 Klaus Kinkel served as Federal Minister of Justice (1991–2), Foreign Minister (1992–8), and Vice Chancellor of Germany (1993–8) in the government of Helmut Kohl. Previously, he had been President of the Federal Intelligence Service (1979–82).

72 Bernd Schmidbauer served as Minister of State from 1991 to 1998. Previously he had been the parliamentary secretary to the Federal Minister for the Environment, Nature Conservation, and Nuclear Safety from January to December 1991.

73 Reinhard Schlagintweit is a politician and diplomat. He served as the Political Director General of the German Foreign Ministry from 1993 to 1999. He joined Foreign Service in 1952 and was assigned to Ankara, Kabul, Bangkok and was ambassador in Jeddah.

74 William J. Clinton, "The President's News Conference with the Prime Minister Yitzhak Rabin of Israel," American Presidency Project, March 15, 1993, http://www.presidency.ucsb.edu/ws/index.php?pid=46339#axzz1l9O0Dw5b

75 The Economic Cooperation Organization (ECO), a reincarnation

of the previous Regional Cooperation for Development (RCD) in the pre-revolutionary period, is an intergovernmental regional organization established in 1985 by Iran, Pakistan, and Turkey for the purpose of promoting economic, technical, and cultural cooperation among the member states. In 1992, the organization was expanded to include seven new members, namely: Afghanistan, Azerbaijan, Kazakhstan, the Kyrgyz Republic, Tajikistan, Turkmenistan, and Uzbekistan.

76 Mohammad Hashemi Rafsanjani (also Mohammad Hashemi), younger brother of former President Akbar Hashemi Rafsanjani, served as the head of the Islamic Republic of Iran Broadcasting (IRIB—Radio and Television), Vice-President in charge of Executive Affairs under his elder brother, and subsequently as member of the Expediency Council.

77 Dr. Rudolf Dolzer served as the Director General of the Office of the Chancellor from 1992 to 1996. He is currently the Director of the Institute for International Law at the University of Bonn, Germany. A profile is available at http://www.mcnairchambers.com/en/members/professor-rudolf-dolzer/profile

78 Martin Indyk served as Assistant Secretary of State for Near East Affairs during the Clinton administration. He is currently the Vice President and Director for Foreign Policy at the Brookings Institution in Washington, DC.

79 Salman Rushdie, the British author of controversial novel *The Satanic Verses*.

80 In May 1995, President Clinton issued Executive Order 12959 prohibiting any US trade with Iran.

81 The American Israel Public Affairs Committee (AIPAC) is a lobbying group that advocates pro-Israel policies to Congress and the executive branch of the United States government.

82 Charles Lane, "Germany's New Ostpolitik: Changing Iran," *Foreign Affairs* (November/December 1995), http://www.foreignaffairs.com/articles/51604/charles-lane/germanys-new-ostpolitik-changing-iran

83 Ali Ahani served as Director General for Western European Affairs at the Foreign Ministry from 1993 to 1998. He is currently serving as Iranian ambassador to France.

84 Kamal Kharrazi, with a PhD in Education and Psychology from the University of Texas, served as Deputy Foreign Minister for Political Affairs in the early 1980s, head of the War Propagation Headquarters until 1989, permanent representative to the UN (1989–97), Foreign Minister (1997–2005), and head of the Strategic Council on Foreign Policy since it was established in 2005 by the Supreme Leader.

85 Seyed Hossein Mousavian, *Iran–Europe Relations: Challenges and Opportunities* (New York: Routledge, 2008), 2.

86 Reviewing the incident of chain murders after Tajzadeh statements,

Islamic Revolution Document Center, December 14, 2011, http://www. irdc.ir/fa/content/15688/default.aspx

87 Ibid., 117.

88 Ibid.

89 Ibid., 119.

90 For a detailed description of the court case and findings, please refer to my book *Iran–Europe Relations: Challenges and Opportunities*.

91 Ibid., 120. This book provides a detailed description of the court case and findings.

92 "Mykonos and the Doubts that Still Remains with Mousavian" (Persian), interview with Seyed Hossein Mousavian, *Deutsche Welle*, September 16, 2012, http://www.dw.de/dw/article/0,,16245110,00.html

93 Hossein Mousavian, *Iran–Europe Relations*, 6.

Chapter 5

1 David Welch's testimony, *Iran and Proliferation: Is the US Doing Enough? The Arming of Iran: Who Is Responsible? Hearings before the US Senate Subcommittee on Near Eastern and South Asian Affairs of the Committee of Foreign Relations*, April 17 and May 6, 1997, http://www.gpo.gov/fdsys/pkg/CHRG-105shrg40187/pdf/ CHRG-105shrg40187.pdf

2 Donette Murray, *US Foreign Policy and Iran: American–Iranian Relations since the Islamic Revolution* (New York: Routledge, 2010), 104.

3 The "Clash of Civilizations" was an international relations theory developed by political scientist Samuel P. Huntington. The theory argues that people's cultural and religious identity will be the primary source of conflict in the post-Cold War era. Huntington presented the theory in a 1993 *Foreign Affairs* article titled "The Clash of Civilizations?" It was later expanded into a 1996 book entitled *The Clash of Civilizations and the Remaking of World Order*. Although the theory was developed by Huntington, the term of "Clash of Civilizations" was coined by the British-American political scientist, Bernard Lewis, in 1990, in an article entitled "The Roots of Muslim Rage," published in *The Atlantic*.

4 "Interview with Iranian President Mohammad Khatami," *CNN*, January 7, 1998, http://www.cnn.com/WORLD/9801/07/iran/interview.html

5 Ibid.

6 Samuel Huntington, *The Clash Of Civilizations and the Remaking of World Order* (London: Free Press, 2002), 258.

7 Ibid., 209.

8 Ibid., 217.

9 Ibid., 310.

10 Peter Waldman, "A Historian's Take on Islam Steers US in Terrorism Fight," *Wall Street Journal*, February 3, 2004, http://online.wsj.com/article/0,,SB107576070484918411-email,00.html

11 "Bill Clinton on Effective Muslim–West Dialogue at the Seventh Millennium Evening," April 12, 1999, http://berkleycenter.georgetown.edu/resources/quotes/bill-clinton-on-effective-muslim-west-dialogue-at-the-seventh-millenium-evening

12 "Message to President Khatami from President Clinton," June 1999, National Security Archive, http://www.gwu.edu/~nsarchiv/NSAEBB/NSAEBB318/doc02.pdf

13 Louis J. Freeh, *My FBI: Bringing Down the Mafia, Investigating Bill Clinton, and Waging War on Terror* (New York: St. Martin's Press, 2005), 20.

14 Jane Perlez and James Risen, "Clinton Seeks an Opening to Iran, But Efforts Have Been Rebuffed", *The New York Times*, December 3, 1999.

15 Government of Iran's response to President Clinton's letter, September 1999, National Security Archive, http://www.gwu.edu/~nsarchiv/NSAEBB/NSAEBB318/doc03.pdf

16 John Lancaster, "US Plans Major Gesture To Iran," *Washington Post*, March 17, 2000.

17 Secretary of State Madeleine K. Albright, "Remarks before the American–Iranian Council," March 17, 2000, http://secretary.state.gov/www/statements/2000/000317.html

18 Saudi Arabia, for example, apparently violates all major human rights values, but Washington has warm relations and long-standing economic and defense ties with the Saudi government. In a clear violation of human rights, Saudi Arabia engaged in a violent crackdown against internal protest, and even sent troops to Bahrain in 2011, where Bahraini protestors were similarly treated. Nevertheless, according to his own testimony, Defense Secretary Robert Gates had "an extremely cordial, warm meeting" with King Abdullah of Saudi Arabia after the Saudis' crackdown. Around the same time, Secretary of State Hillary Clinton announced new sanctions on Iran "to hold accountable those governments and officials that violate human rights."

19 Gary Sick, "The Future of US–Iran Relations," *Global Dialogue* 3, nos. 2–3 (2001), http://www.worlddialogue.org/content.php?id=148

20 "Leader's Speech on the Day of Eid Ghadir at Mausoleum in Mashhad," *Tebyan*, March 25, 2000, http://www.tebyan.net/newindex.aspx?pid=31159&BookID=21743&PageIndex=7&Language=3

21 "Iran's Leader Challenges US and Talks of Re-election Bid," *New York Times*, February 1, 1993, http://www.nytimes.com/1993/02/01/world/iran-s-leader-challenges-us-and-talks-of-re-election-bid.html

22 Profile: Ayatollah Ali Khamenei, BBC, June 17 2009, http://news.bbc.co.uk/1/hi/world/middle_east/3018932.stm

23 "Leader: US Ties Detrimental to Iran," *Press TV*, January 3, 2008, http://edition.presstv.ir/detail.fa/37353.html

24 *Hearing on Nomination of Colin L. Powell To Be Secretary of State, Committee on Foreign Relations United States Senate*, January 17, 2001, http://www.gpo.gov/fdsys/pkg/CHRG–107shrg71536/pdf/CHRG–107shrg71536.pdf

25 US Department of Justice, "Attorney General Statement," June, 21, 2001, https://www.fas.org/irp/news/2001/06/khobar.html

26 Ambassador Ryan Crocker, "Speech on Afghanistan," Carnegie Endowment for International Peace, September 17, 2012, http://www.carnegieendowment.org/files/091712_transcript_crocker1.pdf

27 Michael Hirsh, In the 'War on Terror', Hagel Hasn't Gone with the Crowd, National Journal, Dec 27, 2012, http://www.nationaljournal.com/nationalsecurity/in-the-war-on-terror-hagel-hasn-t-gone-with-the-crowd-20121227

28 David Crist, *The Twilight War: The Secret History of America's Thirty-Year Conflict with Iran* (New York: Penguin, 2012), 428.

29 "Statement by IDF Chief-of-Staff Lt-Gen Shaul Mofaz regarding Interception of Ship Karine A," January 4, 2002, Israel Ministry of Foreign Affairs, http://www.mfa.gov.il/MFA/Government/Speeches+by+Israeli+leaders/2002/Statement+by+IDF+Chief-of-Staff+Lt-Gen+Shaul+Mofaz.htm

30 "Seizing of the Palestinian Weapons Ship Karine A," Israel Ministry of Foreign Affairs, January 4, 2002, http://www.mfa.gov.il/MFA/Government/Communiques/2002/Seizing_of_the-Palestinian_Weapons_ship_Kaine_A_aspx

31 Ibid.

32 Douglas Frantz and James Risen, "A Nation Challenged," *New York Times*, March 24, 2002, http://www.nytimes.com/2002/03/24/world/nation-challenged-terrorism-secret-iran-arafat-connection-seen-fueling-mideast.html

33 Miriam Shaviv, "A Chill Wind from Teheran," *Jerusalem Post*, January 18, 2002.

34 Jack Katzenel, "Netanyahu Rejects Palestinian State," Associated Press, January 17, 2002, http://www.apnewsarchive.com/2002/Netanyahu-Rejects-Palestinian-State/id-ce661123f652ed5a68cce023a0821d62

35 "Reaction of FM Peres to Seizing of the Karine A," Israel Ministry of Foreign Affairs, January 4, 2002, http://www.mfa.gov.il/MFA/About+the+Ministry/MFA+Spokesman/2002/Reaction+of+FM+Peres+to+seizing+of+the+Karine+A.htm

36 Daniel C. Kurtzer, Scott B. Lasensky, William B. Quandt, Steven L. Spiegel, Shibley Z. Telhami, *The Peace Puzzle: America's Quest for Arab–Israeli Peace* (Ithaca, NY: Cornell University Press, 2013), 165.

37 "How Iran Entered the Axis," *PBS Frontline*, http://www.pbs.org/wgbh/pages/frontline/shows/tehran/axis/map.html

38 John H. Richardson, "The Secret History of the Impending War with Iran That the White House Doesn't Want You to Know," *Esquire*, October 18, 2007, http://www.esquire.com/features/iranbriefing1107

39 Ibid.

40 Crocker, "Speech on Afghanistan."

41 "Abbas in Tehran in first visit as President," *Eurasia Review*, August 30, 2012, http://www.eurasiareview.com/30082012-abbas-in-tehran-in-first-visit-as-president

42 "Statement by H. E. Dr. M. Javad Zarif Permanent Representative of the Islamic Republic of Iran before the Security Council," December 23, 2006, http://www.un.int/iran/statements/securitycouncil/articles/

Some in the US and Israel maintain that Iran does not have the right to enrichment of uranium under the Nuclear Non-Proliferation Treaty (NPT). They also argue that some countries that are using nuclear power do not enrich uranium themselves but buy it from other countries that produce enriched uranium. Some others argue that the Non-Proliferation Treaty (NPT) links a member's rights to its compliance with the commitment to apply safeguards and assure the IAEA that it is not seeking weapons. Article IV of the NPT specifically lays out the rights of non-nuclear weapons states, with no exceptions. It guarantees "the inalienable right of all the Parties to the Treaty to develop research, production and use of nuclear energy." The right to produce nuclear energy should include the right to the production of enriched uranium as a critical component for civil nuclear power generation. Otherwise, it should have been clearly exempted. The fact that some countries choose not to exercise that right, instead purchasing enriched uranium from abroad, does not change that right. Article IV of the NPT states that "nothing in this Treaty shall be interpreted as affecting the inalienable right of all the Parties to the Treaty to develop research, production and use of nuclear energy for peaceful purposes without discrimination and in conformity with Articles I and II of this treaty." Paragraph 69 of the final document of the first United Nations General Assembly Special Session on Disarmament in 1978, which was adopted by consensus, states that, "Each country's choices and decisions in the field of the peaceful uses of nuclear energy should be respected without jeopardizing their respective fuel cycle policies or international cooperation, agreements and contracts for the peaceful uses of nuclear energy provided that the agreed safeguard measures mentioned above are applied."

Argentina, Brazil, Germany, Japan, and the Netherlands—all countries which, like Iran, are non-nuclear-weapon parties to the NPT—have uranium enrichment facilities. All five nuclear-weapon parties to the NPT—China, France, Russia, the United Kingdom, and the United States—also have enrichment activities. Iran's nuclear program is carried out under IAEA supervision, and the IAEA has verified that no material is being diverted for military purposes.

43 The Treaty on the Non-Proliferation of Nuclear Weapons, United Nations, May 2–27, 2005, http://www.un.org/en/conf/npt/2005/npttreaty.html

44 Mohammad Javad Zarif, "Tackling the Iran–US Crisis: The Need for a Paradigm Shift," *Journal of International Affairs* 60, no. 2 (2007), http://www.un.int/iran/pressaffairs/articles/Article

45 Seyed Hossein Mousavian, "It Was Not Sanctions That Brought Iran to the Table," *Financial Times*, November 19, 2013, http://www.ft.com/intl/cms/s/0/8d9631f4–510c–11e3-b499–00144feabdc0.html

46 Seyed Hossein Mousavian, *The Iranian Nuclear Crisis: A Memoir* (Washington, DC: Carnegie Endowment for International Peace, 2012).

47 "Straw: US Stalls Accord on Iran Nuclear Program," Alalam News Network, July 5, 2013, http://en.alalam.ir/news/1491728

48 "Interview with Mohamed ElBaradei," *Spiegel Online*, April 19, 2011, http://www.spiegel.de/international/world/spiegel-interview-with-mohamed-elbaradei-egypt-s-military-leadership-is-reacting-too-slowly-a–757786.html

49 Low enriched uranium (3 percent to 5 percent) is used for electricity generation, while 12 percent to 19.75 percent enriched uranium is used in research reactors. High-grade or weapon-grade enriched uranium (90 percent plus) is used for building a nuclear bomb.

50 Greg Bruno, "Iran's Nuclear Program," Council on Foreign Relations, March 10, 2010, http://www.cfr.org/iran/irans-nuclear-program/p16811

51 Semira N. Nikou, "Timeline of Iran's Nuclear Activities," United States Institute of Peace, http://iranprimer.usip.org/resource/timeline-irans-nuclear-activities

According to the *Washington Post*, "President Gerald Ford signed a directive in 1976 offering Tehran the chance to buy and operate a U.S.-built reprocessing facility for extracting plutonium from nuclear reactor fuel. The deal was for a complete 'nuclear fuel cycle'." Dafna Linzer, "Past Arguments Don't Square with Current Iran Policy," *Washington Post*, March 26, 2005, http://www.washingtonpost.com/wp-dyn/articles/A3983–2005Mar26.html

52 Some argue that even under the Shah, the US had some concerns about Iran's nuclear program. The reality is that the differences between the Shah and the US were related only to reprocessing and plutonium separation. There was no dispute about nuclear power plants, the enrichment process, and the Tehran Research Reactor, which used 20 percent enriched uranium. A full report published by George Washington University Archive says:

"By the summer of 1978, Tehran and Washington had overcome differences and agreed to a nuclear pact that met U.S. concerns and the Shah's interest in buying reactors, but the agreement closely restricted Iran's ability to produce plutonium or any other nuclear weapon fuel using U.S. supplied material without Washington's 'agreement.'" William Burr, ed., "US–Iran Negotiations in 1970s Featured Shah's Nationalism and US Weapons Worries," National Security Archive, January 13, 2009, http://www2.gwu.edu/~nsarchiv/nukevault/ebb268/index.htm

This means that despite the restriction on "Iran's ability to produce plutonium," the Shah did not accept that Iran was denied the right to reprocess for peaceful purposes. The disagreement might have been about "using U.S. supplied material without Washington's 'agreement.'" Even this means that Iran could deal with other countries, such as France, and could buy nuclear weapon fuel from the US with Washington's agreement.

A report in the Washington Post noted:

> After balking initially, President Gerald R. Ford signed a directive in 1976 offering Tehran the chance to buy and operate a U.S.-built reprocessing facility for extracting plutonium from nuclear reactor fuel. The deal was for complete "nuclear fuel cycle"—reactors powered by and regenerating fissile materials on a self-sustaining basis. Ford's team endorsed Iranian plans to build a massive nuclear energy industry, but also worked hard to complete a multibillion-dollar deal that would have given Tehran control of large quantities of plutonium and enriched uranium—the two pathways to a nuclear bomb. Either can be shaped into the core of a nuclear warhead, and obtaining one or the other is generally considered the most significant obstacle to would-be weapons builders. (Dafna Linzer, "Past Arguments Don't Square with Current Iran Policy," *Washington Post*, March 27, 2005)

On October 21, 2013 I talked to Akbar Etemad, the head of the Iran Atomic Energy Organization during the Shah's era. He told me that the president of the American company Bechtel came to Tehran and asked him about setting up a joint enrichment project. Dr. Etemad declined the proposal and told Bechtel's president that he had already signed a contract for building an enrichment facility with the French. He told me there was no depute with the US on the wide scope of the nuclear program and that Iran did not let Americans impose any cessation of reprocessing on Iran.

53 Hossein Mousavian, *The Iranian Nuclear Crisis*, 50.
54 Ibid.
55 Maziar Bahari, "The Shah's Plan Was to Build Bombs," *New Statesman*, September 11, 2008, http://www.newstatesman.com/asia/2008/09/iran-nuclear-shah-west
56 Hossein Mousavian, *The Iranian Nuclear Crisis*, 53.
57 Ibid., 54.

58 Shabnam J. Holliday, *Defining Iran: Politics of Resistance* (Farnham: Ashgate, 2011).

59 Jay Loschky, "Most Iranians Say Sanctions Hurting the Livelihoods yet Majority Says Nuclear Power Should Still Move Forward," Gallup, November 6, 2013, http://www.gallup.com/poll/165743/iranians-say-sanctions-hurting-livelihoods.aspx

60 Council of Foreign Relations, "P5+1 Joint Plan of Action with Iran," January 13, 2014, http://www.cfr.org/iran/p51-joint-plan-action-irans-nuclear-program/p31950

61 Suzanne Maloney, "President Obama Urges Saban Forum: Don't Underestimate Political Shift in Iran," Brookings Institute, December 8, 2013, http://www.brookings.edu/blogs/iran-at-saban/posts/2013/12/08-obama-iran-saban-forum

62 Hossein Mousavian, *The Iranian Nuclear Crisis*, 120–1.

63 Iran was only a member of Safeguard Agreement (SA) until November 2003. Members of the SA are not obliged to report their activities until 180 days before the introduction of uranium hexafluoride gas to the centrifuges for uranium enrichment. Iran agreed to provisional implementation of the Additional Protocol (AP) and Subsidiary Arrangement Code 3.1 (SA 3.1) only in November 2003, after the Saadabad Agreement. Iran fully complied with its commitments under SA, AP, and SA code 3.1. After Iran's nuclear file was referred to the United Nations Security Council (UNSC) in 2006, the country withdrew from the AP and SA code.3.1. After withdrawal, Iran built Fordow. Therefore Iran maintains that under the Safeguard Agreement it had no obligation to inform the IAEA about the construction of Fordow. However, the world powers refer to UNSC resolutions claiming that Iran should have suspended, not expanded, its enrichment activities. Fordow was built in response to Israeli and US threats to attack the nuclear facility at Natanz. Iran's decision was based primarily on the need to construct an enrichment facility that could not be destroyed by conventional bombs. Iran's construction of Fordow was therefore a legitimate defensive measure to safeguard its assets against foreign threat.

64 Jonathan S. Landay, "Biggest Hurdle to Deal on Iranian Nuclear Program May Be Talking about the Past," McClatchy DC, October 4, 2013, http://www.mcclatchydc.com/2013/10/04/204292/biggest-hurdle-to-deal-on-iranian.html

65 James Risen and Mark Mazzetti, "US Agencies See No Move by Iran to Build a Bomb," *New York Times*, February 24, 2012, http://www.nytimes.com/2012/02/25/world/middleeast/us-agencies-see-no-move-by-iran-to-build-a-bomb.html

66 Peter Jenkins, "A Manufactured Nuclear Crisis," Inter Press Service News Agency, January 29, 2014, http://www.ipsnews.net/2014/01/manufactured-crisis

67 Michael Oren, "Should Israel Have a Red Line on Iran?," *Boston Globe*, October 9, 2012, http://www.bostonglobe.com/opinion/2012/10/08/israel-red-line-iran-lesses-chances-conflict/KLJSeZx0dRN8tDmDCDztAI/story.html

68 Ibid.

69 "President Says Zionist Regime of Israel Faces Dead End," Iranian President's website, June 3, 2008, http://web.archive.org/web/20110716100837/http://www.president.ir/en/?ArtID=10114

70 Dudi Cohen, "Meridor: Iran Never Called to Wipe Out Israel," *Ynet News*, April 17, 2012, http://www.ynetnews.com/articles/0,7340,L-4216986,00.html

71 "Leader's Speech to Government Officials on the Eid-al-Fitr," Office of the Supreme Leader, November 4, 2011, http://www.leader.ir/langs/en/index.php?p=bayanat&id=3477

72 Jeffrey Goldberg, "Obama to Iran and Israel: 'As President of the United States, I Don't Bluff,'" *Atlantic*, March 2, 2012, http://www.theatlantic.com/international/archive/2012/03/obama-to-iran-and-israel-as-president-of-the-united-states-i-dont-bluff/253875

73 Amir Mohebbian, "Possible Scenarios of Threat against Iran" (Persian), 2011, http://farsi.khamenei.ir/others-note?id=17882

74 Trita Parsi, *Treacherous Alliance: The Secret Dealings of Israel, Iran, and the US* (New Haven, CT: Yale University Press, 2007), 163.

75 Benjamin Netanyahu, *Fighting Terrorism: How Democracies Can Defeat the International Terrorist Network* (New York: Farrar, Straus and Giroux, 1997), 121.

76 Anthony H. Cordesman and Khalid R. Al-Rodhan, *Iran's Weapons of Mass Destruction: The Real and Potential Threat* (Washington, DC: Center for Strategic and International Studies, 2006), 212.

77 Ibid.

78 Ibid., 123.

79 Gil Hoffman and Tovah Lazaroff, "Iran Can Produce Nuclear Bomb by 2005—IDF," *Jerusalem Post*, August 5, 2003.

80 "Assistant Secretary of Defense Vershbow Meets with Senior Israeli Defense Officials," Wikileaks, November 16, 2009, http://wikileaks.org/cable/2009/11/09TELAVIV2482.html

81 Jeffery Goldberg, "The Point of No Return," *Atlantic*, August 11, 2010, http://www.theatlantic.com/magazine/archive/2010/09/the-point-of-no-return/8186

82 David Morgan, "Clinton Says US Could 'Totally Obliterate' Iran," Reuters, April 22, 2008, http://www.reuters.com/article/2008/04/22/us-usa-politics-iran-idUSN2224332720080422

83 "Obama Tells UN: Nuclear Iran Poses Existential Threat to Israel," Jewish Telegraphic Agency, September 25, 2012, http://www.theatlantic.com/magazine/archive/2010/09/the-point-of-no-return/308186/

84 Jeffrey Goldberg, "Obama to Israel—Time Is Running Out"

Bloomberg View, March 2, 2014, http://www.bloombergview.com/
articles/2014-03-02/obama-to-israel-time-is-running-out

85 Hillary Clinton, "America's Pacific Century," *Foreign Policy*, October
11, 2011, http://www.foreignpolicy.com/articles/2011/10/11/
americas_pacific_century

86 David E. Sanger, "Obama Order Sped Up Wave of Cyberattacks
against Iran," *New York Times*, June 1, 2012, http://www.nytimes.
com/2012/06/01/world/middleeast/obama-ordered-wave-of-
cyberattacks-against-iran.html

87 "Statement by the Iranian Government and Visiting EU Foreign
Ministers," International Atomic Energy Agency, October 21, 2003,
http://www.iaea.org/newscenter/focus/iaeairan/statement_iran21102003.
shtml

88 Seymour Hersh, "The Iran Plans," *New Yorker*, April 17, 2006, http://
www.newyorker.com/archive/2006/04/17/060417fa_fact

89 Hossein Mousavian, *The Iranian Nuclear Crisis*, 103.

90 Ibid.

91 Ibid., 107.

92 Ibid., 489, n. 13.

93 George W. Bush, "President Discusses the Future of Iraq," White House,
February 2003, http://georgewbush-whitehouse.archives.gov/news/
releases/2003/02/20030226-11.html

94 John F. Dickerson, "What the President Reads," *CNN*, January 10, 2005,
http://www.cnn.com/2005/ALLPOLITICS/01/10/bush.readinglist.tm

95 Bill Keller, "The Sunshine Warrior," *New York Times*, September 22,
2002, http://www.nytimes.com/2002/09/22/magazine/22WOLFOWITZ.
html

96 Vali Nasr, *The Shia Revival: How Conflicts within Islam Will Shape the
Future* (New York: W. W. Norton, 2006), 212.

97 Copy of the draft edited by Javad Zarif, *New York Times*, April 29,
2007, http://www.nytimes.com/packages/pdf/opinion/20070429_
iran-memo-red.pdf

98 Iran's 2003 proposal, *Arms Control*, http://www.armscontrol.org/
pdf/2003_Spring_Iran_Proposal.pdf

99 Copy of Tim Guldimann's letter, *Washington Post*, accessed February
25, 2014, http://www.washingtonpost.com/wp-srv/world/documents/
us_iran_1roadmap.pdf

100 Copy of the final draft of Iran's 2003 proposal, *New York Times*, April
29, 2007, http://www.nytimes.com/packages/pdf/opinion/20070429_
iran-memo-expurgated.pdf

101 "The 'Grand Bargain' Fax: A Missed Opportunity?," *PBS*, http://www.pbs.
org/wgbh/pages/frontline/showdown/themes/grandbargain.html

102 Michael Rubin, "The Guldimann Memorandum," personal website,

October 22, 2007, http://www.michaelrubin.org/1059/the-guldimann-memorandum

103 Crist, *The Twilight War*, 508.

104 Murray, *US Foreign Policy and Iran*, 126.

105 Hossein Mousavian, *The Iranian Nuclear Crisis*, 144.

106 Implementation of the IAEA's Subsidiary Arrangement and the Additional Protocol would guarantee the maximum level of transparency on nuclear activities.

107 Ibid., 165.

Chapter 6

1 Seyed Mohammad Ali Hosseini, "The Study of Successful Aspects of the Ninth Administration's Foreign Policy" (Persian), Presidential Center for Research and Documents, http://www.presidency.ir/Portal/File/ShowFile.aspx?ID=1cc470a7–74ac–41ed-ab55–1bbae424d3a8 (accessed February 27, 2014).

2 "Ramin: By Raising the Holocaust Issue We Closed the Nuclear File" (Persian), Aftab News, October 7, 2007, http://goo.gl/ltuvev

3 Barbara Slavin, *Bitter Friends, Bosom Enemies: Iran, the US, and the Twisted Path* (New York: St. Martin's Press, 2009), 218.

4 Donette Murray, *US Foreign Policy and Iran: American–Iranian Relations since the Islamic Revolutio* (New York: Routledge, 2010), 135.

5 Lara Jakes, "Look Back at Ahmadinejad's Memorable UN Speeches," September 24, 2013, http://news.yahoo.com/look-back-ahmadinejads-memorable-un-speeches–051914806.html

6 Mahmoud Ahmadinejad, interview with Larry King, CNN, September 22, 2010, http://transcripts.cnn.com/transcripts/1009/22/lkl.01.html

7 Jakes, "Look Back at Ahmadinejad's Memorable UN Speeches."

8 Track II diplomacy is a specific kind of informal diplomacy, in which non-officials (academic scholars, retired civil and military officials, public figures, and social activists) engage in dialogue, with the aim of conflict resolution or confidence-building.

9 "Iran to Welcome Potential US Goodwill: Ahmadinejad," *Press TV*, September 22, 2011, http://www.presstv.com/detail/2012/09/25/263472/iran-to-welcome-potential-us-goodwill

10 Hossein Bastani, "What Does 'Five Times' Emphasis by Ahmadinejad on Talks with the US Mean?" (Persian), BBC Persian, September 30, 2012, http://www.bbc.co.uk/persian/iran/2012/09/120930_l39_analysis_ahmadinejad_iran-us.shtml

11 "No Change in Iran Policy towards US: Velayati," *Press TV*,

September 29, 2012, http://www.presstv.ir/detail/2012/09/29/264160/
irans-us-policy-remains-unchanged

12 Board of Governors, "Implementation of the NPT Safeguards Agreement
in the Islamic Republic of Iran: Resolution Adopted on 4 Feb. 2006,"
International Atomic Energy Agency, February 4, 2006.

13 "The National Security Strategy of the United States," March 16, 2006,
http://nssarchive.us/?page_id=29

14 "$75 Million Sought to Sell Democracy in Iran," *Chicago Tribune*,
February 16, 2006, http://articles.chicagotribune.com/2006–02–16/
news/0602160189_1_iranian-people-president-mahmoud-ahmadinejad-
state-condoleezza-rice

15 Hassan M. Fattah, "US Sets Up a Perch in Dubai to Keep an Eye on
Iran," *New York Times*, November 19, 2006, http://www.nytimes.
com/2006/11/20/world/middleeast/20dubai.html

16 Ibid.

17 "Government in Secret Talks about Strike against Iran," *Telegraph*,
April 2, 2006, http://www.telegraph.co.uk/news/worldnews/middleeast/
iran/1514607/Government-in-secret-talks-about-strike-against-Iran.html

18 On June 30, 2006, the Israeli Air Force launched three air strikes at the
Lebanese town of Qana, killing at least 54 civilians, most of them children.

19 "Secretary Rice Holds a News Conference" (transcript), *Washington
Post*, July 21, 2006, http://www.washingtonpost.com/wp-dyn/content/
article/2006/07/21/AR2006072100889.html

20 Sheila M. Bird and Clive B. Fairweather, "Military Fatality Rates
(by Cause) in Afghanistan and Iraq: A Measure of Hostilities,"
International Journal of Epidemiology 36, no. 4 (2007): 841–46, http://ije.
oxfordjournals.org/content/36/4/841.full

21 Ramin Mostaghim and Louise Roug, "US and Iran to Meet on Iraq
War," *Los Angeles Times*, May 14, 2007, http://articles.latimes.com/2007/
may/14/world/fg-iran14

22 Lionel Beehner, "The Baker–Hamilton Commission (aka Iraq Study
Group)," Council on Foreign Relations, December 6, 2006, http://www.
cfr.org/iraq/baker-hamilton-commission-aka-iraq-study-group/p12010

23 James A. Baker III, Lee H. Hamilton, Lawrence S. Eagleburger, Vernon
E. Jordan, Jr., Edwin Meese III, Sandra Day O'Connor, Leon E. Panetta,
William J. Perry, Charles S. Robb, Alan K. Simpson, *The Iraq Study
Group Report* (New York: Vintage, 2006), xv.

24 Robert Draper, *Dead Certain: The Presidency of George W. Bush* (New
York: Free Press, 2008), xii.

25 Bob Woodward, *The War Within: A Secret White House History,
2006–2008* (New York: Simon and Schuster, 2009), 334.

26 Ibid.

27 Kirk Semple, "US and Iranian Officials Meet in Baghdad: Talks Yield
No Breakthroughs," *Spiegel Online*, May 29, 2007, http://www.spiegel.de/

international/u-s-and-iranian-officials-meet-in-baghdad-talks-yield-no-breakthroughs-a–485377.html

28 Peter Walker, "Iran and US Hold Historic Talks," *Guardian*, May 28, 2007, http://www.guardian.co.uk/world/2007/may/28/iraq.iran

29 Semple, "US and Iranian Officials Meet in Baghdad."

30 Ibid.

31 James Dobbins, "Engaging Iran," United States Institute of Peace, http://iranprimer.usip.org/resource/engaging-iran (accessed February 27, 2014).

32 Helene Cooper and Kirk Semple, "US Officials to Meet with Iranians at Talks on Iraq," *New York Times*, February 27, 2007, http://www.nytimes.com/2007/02/27/washington/27cnd-diplo.html

33 Walker, "Iran and US Hold Historic Talks."

34 Ibid.

35 Semple, "US and Iranian Officials Meet in Baghdad."

36 Project for the New American Century, *Rebuilding America's Defenses: Strategy, Forces, and Recourses for a New Century*, September 2000, http://www.informationclearinghouse.info/pdf/RebuildingAmericasDefenses.pdf

37 John J. Mearsheimer and Stephen M. Walt, "The Israel Lobby and US Foreign Policy," John F. Kennedy School of Government Working Paper No. RWP06–11, March 2006, 1, http://papers.ssrn.com/sol3/papers.cfm?abstract_id=891198&http://papers.ssrn.com/sol3/papers.cfm?abstract_id=891198##

38 Ibid., 13.

39 Aaron David Miller, *The Much Too Promised Land: America's Elusive Search for Arab–Israeli Peace* (New York: Random House, 2008), 96.

40 Jeffrey Goldberg, "Real Insiders: A Pro-Israel Lobby and FBI Sting," *New Yorker*, July 4, 2005, http://www.newyorker.com/archive/2005/07/04/050704fa_fact

41 George W. Bush, *Decision Points* (New York: Crown, 2011), 419.

42 George W. Bush, "President Bush Discusses Freedom Agenda," *Real Clear Politics*, July 24, 2008, http://www.realclearpolitics.com/articles/2008/07/president_bush_discusses_freed.html

43 Ahmad Tavakoli, "Tavakoli Apology to Mousavian," *Alef News*, September 15, 2008, http://www.alef.ir/vdcizvap.t1azq2bcct.html?31861

44 Ahmad Tavakoli, "Accusations of Espionage Were Lies," *Arash Sigarchi News*, September 20, 2008, http://asigarchi.blogspot.com/2008/09/official-apology-to-mousavian.html

45 "Mousavian's Response to Tavakoli's Apology," *Alef News*, September 15, 2008, http://www.alef.ir/vdcizvap.t1azq2bcct.html?31861

46 "Also Attacks Nateq-Nouri," *Roozonline*, April 12, 2009, http://www.roozonline.com/english/news3/newsitem/archive/2009/april/12/article/also-attacks-nateq-nouri.html

47 Ibid.

48 Eskandar Sadeghi-Boroujerdi, "Revolutionary Guards' Political Deputy Accuses Ahmadinejad of Narcissism and Delusion," *Al Monitor*, February 22, 2013, http://iranpulse.al-monitor.com/index.php/2013/02/1416/revolutionary-guards-political-deputy-accuses-ahmadinejad-of-narcissism-and-delusion

49 "Iran Arrests Ahmadinejad Ally," *Voice of America*, June 23, 2011, http://www.voanews.com/content/ahmadinejad-ally-arrested-in-iran---124486554/173051.html

50 Saeed Kamali Dehghan, "Ahmadinejad Allies Charged with Sorcery," *Guardian*, May 5, 2011, http://www.theguardian.com/world/2011/may/05/ahmadinejad-allies-charged-with-sorcery

51 Saeed Kamali Dehghan, 'Iranian Presidential Aide Arrested,' *Guardian*, May 20, 2011, http://www.theguardian.com/world/2011/may/20/iranian-presidential-aide-arrested

52 Saeed Kamali Dehghan, "Mahmoud Ahmadinejad Summoned to Criminal Court," *Guardian*, June 17, 2013, http://www.theguardian.com/world/2013/jun/17/mahmoud-ahmadinejad-summons-iran

53 Ian Black, "Mail Bonding," *Guardian*, November 8, 2008, http://www.guardian.co.uk/world/2008/nov/08/iran-usa

54 "Translation of Ahmadinejad's Letter," *Washington Post*, November 6, 2008, http://www.washingtonpost.com/wp-dyn/content/article/2008/11/06/AR2008110603030.html

55 "Iranians Should Play Role in Global Management," Office of the President, May 19, 2013, http://president.ir/en/48713

56 "Videotaped Remarks by the President in Celebration of Nowruz," White House, March 20, 2009, http://www.whitehouse.gov/the_press_office/videotaped-remarks-by-the-president-in-celebration-of-nowruz

57 "Speech for the Pilgrims to Imam Reza's Shrine (Iranian New Year)" (Persian), Center for Preserving and Publishing the Works of Grand Ayatollah Sayyid Ali Khamenei, March 21, 2009, http://farsi.khamenei.ir/speech-content?id6082

58 Mohamed ElBaradei, *The Age of Deception: Nuclear Diplomacy in Treacherous Times* (New York: Metropolitan Books), 295.

59 Ewen MacAskill, "Obama Sent Letter to Khamenei before the Election, Report Says," *Guardian*, June 24, 2009, http://www.theguardian.com/world/2009/jun/24/khamenei-obama-letter

60 "Ayatollah Khamenei Rejects Talks with US under Pressure," *Press TV*, February 7, 2013, http://www.presstv.com/detail/2013/02/07/287768/no-talks-with-us-under-pressure-leader

61 "Obama Sent Second Letter to Khamenei," *Washington Times*, September 3, 2009, http://www.washingtontimes.com/news/2009/sep/03/obama-sent-second-letter-to-irans-khamenei

62 "Both Ahmadinejad and Rival Mousavi Claim Victory in Iran's Presidential Election," ABC News, June 12, 2009, http://abcnews.go.com/Politics/International/story?id=7821927

63 "Supreme Leader: Protest Leaders Are Responsible for Bloodshed," Center for Preserving and Publishing the Works of Ayatollah Sayyid Ali Khamenei, June 19, 2009, http://english.khamenei.ir/index. php?option=com_content&task=view&id=1155&Itemid=2

64 Shahir Shahidsaless, "Miscalculations Abound in Iran," *Asia Times*, June 26, 2009, http://www.atimes.com/atimes/Middle_East/KF26Ak02. html

65 "Guardian Council Report on Iran Presidential Election," Fars News Agency, July 18, 2009, http://www.iranaffairs.com/files/document.pdf

66 Barbara Slavin, "US Contacted Iran's Ayatollah before Election," *Washington Times*, June 24, 2009, http://www.washingtontimes.com/news/2009/jun/24/us-contacted-irans-ayatollah-before-election

67 Kathy Kiely, "Dear Ayatollah," *USA Today*, June 24, 2009, http://content.usatoday.com/communities/theoval/post/2009/06/68453231/1#. UlhSpFCkrLd

68 "US Showed Support for Iran Protestors: Clinton," *Agence France-Presse*, August 9, 2009, http://www.google.com/hostednews/afp/article/ALeqM5hcI2cEI2R_30663RxlsVetrBx_dg

69 James Phillips, "Iran's Green Movement Revives, Energized by Egyptian Revolt," Heritage Foundation, February 18, 2011, http://blog.heritage. org/2011/02/18/irans-green-movement-revives-energized-by-egyptian-revolt

   Geneive Abdo, "Green Movement 2.0?," *Foreign Affairs*, February 18, 2011, http://www.foreignaffairs.com/articles/67458/geneive-abdo/green-movement–20#

   Ray Takeyh, "The US Must Empower the Green Movement," Council on Foreign Relations, February 17, 2011, http://www.cfr.org/iran/us-must-empower-green-movement/p24155

70 Ibid.

71 Michael H. Posner, "Statement before the Senate Foreign Relation Committee, Subcommittee on Near Eastern and South and Central Asian Affairs on Human Rights and Democratic Reform in Iran," US Department of State, May 11, 2011, http://www.state.gov/j/drl/rls/rm/2011/163123.htm

72 Abdo, "Green Movement 2.0?"

73 Richard N. Haass, "Regime Change Is the Only Way to Stop Iran," *Newsweek*, Januart 21, 2010, http://www/newsweek.com/haass-regime-change-only-way-stop-iran-71005

74 Robert Tait and Julian Borger, "Analysis: Iran Election Statistics Muddy Waters Further," *Guardian*, June 15, 2009, http://www.theguardian.com/world/2009/jun/15/iran-election-analysis-figures

75 The election was rigged. This was admitted by the Guardian Council, but the Council concluded that the irregularities would not have noticeably affected the outcome. The expert judgment of Walter Mebane, who conducted a mathematical analysis of the election, read: "It is important to be clear that none of the estimates or test results in this report are proof that substantial fraud affected the 2009 Iranian election. The results suggest very strongly that there was widespread fraud in which the vote counts for Ahmadinejad were substantially augmented by artificial means. But it is possible that Ahmadinejad actually won, supported by many who might have voted for [the other two candidates] Karroubi or Rezaei instead voting for Ahmadinejad (Mebane 2009)."

Our research found three more extensive statistical analyses on the 2009 election. Ansari points to widespread fraud and casts doubt on the results (Ali Ansari, Daniel Berman, Thomas Rintou, 2009). Ansari's report is refuted by Bozogmehr and Esfandiari (2010). Their analysis concludes that the outcome of the election was a genuine reflection of the will of the Iranian people. In another statistical analysis, Brill concluded that Ahmadinejad had been the actual winner of the election (Brill 2010).

76 Ramin Jahanbegloo, *Iran: Between Tradition and Modernity* (Lanham, MD: Lexington Books, 2004).

77 Jay Solomon, "Iranian Diplomat in US Opens Window on Tehran," *Wall Street Journal*, June 29, 2010, http://online.wsj.com/news/articles/SB1000 1424052748704846004575332754213432126

78 Ibid.

79 Ibid.

Chapter 7

1 "Iran 'Leading' State Sponsor of Terrorism," United States Institute of Peace, August 1, 2012, http://iranprimer.usip.org/blog/2012/aug/01/iran-%E2%80%9Cleading%E2%80%9D-state-sponsor-terrorism

2 Scott Sterns, "US: Iran Remains Leading State Sponsor of Terrorism," *Voice of America*, July 31, 2012, http://www.voanews.com/content/iran_is_leading_state_sponsor_of_terrorism_again/1452064.html

3 William J. Clinton, "Remarks to Future Leaders of Europe in Brussels," American Presidency Project, January 9, 1994, http://www.presidency.ucsb.edu/ws/?pid=49643

4 George W. Bush, "State of the Union Address," Miller Center, University of Virginia, January 29, 2002, http://millercenter.org/president/speeches/detail/4540

5 Secretary of Defense Leon E. Panetta, "Remarks at the Saban Center," US Department of Defense, December 2, 2011, http://www.defense.gov/transcripts/transcript.aspx?transcriptid=4937

6 Greg Bruno, "State Sponsors: Iran," Council on Foreign Relations, October 13, 2011, http://www.cfr.org/iran/state-sponsors-iran/p9362

7 Semira N. Nikou, "Timeline of Iran's Foreign Relations," in Robin B. Wright (ed.), *The Iran Primer: Power, Politics, and US Policy* (Washington, DC: Endowment of the United States Institute of Peace, 2010), 232.

8 Michael T. Kindt, "Hezbollah: State within State," in Michael T. Kindt, Jerrold M. Post, and Barry R. Schneider (eds), *The World's Most Threatening Terrorist Networks and Criminal Gangs* (New York: Palgrave Macmillan, 2009), 128.

9 "Iran Denies Any Involvement in Bombing of US Embassy," *New York Times*, April 20, 1983, http://www.nytimes.com/1983/04/20/world/ iran-denies-any-involvement-in-bombing-of-us-embassy.html

10 "Iran Again Denies Involvement in Khobar Bombing," *CNN*, December 23, 1996, http://www.cnn.com/WORLD/9612/23/briefs.pm/khobar/index. html

11 US Department of State, Bureau of Counter Terrorism, "Foreign Terrorist Organizations," September 28, 2012, http://www.state.gov/j/ct/ rls/other/des/123085.htm

12 Antoine Lahad was the leader of the South Lebanon Army (SLA), a Lebanese militia group that received support from Israel during the 1982–2000 conflict in southern Lebanon. The SLA was engaged against both the Palestine Liberation Organization and Hezbollah from 1984 until 2000, but was dissolved following the withdrawal of Israeli forces from southern Lebanon in 2000.

13 Israel Ministry of Foreign Affairs, "Suicide and Other Bombing Attacks in Israel since the Declaration of Principles," September 1993, http:// www.mfa.gov.il/mfa/foreignpolicy/terrorism/palestinian/pages/suicide

14 Christiane Amanpour, "Iran Justifies Stance on Israel Bombings," *CNN*, March 5, 1996, http://www.cnn.com/WORLD/9603/ jerusalem_blast/03–05/iran_reax/

15 Robin Wright, "The Challenge of Iran," United States Institute of Peace, accessed February 20, 2014, http://iranprimer.usip.org/resource/ challenge-iran

16 United States Department of State, Bureau of Counter Terrorism, "Country Reports on Terrorism," July 2011, http://www.state.gov/ documents/organization/195768.pdf

17 Council on Foreign Relations, "[Michael] McConnell [Director of National Intelligence] Cites 'Overwhelming Evidence' of Iran's Support for Iraqi insurgence," June 28, 2007, http://www.cfr.org/intelligence/ mcconnell-cites-overwhelming-evidence-irans-support-iraqi-insurgents/ p13692

18 Bruno, "State Sponsors: Iran."

19 Peter Finn and Julie Tate, "Mansour Arbabsiar Recalled as Upbeat

about Finances during Summer Encounter," *Washington Post*, October 12, 2011, http://www.washingtonpost.com/national/national-security/mansour-arbabsiar-recalled-as-upbeat-about-finances-during-summer-encounter/2011/10/12/gIQA3nnOgL_story.html

20 Saeed Kamali Dehghan, "Iran Demands Apology from US over Saudi Ambassador 'Assassination Plot,'" *Guardian*, October 31, 2011, http://www.guardian.co.uk/world/2011/oct/31/iran-demands-apology-assassination-plot

21 Juan Cole, "Wagging the Dog with Iran's Maxwell Smart," October 13, 2011, http://www.juancole.com/2011/10/wagging-the-dog-with-irans-maxwell-smart.html

22 I have explained these five episodes in detail in *The Iranian Nuclear Crisis: A Memoir* (Washington, DC: Carnegie International Endowment, 2012).

23 William Lowther and Colin Freeman, "US Funds Terror Groups to Sow Chaos in Iran," *Telegraph*, February 25, 2007, http://www.telegraph.co.uk/news/worldnews/1543798/US-funds-terror-groups-to-sow-chaos-in-Iran.html

24 US Department of State, Bureau of Counter Terrorism, "Foreign Terrorist Organizations," September 28, 2012, http://www.state.gov/j/ct/rls/other/des/123085.htm

25 Seymour M. Hersh, "The Next Act," *New Yorker*, November 27, 2006, http://www.newyorker.com/archive/2006/11/27/061127fa_fact

26 "2nd Blast in 3 days Hits Iranian City," *CNN*, February 16, 2007, http://edition.cnn.com/2007/WORLD/meast/02/16/iran.bombing

27 Homylafayette, "Jundullah Claims Responsibility for Suicide Bombing; 33 Dead," *PBS Frontline*, December 15, 2010, http://www.pbs.org/wgbh/pages/frontline/tehranbureau/2010/12/suicide-bombers-kills-at-least–30-in-chabahar.html

28 Sam K. Parks-Kia, "Abdolmalek Rigi—Who Is He?," *Press TV*, February 26, 2010, http://edition.presstv.ir/detail/119561.html

29 Tim Shipman, "Bush Sanctions 'Black Ops' against Iran," *Telegraph*, May 27, 2007, http://www.telegraph.co.uk/news/worldnews/1552784/Bush-sanctions-black-ops-against-Iran.html

30 Mark Perry, "False Flag," *Foreign Policy*, January 13, 2012, http://www.foreignpolicy.com/articles/2012/01/13/false_flag

31 Sam Sedaei, "Incomprehensive Choices on Iran," *Huffington Post*, July 31, 2007, http://www.huffingtonpost.com/sam-sedaei/incomprehensive-choices-o_b_58548.html

32 Seymour M. Hersh, "Preparing the Battlefield," *New Yorker*, July 7, 2008, http://www.newyorker.com/reporting/2008/07/07/080707fa_fact_hersh

33 Ibid.

34 Seymour M. Hersh, "Our Men in Iran?," *New Yorker*, April 6, 2012, http://www.newyorker.com/online/blogs/newsdesk/2012/04/mek.html

35 David E. Sanger, "Obama Order Sped Up Wave of Cyberattacks against Iran," *New York Times*, June 1, 2012, http://www.nytimes.com/2012/06/01/world/middleeast/obama-ordered-wave-of-cyberattacks-against-iran.html

36 Patrick Disney, "Kicking the Hornets' Nest: Iran's Nuclear Ambivalence and the West's Counterproductive Nonproliferation Policies," *Nonproliferation Review* 19, no. 2 (2012): 175.

37 "Hamas Sweeps the Election Victory," *BBC NEWS*, January 26, 2006, http://news.bbc.co.uk/2/hi/4650788.stm

38 Adam Shatz, "In Search of Hezbollah," *New York Review of Books*, April 29, 2004, http://www.nybooks.com/articles/archives/2004/apr/29/in-search-of-hezbollah

39 "US Terrorism Report: Iran and Hizballah, Hamas," United States Institute of Peace, August 23, 2011, http://iranprimer.usip.org/blog/2011/aug/23/us-terrorism-report-iran-and-hizballah-hamas

40 Marwan Bishara, "Gauging Arab Public Opinion," *Aljazeera*, March 8, 2012, http://www.aljazeera.com/indepth/opinion/2012/03/20123793355501965.html

41 Related to the Hashemite clan, to which Prophet Mohammad (PBUH) belonged. I am a Sayyid (persianized as Seyyed or Seyed). This is an honorific title indicating that the person is a descendant of the Prophet Muhammad.

42 The world's largest lake, in the north of Iran. Its coast offers sandy beaches, lush vegetation, and spectacular natural scenery.

43 A city in the south of Iran.

44 US Department of Justice, "Attorney General Statement," June 21, 2011, https://www.fas.org/irp/news/2001/06/khobar.html

45 Suzanne Maloney, *Iran's Long Reach: Iran as a Pivotal State in the Muslim World* (Washington, DC: United States Institute of Peace, 2008), 26.

46 Daniel Benjamin and Steven Simon, *The Age of Sacred Terror: Radical Islam's War Against America* (New York: Random House, 2003), 132.

47 Geffery Charlston, ed., *United States Military History 1865 to the Present Day* (Farnham: Ashgate, 2006), 125.

48 "Perry: US Eyed Iran Attack after Bombing," UPI, June 6, 2007, http://www.upi.com/Business_News/Security-Industry/2007/06/06/Perry-US-eyed-Iran-attack-after-bombing/UPI-70451181161509

49 Israel Ministry of Foreign Affairs, "Acquisition of Israeli Nationality," accessed February 21, 2014, http://www.mfa.gov.il/mfa/aboutisrael/state/pages/acquisition%20of%20israeli%20nationality.aspx

50 Robert Fisk, *The Great War for Civilization: The Conquest of the Middle East* (New York: Vintage Books 2007), 128.

51 Fayziya Madrasa (Seminary) in Qom and Talibiya Madrasa in Tabriz were simultaneously attacked by the secret service agents of the Shah a few days prior to the speech.

52 "Historic Speech of Imam Khomeini [ra] in 1963," *IBN TV*, http://www.
    ibn-tv.com/2011/06/historic-speech-of-imam-khomeini-ra-in–1963
    (accessed February 21, 2014).

53 Stephen M. Walt, "Well, duh …," *Foreign Policy*, September 18, 2011,
    http://walt.foreignpolicy.com/posts/2011/09/18/well_duh

54 For a list of further vetoes, please visit "UN Security Council: US Vetoes
    of Resolutions Critical to Israel," http://www.jewishvirtuallibrary.org/
    jsource/UN/usvetoes.html

55 United Nations Security Council, "Lebanon: Draft Resolution,"
    March 11, 1985, http://www.un.org/en/ga/search/view_doc.
    asp?symbol=S/17000

56 United Nations Security Council, "Burkina Faso, Egypt, India,
    Madagascar, Peru, Trinidad, and Tobago: Draft Resolution,"
    September 12, 1985, http://www.un.org/en/ga/search/view_doc.
    asp?symbol=S/17459

57 United Nations Security Council, "Algeria, Argentina, Nepal, Senegal,
    Yugoslavia, and Zambia: Draft Resolution," January 29, 1988, http://
    www.un.org/en/ga/search/view_doc.asp?symbol=S/19466

58 United Nations Security Council, "France, Portugal, Sweden, and United
    Kingdom of Great Britain and Northern Ireland: Draft Resolution," March
    7, 1997, http://www.un.org/en/ga/search/view_doc.asp?symbol=S/1997/199

59 United Nations Security Council, "Qatar: Draft Resolution," July 12,
    2006, http://www.un.org/en/ga/search/view_doc.asp?symbol=S/2006/508

60 United Nations Security Council, "Afghanistan … Zimbabwe: Draft
    Resolution," February 18, 2011, http://www.un.org/en/ga/search/view_
    doc.asp?symbol=S/2011/24

61 Robert Burns, "Obama Opens Long-Shut Talks on Mideast Peace,"
    AOL, September 1, 2010, http://www.aolnews.com/2010/09/01/
    obama-opens-long-shot-talks-on-mideast-peace

62 "US 'Deeply Disappointed' in Israel Settlement Move," Reuters,
    November 2, 2011, http://www.reuters.com/article/2011/11/02/
    us-palestinians-israel-usa-idUSTRE7A142K20111102

63 "Kerry Reaffirms: US Views Settlements as 'Illegitimate,'" November
    6, 2013, http://news.yahoo.com/kerry-reaffirms-us-views-settlements-
    illegitimate–142708943.html

64 http://www.telegraph.co.uk/news/worldnews/middleeast/
    israel/10613055/John-Kerry-labelled-anti-Semite-for-warning-of-
    possible-boycott-of-Israel.html

65 Khaled Abu Toameh, "Peace Process Clinically Dead, Israel Responsible,"
    Jerusalem Post, June 17, 2012, http://www.jpost.com/MiddleEast/Article.
    aspx?id=274161

66 Palestine Liberation Organization, Negotiations Affairs Department,
    "Special Focus: Occupied East Jerusalem," http://www.nad-plo.org/
    etemplate.php?id=344 (accessed February 24, 2014).

67 "Supreme Leader's Inaugural Speech at the 16th Non-Aligned Summit,"
   Center for Preserving and Publishing the Works of Grand Ayatollah
   Sayyed Ali Khamenei, August 30, 2012, http://english.khamenei.ir/index.
   php?id=1668&option=com_content&task=view
68 "Iran: Chronology of Events: June 1989–July 1994," Refworld, January 1,
   1995, http://www.unhcr.org/refworld/country,,IRBC,COUNTRYREP,IR
   N,,3ae6a8170,0.html
69 Reynaldo Galindo Pohl, "Final Report on the Situation of Human
   Rights in the Islamic Republic of Iran," United Nations High
   Commissioner for Human Rights, February 2, 1994, http://www.unhchr.
   ch/Huridocda/Huridoca.nsf/0/3b10d2ce0deea2348025673700654bed?Op
   endocument
70 Hossein Mousavian, *Iran–Europe Relations*, 47.
71 Ibid.
72 See note 85, Chapter 4, p. 316.
73 Saeed Rajaee Khorasani, a professor of philosophy, served as the
   permanent representative to the UN (1981–7), deputy and head of the
   Human Rights Subcommittee at the 3rd Majlis, and lecturer at Islamic
   Azad University (Tehran). He passed away in fall 2013.
74 See note 73, p. 316, Chapter 4.
75 Barbara Slavin, "Congress Not Won Over by Rouhani Victory in
   Iran," *Al Monitor*, June 18, 2013, http://www.al-monitor.com/pulse/
   originals/2013/06/congress-iran-election-rouhani-skeptical-sanctions.html

Chapter 8

1 Kayhan Barzegar, "Roles at Odds: The Roots of Increased Iran/US
   Tension in the Post–9/11 Middle East," *Iranian Review of Foreign Affairs*
   1, no. 3 (2010): 85–114.
2 *Machtpolitik* (German), or power politics, is a state of international
   relations in which sovereigns protect their own interests by threatening
   one another with military, economic, or political aggression.
3 Fawaz A. Gerges, *America and Political Islam: Clash of Cultures or Clash
   of Interests* (New York: Cambridge University Press, 1999).
4 Bernard Lewis, "Islamic Revolution," *New York Review of Books*, January
   21, 1998, http://www.nybooks.com/articles/archives/1988/jan/21/
   islamic-revolution
5 Craig Timberg, "Gates Has 'Warm' Meeting with Saudi Arabia's
   King Abdullah," *Washington Post*, April 6, 2011, http://www.
   washingtonpost.com/%20world/defense-secretary-gates-arrives-in-
   saudi-arabia-for-meeting-with-king-abdullah%20/%202011/04/06/
   AFV6iXnC_story.html
6 Hassan Rouhani, interview with *Mehr Nameh* magazine (Persian),

Center for Strategic Research (Iran), May 7, 2012, http://www.csr.ir/Center.aspx?lng=fa&subid=-1&cntid=2497

7 Martin Malek, "Russia, Iran, and the Conflict in Chechnya," *Caucasian Review of International Affairs* 2, no. 1 (2008): 25–34.

8 See pages 193–7 (Chapter 5) of the book under the title "Iran's Proposal: Too good to be true" and the corresponding notes 97–104.

9 Mohamed ElBaradei, *The Age of Deception: Nuclear Diplomacy in Treacherous Times* (New York: Metropolitan Books), 132.

10 "The Organization of the Islamic Conference," accessed February 28, 2014, http://fimforum.org/en/library/OIC_Overview_and_Analysis.pdf

11 "Leader Reiterates Pessimism about Possibility of Deal with US," Fars News Agency, February 17, 2014, http://english.farsnews.com/newstext.aspx?nn=13921128001246

12 "Rereading the Orders of the Revolution's Supreme Leader" (Persian), *Mashregh News*, April 5, 2012, http://goo.gl/M5bFJe

13 Jeffrey Goldberg, "Obama to Iran and Israel: 'As President of the United States, I Don't Bluff,'" *Atlantic*, March 2, 2012, http://www.theatlantic.com/international/archive/2012/03/obama-to-iran-and-israel-as-president-of-the-united-states-i-dont-bluff/253875

14 *Times* editorial board, "No New Iran Sanctions Now," *Los Angeles Times*, November 17, 2013, http://www.latimes.com/opinion/editorials/la-ed--iran-house-sanctions–20131117,0,6728477.story#axzz2mT0tJ5I4

15 Mohamed ElBaradei 2014, Hassan Rouhani, The Time, April 23, http://time.com/70838/hassan-rouhani-2014-time-100/

16 Seyed Hossein Mousavian, "It Was Not Sanctions That Brought Iran to the Table," *Financial Times*, November 19, 2013, http://www.ft.com/intl/cms/s/0/8d9631f4–510c–11e3-b499–00144feabdc0.html#axzz2mSviTVYN

17 Ibid.

18 Secretary of Defense Leon E. Panetta, "Remarks at the Saban Center," US Department of Defense, December 2, 2011, http://www.defense.gov/transcripts/transcript.aspx?transcriptid=4937

19 "Weighing Benefits and Costs of Military Action against Iran," Iran Project, accessed February 28, 2014, http://www.wilsoncenter.org/sites/default/files/IranReport_091112_FINAL.pdf

20 Eugene Gholz, "The Strait Dope," *Foreign Policy*, August 24, 2009, http://www.foreignpolicy.com/articles/2009/08/12/the_strait_dope

21 Bradley S. Russell and Max Boot, "Iran Won't Close the Strait of Hormuz," *Wall Street Journal*, January 4, 2012, http://online.wsj.com/article/SB10001424052970204632204577130834200656156.html

22 Alireza Nader, "Will Iran Close the Strait of Hormuz?," Rand Corporation, October 2, 2012, http://www.rand.org/blog/2012/10/will-iran-close-the-strait-of-hormuz.html

23 Geoffrey Kemp and John Allen Gay, *War with Iran: Political,*

Military, and Economic Consequences (Plymouth: Rowman & Littlefield, 2013).

24 David Blair, "Robert Gates: Bombing Iran Would Not Stop Nuclear Threat," *Telegraph*, May 1, 2009, http://www.telegraph.co.uk/news/worldnews/middleeast/iran/5257343/Robert-Gates-bombing-Iran-would-not-stop-nuclear-threat.html

25 "Rouhani Demands End to Securitized Atmosphere," YouTube, June 1, 2013, http://www.youtube.com/watch?v=NBX_VGddTYM

26 "Without Investment We Will Become the Importer of Oil and Related Products" (Persian), *Aftab News*, April 5, 2011, http://aftabnews.ir/vdchqknzm23nizd.tft2.html

27 "Sanctions Take Toll on Iran's Oil Industry," United Press International, April 28, 2011, http://www.upi.com/Business_News/Energy-Resources/%202011%20/04/28/Sanctions-take-toll-of-Irans-oil-industry/UPI-60311304016515

28 "Forming Huge Oil Consortiums Necessary, Ghasemi Says," *Tehran Times*, November 29, 2011, http://www.tehrantimes.com/index.php/economy-and-business/1948-forming-huge-oil-consortiums-necessary-qasemi-says

29 "Surprising Success of Iran's Universities," *Newsweek*, March 13, 2010, http://www.thedailybeast.com/newsweek/2008/08/08/the-star-students-of-the-islamic-republic.html

30 Patrick Clawson, "Much Traction from Measured Steps: The Iranian Opposition, The Nuclear Issue, and the West," Washington Institute for Near East Policy Paper No. 100, January 2010, http://www.voltairenet.org/IMG/pdf/Iranian_Opposition.pdf

31 Ben Piven, "Map: US Bases Encircle Iran," *Aljazeera*, May 1, 2012, http://www.aljazeera.com/indepth/interactive/2012/04/2012417131242767298.html

32 *World Factbook* (Washington, DC: Central Intelligence Agency), accessed February 28, 2014, https://www.cia.gov/library/publications/the-world-factbook/rankorder/2001rank.html

33 "Iran's Population Reached 77.1 Million" (Persian), Fars News Agency, February 21, 2013, http://www.farsnews.com/newstext.php?nn=13911203000204

34 Middle East expert Robert Baer has written that "*takfiri* generally refers to a Sunni Muslim who looks at the world in black-and-white; there are true believers and then there are nonbelievers, with no shades in between. A *takfiri*'s mission is to re-create the Caliphate according to a literal interpretation of the Qur'an." Robert Baer, *The Devil We Know* (New York: Crown, 2008), 123.

35 Mark Perry, "False Flag," *Foreign Policy*, January 13, 2012, http://www.foreignpolicy.com/articles/2012/01/13/false_flag#sthash.SgpybvqT.dpbs

36 "Israel's Mossad Trained Assassins of Iran Nuclear Scientists, Report

Says," *Haaretz*, February 9, 2012, http://www.haaretz.com/news/diplomacy-defense/israel-s-mossad-trained-assassins-of-iran-nuclear-scientists-report-says-1.411945

37 Gary Sick, "The Future of US–Iran Relations," *Global Dialogue* 3, nos. 2–3 (2001), http://www.worlddialogue.org/print.php?id=148&PHPSESSI D=c1bb07f3f361a535a2ab275fca4f756

38 Seyed Hossein Mousavian, "What Kerry Needs to Know about Iran," *Financial Times*, February 25, 2013, http://www.ft.com/cms/s/0/4b77d996–7f41–11e2–97f6–00144feabdc0.html#axzz2czIH1ujV

39 Shahir Shahidsaless, "A Chance at Last," *Majalla*, September 10, 2013, http://www.majalla.com/eng/2013/09/article55245306

40 Ibid.

41 Hossein Mousavian, *The Iranian Nuclear Crisis*, 125, 241, 242, 248, 349.

42 Jacob Bercovitch, "Mediation in International Conflict: Theory, Practice, and Developments," in I. William Zartman (ed.), *Peacemaking in International Conflict: Methods and Techniques*, rev. edn (Washington, DC: United States Institute of Peace Press, 2007), 168.

43 Ibid., 170.

44 Ibid.

45 Ibid., 177.

46 Ibid., 175.

47 Christa Case Bryant, "The Man behind Secret US–Iran Talks, Sultan Qaboos," *Christian Science Monitor*, November 24, 2013, http://www.csmonitor.com/World/Middle-East/Olive-Press/2013/1124/The-man-behind-secret-US–Iran-talks-Sultan-Qaboos

48 William Green Miller and Seyed Hossein Mousavian, "Iran Nuclear Talks: Citizen Diplomacy Would Build Trust," *Christian Science Monitor*, April 5, 2013, http://www.csmonitor.com/Commentary/Opinion/2013/0405/Iran-nuclear-talks-Citizen-diplomacy-would-build-trust

49 http://www.al-monitor.com/pulse/originals/2014/03/aipac-policy.html#

50 See Resolution 1373, Addendum 2.

51 Frank N. Von Hippel, Seyed Hossein Mousavian, Emad Kiyaei, Harold A. Feiveson and Zia Mian, "Fissile Materials Control in the Middle East," International Panel of Fissile Materials Research Report No. 11, October 2013, http://fissilematerials.org/library/rr11.pdf

52 "Zarif and Pelosi's Daughter on Twitter,"*Mashregh News*, September 5, 2013, http://goo.gl/LnWV5B

53 "U.S.-Iran trade still thrives 2012," United States Institute of Peace, The Iran Primer, April 2010, accessed March 5, 2014, http://iranprimer.usip.org/blog/2012/apr/10/US–Iran-trade-still-thrives-0

54 Patrick Clawson, "U.S. sanctions," United States Institute of Peace, The Iran Primer, accessed March 5, 2014, http://iranprimer.usip.org/resource/us-sanctions

55 Bijan Khajehpour, "Iran's pivot to the East," *Al Monitor*, July 19,

2013, accessed March 5, 2014, http://www.al-monitor.com/pulse/ar/contents/articles/opinion/2013/07/iran-trade-west-asia-economy.html#

56 "Iran's growing dependence on China," United States Institute of Peace, November 14, 2011, accessed March 5, 2014, http://iranprimer.usip.org/blog/2011/nov/14/iran%E2%80%99s-growing-dependence-china

57 Khajehpour, "Iran's pivot to the East."

58 Ibid.

59 "Looking toward the East" (Persian), *Tejarat Magazine*, December 7, 2013, http://tejarat.donya-e-eqtesad.com/fa/packagestories/details?service=economy&story=2d4d851d-c750–46a9–81b6–6c2e9fd2afa2 (accessed March 5, 2014).

60 Nikolai Bobkin, "Iran and China: friendly relations based on pragmatism," *New Eastern Outlook*, February 21, 2014, http://journal-neo.org/2014/02/21/rUS–Iran-i-kitaj-v-osnove-druzhestvenny-h-otnoshenij-pragmatizm/ (accessed March 5, 2014).

61 "Total trade between Iran and China $40 billion" (Persian), *Mehr News*, February 23, 2014, accessed March 5, 2014, http://www.mehrnews.com/detail/news/2242216

62 "Iran, China finalize roadmap to double bilateral trade, *Tehran Times*, February 24, 2014, accessed March 5, 2014, http://www.payvand.com/news/14/feb/1157.html

63 Mohammad Reza Kiani, "Revisiting the Iran–EU relations," Institute for Middle East Strategic Studies, accessed March 5, 2014, http://en.merc.ir/default.aspx?tabid=98&ArticleId=309